SHIPPING AND DEVELOPMENT IN DUBAI

SHIPPING AND DEVELOPMENT IN DUBAI

Infrastructure, Innovation and Institutions in the Gulf

Keith Nuttall

I.B. TAURIS
LONDON • NEW YORK • OXFORD • NEW DELHI • SYDNEY

I.B. TAURIS
Bloomsbury Publishing Plc
50 Bedford Square, London, WC1B 3DP, UK
1385 Broadway, New York, NY 10018, USA
29 Earlsfort Terrace, Dublin 2, Ireland

BLOOMSBURY, I.B. TAURIS and the I.B. Tauris logo are trademarks
of Bloomsbury Publishing Plc

First published in Great Britain 2022
This paperback edition published 2023

Copyright © Keith Nuttall, 2022

Keith Nuttall has asserted his right under the Copyright, Designs and Patents Act,
1988, to be identified as Author of this work.

For legal purposes the Acknowledgements on p. ix constitute an extension
of this copyright page.

Series design by Adriana Brioso
Cover image: Jebel Ali port, Dubai, UAE. (© NASSER YOUNES/AFP/Getty Images)

All rights reserved. No part of this publication may be reproduced or transmitted
in any form or by any means, electronic or mechanical, including photocopying, recording,
or any information storage or retrieval system, without prior permission in writing from
the publishers.

Bloomsbury Publishing Plc does not have any control over, or responsibility for, any
third-party websites referred to or in this book. All internet addresses given in this
book were correct at the time of going to press. The author and publisher regret any
inconvenience caused if addresses have changed or sites have ceased to exist, but
can accept no responsibility for any such changes.

A catalogue record for this book is available from the British Library.

A catalog record for this book is available from the Library of Congress.

ISBN: HB: 978-0-7556-4162-8
PB: 978-0-7556-4166-6
ePDF: 978-0-7556-4163-5
eBook: 978-0-7556-4164-2

Typeset by Deanta Global Publishing Services, Chennai, India

To find out more about our authors and books visit www.bloomsbury.com and
sign up for our newsletters.

To Lynn, William, James, Emma – and George

CONTENTS

List of figures	viii
Acknowledgements	ix
INTRODUCTION	1
Chapter 1 DUBAI: ORIGINS AND EMERGENCE (1833–1958)	15
Chapter 2 TAKE-OFF: CREEK, CONTAINERIZATION, CONNECTIVITY (1958–71)	41
Chapter 3 EXOGENOUS IMPACTS AND THE LOGISTICS REVOLUTION (1971–90)	71
Chapter 4 SUCCESS: GOOD LUCK OR GOOD MANAGEMENT? (1990–2004)	107
Chapter 5 THE NEW CHALLENGES OF THE TWENTY-FIRST CENTURY (2004–PRESENT DAY)	135
CONCLUSION	165
Notes	179
Bibliography	201
Index	215

FIGURES

1	Map of the Gulf in the nineteenth century	102
2	First ship call at Port (Mina) Rashid, Dubai – MV Sirdhana November 1970	103
3	HH Shaikh Rashid al Maktoum, Ruler of Dubai, opening the Port Rashid Container Terminal in November 1980	104
4	Aerial photograph of Port Rashid circa 1981	104
5	Containership 'Tor Bay' – Built 1982, overall length 200 metres, capacity circa 2000 TEU (twenty-foot equivalent unit containers)	105
6	Containership 'CMA-CGM Jacques Saade' – Built 2019/20, overall length 400 metres, capacity circa 23,000 TEU	105

ACKNOWLEDGEMENTS

In my professional career in the shipping and, subsequently, the ports industries, spanning several decades, one of my first postings in the early 1980s was to Dubai, for three years. I returned twice more to live in Dubai and Sharjah in the 1990s and for nearly ten years at the beginning of the twenty-first century. During these years, there were visits throughout the Middle East region, the Arab Gulf States, Iran, Iraq, Syria and Lebanon. My profession also required me to spend time in South Asia, Southeast Asia and the Far East. I was therefore fortunate to be able to observe – and play a small part in – the remarkable transformation of Dubai and the UAE during this formative period and, thanks to my business travels worldwide, make comparisons with other regional and international centres.

This book, therefore, includes much personal experience of Dubai's emergence and that of the Gulf and wider region, in addition to specific research carried out more recently. I have also drawn on the attitudes and opinions of many UAE residents as well as friends and (ex)colleagues in the ports and shipping industry, to whom I am grateful.

I would like to thank, in particular, George Chapman (and his daughter Vanessa) in Dubai, Tim Power of Drewry Maritime Research in London, Janet Porter of Lloyds List/Containerization International, the staff of the National Archives in Kew, the staff at the HSBC (BBME) archives in London, Cambridge University Press Archive Editions staff, and members of Gulftainer in Sharjah for their help, useful contributions and information.

I must also thank the teaching and supervisory staff at two great British educational institutions, Birkbeck College (University of London) and the University of East Anglia, for resuscitating and polishing my long-buried academic aspirations.

INTRODUCTION

Dubai became part of the United Arab Emirates (UAE) in 1971, but in the middle of the twentieth century, it was an independent little-known statelet, a small town on a sandy inlet in the British-protected territory of the Trucial States in southern Arabia, dependent on subsistence fishing, agriculture and small-scale trade. The major trading centres in the Middle East region were long-established cities, such as Basrah, Beirut and Aden. In the mid-1950s, the nine-mile-long creek on which Dubai was built and on which its dhow-based trading prosperity depended was silting up. Shaikh Rashid Bin Saeed Al Maktoum (the de facto ruler, acting as regent for his ailing father) arranged for a bank loan of half a million pounds sterling from the British Bank of the Middle East (BBME), persuaded merchant families to contribute to the dredging in 1958 and later, with a loan from Kuwait, expanded it further.[1] The creek today is still handling dhow traffic, but the Emirate's main shipping operations are handled by Jebel Ali port, established on a green-field site, which was opened in 1979. This facility is, at the time of writing, the world's ninth largest container port, handling over 15 million container TEUs[2] in 2017 and it also serves the 57-square-kilometre Jebel Ali Free Zone (JAFZ), the world's largest free-zone complex, with over 7000 registered companies. Dubai's first all-weather airport was completed in May 1965, and in September 2014, this much-expanded facility overtook London Heathrow as the world's busiest international hub with around 70 million passengers annually.[3] Basrah, Beirut and Aden are but shadows of their past pre-eminence, overtaken and displaced as regional centres by a remarkably dynamic and evolving Dubai.

In April 1956, Malcolm Mclean's Pan-Atlantic Steamship, the 160-metre-long, 10,500 gross registered tonnage (GRT) *Ideal X*, carried fifty-eight containers from New York to Houston. This revolutionary way of carrying cargo in containers inaugurated what was to become the complete transformation of the cargo shipping industry. Comparatively, in 2015, as an example, Mediterranean Shipping Company (MSC) launched the *MSC Oscar*, a container ship nearly 400 metres long, with a GRT of 192,237 able to carry 19,224 TEUs. In April 2020, Hyundai Merchant Marine (HMM) squeezed out even more capacity with the *HMM Algeciras*, 400 metres long and with a capacity of nearly 24,000 TEUs – the world's biggest at the time of writing. These developments too reflect the dramatic evolution in logistics and cargo transportation.

This book argues that the wholehearted adoption by Dubai of this transformative and disruptive technology – containerization and related port, shipping and airline logistics deriving from it – was the most significant example of the Emirate's approach to development. The focus on infrastructure was a paradigm shift, a 'milestone event . . . (with) systemic and durable impact',[4] which has been the initial main driver in the development, evolution and transformation, not only of Dubai but of the whole region. Together with Dubai's follow-up policies, creating effective institutions and pursuing and encouraging innovation, the process has served as an example for other emerging states, creating a luminary of successful globalization.

How has this small city achieved such remarkable, wide-ranging economic success, compared not only with the perennially under-achieving Middle East and North Africa (MENA) region but with other late-developing states as well? Why, uniquely until recently in the region, has it adopted a policy of development diversification for several decades, that has been the catalyst for success?

The research, empirical evidence and personal experience in this book add to the limited body of work on Dubai and the Gulf in two main ways. Firstly, it highlights that the experience of Dubai is very different from the developmental evolution of other Arab Gulf states, which, focussed almost entirely on oil and gas, emerged and have remained primarily as rentier states.[5] Most of the limited amount of academic literature on the Gulf deals with these rentier states, the nature and survivability of monarchical government, and the democracy deficit. There are also individual country histories, but little on the distinctive trajectory of Dubai, whose rulers, I will argue, pursued a top-down strategy, embedding citizens in an entrepreneurial drive very different in approach to that of their immediate neighbours. The Gulf states share many common traits of language, religion, tribal origins and social structures, but their attitudes and approach to development and engagement with the outside world differ very considerably. Broad-brush descriptions linking these states into one simplistic 'Gulf' package are entirely misplaced.

Secondly, the work emphasizes the pivotal role of containerization and infrastructure in creating the framework for Dubai's economic take-off. Once again, this is a subject that is woefully under-researched with little literature on the role of containerization in general, let alone its impact in being the enabler of the globalized movement of goods – of globalization. When we consider that 90 per cent of worldwide trade moves by sea and, according to the World Bank, worldwide container port volumes were 750 million TEU in 2017 (up from 560 million in 2010),[6] it is remarkable that so little academic attention has been paid to the impact of maritime transport on development. This book aims to correct this imbalance as far as Dubai and the Gulf are concerned. It is now increasingly accepted by most emerging economies throughout the world, that effective development, the smooth movement of products and the consequent reduction of costs, is dependent on effective infrastructure – interconnected port, road and rail facilities. That this is so understood and is a major plank of China's recent 'Belt and Road' initiative is testament in part to the example and success of Dubai. The questions this study seeks to answer are why and how Dubai pursued such a policy so distinctively, thoroughly and persistently.

It is not widely appreciated how much Dubai has dominated the Gulf (and the wider region) with its trading and logistics activities and those activities such as tourism that evolved and grew out of them. Consumer goods for the Upper Gulf states are often carried in containers relayed over Dubai; Oil Pipeline Project cargo for Iraq's oilfield development, for example, is aggregated in Dubai from worldwide sources before shipment to the Iraqi port of Umm Qasr; hundreds of companies based in Dubai's Free-zones use Dubai as a base to serve the region with spare parts and products; containers for South Asian and African ports are relayed via Dubai from mega-container ships on core routes, such as Europe/Gulf or Far East/Gulf, onto smaller 'feeder' vessels; business and personal shoppers from East Africa, Asia and the Gulf visit Dubai via the world's biggest airport hub (often on Dubai's – and one of the world's biggest – airlines) to find the best range of goods and to spend time in a safe and relaxed environment. The development of the ports and airports was followed by the investment and expansion of free-trade zones and subsequently by free-zone clusters. This study examines how these innovative developments have taken place and why the success of this multifaceted effort and the attitudes and approach behind it are what distinguishes the Emirate from many of its neighbours.

This book will assess how Dubai's actual or potential rivals failed to adopt similar measures either at all or as thoroughly, and why only in recent years have they started to pursue similar diversification strategies (using the 'Dubai Model'[7] as a guide), away from simple dependence on oil and gas revenues.

The conventional theories of authoritarian (Gulf oil monarchy) development (or stagnation) and (oil) 'rent' distribution (Beblawi and Luciani,[8] Ayubi,[9] Gray[10]) on the Middle East do not account for the emergence of Dubai as an increasingly important player on the world political and economic stage. They highlight the conventional oil monarchy policy of relying primarily on the revenue from oil ('rent'), which is then distributed to their populations as 'cradle to grave' benefits. Such regimes as Kuwait for example, have (until recently), made little effort to diversify their economies, assuming that their ample fossil-fuel reserves would sustain them. However, this 'oil-curse' approach has ensured that, as Ashraf Mishrif highlights, 'despite financial wealth and relative economic and political stability in most Gulf Co-operation Council (GCC) countries, the decline in oil prices has exposed the structural weaknesses of Gulf economies in their heavy dependency on oil and gas and the inevitability of bringing about radical changes in the economic system'.[11]

This study is important because it emphasizes how Dubai, without huge oil reserves, pursued pragmatic, multi-layered development policies and diversification efforts, based on the building blocks of liberal trading links that it had long espoused, focussing on joined-up transport logistics. The book will investigate how and why such deliberate – not accidentally successful – policies have enabled Dubai to become the primary regional *entrepot*, distribution centre and airline hub. Significantly, I will argue, an *entrepot* not only for the Gulf but also for parts of South Asia and East Africa too, transforming and influencing the way in which the wider region adapts and develops.

The findings also seek to explain how, despite a lack of 'endowments', Dubai has succeeded in competing successfully, despite being surrounded by resource-rich, larger neighbours. They also challenge the forecasts of some regional specialists such as Christopher Davidson,[12] who have suggested that all Gulf monarchies might collapse (soon) because of failures to react to changing political ('Arab Spring') and economic (lack of diversification from oil and gas based) rentier policies – Huntington's 'Kings' Dilemma'.[13]

It is therefore my contention that the modern history of Dubai and its development occupies a unique and important place in the topography, not only of the Gulf but in the wider world of emerging economies. The impact of Dubai and the policies it has adopted have transformed and continue to transform the Gulf, both by direct example and because others have increasingly emulated them.[14]

Sources and methodology

The arguments in the book are drawn from primary and secondary sources; empirical evidence (some of which is based on my own experience of living in and working with the Gulf region for several decades); and interviews with senior, long-standing Dubai residents, Emirati and expatriate.

This is not intended to be a comprehensive history of the sub-region of the Middle East known as the Gulf. The work makes reference to the various theories and analyses of political, social and economic activity in the region, but in interpreting the evidence I have adopted a largely 'Historical Institutionalist' approach – assessing real-world questions within a historical focus. This approach looks at institutions (in this case, those of Dubai) within a historical context and the rules within which they operate, the ways they react to events, the individuals who shape these decisions, the ideas that motivate them, whether they learn from the past and from others – the factors influencing progression along a particular path. The core assumption is that, in order to understand how Dubai has evolved distinctively, two main strands of research are required, to determine *why* Dubai pursued this path and *how* it did so.

Firstly, focussing primarily on the *why*, historical analysis of Dubai's history and that of its neighbours must be undertaken to illustrate, compare and contrast the developmental attitudes and strategies adopted. Why did Dubai, (uniquely), pursue such policies and was this approach a result of local rulers' attitudes, or that of the British protecting power? Were such policies pursued by succeeding rulers and if so why? Such analysis makes reference to the distinctive nature of the structures of power and decision-making in the Gulf, by regional specialists such as Herb,[15] Linz[16] and Lucas,[17] on monarchical authoritarian rule in the Gulf – links between rulers and ruled,[18] including possible coercive policies,[19] the role of migrants,[20] how the economy works and how Dubai 'exports' its model and its 'soft power'.[21] Very pertinent to this analysis is why Dubai and the UAE were virtually unaffected by the 'Arab Spring' upheavals,[22] of 2011, and what has been the impact of regional disputes. Such tensions, often stoking differences between

Sunnis and Shia, are highlighted, for example, by Toby Matthiesen's *Sectarian Gulf*,[23] putting into sharp focus a key element of this book's argument how the spirit of tolerance and a willingness to trade equally with anyone has contributed so much to Dubai's success. However, as there are few if any complete studies on the role of infrastructure and ports, airports and shipping in Gulf development, this work, while focussing on the distinctive nature of Dubai, also contrasts and compares the development of Gulf neighbours.

Dubai's formative years occurred initially during the period of British protecting power, effectively from the 1830s to 1971 when the independent United Arab Emirates was created from the separate Trucial States of which Dubai was one. However, policy direction established during the latter stages of this period was maintained and expanded post-independence. I have therefore relied heavily on the UK National Archives (UKNA) and the reports sent privately between British officials in Dubai, the Gulf Political Head Office in Bahrain and London, to determine how much of an influence, if any, British officials had in shaping Dubai's distinctive development. These documents, because they are written from a British perspective, provide useful insights on how the British saw their role, their influence, and the capabilities and personality of the Dubai ruler(s) and those of the other Trucial States. This, we should remember, was at a time when Dubai had not achieved the status it has today but was simply a small statelet, without significant oil wealth, among others potentially more significant in the region. One of the key questions considered is whether the British saw Dubai as the emerging centre of the Trucial States and, increasingly, the Gulf, or was this not at all clear? Was there a long-term 'cunning plan' by the British that favoured Dubai? Or was it simply the fact that Dubai and its ruling family were prepared to take investment decisions that improved Dubai's position as a trading and business centre when others weren't? The records and correspondence of the British Bank of the Middle East, for many years the only bank permitted in Dubai, are another interesting window on how officials working with the Ruler of Dubai saw his attitude to work and development, compared with other Trucial States.

Prior to the 1950s, pertinent primary and secondary sources are not plentiful, as Julian Walker has highlighted, 'until after 1947 there were virtually no British official written documents available on the (Trucial) coast'.[24] Accounts that do exist tend to feed off each other, as the main original source works are archives from British Foreign and India offices, or compilations from the archives, such as Anita Burdett's *Records of Dubai*,[25] supplemented by some business histories and personal recollections, such as Wilfred Thesiger's travels in the late 1940s in the Arabian Peninsula described in the classic *Arabian Sands*.[26] Older works on the region include the *Gazetteer of the Persian Gulf*, published in 1908 by the Government Printers in Calcutta, compiled and written by J G Lorimer.[27] This monumental work, unequalled in detail and scope even today, was produced by the British Government of India to provide information for British officials increasingly involved in this largely unknown area at the time, and it provides much valuable background information about Dubai and its neighbours' early years. It also, as an impartial reference work, illustrates the reasons why, even at the beginning of the twentieth century, Dubai had begun to acquire its reputation for commercial acumen. It is important to stress again that Dubai was, until the middle of the twentieth century, a small settlement, existing initially on what could be caught from the sea, subsistence basic agriculture, pearling and increasingly some trade, utilizing its long, sheltered, sandy creek. I am fortunate to have had access to the unpublished memoirs of George Chapman, who arrived in Dubai in 1951 and, as a Gray Mackenzie (trading and agency company) employee, became responsible for shipping and related matters in Dubai and worked closely for many years with Shaikh Rashid Al Maktoum. Retiring in 1981 as Gray Mackenzie managing director in Dubai, (but still living in Dubai at the time of writing), his reminiscences give an interesting perspective, at this formative period in the Emirate's development, from someone close to the heart of the decision-making process.[28] His account, particularly his assessment of Shaikh Rashid, with whom he worked for over thirty years, reinforces the other primary and secondary sources, which include general histories covering the (then) Trucial States, pre-1971 independence and the formation of the United Arab Emirates.

Secondly, focussing on the *how*, it is also essential to show the development of the history of the Liner Shipping industry (i.e. cargo-ships operating to fixed schedules), the ports industry overall and the aviation industry throughout the Gulf to illustrate how distinctive the actions and responses of Dubai were,[29] and continue to be.[30] Until now, there has been no detailed study of the importance of container shipping in the region and the impact that it had in globalizing Gulf states. Therefore, this study examines the historical developmental progress of Dubai and the importance of logistics infrastructure-focussed expansion, which has had such a transformative impact throughout the world. This shows the attitude of Dubai in reacting to the containerization revolution in shipping – 'the handmaid of globalisation'– described in Marc Levinson's seminal study,[31] aviation and the subsequent diversifying and supplementary innovations such as free-zone expansion, tourism and brand creation that followed. Assessing the development of containerization and container ports in the area is also a useful tool for measuring and contrasting the attitude of Dubai's neighbours to diversified development. It is necessary to examine the evidence to assess other regional states' focus on oil and gas extraction and sales and why they did not seem particularly interested in diversifying and pursuing and expanding trade. Did Dubai, therefore, benefit from the lack of concerted competition to its developmental path? It is also essential to illustrate the impact of regional strife, directly or indirectly on neighbouring states, and the effect this had on their development and attitude to investment. As a stable centre, Dubai was able to benefit from problems elsewhere – but was this only because it had invested in and created the facilities that offered alternatives? This book assesses why and how other states did not adopt Dubai's approach.

Sources for the shipping, ports and aviation portions of this work are obtained from specialist organizations (such as Drewry Maritime Research in London), from organizations in the region where I have contacts or from interviews with representatives of companies such as *Emirates Airline* or *Dubai Ports World* (DPW). It should be highlighted at this point that a large part of my working life has been spent working in and with Dubai, initially in 1981. I am therefore able to bring my own knowledge and experience of Dubai's development and that of the shipping and ports industry throughout the region. There are very few, if any, primary or secondary sources dealing with modern cargo shipping and modern container ports in the Gulf, other than occasional and isolated articles. The study tries to avoid using too much shipping and ports industry terminology, but where this is essential, I have explained the references as clearly as possible. I have felt it necessary to provide some statistics to reinforce and clarify, empirically, points and trends that support my arguments. For example, I have used tables to emphasize the difference between annual growth in cargo volumes in Dubai compared with those of other locations.

The sources, either primary or secondary, that I have used for this history of how Dubai developed using infrastructure, trading and logistics, are in English, not Arabic. There are four main reasons for this. Firstly, there are no comparable primary source and Dubai government records (to those of the UK National Archives) for the period under study, because at the time such major developmental events were taking place, British stewardship involved the creation of a modern state with most record keeping in English. The comprehensive British bureaucratic records (primarily the UK National Archives) are in English. Secondly, the British administrative and bureaucratic structure which assisted in the creation of the modern Dubai state was staffed by British expatriates at senior level, plus (usually) English-speaking South Asian (Indian) managers and clerical staff, with some local and expatriate Arab (and English-speaking Sudanese) staff. Government records, reports and minutes of meetings were in English, because there were a few educated Arab clerical staff available. Even today, over 90 per cent of Dubai residents are non-native Emiratis, with English being the primary language of communication. Those academic works written by Arabic speakers, that I have sourced, are invariably written in English. Thirdly, the growth of Dubai's role as a shipping and aviation centre enhanced and perpetuated the role of English as the international communications and documentation of these industries are invariably in that language. Any secondary sources, reports, articles and literature relating to ports and shipping (the 'how') are in English. Fourthly, there are a few significant memoirs of senior Arab players during these formative years and those that are available, such as the works by the Ruler of Sharjah, by Shaikh Mohammed of Dubai or by Easa Saleh Gurg, are all in English editions, to gain a wider readership. Interviews with senior Emiratis, carried out during the course of this research, took place in English, which they spoke flawlessly. Dubai has long regarded itself as a globalized 'world city', which entails communications, websites, academic sites and articles to be written or expounded in English, as well as in Arabic. For this focussed study on the modern evolution of Dubai and the logistics industry, sources in English predominate.

Sources and literature

This section considers the secondary sources, their contribution and how this book complements the existing literature.

The emergence and evolution of the region in the nineteenth and twentieth centuries are revealed in more general works and travel literature. Earlier and more general works on the Gulf invariably do highlight the importance of trade and initially low-level European maritime trade. For example, the English East India Company established a 'factory' (trading base/warehouse) in Gombroon, Persia, now Bandar Abbas in Southern Iran, as far back as 1623, which expanded in the nineteenth century particularly as the waterway became a critically important line of communication (through Syria, Baghdad and Basrah) for the British route to and from India. The British then came to dominate the Gulf in the first half of the nineteenth century after the campaigns against piracy (or to remove trading rivals, according to Shaikh Sultan Al Qasimi's *The Myth of Arab Piracy in the Gulf*),[32] and the signing of treaties with the lower Gulf Shaikhs from 1820 onwards. General histories covering the early years include Frauke Heard-Bey's *From Trucial States to United Arab Emirates*[33] and Donald Hawley's *The Trucial States*,[34] which are valuable in setting out the often fractious and sensitive environment from which Dubai emerged, particularly in revealing that other neighbours (such as Sharjah) were bigger and richer with better facilities in the first half of the twentieth century. Such works, regardless of author, were written several decades ago but all agree that there was nothing pre-ordained about Dubai's success, that the development path was very distinctive and that attitudinally, the ruling family's approach to involvement in long-term planning was significant. I certainly argue that Dubai's more proactive stance to attracting business is key to understanding its success.

Jonathan Raban's 1979 travelogue *Arabia through the Looking Glass*[35] clearly pinpoints this aspect of Dubai with its creek, 'the main artery of the city's life . . . getting on with what it always did. Dubai was different . . . Indians, Iranians, Pakistanis, Arabs congealed into the careless cosmopolitanism of an old port which has always been used to beaching the tidewrack of the Gulf and Indian Ocean'. Such works are a useful reminder that the Gulf was historically well-linked with communities throughout the Indian Ocean for centuries – particularly that these Gulf *littoral* communities faced 'outwards' across the sea so they were familiar with outsiders and used to trading with them. They also remind us that the region was competitive, with fluctuating fortunes – small communities existing on pearling, fishing and small-scale trade interspersed with bigger centres (traditionally in Iraq or Persia), whose fortunes ebbed and flowed. Again, there was nothing to suggest that Dubai was automatically destined to grow and prosper, but each of these contributions highlight – as does Michael Field's 1984, still unmatched study of Arabian business families, *The Merchants* – that 'Dubai pulled itself up by its own bootstraps without any oil revenues until 1969 . . . and the foundation of Dubai's prosperity has been trade – quite different from any other oil state'.[36] I very much agree with this assessment.

Dubai developed differently. These elements emerge clearly – albeit rather too hagiographically – in the case of biographies about the transformative ruler (1958–90) Shaikh Rashid Bin Saeed Al Maktoum from Abbas Makki's *Rashid: The Man Behind Dubai*[37] and Graeme Wilson's substantial *Rashid's Legacy*.[38] However, a more nuanced account by Easa Saleh Al Gurg (later UAE Ambassador to the

UK) – *The Wells of Memory*,[39] of growing up in a rapidly modernizing Dubai in which as a young educated Dubai national (of Persian based Arab origins) he was interacting with the remarkable Dubai ruler, Shaikh Rashid, has much to reinforce these points, while giving us a different, non-British-sourced perspective.

This book suggests that British pacification of the Gulf in the early nineteenth century replaced the potential hegemony of some existing regional powers and allowed smaller centres the opportunity to develop. The existing Gulf and Indian Ocean links remained but evolved variously, as trading patterns and conditions changed for political or economic reasons. As always, in a competitive environment, some centres prospered, some fell away. The question is why some, like Dubai, thrived under an umbrella of distant British protection, and I will argue that this was only because of the efforts they made and the attitude to trade and business that they adopted. I will also argue that the Dubai ruler (from 1958) Shaikh Rashid Bin Saeed Al Maktoum played a particularly skilful role in pursuing development policies for the benefit of Dubai, with determination, subtlety and charm. Dubai's 'sense of place' as a city of merchants can be seen in works illuminating the crucial trading and maritime mentality which distinguished Dubai from many of its neighbours. Abdul Sherriff's *Dhow Cultures of the Indian Oceans*,[40] Stephanie Jones' *Two Centuries of Overseas Trading*[41] (about the Inchcape/Gray Mackenzie agents and traders in Dubai and the Gulf), James Onley's *Britain and the Gulf Shaikhdoms 1820-1971*[42] and Nelida Fuccaro's recent writings on Gulf port cities are useful examples in setting the scene. This book focusses on how it was that Dubai reacted distinctly and effectively to out-compete other centres and achieve its pre-eminence, within the evolving structure of Indian Ocean and Gulf trading links, despite the lack of wealth, size or natural endowments.

Modern studies

There has been little work produced that illustrates the crucial correlation between the transformation of shipping, ports and logistics in the Gulf and Dubai's remarkable emergence, particularly from the 1970s onwards, other than by Broeze, nearly twenty years ago with a chapter on Dubai in *Harbours and Havens: Essays in Port History*,[43] partially in Ramos' 2010 work, *Dubai Amplified: The Engineering of a Port Geography*,[44] and more recently in Kamrava's 2016 edited *Gateways to the World*.[45] Though there have been an increasing number of studies in recent years on the Gulf region, 'the middle east is poorly served by academic literature and the Gulf particularly ill-served',[46] only a handful have focussed specifically on Dubai and there is still surprisingly little written on recent history. Indeed the *Financial Times* review of Christopher Davidson's book on Dubai in October 2008, quoted on the back cover, actually refers (even in 2008) to it as a 'history of an obscure [sic] part of the Gulf'.[47] This point is repeated (about Dubai) in a recent work on economic diversification, 'despite the uniqueness of this case, little attention has been paid to the success story in the heart of the oil-rich GCC countries'.[48] Problems continue to exist with the availability of data and its reliability and, in recent years, the blurring together of Dubai and the rest of the UAE. These more detailed studies do focus much more on the impact and impetus of Shaikh Rashid and his successor ruling sons – in particular, Davidson's aforementioned, prescient volume *Dubai: The Vulnerability of Success*, Jim Krane's colourful, anecdotal, more folksy *Dubai*;[49] Syed Ali's more critical, though often journalistic, *Dubai: Gilded Cage*;[50] and Hvidt's long article in the 2009 IJMES, *The Dubai Model*,[51] not forgetting Mike Davis' critical polemic on Gulf capitalism *Fear and Money in Dubai*.[52] Davidson made an entirely rational case about the risks for the freewheeling, entrepreneurial Dubai in a region where Abu Dhabi's oil wealth and land area are more stable and more likely to outlast the business plans of its fellow, now virtually oil-less, Emirate. However, there is little emphasis on the wider implications of the diversification into the shipping and air-transport revolution that has impelled Dubai to firmly established, regional trading hegemony – which (ironically) Abu Dhabi is now also embracing. Any analysis of Dubai cannot avoid scrutinizing the structures of power that allow this freewheeling, laissez-faire economy to continue to thrive without coercing its citizens or without anyone 'kicking away its ladder',[53] especially as its 'All in the Family' rule seems at first glance to mirror those of other Gulf monarchies. Nor can such a study ignore the weaknesses, shortcomings and potential pitfalls of the 'business state' mentality and ruling structure highlighted by Davis and Khalaf, Al Shehabi & Hanieh.[54] The current ruler, HH Shaikh Mohammed Al Maktoum, in his several books, including *Flashes of Thought*,[55] inevitably has a different, more optimistic perspective that allows us to get some insight into his vision for the Emirate and how he wants it implemented.

The literature on Dubai up to now has been sparse and, with one or two honourable exceptions, has tended to fall into the exotic location travel literature category, the part of a broad-brush regional review, the 'shock-jock' expose of capitalist abuses or referenced in works on monarchical survival. This book is focussed more on how and why Dubai pursued such an independent path. Why did it develop its infrastructure and its trading networks, and what were the events, internal and external, that influenced what happened? How was it that Dubai (and nowhere else) focussed so singularly on containerization and transport logistics? Why did Dubai expand its airport so spectacularly and – in defiance of conventional economic logic – start up an airline from scratch? What was the impetus that made Dubai create a huge tourism industry from a standing start and establish free-zones to complement its ports? This study answers these questions – which have a crucial bearing on how other states approach development – as Dubai's model, linked to the globalized world is now increasingly studied by other emerging economies. Of course, such a developmental path was not without its risks and mistakes – this study illustrates them too.

Dubai was regularly affected by external regional conflicts and disputes. However, we need to assess what impact these events had on Dubai and whether it benefitted because it was increasingly the preferred location to which people and companies re-located, 'voting with their feet', or because it had the foresight to create the right institutions, infrastructure and opportunities. It is crucial also to set out the reasons why and how Dubai created an environment that was attractive for people from all over the world to live in and work.

Shipping and logistics literature

The early literature about Dubai explained how the town adopted user-friendly approaches to attract merchants to trade and settle in the early twentieth century. Other specific literature on the shipping lines and trading companies throws light on the trading and economic development of the region and why Dubai came to be a centre of importance – and others declined, with works by Jones,[56] Blake,[57] Morton,[58] Griffiths,[59] Fuccaro[60] and Kamrava,[61] more recently. These works are useful in focussing attention on the environment and technological changes as Dubai gradually emerged to supplant other centres. What is virtually unexplored is the way and extent to which Dubai seized the opportunity from the 1970s onwards to invest and develop its ports infrastructure as containerization expanded – and subsequently to redefine air travel too. The worldwide container revolution, and its dramatic impact on ports, trades and people, is emphasized and explained in only a few works, such as Levinson's *The Box*, by now, the standard, and virtually only, explanation of the worldwide container trade revolution (Boxes=Containers); Cudahy's *Box Boats*;[62] *The Globalisation of the Oceans* by Broeze;[63] the economic impact illustrated by Hoosteval;[64] as well as more general works such as Rose George's,[65] or Horatio Clare's,[66] accounts of life on a modern container ship. There is no history of the progress and impact of containerization in the Gulf – until now.

However, in order to appreciate the scale of Dubai's achievement, this study charts in some detail the monumental changes in the shipping, ports and logistics industry from the 1960s onwards, illustrated briefly in the second paragraph of this introduction, and how and why Dubai capitalized on them. This study of Dubai's focus on logistics and technological innovation reveals the impact that such policies had in creating an environment which allowed the Emirate to flourish in the new globalized, economically interdependent world.

Understanding the cargo/container shipping and ports industry (and airports and airlines) is crucial to our appreciation of how and why Dubai came to dominate the region logistically. In developing this argument, it is necessary to show the very modest beginnings of Dubai's port and trading activity and how they evolved. Port cities are inevitably affected by three main factors: their locations, the (political and economic) environment in which they operate and their response to and anticipation of the needs of their actual or potential customers. However, locations can become less (or more) attractive if trade conditions change; the political and economic environment can destroy (or benefit) a port's existence and providing what customers require can establish a port from small beginnings – or with indifference and lack of forward-thinking cause it to atrophy. In other words, as always, there are some factors that are impossible to overcome, but most of the time it is making the most of what you have and providing the facilities that your customers want – or this is what should be the case. This study assesses Dubai's approach to the creation of the transport and logistics industry (ports/support facilities to 'add value'/airports/airlines) to determine how this approach was pursued. It will be highlighted that other states did make some efforts to establish better ports and airports, but factors such as politics, inertia and lack of initiative produced results that fell far behind those of Dubai.

To sum up

This work aims to answer the questions of how and why infrastructure, innovation and institutions account for the distinctive rise of Dubai – and why this development did not happen on a similar scale in its neighbours' territories.

It highlights how Dubai's policies were from the beginning designed to expand and develop Dubai as a trading hub, not just to collect 'rent'. These policies gradually evolved into an economy which is complex and diversified based on its traditional strengths as a shipping, transport and trading centre. I will argue that this development did not 'just happen' or come about by accident. It took place because Dubai tapped into the rapidly changing world of transport logistics – the container revolution; the increase in the size of container ships; the way in which Liner Shipping operated; providing user-friendly facilities within free-zones unhindered by the standard existing bureaucratic constraints and by innovation and investment in airports, (an airline) and tourism.

The study also highlights that we cannot ignore that Dubai's policies and investment paths have not always succeeded, as the impact of the global crisis in 2007–8 showed dramatic effect, when its debt-fuelled investments in the overheated property market threatened to derail the Emirate's economy completely. Without the natural fossil-fuel resources of its neighbours to fall back on, as Christopher Davidson has stressed,[67] its expansive business plans always involved inherent risk, both from internal and external factors. I will argue that Dubai's development has always involved risk – borrowing to dredge the creek, creating Jebel Ali from bare sand, establishing Emirates Airline from scratch and establishing a tourist industry in a region that had never been contemplated as a leisure industry option. However, these were calculated risks, 'playing the long game', enhancing the ability of Dubai to compete. Over the last half-century, the region in which Dubai is based has been convulsed by several regional conflicts and international downturns. The fact that Dubai has survived these crises, surmounted them and continued to innovate and expand, is testament to the quality and depth of the economic and governance structures it has put in place.

As it has developed a brand, Dubai has faced accusations of superficiality and brashness, 'the Las Vegas of the Middle East' and, during its downturn, experienced gleeful schadenfreude from Western states. Much of the vitriolic reaction seemed to go above and beyond the appropriate critiques of an economy which had over-reached and borrowed too much. At the time of the global financial crisis, Western media reports on Dubai focussed on the failures in a patronizing, 'cars abandoned at the airport', way, revisiting the stereotypical orientalist[68] image of a yet another collapsing Middle East state, run by (implicitly) incompetent Arabs – even though Dubai was modelled on 'western' forms of capitalistic development. The irony was, of course, that most other Western economies had imploded too, because, like

Dubai, hubristically and overconfidently, they had over-borrowed and/or placed faith in, it transpired, barely understood financial investment models.

The case being put forward here is that as a small developmental economy, Dubai is in fact providing an exemplar, despite its mistakes, of how to survive without resources in a globalized world by focussing on professionalism and innovation, by the creation of a market, an entrepot and logistics services serving a wide region. The risks remain: patrimonial family rule is subject to change; the region is volatile; competition is rising; and Dubai depends on investors and visitors continuing to regard the city as a reliable, neutral safe haven. The professionalism and effectiveness of its institutions will give it a good chance of continuing to surmount the obstacles as it has done in the past. Crucially also, in a region and Arab world beset by economic and political failure, Dubai's success – latterly within the UAE – sets an example of what can be achieved – 'warts and all' – by highlighting worldwide that Arab states can not only work but also be showpieces of development. The study will also argue that by choosing to focus on transport logistics as a basis on which to develop and diversify, in this increasingly nationalistic, but still globalized world, there still exists the power, contrary to many narratives, to influence events rather than being swept along by them. I will argue that Dubai did not need to engage with modern globalization, but has individually, nationally and regionally chosen to be part of it on its own terms (in comparison to many of its neighbours who have sought to keep it at bay). It has succeeded by its own developmental and marketing efforts, to the extent that it is the benchmark in a very wide region as the place to work, live and play – the 'Dubai model' to be studied and emulated.

As indicated earlier, following this introduction, there are five main chronological sections. Chapter 1 explains the origins of Dubai, the conditions and environment that shaped its initial development in the prevailing economic and political landscape, followed by describing and analyzing the slow growth of the town in the early twentieth century and the economic crisis caused by the collapse of pearling. The impact of the rule of Shaikh Rashid Bin Saeed Al Maktoum from 1958 and the development of the modern shipping and ports industry is covered in Chapter 2. This chapter focusses particularly on the containerization 'revolution' and the impact this had on shipping itself and on ports, linked with the take-off into 'modern Dubai' initiated by Shaikh Rashid Al Maktoum in the 1950s and 1960s, emphasized by the creek expansion, the construction of Port Rashid and the airport. Chapter 3, covering the period from 1971 to 1990, highlights the dramatic impact of Jebel Ali and Free-zones, together with the external events, which so influenced and shaped Dubai in these turbulent decades. The chapter also takes stock of the competitive environment in the region and assesses and contrasts the responses of other regional states to developmental, shipping and logistical challenges, compared with those of Dubai. Chapter 4 reviews the period in the years after the liberation of Kuwait in 1991 and the geopolitical developments in the region and the internal processes, which cemented Dubai's reputation and transition from a small port of minor importance to the regional business, financial and shipping hub. Chapter 5, highlighting the years after 2004 to the present day, reflects on the new challenges to Dubai, which unexpectedly arose in the early years of this century, beginning with the arrival of a more assertive Abu Dhabi and the Global Financial Crisis of 2007–8. This chapter also explains innovations such as the free-zone cities and tourism, introduced in Dubai to supplement, complement and 'add value' to the initial port and airport developments. The Conclusion pulls together the arguments to focus on what has made Dubai so distinctive and different. To add clarity, there are maps of the Gulf as it was in the nineteenth century and as it is now, together with illustrations of shipping developments and the evolution of Dubai.

Chapter 1

DUBAI

ORIGINS AND EMERGENCE (1833–1958)

It is difficult to overstate the role of the ocean in the rise of the modern world-system.[1]

Beginnings

When some members of the Bu Falasah (Bani Yas) tribe determined in 1833 on *hijra*, or migration,[2] to leave Abu Dhabi, as a result of internal feuds and establish themselves about 150 km north, up the Arabian Gulf coast in Dubai, Dubai was still only a small participant in the commerce of the region. This exodus had a sizeable impact, 'doubling the town's population'[3] to around 2000 people. The new arrivals, like the established inhabitants, lived around the sheltered, though shallow sandy creek relying on fishing, supplemented by dates, with some goats and camels supplying milk and meat – and pearling as the only source of revenue. However, the Gulf itself was part of a long-established pattern of pragmatic trade and tolerance of other cultures, and for centuries, links between port settlements in the Indian Ocean *littoral* had flourished, including trading for necessities between themselves and goods from larger centres further afield. Indeed, 'from 1500 the Indian Ocean emerged . . . as the locus of early modern trade between Africa, Asia and Europe. Global historians increasingly acknowledge the Indian Ocean international system as "ground zero" for early modern globalization'.[4] We should not therefore lose sight of the fact that the rise of Dubai and its economic liberalism is far from an aberration, more a return to an example of the multifaceted diversity of contacts and trading that had flourished in the region for centuries.

Regional specialists, such as Fuccaro, Potter, Sheriff[5] and Villiers,[6] have established that, owing to poor inland communications through difficult terrain and weak overall control by colonial Ottoman or Persian overlords, Gulf port towns and their trades were orientated outwards. Until the age of steam in the mid-nineteenth century, trade was dependent on the monsoon winds and, as Potter emphasizes, 'it is quite clear that the prosperity of Gulf ports was built on commerce ... the seaborne trade with China, India and East Africa'.[7] Dependent on the sea for their very existence, these Gulf settlements – even small centres like Dubai – included cosmopolitan inhabitants from all the societies and peoples surrounding the Indian Ocean and the Gulf, who could and would move if conditions were felt to be better or more secure elsewhere (security and stability were particularly important). As with anywhere else in the world, conditions did change, trading routes altered, and political factors intervened. Those centres that were flexible and adaptable survived and prospered best.

For trading and commerce, in the middle of the nineteenth century, the Gulf coastline of the Arabian Peninsula was still economically of little interest (apart from the inner Gulf pearling-centre island of Bahrain), with the major trading ports being in Southern Persia and Basrah (Mesopotamia – now Iraq). Dubai was still an insignificant, now independent, small town, having succeeded in precariously balancing itself between its erstwhile overlords in Abu Dhabi and the powerful Qawasim of Ras al Khaimah. There were two main reasons how it had succeeded in doing so. The first reason was that the Qawasim who had been the major maritime power in the region had lost most of their military strength, as a result of clashes with the British, as shown for example by Fuccaro.[8] It therefore suited the chastened and weakened Qawasim, though still controlling land territories covering much of the northern and eastern parts of the peninsula (stretching down to Sharjah town just north of Dubai), as well as large swathes of the southern coast of Persia including ports such as Lingah, to have a small and unthreatening, independent Dubai divorced from Abu Dhabi, as a buffer between them and their rival power. Although disputes continued for decades with tribal and regional alliances changing regularly, Dubai managed to retain its separate status.

The second reason that Dubai survived independently was that the British defeat of the Qawasim and the destruction of their fleet in 1819 was followed by the first of a series of truces (from January 1820), in which the local rulers agreed to 'a cessation of plunder and piracy on land and sea for ever'.[9] This truce, agreeing to stop hostilities, was followed by a second in 1835 during the (vital) pearling season, signed by the rulers of Sharjah, Ajman, Abu Dhabi – and Dubai, with a third for ten years, agreed in 1843. Such was the success of these measures that in May 1853 the 'Perpetual Maritime Truce' was signed by the rulers of Abu Dhabi, Dubai, Ajman, Ras al Khaimah and Umm al Quwain agreeing that 'from this date and hereafter, there shall be a complete cessation of hostilities at sea between our respective subjects and dependents, and a perfect maritime truce shall endure between ourselves and between our successors, respectively for evermore'.[10] Dubai was therefore now also being treated as a separate entity in the agreements with the de facto new regional overlords, the British, and was a signatory to treaties designed to prevent further hostilities – a message certainly not escaping the notice of its rulers as they assessed the changing political and economic landscape. As Glen Balfour-Paul highlights, there was another significant result of the truces as 'the outcome of Britain's treaties with whatever Shaikhs they found locally in charge at the time (was that) their separate authority was legitimized and perpetuated'.[11]

1. Dubai: Origins and Emergence (1833–1958)

Dubai's strategy was already beginning to take shape and can be summed up as taking three discernible directions, as outlined by Andrea Rugh.[12]

1. Maintain independence from other regional powers (e.g. between the Qawasim and Al Nayan of Abu Dhabi).
2. Exploit outside opportunities, if possible, to boost the economy.
3. Keep family challenges under control and keep good relations with the British (who would therefore be more inclined to intervene favourably if required).

These sensible policies were to be maintained for the next 150 years.

With British power having secured the 'pacification' treaties and established the 'Trucial Coast' in place, and by so doing, preserving the independence of fledgling Dubai, the reasons for the British being in the region at all and their impact need to be reviewed.

The English, later British, East India Company (EIC), having established themselves in Shiraz and Isfahan in 1617, first set up a 'factory' (warehouse/trading post) in the Gulf at Gombroon (now Bandar Abbas) in Persia in 1623, having assisted the Persians to re-take Portuguese ports or strongholds at the mouth of the Gulf in 1622. Political and economic uncertainty provoked the establishment of a replacement EIC headquarters in Basrah in 1723, but subsequently a 'British Resident' representative was based in Bushire on the Persian coast – the entry port for the caravan routes into the interior of Iran. From 1763 (until transferred to Bahrain in 1946), the primary British representative in the Gulf was based in Bushire, reflecting the commercial and political importance of the country (compared with the 'barren wastes' on the other Gulf coast) – particularly as the Persian Imperial *firman* (edict) of 1763 confirming the residency gave the EIC 'a monopoly on the import of woollens into Persia, freedom from taxes and a promise that no other European nation would be allowed to establish a trading station there'.[13] Dominating the most economically important sectors in the Gulf, the British were therefore in a strong commercial and political position and these factories, and that at Basrah in Mesopotamia from 1635, administered from Bombay, 'formed the basis of British economic activities in the Gulf for a hundred and fifty years'.[14]

Persian naval resources were meagre, having no maritime tradition, depending on coastal Arabs for manpower and shipbuilding knowledge and having to import timber from the Caucasus. The Qawasim, however, based in Ras al Khaimah on the Arabian side of the Gulf, were a far from negligible maritime power and also controlled the territory inhabited by Arabic-speaking people of Arab descent on the eastern part of the south coast of Persia, in towns such as Lingah, Sinas and Charak, ruled by a Qawasim Shaikh, under only nominal control from Tehran.

HH Shaikh Sultan al Qasimi (the current ruler of Sharjah) and a direct successor of the 'Qawasim' (plural of 'Qasimi') is quite clear that "In my view the East India Company was determined to increase its share of the trade of the Gulf by all possible means",[15] challenging the orthodox view that EIC/British antipathy towards the Qawasim was because of their piracy and attacks on British ships. Certainly, it appears that almost every incident affecting British or EIC ships was reported to London as being attributed to Qawasim predations, accurately or otherwise, as Belgrave admits.[16]

J.B Kelly's more standard approach accepts that though the (Trucial States) coast was known as the 'Pirate Coast' due to the exploits of the Qawasim, 'it must be said that their reputation was largely earned as a result of incidents arising out of their protracted struggles with the rulers of Muscat' (but that it was hardly surprising if they had resorted to piracy), 'in view of the harshness and poverty of their lives'.[17] Additionally, they appear to have been influenced by Wahabis who, emerging from the central Arabian deserts around 1800, but without any maritime presence, reached an agreement with the Qawasim two years later for joint action against their Omani enemies, as Potts records.[18] The Wahabis were fundamentalist, conservative and intolerant of foreigners – and other Muslims who did not comply with their austere interpretation of Islam.

It is also likely that Qawasim trading activity, focussed on Qishm (Kish) island in Southern Persia, would have had some impact on the effective duopoly enjoyed by the British/Persian centre in Bushire. However, as highlighted by Frauke Heard-Bey, by the end of the eighteenth century, they had already lost much of their earlier dominance due to British competition, inter-Arab warfare (against Oman) with a major impact on trade and particularly pearling revenues. 'Having a much narrower economic base than their Omani enemies they relied more and more on the supplies captured from Omani trading vessels . . . eventually this behaviour . . . led the Qawasim to attack and capture even ships flying British colours.'[19]

Certainly, British concerns in the early decades of the nineteenth century were now primarily focussed on the fact that one of the routes to, 'jewel in the crown', India from Great Britain passed through the Gulf (via the Mediterranean, Syria and Iraq) and though the regional disputes clearly involved elements of trade competition, intra-regional power struggles – and presumably at least some attacks on merchant vessels by 'pirates' – it was essential that the sea-lanes to and from India were protected. As Noura al Mazrouei has emphasized in the context of relations with Saudi Arabia, 'before the oil era Britain focused mainly on the coastal areas . . . and intervened . . . in cases impacting on the stability of the coast'.[20] Accordingly, in December 1819, after the failure of 'reconciliation' efforts in 1806, and further, smaller 'warning-shot' punitive expeditions in 1809 and 1816, Ras al Khaimah, the capital of Qawasim power, was attacked and destroyed by a flotilla assembled in Bombay comprising several warships accompanied by 3500 sepoys (native Indian soldiers). Supported by around 4000 Omani troops, who were only too anxious to assist in the removal of a major regional rival, the joint force also burnt or removed the Qawasim fleet and as part of the campaign, destroyed Qawasim ships and fortifications along the coast as far as Sharjah and in the Qawasim possessions in Southern Persia, as highlighted by Shaikh Sultan Al Qasimi.[21] Sir William Keir, in command of the expeditionary force, having won the battle, realized that his instructions did not extend to what action should be taken once the Qawasim were defeated and so, after working on the problem for a month, he put together the first of the truces (treaties of peace) signed by the local rulers in January 1820. As Charles Davies' investigation into Qasimi piracy in this period concludes, 'the eventual political settlement was in many ways (an) extempore production . . . it would be difficult to argue that there was an effective, overall and conscious stratagem or concerted policy behind Britain's experiences in the Gulf during these years . . . the evidence seems to point to piecemeal even ad hoc development'.[22]

With the Qawasim removed as a threat, for the British, the Gulf was now *mare nostrum* and would remain so for the next century and a half.

We can draw several conclusions from the political and economic environment in the Gulf in the mid-nineteenth century after the destruction of the Qawasim and the signing of the various peace agreements. Firstly, that the British arrived in the Gulf as traders, supplicants clinging to small trading posts, initially in the form of the East India Company early in the seventeenth century then, after 1858, represented and directed by the Government of India on behalf of the British Crown. By the end of the eighteenth century, they had outlasted and ousted their European competitors (with European politics having an impact) and, as a result of internecine and regional conflicts on the Arab and Persian sides of the Gulf, were in a strong economic (and political) position thanks to beneficial treaties with Persian rulers. At this time, there was little or no interest in the (mainly) small subsistence-level hamlets on the *terra incognita*, Arab Gulf Coast.

Secondly, this economic involvement and increasing economic strength inexorably led also to political (and military) power, and this was ruthlessly used in 1819 to eradicate the maritime threat of the Qawasim, who may have been an economic irritant and also were, more importantly, difficult to control and monitor, were linked to potentially threatening austere and xenophobic Wahhibis emerging from the hinterland, and whose ships were certainly a major source of concern to all shipping in the lower Gulf, including those on the vital corridor to India. Philip Macdougall in his study of maritime activity in the region comments that at the beginning of the nineteenth century a major objective for the Wahabis

> was the Arabian coast of the Gulf, for if these territories also succumbed it would not only permit the establishment of a large Muslim state, but would, through the commercial activities of the Arabs living there, would allow Wahhabism, to be exported to the coasts of Africa and India. Around 1805, the Qawasim acceded to the Wahhabis, religious teachers teaching the new faith and encouraging a seagoing campaign that had the dual objective of plunder and the extinguishing of those not converted to the Wahhabi faith.[23]

Thirdly, having removed any potential threats, the truces and treaties of 1820, 1835, 1843 and 1853 signed between the British and local rulers were not particularly punitive, as the British were not interested in this barren desert area and simply wanted it to remain peaceful and unthreatening. Indeed, when the 1853 agreement expired, the rulers demanded that it be renewed in perpetuity in order that pearling and trade continue to be protected.[24] These policies succeeded in eradicating much of the tribal warfare that had debilitated the region and allowed stability. 'Stability meant wealth and as coastal dwellers found their circumstances improving, their way of life became more attractive to the Bedu (desert dwelling nomads) who settled and took up trades such as pearling and fishing . . . as a result, Dubai's population swelled.'[25] Pearling, virtually the only revenue-earning activity on the Arab coast, would particularly benefit from peaceful conditions.

Fourthly, the signing of the treaties with the leaders in place at the time legitimized them more definitively and set in motion the rule of these family dynasties in the new time of peace. Indeed, it also 'gave members of the ruling families a considerable stake in maintaining the (new) status quo',[26] particularly so when, traditionally, a ruling tribal family was by no means guaranteed to be allowed to stay in power by other members of the tribe. 'The Treaty system strengthened his position and assured the continuity of his influence. With time it became a guarantee. Most important, it contributed to the institutionalization of his position.'[27]

Fifthly, Dubai's ruler being a signatory to the treaties and the agreements of non-aggression confirmed its status as an independent town – with the British as guarantors.

Finally, it was evident that the British were now the dominant, unchallenged power in the Gulf, very much based on control of the sea.

In setting out this *tour d'horizon*, I have sought to establish that the expansion and separation of Dubai in the 1830s was fortuitously timed for the newly independent town because it coincided with conditions in the region that had seen the British establish themselves as the paramount power by the removal of all potential rivals and the imposition of peace on the feuding tribes of the coast. Without this presence and impact, it seems very likely that small, feeble Dubai would have been in due course swallowed up by the (still) powerful Qawasim or by Abu Dhabi. But the weakening of the maritime, outward-looking Qawasim, the land-based focus of the Al Nahyan Bani Yas of Abu Dhabi more on their desert domains (particularly the oasis of Buraimi) and the fact that they were both committed to peaceful activity allowed Dubai the breathing space to survive and grow. The British presence also kept at bay and staved off, as far as all the small Shaikhdoms were concerned, the potential territorial ambitions of the Wahhabis, subsequently Saudis, who continued to encroach and assert their influence in the ill-defined border areas of the desert, particularly in the strategic oasis of Buraimi.

Equally, the Qawasim in Ras al Khaimah (RAK) and Sharjah were (understandably) resentful of their diminution in status, but the 'levelling of the playing-field' meant that there were opportunities for Dubai and indeed all other towns, in an environment where peaceful maritime trading was now encouraged by the *Pax Britannica/Arabica*. British policy, based on the need to control the shipping routes both in the Gulf area and particularly to and from India, without risk of piracy and maintain peace to allow trade to thrive, therefore indirectly allowed Dubai to survive, and the presence of another signatory, dividing Qawasim and Abu Dhabi territories, well-aware of the usefulness of British protection, was a useful side effect, as highlighted by Davidson.[28]

The fact was that the signing of the various treaties proved remarkably beneficial for the various new 'Trucial States'. 'It is evident from the history of British relations with the Shaikhdoms that the treaties were not imposed on the Rulers as a result of conquest, but, were concluded in consequence of special requests by them for British protection',[29] stresses Husain Al Baharna. James Onley makes the same point: 'The Rulers actively sought British protection; the Pax could not have been established in the first place without their approval and support.'[30] It is not difficult to see why. All the rulers benefitted from the maintenance of a peaceful status quo, admittedly, in particular the smaller and weaker Shaikhdoms (Dubai, Umm al Quwain, Ajman) who had previously been dependents, tacit or otherwise, of bigger powers and now saw their independence – and family dynasties – assured. Also, peaceful relations allowed a focus on money-making enterprises of pearling and trading, without which the Shaikhdoms would be entirely without revenues. Even the Qawasim, now a spent military force, and who may well have mused over 'what might have been' if they had not over-reached themselves, retained their possessions on both sides of the Gulf.

Qawasimi Lingah, or Lengeh in particular, on the Persian coast, was to remain one of the key trading centres for decades to come. 'After the British put an end to their maritime violence in 1819, the Qawasim did their best to develop Lingah as a commercial centre, at which they were successful.'[31] Indeed Lingah remained the key lower Gulf entrepot until around 1900, rather weakening the argument of those who felt British anti-Qawasim action was because of the desire to remove commercial rivals. This was highlighted during the 1863 visit of Lewis Pelly (British Political Resident based in Bushire 1862–72), when Lingah is described as being unwalled, with a population of 8000–10,000 people, ruled by a Shaikh, 'an Arab of ancient descent, and the place enjoys considerable prosperity owing to there being neither import nor export duties. The bulk of the trade is with the maritime Arab ports to which goods from Bombay and Kurrachee (Karachi) are conveyed in small coasting craft.'[32] Lingah, controlled and ruled by the Al Qassimi, thus remained the major relay and transhipment port of the Southern-Gulf throughout most of the nineteenth century, 'benefitting from the fact that ... trade with India between 1845 and 1865 quintupled, while between 1861 and 1865 it tripled',[33] thanks in part to better, more reliable steamship connections, with regional inhabitants controlling the on-carrying distribution out of Lingah from the main-line vessels calling there, to other regional ports.

It is clear therefore that, far from imposing punitive treaties on a collection of unwilling (though some were more willing than others) participants, or destroying commercial rivals, the British actions had the effect of diminishing intra-gulf tribal hostilities, stopping attacks on shipping, pearlers and fishing boats and this had been welcomed by (most of) the ruling families – with the peace dividend for all regional inhabitants being in the ability to trade, fish or pearl-dive with less fear of attack. The British presence was low-key, with the Gulf Resident/Political Resident, responsible for the whole Gulf, based in Bushire, visiting the Shaikhdoms only once a year and maintaining subordinate 'native' (i.e. non-British) political agents throughout the region – in Qawasim Sharjah (reflecting its continuing importance) for the Trucial States from 1823. A small squadron of warships was based in Bushire on anti-slavery duty and as a potential mobile response 'big stick' in case of need, but otherwise the resident trod softly and the Shaikhdoms were largely left alone, with 'the traditional institutions of the area (left) intact',[34] but the inhabitants well-aware of the possibility of gunboat-diplomacy.

It's the (maritime) economy

With tranquillity imposed, the focus of this chapter now falls on the economic conditions and development of the Gulf in the late nineteenth century and the gradual emergence of Dubai.

The economic activity in the Gulf remained centred on two main activities: pearling and trading. For the small centres on the Arabian coast, pearling was almost the only occupation other than those of subsistence, such as fishing or basic agriculture. As an illustration of the importance of pearling, Hawley records the estimates in the 1830s when about 700 boats were from the Trucial coast, each with a crew of seventeen or eighteen;[35] however, by the beginning of the twentieth century, Lorimer estimated numbers as over 1200 boats:[36]

Ajman – 40 boats
Abu Dhabi – 410 boats
Dubai – 335 boats
Umm al Quwain – 70 boats
Sharjah (including Ras al Khaimah) – 360 boats

Pearling represented by far the dominant share of employment, as for example, Dubai's population at this time according to Lorimer was around 10,000–12,000 people and those working on the pearling fleet (circa 5000 to 6000) would thus have represented a sizeable share of the total, virtually all able-bodied men and older boys, albeit boosted by seasonal outsiders. Revenues were considerable, reported by Lorimer as averaging (in rupees):

In 1873–905, annually, Trucial States area 4,150,398 and Bahrain 3,837,359
In 1905–1906, Trucial States area 8,000,000 and Bahrain 12,603,000

Dionisius Agius states that at this time, 10 rupees were worth about £1 sterling,[37] making the Trucial Coast production worth around £800,000 in 1905–6, a very substantial sum indeed. Pearling would continue as the major employer until the 1930s and 1940s, when worldwide recession, the arrival of Japanese cultured pearls and alternative work in the fledgling oil industries became available. Agius quotes statistics for Bahrain showing 917 pearling Dhows in 1907, reduced to 69 in 1947.[38] Those who benefitted from the pearling trade were few – the rulers (who levied a tax on boats from their territories), and the pearl merchants and agent intermediaries, who made the bulk of the profits. For the divers and seamen, who performed the hard and dangerous work, 'the sweated labour of the sea ... battened upon by a sequence of exploiters',[39] the rewards were meagre indeed. It is also evident from these statistics, based on the number of boats and thus the number of pearl buyers, that Dubai had become a much bigger centre in the seventy years since its independence, though still of little importance in the wider world. The beginning of its transformation would be the result of external trade and politics.

The trading ports in the second half of the nineteenth century in the Gulf were still the same centres that had flourished for the last hundred years: Basrah (southern Mesopotamia and gateway to the interior and Baghdad, using predominantly British smaller vessels on the Tigris/Euphrates rivers); Bushire (entry and caravan-route point for the interior of Persia and the major cities of Isfahan, Shiraz and Tehran); Lingah (trans-shipment only) and the Arab Emirate of Mohammerah (on the Persian side of the Shatt-Al Arab-River, another entry point for Tehran and Isfahan and re-named as Khoramshahr in the reign of Reza Shah); as well as Bahrain, Bandar Abbas and Muscat to a lesser degree. 'The area became a supplier of raw cotton ... Bushire and Basrah became significant market for British goods ... (and) from the hinterland of these ports came pearls, silk, nuts, spices, dates and other dried fruit, wool and carpets.'[40] Lingah, however, unlike Bushire with its caravan routes into the interior of Persia, was a purely transhipment port (as noted by Pelly above) whereby goods from Bombay or Karachi, for example, were discharged and relayed on to smaller craft serving smaller regional ports. Trade moved in and out of the Gulf on the main routes from Great Britain and Europe, mainly via the Red Sea and the Suez Canal (after 1869) and, also, to and from Britain's Indian Empire, particularly the ports of Karachi and Bombay.

The technological change that had promoted the Industrial Revolution had extended to shipping and the emergence of steamships, from the 1830s onwards, on deep-sea routes (though hampered in the early stages by inefficient engines and lack of coaling stations which initially restricted their range, compared with sailing ships) and supported the expansion of increasingly global trading patterns. Transport by sea was becoming faster and more reliable, with four main factors identified by Martin Stopford,[41] which accelerated the changes:

1. The Steam Engine, which meant that ships were no longer at the mercy and vagaries of the wind
2. Iron Hulls, which were more efficient and effective in protecting cargo and allowed larger ships to be built
3. Screw propellers, which made ships more reliable, faster and seaworthy
4. Deep sea cable networks, which allowed traders, governments and shipping companies to communicate more efficiently and quickly

Also, the expansion of the British Empire and trade routes necessitated improved communications and 'the British Government had a strong interest in perpetuating and expanding mail routes, but for the private operator, mail steamship services were rarely profitable (due to high costs) but Government subsidies ... could help to offset these costs'.[42] Accordingly, a policy of subsidies was developed by the British government (costing around £1 million annually overall), and in 1862 with the support of Sir Bartle Frere, the governor of Bombay, a subsidized mail contract was awarded to the newly formed British India Steam Navigation Company (BI) from Bombay and Karachi to Basrah and intermediate ports. Initially, from 1863, the service operated with only eight sailings a year, but by 1866 it was operating on a fortnightly basis calling Muscat, Bandar Abbas, Bushire and Basrah with Lingah and Bahrain alternately or on inducement.[43]

Though the new BI service was a private company, commercial proposition, expanding the network of the line's services, it may also, in part, be seen as an example of how the Government in India (as an arm of the British Government) 'assisted (British) private enterprise in opening up new areas to British trade and to British political influence',[44] in this case by selecting the BI to receive the mail-contract subsidy. Mail subsidies provided a 'regular income stream' on which lines could depend, allowing them to develop trades which might otherwise have been ignored or served less well, 'in an era in which sea power was so integral a part of international trade and diplomacy, contracts acted as a multi-functional mechanism for carrying out those purposes'.[45] Other major states adopted similar policies. Of course, state subsidies are nothing new and even today discussions revolve around Chinese manufacturing subsidies or even whether Gulf airlines receive preferential treatment or not. In the case of the BI steamships in the 1860s, there can be no doubt that this subsidized 'head start' (or 'confirmed revenue stream') in establishing expensive, new-technology services was a major assistance for the line in competing with actual and potential rival lines, even if we must accept that starting such a risky and expensive shipping service on a new route needed all the help it could get. There is also no doubt that British commercial interests benefitted from such intra-imperial links. The next step was to establish a professional land-side network of agents in the Gulf.

The arrival of steamships was to transform the trade in the Gulf. Regular steamship services operating on a known schedule and no longer at the mercy of the winds and tides required a more professional and systematic approach by those dealing with them on land and as 'there would clearly be a need for agents at the proposed ports of call, (so), a small group of British individuals grasped this new opportunity'.[46] These individuals were connected to the original Mackinnon Mackenzie company formed in Calcutta, out of which had arisen the BI. The two partnerships, Gray Mackenzie and Company (GM) and Gray Paul and Company, effectively divisions of the same business, later merged to become simply Gray Mackenzie, established agencies in the Gulf with 'the ports covered being Basrah, Mohammorah (Khorramshahr), Bushire, Bandar Abbas, Lingah, and Dubai'.[47] Griffiths implies that Dubai was included in the 1860s along with, for example, Basrah in 1869, but with no steamer calls, and according to George Chapman, the port was not actually added on the Gray Paul agency network until 1891. BI whose agents were Gray Paul commenced ad hoc calls in that year.[48]

We have established, therefore, that the Gulf trades in the latter part of the nineteenth century were beginning to be transformed by the introduction of, British dominated, steamship lines and the attendant network of professional agents at the main ports to deal with them. Though statistics are somewhat uncertain in the early years, it is readily apparent that volumes of tonnage handled and numbers of sailings by BI in particular, but other services also, dramatically increased. The bigger steam ships called fewer ports, but the overall trade increased, and this benefitted the smaller, local, 'feeder' vessels, 'local shipping maintained a solid profile . . . the continuation of inter-coastal trade was also assisted by the size of British ships which could only approach large harbours'.[49] (Actually, this quotation implies that these larger ships actually 'berthed' alongside a quay when in practise due to a lack of suitable ports they invariably anchored off the coast with cargo brought ashore in small craft, for example at Lingah and Dubai – but the point remains a valid one.)

As an illustration of trade volumes, the following figures are extracted from Saldanha quoted by Jones:

Tonnage discharged by BI ships / Numbers of BI calls / % of Total tonnage handled by BI

Bushire 1873	26,000 / 26 / 62%
Bushire 1886	97,000 / 108 / 93%
Bushire 1900	133,00 / 111 / 98%
Bandar Abbas	1873 26,000 / 26 / 84%
Bandar Abbas	1886 95,000 / 107 / 95%
Bandar Abbas	1900 135,000 / 101 / 96%
Lingeh 1873	26,000 / 26 / 85%
Lingeh 1886	63,000 / 78 / 100%
Lingeh 1900	86,000 / 78 / 98%

Source Saldanha.[50] (Quoted by Jones)[51]

Therefore, by the beginning of the twentieth century, the trades in and out of the Gulf had expanded and were well established with, according to Lorimer,[52] lines operating as listed:

The BI– with weekly services to and from Karachi and Bombay (with the UK served via Karachi)
The Bombay and Persian Steam Navigation Company (Moghul Line) – to and from Bombay (irregular)
Persian Gulf Steam Navigation Company – UK (monthly)
Messageries Maritimes – Marseilles (irregular)
Russian Gulf and Persian – Odessa (Monthly)

This report is supplemented and updated by the 'Cabinet Survey of Shipping in the Gulf for 1907' by the director of Naval Intelligence (DNI), quoted by Burdett,[53] showing other services from the UK to and from the Gulf:

The BI (cargo relayed at Bombay or Karachi)
Anglo-Algerian (Frank C Strick) – monthly
Bucknell Steamship
West Hartlepool Steam Navigation Co.
And from Hamburg, Hamburg-America Line (Monthly)
Basrah dominated the volumes of cargo handled. 'Ninety percent of the cargoes are shipped at Basra; steamers seldom wait more than a day at any other Gulf port.'[54]

Until the end of the nineteenth century, Dubai remained a small port town, growing in size, but still as we have seen, dependent almost entirely, on pearling. This was about to change under the rule of Shaikh Maktoum bin Hashar al Maktoum (1894–1906) whose policy was 'liberal and enlightened and resulted in the rapid growth of the port of Dubai, which after 1902, assisted by the decadence (decline) of Lingah, became a regular port of call for steamers and the chief commercial emporium of the Trucial coast'.[55] Certainly, the DNI report shows that in 1907, Dubai was then a regular call on the BI service Number 14 from Bombay and Karachi (that called at several ports in the Gulf, including, still, Lingah), with the faster mail service (Number 13), calling only Basrah, Mohammerah (Khorramshahr) and Bushire.

Lingah was, as previously described, a well-established port on the south coast of Persia, in a coastal *littoral* of ethnic Arabs with close links to those on the Arab shore. It was ruled by an Al Qasimi Shaikh until 1887[56] as a hereditary administrator, with his official responsibility being to collect taxes and duties and maintain law and order, until, as Floor confirms, the central Persian government started to exert its control over the (virtually autonomous) region. Lingah had no important hinterland links to the interior of Persia and its trade depended on pearls and the relay (trans-shipment) of goods, mainly from India, from large vessels on to small craft for regional distribution. Such a system can only survive if costs are kept to the minimum with low duties and lengthy (free) storage times for the cargo and, until 1900, the port had flourished in just such a laissez-faire way because of the lack of central government supervision with control of revenues farmed out to local officials. However, from *Nowruz* (21 March) 1900, the new (Belgian) controller of customs for the Persian government implemented a new state policy for improving and modernizing revenue collection, to enhance import duties, to stimulate exports and to remove internal road tolls (*octroi*). Lingah and other southern ports (such as Bushire) were forced to apply a uniform 5 per cent duty which was unpopular locally, but for the central government, showed a sizeable increase in direct revenue. Lorimer reports that in 1900–1, net revenue was 320,000 tomans (a major Persian currency unit, then divided into 10,000 dinars), compared with less than 250,000 tomans in the previous year.[57] Worse was to follow for relay-dependent Lingah, as in 1902, duties on re-exported wheat and barley were increased to 15 per cent (if not shipped within twenty days) and for rice and ghee to 10 per cent on the same basis – these and all other products having already had to pay the new 5 per cent import duty. These measures effectively destroyed the ability of the merchants to make money (on an operation which depended on low costs and long free or cheap storage times), and if there was no money to be made, the port could not flourish. The new customs officials showed little consideration for the difficulties of the Lingah merchants and, 'as a result of the new customs regulations, goods at Dubai were 10% cheaper than at Lingah. Shipping companies and merchants found out that on the other side of the Gulf there were none of the restrictions and formalities required by Persian/Iranian customs and that it was a paying trade'.[58] Floor also attributes the problems of Lingah to a customs arrangement involving standard centralized revenue collection, with Russia in 1903, agreed by Iran with its largest trading partner without too much consideration of the impact on a port not involved in Russian trade, not involved in trade to the interior of Persia and almost entirely dependent on relay trade to the Arabian coast. 'As a consequence, its importance as the port of trans-shipment for the Arab coast immediately declined'.[59]

It is important to emphasize that it was the merchants who controlled the various businesses and the nature of activity in Lingah being transhipment, such services were portable and transferable, that could very easily be carried out in another port town in the same Gulf-gateway area. Very astutely, the ruler of Dubai invited merchants (who as we have seen, were Arab speaking with close cultural and familial links) to move their transferable skills and connections to Dubai, where they were provided with land and re-settlement assistance and low or zero tariffs, to re-create the transhipment entrepot of Lingah in Dubai. Lorimer records in 1908 that 'the trade of Lingah has now in large measure passed to Dubai'.[60] This included smuggling (of tea and coffee for example) into the now high-tariff areas of Persia, and of equal if not more importance – steamship calls (twenty-one in 1902 mainly by the Bombay and Persia company) had commenced at Dubai, and from 1904 the dominant BI cargo service started to call Dubai regularly, as well as Lingah. Dubai's status as a trading centre was being enhanced, with re-exports for other Gulf ports being trans-shipped and cargo for the interior of the Trucial States moving inland.[61] In 1905–6, Heard-Bey records that thirty-four steamships visited Dubai and unloaded around 70,000 tons.[62] Although the decline of Lingah clearly occurred over a period of some years and some services, particularly the BI, continued to call,[63] its heyday as the lower Gulf cargo relay centre was now in the past, from having trade, 'in the order of one million pounds (in the 1890s), after the imposition of the new uniform customs tariff . . . its trade dropped to £250,000 and Dubai became the emporium for the Arab coast'.[64]

What is also significant is that large numbers of these merchants, including the Pearl merchants, moved to Dubai when, presumably, they could have transferred their activities to, for example, Sharjah, which, less than 30km north of Dubai, also had a creek for small craft and, ruled by the Al Qasimi ruling family, a long, familial and close connection with Lingah. As previously emphasized, the cosmopolitan nature of Gulf trading centres meant that traders, merchants and craftsmen were perfectly capable of moving to rival centres if working and business conditions – such as tax or duty increases – became untenable. It is impossible to avoid the conclusion that most of these business people moved to the place that they felt would provide the best location, commercially and geographically to live and to develop their trading businesses, prompted by the proactive stance of Dubai ruler Shaikh Maktoum al Maktoum, who clearly understood what such merchants would require and ensured that the right facilities were provided. The ruler removed the 5 per cent customs duty in Dubai in 1904 and the city became a free-port with no customs duties. As had been the case in Lingah, the ruler received some revenue each year from a merchant who was permitted to act as a 'revenue-farmer' to recover charges where he could.[65] According to Wilson he 'began a systematic programme aimed at the most influential merchants; he abolished most tariffs . . . and sent personal envoys to the most important members of Lingah's merchant community. If the largest merchant operations could be brought to Dubai . . . then medium and small businesses would follow.'[66] It is also reasonable to take the view that the merchants also felt comfortable moving from the uncertain political and commercial future of Lingah to an entrepreneurial Dubai that ruled itself but effectively operated under the umbrella of British protection. As James Onley emphasizes, 'Protection was one of the greatest concerns of Gulf merchants before the 20th century . . . to gain protection . . . members of business families frequently allied themselves with European governments or companies'.[67] For business people, stability and clarity are perhaps the most essential components of all, and, astute as they were, the merchants of Lingah could see that a more secure future lay in Dubai, replicating the laissez-faire conditions of Lingah and geographical convenience without the political uncertainty.

There can be no doubt that this migration of merchants from Lingah is a seminal event in the history and development of Dubai, reflecting as it does, those qualities which would come to distinguish the Emirate in the following years. These would include taking the initiative innovatively, acceptance of outsiders who would participate constructively in the growth of Dubai, being aware of the importance of stability and taking a long-term view and adopting an overall flexible approach to ensure that business people were encouraged to settle. It also marks the first incidence of Dubai taking steps to shape its own future. The new settlers gradually assimilated into the life of Dubai. They retained not only, for example, in 'Bastakiya' the area of Dubai given to them (named after the town and region of Bastak in Southern Persia, inland from Lingah), some of their traditional building styles with a cooling tower – the *badgir* or 'windcatcher' known as a *barjeel* in Arabic – but also the trading and personal links with Persia (and the rest of the region) that would endure and be of great benefit to the city's economy in years to come. The lessons of Lingah, the impact that over-regulation and bureaucracy could have in a competitive marketplace and the importance of having a stable and welcoming environment that would encourage people to settle were well learnt and continue to resonate today.

What the British did next

At the end of the nineteenth century, rivalries between the various imperial powers were intensifying and there were increasing attempts by France (coaling stations and trade), Russia (pressure on Persia felt to be another part of 'the Great Game' encircling India) and Germany (influence and trade) to take an interest in the Gulf, which the British had had more or less to themselves for decades. Accordingly, and certainly not coincidentally, in 1892, the Trucial rulers of Abu Dhabi, Dubai, Ajman, Sharjah, Ras al Khaimah and Umm al Qaiwain agreed to sign a supplementary treaty with the British on behalf of themselves and their successors agreeing not to enter into any agreement or communication with a foreign government, confirming that no foreign power representative would be allowed to take up residence in their territories, and also that they could not sell, lease or give occupation to any government except the British.

In addition to this 'ring-fencing' of the Arab Shaikhdoms, prestige and 'face' in diplomacy were very much part and parcel of the methods of imperial control, and also as a means of deterrence. It was essential 'for Britain to assert its power and demonstrate it was both capable and willing to exercise force'[68] to maintain the belief that the British were in control of the Gulf and if the loose reins of informal empire were to be maintained. British imperial concerns, at this time, tended to revolve around Russia and its supposed aim for 'warm-water' ports. Persia was regarded as a bulwark against these encroaches and there had even been a brief Anglo-Persian war in 1856-7 when the Persian government had seemed to be inclining towards Russian concessions. The arrival of a Russian cruiser *Askold* on a Gulf visit in 1902 concentrated minds decisively. Should there still be any doubt remaining that the British government intended to hermetically seal off the Trucial States at a Governmental level, from outside (non-British) influence, the Foreign Secretary Lord Lansdowne in 1903 spelled it out in clear Monroe Doctrine style, that it was the intention 'in the first place to protect and promote British trade in these waters... and that we should regard the establishment of a Naval Base or fortified base by any other power as a very grave menace to British interests and we should certainly resist it with all the means at our disposal'.[69] Lord Curzon, the viceroy in India, also made a state visit to the Gulf in 1903, his ship accompanied by four warships and held a *durbar* in Sharjah, reminding the Trucial Shaikhs with much pomp and circumstance and high-flown rhetoric of how Britain had ended violence, ensured their independence and was committed to their protection.

It is worth emphasizing again here that though the British successfully staved off other foreign involvement, the treaties with the Gulf rulers also specifically confirmed that Britain would not interfere in their internal affairs and this had the effect of ossifying the regimes and internal political systems of these 'protected states' where the sovereignty of the ruler was recognized. 'The indeterminate status of the Gulf Shaikhdoms, bears in retrospect all the marks of that scrupulous imprecision characteristic of so many of Britain's imperial contrivances... and that the British made up the rules as they went along',[70] which in a fluid environment, where vague 'spheres of influence' were regarded as the norm, seems very much an accurate assessment.

Dubai was therefore left much to itself as the twentieth century commenced but in the seventy years since its 're-foundation' as an independent Shaikhdom:

- It had been legitimized and 'officially recognized' as such, by virtue of the Al Maktoum ruler being a signatory to the treaties with the British.
- As one of the 'protected states', its security was guaranteed by the British.
- It had taken advantage of political problems in Persia and had deftly attracted many powerful economic migrants to settle in Dubai who welcomed the stable and secure entrepreneurial climate. The business controlled by such merchants resulted in 'a remarkable development in commerce'[71] and the start of regular steam vessel calls after 1902.

However, we should not overstate the scale of development even if the first faltering steps had been taken. Dubai was still a small town, albeit substantially larger than before and, like the rest of the Trucial Coast, would remain so for decades to come. Lorimer's survey highlights that the town had a population of around 10,000 people of Arab, Persian, Sudanese and Baluchi origin in the main. There were 335 pearling boats, 50 fishing boats and around 20 'seagoing' boats for more distant trading. The only exports were pearls, pearl-shell and dried fish with imports being primarily dates, rice, piece goods, spices, coir, metals and timber. At this stage and for many years yet, pearling predominated above all else (occupying the bulk of the local male population in the season) and Lorimer records that Dubai (with its 335 boats) had made such strides in establishing itself in this trade that by the end of the nineteenth century the estimated exports were worth 100 lakhs (a lakh is 100,000) of rupees per annum.[72] However, as indicated earlier, the big profits were made elsewhere. 'The Bank of England's records show that in 1917 on the Mumbai (Bombay) market, a gram of Gulf pearls was worth 320 grams of gold.'[73]

Despite Dubai continuing to develop itself as a commercial centre, its economy and that of other Arab Gulf towns continued to be almost completely dependent in the pre-oil years on this single primary product – pearls, as Lorimer, Walker and Davidson among others have emphasized. Consequently, when a combination of the worldwide economic depression and the Japanese development of (cheaper and more reliable supply) cultured pearls in the mid-1920s occurred, Dubai and the region were very adversely affected, as a result of lack of demand from the usual buyers and a collapse in prices. However, as Julian Walker has emphasized, though the merchants and those directly involved in pearl fishing were greatly impoverished, at this time, the rulers such as those in Sharjah and Dubai were starting to receive new sources of income such as payments for oil exploration concessions and civil and military aviation agreements (payments for aircraft landing strips or flying-boat calls). Dubai, in particular, 'boosted by . . . Lingah merchants, the introduction of a Mail Steamer service as well as her Ruler's encouragement of trade grew enormously in population and power. Not only did it attract migrants from other parts of the coast, but also immigrants from abroad. . . . The town of 35,000 people in 1950 was far more cosmopolitan than the village . . . in 1905.'[74] The schedule of the British India Line (BI) in 1947 shows two services now calling Dubai (and Sharjah) regularly from the sub-continent Programme A and Programme B, with no Lingah,[75] confirmed by a letter from George Chapman working for the BI agents, Gray Mackenzie in 1952, responding to a query about a supply of drinking water for the new Political Agency in Dubai: 'there are four mail steamers calling here during a month, two proceeding northwards and two southwards'.[76] Even at this time, Dubai 'time in port' on the inward discharge cargo call was timetabled at ten or eleven hours, with Sharjah only requiring two hours – clearly an indication of cargo volumes. Burdett's compilation of the records shows that by 1960, the BI service to the Gulf from Bombay and Karachi was operated on a fixed weekly service, by five ships carrying not only cargo but migrant working passengers. Significantly, Dubai now was a weekly service, but Sharjah was monthly at best. Other services too, including Strick Line from Europe, were operating regular services including Dubai, in the Strick case as one of about ten ports of call in the Gulf, requiring a month or more spent in the Gulf![77]

Walker also highlights, from his own experience as a political officer in Dubai, that there was a regular flow of itinerant workers through Dubai, in particular, once oil exploration began in earnest from the 1950s and the city benefitted by providing transport, accommodation, food and support services to such workers in transit. These workers, from India and Pakistan, travelled on British India Line ships, which from the late 1940s included the four newly built (1947) 'D' class ships for the Gulf trade to and from South Asia, 'Daressa', 'Dara', 'Dumra' and 'Dwarka', this latter ship being destined to be the last of the line, remaining in service until 1982. Shallow drafted and designed to carry air-cooled fruit to the Gulf, they specialized in carrying large numbers of passengers (labourers and other workers moving to the Gulf for work), mainly, cheaply, on-deck, accommodating until 1977, up to 1537 passengers per sailing in this way.[78] Additionally, after 1947, when the Indian Government restricted and levied duties on official Gold imports (considered essential by most Indians for dowry payments, jewellery and as a tangible and transferable asset), 'the Emirate (became) a base for informal [sic] gold trading with the sub-continent'[79] and 'the merchants of Dubai ... were ready to take advantage of the resultant opportunity [sic] .... This brought ... prosperity to the coast.'[80]

To sum up, so far, if, in its early years, Dubai survived as a result of the pacifications and treaties imposed by the British, particularly on the major powers of the region, it is clear that by the early years of the twentieth century, the Emirate was beginning to exert itself in its own right, proactively and imaginatively in ways that would be familiar a century later. Reacting to an opportunity created by the heavy-handedness of Persian administration in the south of the country, which effectively removed the ability of Lingah to continue to operate as the flourishing transhipment hub as it had for most of the nineteenth century, Lingah's merchants were persuaded to decamp to Dubai with their transferable skills and contacts due to promises of good living conditions, light-touch bureaucracy and taxation and safety and security. Merchants from Southern Iran continued to migrate to Dubai throughout the first half of the twentieth century, helping to establish and expand not only the Emirate's reputation for trade in goods and pearls but also its reputation for accepting and working with people from elsewhere, in particular, cementing its close relationship with Iran that was to be of such benefit in the future. The growth of Dubai and its new role, replacing Lingah as the relay centre and entrepot for the Arab Gulf Coast (and for smuggled goods to Iran), provided the opportunity for steamships (particularly those of BI) to call regularly from the end of the nineteenth century. Although with the decline in pearling activity, progress and expansion were slow until the 1960s, by this time, Dubai was the recognized centre of the region, looking 'every week a little more like the capital of the six northern Trucial States . . . its 15 berth deepwater harbour and vast new airport terminal are well on the way to completion and work on the 393 bed hospital is about to start'.[81] It is from this time, during the rule of Shaikh Rashid al Maktoum, who became ruler in 1958, that Dubai's progress accelerated, linked to developments in the shipping industry which will be examined in more detail in the following chapters.

The beginnings of infrastructure development

As previously highlighted, in Dubai, the Creek remained the centre of cargo-handling activity, which entailed in the early 1950s, 'two small tugs, three barges and several wooden *tishallahs* (small sailing boats) to handle cargo from ships that anchored two to three miles offshore . . . with the channel reduced to a depth of two and a half feet at low water'.[82] The Creek in Dubai was (and is) an inlet into the sandy coastline, created by wind and tidal erosion. By the early 1950s, the silting-up of the Creek was a becoming a major concern, 'particularly in the winter months when the mouth of the creek would move some six or seven hundred yards . . . boats were running aground, capsizing and even sinking',[83] as without the creek, Dubai's ability to retain its position as a trading centre would disappear. The Regent and acting ruler, Shaikh Rashid al Maktoum, consulted with the British political agent in Dubai and in January 1955 Halcrow and Partners produced a report (responding to a request made by the Agent in June 1954) 'ascertaining what measures could be best adopted for the improvement of the harbour of Dubai'.[84]

The British residency in Bahrain (regional Head Office for the Gulf), in a report to the Foreign Office in London, recommended only a few weeks later that 'commercially it would seem definitely necessary that (Dubai) should survive and probably develop, (as) in the event that oil is found in the neighbouring Shaikhdoms, the port of Dubai would be the normal port of entry'[85]. The recommended works to improve the creek were estimated to cost the then substantial sum of around £400,000 (£388,000) – around £8.5 million today – and as this figure was substantially beyond the resources of the Dubai government, some months elapsed as both British Political Offices in the Gulf and Shaikh Rashid manoeuvred to find the money. The former clearly were feeling at times that Shaikh Rashid was letting them do most of the work, particularly in dealing with other regional rulers who might assist with gifts or loans, which for the initial softening-up indeed, he probably (not unreasonably) was, at least in part due to his delicate position as acting regent for the ruler, his ailing father, 'however if we did not undertake this, nothing would be done'.[86] Eventually, though the merchants of Dubai raised an initial £35,000 as a contribution to a 'Creek Bond', initiated by Shaikh Rashid as a way of raising funds from those whose livelihoods were most at stake, the ruler of Kuwait (and the Emir of Qatar) agreed to assist and contributed the required funds as a loan – a loan guaranteed by the British Bank of the Middle East (BBME) in Dubai.[87] BBME reports to London confirm that Shaikh Rashid did actually play his part, returning from a visit to Kuwait in mid-1956 and advising the BBME manager 'that he (had been) . . . promised the money for the creek scheme'[88] and in early 1957 BBME Dubai also advised London that the Government of Qatar had remitted £100,000 in favour of Shaikh Rashid's Creek Account,[89] 'as a free gift'.[90]

The Creek was dredged in 1958-9 by the Austrian company Overseas AST, ensuring that Dubai was no longer at risk of its waterway silting up, and, also now being able to take in a larger craft. Significantly, Chapman records that the sizeable works, including 'widening the creek with explosives', caused considerable disruption, but the ruler 'was a constant visitor to the project sites, often dropping in to check progress, three, four or five times a day'.[91] It is apparent from such reports and others that Shaikh Rashid not only identified with the works but had the initiative, energy and determination to drive them personally, including the decision to use the dredged and excavated rock and silt for repair and land reclamation, which was then sold off to businesses.[92] That the blocking of the creek and of commercial traffic was a real threat with major consequences is illustrated by the example of neighbour and rival, Sharjah.

At this point, it is an appropriate opportunity to assess and compare briefly the position of other Trucial States and other Gulf States in the middle of the twentieth century

Sharjah

Halcrow had been asked to produce a report on harbour development prospects in Sharjah as well as Dubai, but their report of January 1955 highlighted that in Sharjah, due to silting, 'most of the supplies required for the town are imported through Dubai'[93] and that very major investment would be needed. The Political Agency in Dubai clearly felt that though some limited assistance should be given, Sharjah would be quite unable to repay it. The facts were that not only was Sharjah's Trade now less than Dubai's and given less prominence by the ruler, with merchants deserting the Emirate for its near neighbour Dubai,[94] but the British Political Agency for the Trucial States based in Sharjah since 1823 had moved to Dubai in 1954, reflecting the expansion of commercial and oil-related activities based there. It is clear from the wording in the British records that as the shift of the political headquarters to Dubai had shown, Sharjah was now (commercially) less important than its neighbour and any Sharjah scheme was 'definitely impossible financially and not warranted commercially'.[95] Though there were efforts made to ensure that Sharjah would get 'freeport' facilities at Dubai, some money to be provided for surveys on Sharjah's east coast for the port of Khor Fakkan and some assistance with other Sharjah pier and causeway projects, it is evident that the

British had decided to put their support only behind major development in Dubai – an entirely logical decision.

As described previously, this changed political and economic environment contrasts greatly with the nineteenth century and the powerful Qawasim maritime power based in Sharjah and Ras al Khaimah and even the first half of the twentieth century when the British Political Agency, the main civil and military airport for the Trucial States and the main base for the Trucial Oman Scouts were all based in Sharjah. However, in 1954 the agency was transferred to Dubai, in 1960 Dubai opened its own airport and in 1960, too, the Sharjah creek silted up almost completely resulting in Dubai gaining (even) more business and the ruler of Sharjah (Shaikh Saqr Bin Sultan Al Qasimi) admitted that as a result 'people were leaving'.[96] The opening of an expanded Dubai airport in May 1965 further incensed Shaikh Saqr as the modern facility immediately attracted most of the civil/business traffic (as Dubai was the bigger business centre), particularly the services of Bahrain-based Gulf Aviation who had been calling Sharjah.[97]

It is clear, however, that as early as 1948 (following the transfer of British regional jurisdiction from India to London after Indian independence), there were concerns about the future of Sharjah and that Dubai was progressing more effectively, as illustrated by the recommendation in a letter from the Gulf Residency in Bahrain to London that Dubai would be a better location for the office of the political officer. It is worth quoting some of the communication to understand the rationale:

> With regard to the site, the Political Officer Trucial Coast at present resides at Sharjah which has been the headquarters of our representative on the Trucial Coast since 1823. At that time it was a prosperous port . . . since then, owing to family strife and a succession of weak rulers, the sheikhdom has split into numerous pieces and the port, as a result of misrule and the silting up of the creek, is moribund. Dubai is now commercially, far and away the most important port on the Trucial Coast. The Shaikh maintains good order and trade flourishes. The post office is situated here and also the head office of Petroleum Concessions Ltd. Gray Mackenzie (shipping agents) have an office and we maintain a dispensary with an Indian doctor. The only arguments for retaining our headquarters at Sharjah, which is ten miles away are that the airport and telegraph office are there, and I do not think these outweigh the arguments in favour of transferring to Dubai.[98]

Subsequent exchanges of letters admit concern about 'the possible loss of prestige to the Shaikh of Sharjah, when we move, after maintaining our headquarters in his state for the last 100 years. Nevertheless, the rising political and economic importance of Dubai outweighs these considerations'.[99] The fact that the ruler of Dubai offered a prime site on Dubai creek adjacent to the ruler's house free of charge[100] only made the decision easier.

I highlight these communications, assessing the condition of Sharjah in the late 1940s and highlighting that the focus was already moving to Dubai, because the official political interaction between the ruler of Sharjah and the British political officers became increasingly strained in the 1950s. However, at a personal level it seems there was clearly often a close relationship between the political and commercial expatriates and a man who spoke English well, wrote poetry and was 'a modern man' with a sense of humour, as confirmed by Donald Hawley and Neville Green.

Though there were sound economic and financial reasons for the British policy of focussing resources on Dubai, the ruler of Sharjah, Shaikh Saqr al Qasimi, conscious of past glories, chafing under the constraints of the system within which he was increasingly a minor player and resenting how Dubai was increasingly economically pre-eminent, tried to pursue projects independently (with outside funding if possible), rather than working with the British Political Agency. This was despite the still valuable presence of a Royal Air Force base on his territory (for which the British paid an annual sum) and the main Trucial States airport in the same location. A BBME letter to London from the Dubai manager in June 1956 records that 'Shaikh Sagr (Saqr) of Sharjah is not always co-operative with the Political Agency'.[101] Though this attitude was perhaps understandable, it simply reinforced the belief of British officials that they had made the right choice in placing more emphasis on increasingly commercially successful Dubai and working with its more constructive neighbour Shaikh Rashid. Shaikh Saqr took no action to resolve the increasingly parlous state of the Sharjah creek, unwilling to work together with the British authorities to obtain finance and contracts with companies to work on the problem, and in 1960 a particularly strong *shamal* (windstorm) combined with the tide closed the creek completely. Chapman records that because of the silting, 'we didn't handle any more cargo in Sharjah until 1963'.[102]

Abu Dhabi

The development of the largest of the Trucial States followed a very different path than its neighbour. 'Unlike Dubai, where prominent merchant families had been established for generations, Abu Dhabi's business community was more of a post-oil boom phenomenon and therefore, lacked the roots, scope and energy of its Dubai counterpart.'[103] During the pre-oil 1950s, Abu Dhabi was a backwater, 'a poor place consisting mainly of palm frond *barastis,* (basic shelters or huts), and a small market',[104] with the British Political Agency in Dubai (from 1954) and the Gulf Residency in Bahrain, maintaining a consistent line in annual reports about how Dubai was developing, and how Abu Dhabi was not. The following excerpts give the general tenor. The Bahrain residency reported, 'in Abu Dhabi where there was a serious crisis in relations between the ruler (Shaikh Shakhbut Bin Sultan Al Nahyan) and his family, mainly owing to his parsimonious character'.[105] For 1955, 'During the period under review (1955) Dubai has maintained and strengthened its position as the centre of trade and maritime communications for all the Trucial States.'[106] Yet again, in 1956, 'Dubai has made great progress with the institution of a municipal council, the improvement of the customs authority, the establishment of a local police force and considerable progress on the harbour improvement scheme.'[107] The report for 1959 emphasizes the differences: 'Dubai strengthened her position as the "capital" of the Trucial States in 1959. The ruler showed commendable enthusiasm and energy' (with a new airport planned, telephones hoped for in 1960 and electricity in 1961). In Abu Dhabi, the ruler was reported to be spending most of his time inland at the Buraimi oasis.[108]

The rest of the Gulf at the end of the 1950s

Oman

Oman is a large country with a coastline over 2000 km in length. In the history of the Gulf and Indian Ocean, Oman has long played a major role as a maritime power,[109] and Omani merchants have, for centuries, interconnected with other trading regions as far as China from ports such as Sohar on the Batinah coast – an example of such a trading voyage was re-created by Tim Severin.[110] By the end of the seventeenth century, actual Omani control, after expelling Portuguese garrisons, extended to the East African coast and the island of Zanzibar,[111] as well as the enclave of Gwadar in present-day Pakistan, near the Iranian border, across the straits from Oman.[112] As early as 1646, the British East India Company (EIC) sought trading privileges in Sohar, acknowledging the strength of Omani naval and trading activity in the Indian Ocean. Anglo-Omani relations continued to develop and in 1798 and 1800 were cemented by a Treaty of Friendship and Mutual support, to be 'unshook till the end of time',[113] in part a response to concerns about the aggressive efforts of Wahhabi rulers from the central part of the peninsula (Nejd) to impose their austere form of Islam on their more pragmatic neighbours. Wahhabi influence had extended to the Qawasim, themselves a significant regional naval power rivalling that of Oman and with whom in the early nineteenth century there were regular conflicts on land and sea. As described earlier, the British desire to be rid of the threat posed by the Qawasim (piratical or not), particularly if allied with Wahhabis expanding their area of control, coincided perfectly with the Omani desire to be rid of a powerful rival, and accordingly British and Omani forces fought together at the destruction of the Qawasim fleet and capital Ras al Khaimah in 1819.

Despite the close relationship, Oman stayed aloof from the protective treaties signed by the British in 1820 with the lower Gulf shaikhdoms that bound them to Britain and, perhaps recognizing that such agreements protected the small statelets from outside interference which included that of a now locally unchallenged Oman, the Sultanate focussed attention on its presence in East Africa. However, such an apparent resurgence concealed the onset of long-term decline as, closed-off from the Gulf, 'in effect, Oman was simply left out of the action as trade no longer passed through its formerly thriving port cities'.[114] The transfer of the Sultan's court from Muscat to Zanzibar in 1840, and the value of the clove trade from Zanzibar in the 1860s 'already approaching £100,000 per year',[115] was clear evidence of where the new economic focus lay. Muscat was included as a port of call on the fortnightly BI steamship service into the Gulf from the 1860s onwards because of its role as an entrepot for the wool trade, residual intra-regional trade, the links with Zanzibar and perhaps as a political gesture to an old ally, but the reality was that it was increasingly a backwater. In the 1950s, under the rule of conservative Sultan Said Bin Taimur, and with the interior of the country still controlled by his religious opponents, this situation had not changed.

Bahrain

Bahrain has had a long pearling and merchant trading history with major Gulf trading companies such as Y B A Kanoo and Inchcape/Gray Mackenzie based or headquartered there, in the case of Gray Mackenzie (Gray Paul), since 1883. Stephanie Jones, using the statistics from Saldanha, highlights that Bahrain in the late nineteenth century was a major though not always regular port of call by BI steamers, primarily because of the pearl business (exports to India), which locally employed '4500 boats manned by 74,000 men .... By 1905/6 the trade was worth nearly £1.5 million'.[116] The British (Regional Head Office) Gulf Residency was based on the island from 1946 until (Bahrain independence) 1971, inevitably resulting in the state being regarded as the British Headquarters for the region with attendant (mainly British) military and commercial clusters established alongside. The collapse of the pearling trade in the 1930s was replaced by the early discovery of oil in 1931 and its export from the 1932 funded development of infrastructure with diversification that would eventually include the foundation of Aluminium Bahrain (ALBA) which started production in 1971; the establishing of Bahrain-based Gulf Air in 1974 by the Governments of Bahrain, the Emirate of Abu Dhabi, Oman and Qatar from the foundations built by pioneer, Gulf Aviation (founded in 1950 and based in Bahrain); the creation of the Arab Shipbuilding and Repair Yard (ASRY) in 1977 and a port, Mina Salman with a container terminal from 1979.

However, there were warning signs by the late 1950s, and as early as 1960, in the annual review sent to London, the Resident was reporting that 'the economic future of Bahrain continues to be a source of concern. The ruler is quite unwilling to accept that developments have taken place elsewhere in the Gulf which have undermined Bahrain's position as the trading centre of the area'. The same report reflected on 'the development of Dubai and the drive and energy of its merchants combined with the liberal policies of Shaikh Rashid'.[117] Bahrain was still, at this time, the established business and transportation centre of the Arab Gulf – but this was not to last.

Qatar

Qatar remained under British protection, under the terms of a Treaty signed in 1916, and this is likely to have ensured that the small, thinly populated peninsula did not fall into the hands of Saudi Arabia. The economy was wholly dependent on pearling and the collapse of this industry in the 1930s led to an exodus of population late in the decade, to Bahrain and Eastern Saudi Arabia. However, oil was discovered in 1939 and exports commenced in 1946. Internecine disputes among the Al Thani ruling family continued, increasingly about the distribution of oil revenues from the 1950s onwards, but British advisors stationed in Doha from the start of the decade encouraged modest efforts to develop the administration and develop services and education. There was no attempt to develop a further economic base, as the Rentier income from oil (and gas) was very substantial, particularly as the Qatari population was numbered only in some thousands.

Kuwait

Kuwait is a small state in the Northern Gulf, on the border with Iraq, where (easily extractable) oil was first discovered in 1938, with exports commencing in 1946 (as recorded on the Kuwait Petroleum Corporation Website). The state has a long seafaring and mercantile tradition,[118] but these elements declined rapidly as the revenues from one of the world's largest oil reserves (nationalised in 1975) increasingly dominated the economy, with the small (measured in 200,000 or 300,000 even in the 1960s and 1970s) population receiving generous lifelong subsidies. The fact is that though Kuwait had once been an important trading location, acting as a conduit for Gulf/Levant trade and with trading vessels sailing throughout the Indian Ocean, the arrival of vast oil revenues from the 1940s onwards with rentier payments to all citizens gradually diminished the appetite for and role of all other activities apart from a small number of major merchants and the oil industry – the latter dominated by foreign labour from the 1960s and 1970s.

Saudi Arabia

On 27 September 2017, Saudi Arabia announced that women would, for the first time, be allowed to drive cars. The fact that this momentous decision had to wait until 2017 to be implemented is in itself a powerful indicator of the attitudes and restrictions prevailing in the Kingdom which, together with its focus on the utilization of its vast oil wealth and the fact that the Kingdom has coastlines in the Red Sea and the Gulf, ensured that it has never been a challenger to Dubai as the Gulf's business centre, despite its far greater size and population. However, Saudi planners began early to start assessing how to develop the kingdom's economy using the oil first discovered in 1938 and exploited by the newly named Arabian American Oil Company (ARAMCO) from 1944, the American shareholders agreeing to relinquish 50 per cent control to the Saudi government in 1950, with the company eventually becoming fully Saudi owned in 1988.

A unified state only since 1932 and dominated by the austere Wahhabi Muslim faith emanating from the inland areas of the Nejd, Saudi economic policies were, in contrast to those of Dubai, inwardly focussed on developing the oil industry – there was little or no interest in developing the kingdom as a centre for trade. In part, this policy was driven by the conservatism of an inland desert-dwelling people in a large country of 830,000 square miles, who had had, unlike many of their smaller Gulf neighbours on the coast, little interest in participating in intra-regional trading links, particularly as such contacts involved interaction with non-Muslim, infidel foreigners, and also the determination of the Government as self-designated protector of Islam's holiest places, to preserve the Islamic identity of the country. Religious suspicions of the Shia minorities in the east of the country also played a part in keeping the Gulf littoral under-developed. Until the industrialization policy of King Faisal determined on the creation of Jubail industrial zone and port in 1975, the only Saudi port of any size on the east (Gulf) coast was in the newly (1930s) established town of Dammam, serving, what since the 1940s had been the oil-rich eastern provinces. Dammam and the neighbouring town of Dhahran expanded considerably after Aramco began building camps for oil workers, to the extent that it became a quintessential 'company town', planned and constructed by the Oil industry, though 'the city has transformed itself from a sterile company town . . . into a thriving secondary port city today'.[119] Comparatively, Jeddah on the Red Sea had a much longer history of exposure to foreign activity as for centuries, albeit restricted, it was the main entry point for the (only Muslim) *haj* pilgrims en route to Mecca, with the capital Riyadh, until the latter years of the twentieth century, a small and isolated parochial backwater.

Dammam, then, from its first inception was created to serve the oil industry and to provide an entry point for consumer goods into the Eastern Provinces of Saudi Arabia, with no intention or prospect of acting as a regional distribution centre with the suspicious and restrictive nature of Saudi cargo-handling regulations giving no opportunity for expansion.

Iran

Although, as previously described, Iran's ports such as Bushire and Bandar Abbas (historic 'Gombroon') have a long and distinguished history, and 'BI's fortnightly service (in 1866) between Bombay and the Gulf called at the ports of Bombay, Muscat, Bandar Abbas, Bushire and Basra',[120] any account of Iran's recent history, and certainly that of its involvement in transport and logistics, has to be dominated by the impact of the Islamic revolution in 1978-9, the near-decade-long war with Iraq (1980 to 1988) and the UN sanctions imposed on the regime in more recent times. However, by the time of Shaikh Rashid's accession in Dubai in 1958, Iran was, under Shah Muhammed Reza Pahlavi, engaged in huge state expansion, as a result of oil production which was expanding to become one of the world's largest. Oil revenues fuelled a massive growth in imports, with ports such as Bandar Shahpour, at the head of the Gulf with easy inland access to Tehran, being expanded.

Iraq

Historically, stretching back into antiquity as the port for Mesopotamia, in the nineteenth century with the advent of steamship services from India such as that of the BI, where Basrah was the Gulf terminus[121] and the operation of riverine steamers by Lynch Brothers to and from Baghdad,[122] 'Basrah was one of the most important Gulf ports . . . with (eg) in 1901-04 goods worth £1.5 million imported from Europe and North America... and seaborne exports (which) included wool, cereals, dates, liquorice root and horses . . . .'[123] Basrah's position, about 100km from the sea, on the shallow and oft-changing channels of the Shatt-Al-Arab, would become a hindrance to trade as ship sizes increased. By the late 1950s, the constitutional monarchy installed by the British in the 1920s, despite creating the framework of a modern state, developing oil exports and expanding airports and the main port of Basrah, was increasingly at bay in an era of Arab nationalist feeling. In July 1958, a group of army officers overthrew the government.

Chapter review

In retrospect, it is easy to judge the accession of Shaikh Rashid in Dubai as a watershed moment – as the beginning of the dramatic era of expansion that was to transform the Emirate – and the region. However, at the time, the new ruler, despite experience as Regent during his father's increasing incapacity, was an unknown quantity, coming to power at a period of unprecedented upheaval in the Arab world and the region. This included the increasing impact of oil (exported from Bahrain, Kuwait, Saudi Arabia and Iran since the 1930s and 1940s) and its revenues; the apparent progress of a militarily and economically powerful Iran under the Shah after the upheavals of 1953 and the removal of Prime Minister Mossadeq with American and British collusion; the revolution in Iraq in 1958; the Suez crisis of 1956 and a wave of nationalist Arab sentiment, often linked with anti-colonialist/anti-British feeling.

However, as the new ruler of a small independent Trucial State, dependent on trade, Shaikh Rashid's perspective and focus were rather different. Firstly, his plans for expanding the creek on which Dubai's trade depended, to improve its competitive position, were finally coming to fruition. Sharjah was no longer a serious rival, with the British Political Office transferring to Dubai in 1954 and its creek getting blocked. The future prospects for Dubai were looking very bright, with Sharjah not a competitive threat and Abu Dhabi, at the time ruled by a parsimonious conservative ruler who opposed all change, apparently indifferent. Secondly, Shaikh Rashid had no illusions about the ability of his tiny state perched on the edge of the Gulf to resist the circling powers. The memories of Saudi incursions in Buraimi in 1955, repelled by the Trucial Oman Scouts, were a powerful reminder. Shaikh Saqr of Sharjah might harbour illusions about the return to glory of the Qawasim with the promised assistance of the Arab League, but this would not benefit Dubai, and the fate of other ruling dynasties (in Egypt or Iraq) at the hands of republicans was, despite promises of Arab unity, hardly a powerful argument for change for the Al Maktoums. British protecting power, despite setbacks, had survived for over a hundred years and seemed in no hurry to depart the Trucial States. Shaikh Rashid therefore concentrated on economic policies and took his opportunity to develop his state and its trading infrastructure while he had the security and the opportunity.

Chapter 2

TAKE-OFF

CREEK, CONTAINERIZATION AND CONNECTIVITY (1958–71)

That simple metal box was what we today label a disruptive technology.[1]

The liner shipping industry in the mid-twentieth century – Introduction

Many writers and journals focussing on world affairs, particularly trade and globalization, such as Levinson, Broeze and *The Economist*, to name but three, agree that maritime transport is one of the world's most important industries,[2] despite its 'invisibility in academic debates or mainstream economic or economic history journals'.[3] 'For anyone interested in the growth and development of the world's economy, knowledge of the history and mechanisms of shipping provides important insights'.[4] Even less has been written, with a handful of honourable exceptions such as those indicated earlier, about containerization – the unitization and standardization of cargo shipping from the late 1960s onwards that enabled globalization. More popular works on globalization such as Thomas Friedman's, *The World Is Flat*, despite listing ten major 'world flattening factors', actually fails to include containerization directly despite covering many of the impacts that containerization created.[5] Perhaps part of the reason for these oversights is that 'many world-changing inventions hide in plain sight . . . as they quietly reorder everything . . . yet this simple no-frills system for moving things round the world has been a force for globalisation more powerful than the World Trade Organisation'.[6] *The Economist* highlights that 'between 1985 and 2007 trade volumes rose at around twice the rate of global GDP; in the 1990s the world's largest container ships only had space for 5000 or so containers now it boasts giants like the Munich Maersk (21,000 containers); the global logistics industry had revenues of USD 4.3 trillion in 2014'.[7]

Nowhere is the influence of the containerization revolution more clearly illustrated than in the development of Dubai and the Gulf. As we have seen, the evolution and expansion of shipping had a major impact on the Gulf in the nineteenth and first half of the twentieth centuries as steamships replaced sail.

However, the most dramatic change – the 'disruptive technology' – was with the arrival of containerization in the region during the 1970s, a revolution providing opportunities which Dubai, above all, was to develop and exploit.

The impact of containerization worldwide was so revolutionary because, in the space of two decades, it completely and utterly transformed the cargo shipping, ports and distribution systems that had evolved gradually over centuries. In the same way that the introduction of the British 'Dreadnought' Battleship in 1906 made obsolete all other capital warships[8] and therefore 'levelled the playing-field', containerization meant that cargo-shipping lines who had painstakingly built up their fleets, networks, procedures and market positions quickly realized that the way was now open for new operators to enter the market bringing in radical attitudes and skills. Previous company reputations burnished over many decades now counted for little in the new world of a different type of integrated shipping service and difficult investment decisions had to be made as the sheer cost of replacing conventional fleets and building new container-carrying ships began to be appreciated, costs that individual lines would find difficult to shoulder on their own. Containerization accelerated the consolidation of the shipping industry as individual companies were forced to work together or amalgamate by the cost of and scale of investment in new ships, equipment and technology.

Similarly, ports established for centuries increasingly realized that new facilities were required, new attitudes and sometimes, that they were no longer ideally placed to cater to the new types of ships and revised trading patterns. For example, upriver ports established in cities for centuries, such as (the pool of) London, rapidly became unviable in the 1960s as the changing requirements of containerized trades, bigger trucks, larger areas in the port to stack containers and bigger ships forced a search for better, spacious, easily accessible, deep-water locations. New ports emerged, such as Felixstowe on the UK east coast (now handling around 4 million TEUs per annum), highlighted on the port website as 'opening on 1st July 1967 . . . it was the UK's first purpose-built container terminal . . . chosen because of its proximity to the main shipping lanes and the major ports of North Europe'.[9] As always, change provides opportunities and some (ports) responded better than others. In the Gulf, Dubai was one of them.

Broeze encapsulates these momentous changes well.

> Containerization revolutionised liner (i.e. cargo ships operating on regular schedules), shipping in all its physical, functional, organisational and human aspects. It industrialized the process of cargo handling and propelled the liner business into the modern worlds of computer and information technology. It was based on . . . the homogenisation of cargo into standardised units . . . in-order to increase productivity and reduce ships' time in port; and the use of such standardised units to produce an effective multi-modal, sea and land system with door to door transport from producer to consumer.[10] As Broeze emphasizes, so too does Craig Martin, 'central to this (worldwide containerization) is the standardization of infrastructure',[11] and Heins, 'standardisation of the container on a worldwide basis, so that users throughout the world would be working

with the same object and could handle a container from any source with the assurance it would fit their equipment'.[12]

In the 1970s, the transformation of the industry started to gather momentum (though of course the process of containerizing took longer in some areas of the world than others), with Broeze tabulating the early stages of containerized services on North/South routes as follows (selected).[13]

1972 – Europe – East Asia
1974 – USA –   Middle East/India
1977 – Europe – Middle East
1978 – Japan –   Middle East

Until this time, the process of handling general cargo was in many respects virtually unchanged for centuries. Quantities of cargo were delivered to the quayside by a variety of means, to be handled in individual pieces, in bundles or loaded in boxes or chests (all such general cargo was known as 'loose' or 'breakbulk'), and loaded by shore and/or ship cranes and/or port labourers onto the ship where, depending on the mix of cargo, it was stowed, usually under-deck in hatches. Such complexity required a detailed 'stowage plan' to be produced by the ship (both for stability reasons and, also, to advise destination ports what was to be discharged and where on the ship it might be found). Such processes were labour-intensive, slow and the nature of the operations meant that cargo was often identifiable (which inevitably resulted in a lack of security and thus often some 'pilferage') and prone to damage or loss. Insurance rates were therefore high, as damage was frequent and the proportion of losses of certain products (such as alcoholic drinks or cigarettes) were regarded as normal. Productivity was thus very dependent on the professionalism and competence (or not) of port labour intertwined with that of the ship and the availability of shore (and ship) handling equipment. Cargo operations were therefore piecemeal, unstandardized, and costly with a consequent problem in maintaining precise schedules for the shipping services.

> Cargo was laboriously loaded and unloaded from a ship's hold in small batches. Then it was often stored and sorted in a warehouse before being distributed by the inland transport system. The port acted not so much as a conduit for trade but as a potential bottleneck, where action (or inaction) by any of the wide variety of people handling the break-bulk cargo could delay or disrupt the transport process.[14]

Depending on these factors and the volume of cargo to be loaded or unloaded (usually both), it was not unusual even in developed country ports for conventional cargo liners to be in port for several days or weeks, as the following extract from an account of a Holt Line vessel call at Singapore in the 1960s reveals. 'For those four days in port we took bites out of the "general" with which our 'tween decks and holds were filled, landing cartons and boxes, cases and crates, drums of cables and drums of chemicals, bags and bales, cars, lorries, personal effects, spirits, beers, foodstuffs and odd pieces of machinery.'[15] Not only were cargo operations slow and complex, that could be affected by many factors hindering the speed and efficiency of the process, but ships were, until the last quarter of the twentieth century, still relatively small. 'Around 1880 an average cargo vessel measured about 500 Gross Registered Tonnage (GRT) or could load some 700 Dead Weight Tons (DWT); by 2008 . . . the respective averages had grown by a factor of 30.'[16] Even in 1970, just on the cusp of new containerization age, the first ship to berth at the newly inaugurated Port Rashid in Dubai was the 1947-built BI cargo/passenger vessel SS (steamship) Sirdhana with a GRT of 8608 tons, still operating on the Bombay/Gulf service but approaching obsolescence.[17] Bearing in mind that the biggest containerships in the second decade of the twenty-first century can have a GRT of 192,000 tons (e.g. *MSC Oscar*, built in 2015), the size and capacity increase over such a ship as 'Sirdhana' only just over forty years later is at a factor of around 22, or expressed in another way, that one, new, containership is the equivalent of twenty-two conventional cargo ship 'Sirdhana's. Containerization and standardization encouraged the growth in size of container ships which being simpler could be operated by smaller crews (regardless of vessel size) and be handled by fewer port side workers – and handle hundreds of containers (and thousands of tons) in hours rather than days or weeks.

For the shipping industry, like any other commercial activity, the aim was (and is) to provide a service to customers, to make money and to carry cargo as efficiently, cheaply and quickly as possible. The more voyages undertaken quickly (less port time), the better the returns and the happier the customers who wanted their cargo as soon as possible. However as indicated earlier, there had been relatively little progress in making these efficiencies and even by the middle of the twentieth century, changes had been slow and incremental. Cargo ships were now usually powered by diesel engines rather than steam (or sail); they were bigger but not dramatically so; they were built of steel rather than iron or wood and were faster and more reliable, but cargo handling remained slow, labour-intensive and complex.

The sea-lanes of the world in the 1960s and 1970s were still dominated by the established, traditional shipping companies of the main trading nations, such as: The Peninsular and Oriental Steam Navigation Company (P&O) from the UK; Hapag Lloyd (West Germany): Nippon Yusen Kaisha (NYK) of Japan; Nedlloyd from the Netherlands; Waterman and Lykes lines (USA). Unregulated cargo-liner services were (and are) always affected by 'the classic problems of . . . large capital units, an overall excess of capacity, seasonal fluctuations in cargo and a cargo imbalance between the two trade legs. How then . . . to maintain competition but find a way to keep that competition between reasonable limits?'[18] In order to cope with the unfettered competition that had threatened the very existence of the regular East-West cargo-liner services that had begun operating in the late nineteenth century, the lines grouped together and formed 'Conferences', the first being the Calcutta/Europe Conference in 1875 quickly followed by the Far Eastern Freight Conference (FEFC) in 1879. These agreements between lines involved agreed numbers of sailings, mutually agreed freight rates and often, earnings paid into a common 'revenue pool' for later distribution in agreed ratios. Such groupings were essentially providing a way of keeping the impact of supply and demand under control, by sharing the impact among lines in a structured manner. However, while providing good collective services to customers and ensuring that the lines' financial uncertainty was ameliorated, such groupings were inevitably considered as restrictive cartels by other non-member lines and some shippers' organizations, particularly as such measures usually did stabilize freight rates and favoured the members to the detriment of 'outsiders', especially as Letters of Credit (L/Cs) increasingly stipulated 'Shipment required by Conference Vessel'.

This then was the cargo shipping environment at the onset of the containerization revolution in the late 1960s and early 1970s. An industry steeped in tradition and conservatism, which had, on most major routes, 'cartelised' the trade ensuring that traditional, established lines dominated, diminishing the usual impact of 'supply and demand', and whose procedures and attitudes remained much as they had for the previous century. Ships would meander along trade routes such as the ones to the Gulf, calling at several ports, sometimes others, unscheduled, to load 'inducement' cargo taking months to complete a round voyage. The system was slow, labour and paperwork intensive with cargo delivery for customers lengthy and unreliable. This 'old order' of traditional lines and ports was to be swept away by the impact of containerization, 'the most profound development in cargo liner trades since the change from sail to steam',[19] which in turn enabled, by providing efficient and cost-effective transportation as an essential building block, the global growth benefitting from a rules-based system of international trade and investment, established in the post-war 'liberal world order'. For Dubai, the onset of containerization at a time when the Emirate was in the process of building up its infrastructure was an opportunity – albeit a risky one – to invest in a new technology to ensure its place as a focal-point trading centre and to outpace and outflank potential rivals, by being more efficient in handling cargo.

Though there are many examples of individual and isolated attempts over the centuries to make it easier to move goods over land and sea by forms of unitization identified for example by, writers such as Levinson,[20] Burrell,[21] Donovan and Bonney,[22] and Klose,[23] it is overwhelmingly agreed that it was the trucking company owner and radical innovator Malcolm McLean, who, increasingly frustrated by delays to his trucks on the US highways of the 1960s and the inefficiencies and slowness of loading and unloading cargo manually, transformed the industry – and the world – by investigating and developing ways of moving trucks directly on and off ships. On 26 April 1956, the converted tanker 'Ideal X' was loaded with fifty-eight specially designed metal containers from trucks in New Jersey, New York and five days later discharged them onto trucks waiting in Houston, Texas. Mclean had not only started the process of moving cargo intermodally (that is, by land and sea in one 'though-transport' operation) but he had also recognized that it was cheaper (than the trucks-by-road option) moving freight to Houston from New York using tankers that, having discharged their oil cargo, were sailing back empty to Houston. Secondly, instead of merely loading trucks onto the ships, he had commissioned the design of special steel containers which, unlike truck chassis, could be stacked on top of each other on the platform built above the deck of the tankers, again, more cost-effective and efficient. These containers were the same size as a standard US road trailer, 33 feet long by 8 feet high and 8 feet wide.

Mclean was dedicated to the cutting of costs, to enable him to compete (initially as a trucker, with other trucking companies and the railways) encapsulated in his famous aphorism, referenced by Oliver Allen: 'you know what freight is? It's something added to the cost of the product'.[24] In late 1957, he replaced the converted tanker ships with 'C2' cargo ships that could carry 226 containers. The cost and time savings were dramatic. Shipping companies had long recognized that the more time spent in port, the more costly the operation, as ships make money by performing more voyages at sea and not by incurring costs in port. Mclean's new Pan-Atlantic service, using the bigger and more suitable 'container ships' on the service to Miami and Houston from New York transformed the costings. As highlighted by Brian Cudahy, for cargo operations, 'A conventional break-bulk cargo-ship would typically require 150 or more longshoremen (dockworkers/stevedores) working for at least four full days. With a containership (such as the C2) the same task could be accomplished by a crew of 14 in a little over an eight-hour shift.'[25] The cost comparison (for port labour) as calculated by Cudahy would be around USD 15,000 for the conventional operation in this case, but only USD1,600 for the new container system – even without taking into account that ship's port time was reduced by over three days, and three days being saved on each voyage also meant more revenue-earning voyages per annum were possible. By proving the system worked and that by stopping the handling of cargo piece by piece on the dockside, ship loading and discharging time would drastically diminish, cargo in-transit time would reduce and cargo damage and pilferage would almost disappear (reducing insurance costs) he set in motion the dramatic reductions in cost and improvements in efficiency that allowed the great leap forward of the logistics industry. Indeed, 'thanks to the efficiency of the container system, transport costs have sunk so low that it is generally less expensive to have a product manufactured in various locations and then transport it.'[26] It is these revolutionary changes that made containerization the handmaiden of globalization providing the opportunity for the lean, hungry and innovative (like Dubai) to become part of the process rather than an onlooker.

New services to Puerto Rico, and the first transatlantic containership service (in the spring of 1966) followed, but as highlighted by Levinson, the worldwide roll-out of containerization was protracted despite its clear cost saving, not only because of uncertainties about its viability on some trades but because of the need to agree on common standards for container sizes and associated technical, safety and loading conditions. Clearly, in view of the costs involved to re-equip ships and ports for containerized cargo, companies would not take expensive re-tonnaging action until it was clear that standards had been universally agreed to. As Levinson and Martin confirm, only in 1970 after several years of complex work involving the many and varied member nations was the final International Organisation for Standardization (ISO) report produced. The US Federal Maritime Board began first initiatives towards standardization in 1958, followed by the American Standards Association,[27] who announced the standard dimensions in 1961 (based on the limitations of road-trucks), subsequently agreed at the Paris ISO summit meeting in 1964 and subsequently re-confirmed in 1967 and 1969. Standard containers are 8 feet wide and 20 feet long (TEU – Twenty Foot Equivalent Unit) or forty feet long (FEU = 2 x TEU) with heights either 8 feet 6 inches or (introduced in later years) 9 feet 6 inches (known as high cubes, used for volume, low weight cargo in 40 foot containers). Even though McLean's Sea-Land Company soldiered on with their own 35-feet-long containers for some years, standardization was an absolutely essential part of the containerization revolution, allowing ships, equipment, trucks, trains and ports to be compatible with one another, ensuring speed and greater efficiency of operation, 'the container, in effect constructs a cohesive network out of disparate parts'.[28]

However, what provided the major impetus and the realization of containerization's merits on a major scale was the decision by the US military to award a USD70 million contract to McLean's company (now called Sea-Land) in March 1967 to provide a seven-ship container service to supply American forces in Vietnam.[29] The impact of a modern war on the logistics supply chain was something that even the American military planners failed to gauge, but, unwilling to accept they might be wrong and need a more radical solution, it was only when the congestion and delays at Vietnamese ports during 1966 reached serious levels and costs of flying in supplies rose steeply that the policy changed. As emphasized by Levinson, the arrival of the first large(r) containership 'Oakland' at Cam Ranh Bay in November 1967 carrying 609 x 35-foot containers, 'as much cargo as could be carried on ten average breakbulk ships hauling military freight to Vietnam',[30] transformed the situation and the delays and congestion disappeared. Containerization worked to reduce costs, lessen cargo pilferage and improve efficiency of supply when facing logistical bottlenecks. This was a lesson that would be learnt in other congested areas, particularly the Gulf. Significantly, the ruler of Dubai, having announced the development in 1976 of the Jebel Ali vast port project, signed an agreement with McLean's Sea-Land Company, as the world-leader in containerized transport, to operate it (albeit also to avoid a monopoly by George Chapman's, Gray Mackenzie and Co. who already operated the existing Port Rashid).

Despite their concern about the costs and immense implications of containerization, the traditional carriers actually responded with remarkable speed and prescience. In 1965, four of the major traditional British shipping companies – the Peninsular and Oriental Steam Navigation Company (P&O); Alfred Holt; British and Commonwealth and Furness Withy – agreed to combine their container shipping interests in a new company, Overseas Containers Limited (OCL), realizing that each of them alone could never hope to bear the costs of containerization. The new venture was the first of the many amalgamations in the shipping industry that were to follow, the second, in 1966, being the formation of Associated Container Transport (ACT), comprising Ellerman Lines; Blue Star; Ben Line; Harrison Line and Port Line. Also, in (April) 1966, Malcolm McLean's Sea-

Land commenced a Transatlantic container service which 'astonished the shipping world: cargo sent to Europe arrived at its destination fully four weeks earlier than its equivalent had before'.[31] OCL ordered six 1900 TEU containerships for the Europe/Australia trade in 1968 (each replacing four or five conventional ships) and in March 1969 the first of these new vessels, 'Encounter Bay', inaugurated the first fully cellular (all container) service to Australia and New Zealand from the UK and North Continent. 'The efficiency gains from containerizing liner shipping were to be considerable. In 1968 more than fifty British break-bulk cargo liners worked in the UK & North Continent – Australia trade. Nine container ships were to take over 80% of their trade, carrying it faster at sea and loading and discharging it faster in port'.[32]

The impact of containerization was to be felt in several different ways; first, the reduction in costs and the improvement in service speed and reliability led to a growth in cargo volumes; secondly, the demands of new technology, different and bigger ships, new cargo-handling methods and changing patterns of trade made some ports obsolete, particularly those, as highlighted earlier, in upriver (narrow, shallow, restrictive, tidal) locations such as the Pool of London near Tower Bridge. Thirdly, the simplified and mechanized nature of containerization needed considerably fewer dock workers, resulting in difficult transitions particularly in Europe, Australia and the United States for the established, heavily unionized large workforces, which were decimated by the changes. Established ports such as Liverpool, increasingly in the wrong geographical location in an increasingly East/West trading pattern, trade with Asia and continental Europe, failing to invest in new equipment and provide deep-water berths and suffering from a reputation for poor working practices and difficult labour relations, lost much of their business, sometimes to new purpose-built container ports such as the aforementioned, Felixstowe on the UK's east coast. Fourthly, the greater reliability of container ships to maintain their schedules as a result of lines now being able to calculate port-stay times accurately, kick-started another logistics revolution, that of using container ships themselves as floating warehouses. This innovation, developed by Japanese exporters to Europe, was labelled 'Just-in-time' (JIT) and involved reducing the inventory costs of storing imports on land, by using reliable container services operating on fixed published schedules to deliver goods shortly before they were required, rather than storing them in large warehouses on arrival and at point of origin. Regular services, several each week, with the precise date of arrivals at ports known weeks or months in advance transformed the logistics and distribution industry. This process enabled dramatic improvements in efficiencies and cost savings for producers and end-users by eliminating warehouse storage needs, improving forecasting disciplines and reducing excess manufacturing. Exporters and end-user customers benefitted from faster, more efficient – and thus cheaper transport costs (linked with cheaper containerized shipping costs). Newcomers such as Dubai, without the burden of inheriting long-established, now obsolete vast storage infrastructure, could transition swiftly into the integrated, intermodal age. This radical re-ordering of the logistics chain was only possible because of containerization.

Vernon Rolls in his unpublished history of the Far Eastern Freight Conference (FEFC) highlights the comparison between the conventional services provided by FEFC lines in 1975 and container services in 2005 on the North Europe to Far East services:

Conventional (1975) and Container (2005) Liner Services Comparison[33]

	1975	2005
Sailings per month	31	82
Freight Tons* / (TEU) per month	40,000* TEU	352,000 TEU
Fastest Transit (Days)	20–25	20

(*Freight Tons converted into TEU at 20 Freight Tons per TEU)

Clearly, by 2005 though the average transit times are only marginally better, there are dramatically more services, more frequently, with more capacity.

Finally, ships themselves and the shipping companies changed. Ships became bigger, specifically designed to carry containers and companies increasingly adopted the logic of economy of scale, that the fixed costs (of a ship) could be offset by carrying more containers, which would reduce the 'slot cost' (cost of carrying each container) and thus enable them to be more competitive. Fixed costs represent crew costs, ship operating costs/insurance/finance depreciation and amortization. In other words, put simply, for example, a ship carrying 1000 TEU with fixed costs of (say) USD 5000 per day would have a slot cost of USD 5 per TEU. A bigger ship of 20,000 TEU with fixed costs of USD 20,000 per day would have a slot cost of USD1 per day. This logic, of bigger ships allowing lower costs, however, depends on filling the ship, which does not always happen, leading to lines cutting freight rates, which undermines the cost savings. However, the economy of scale logic determines that the bigger ships can (on major trade lanes) outlast, over difficult times and out-compete, smaller, more expensive ships, so ship sizes are still increasing at the time of writing, with those carrying over 20,000 TEU being built and delivered.

As a comparison, a container ship launched in 1982, OCL's 'Tor Bay' was 220 metres long and carried 1,900 TEU. In 2015, MSC launched the 'MSC Oscar' at 400 metres long, able to carry 19,000 TEU, requiring a minimum depth of water under the keel of 16 metres and much bigger container gantry cranes onshore. Some ports adapted to meeting these ever-more challenging equipment, draft and technological requirements; others didn't. Dubai wholeheartedly responded, to invest ahead of demand. The shipping companies themselves responded in different ways, but one of the greatest changes was and has been the amalgamation of lines, continuing the process begun at the very start of the containerization era, reflecting the need to achieve economies and cost reductions in an era of low rates that the lines themselves have created. In 2016–7 alone, Hanjin (Korean) went bankrupt; Japanese lines NYK, K Line and MOL amalgamated; Maersk took over Hamburg Sud; Hapag Lloyd took over United Arab Shipping Company (UASC) and the Chinese line COSCO took over Orient Overseas Container Line (OOCL)

– 'four weddings and a funeral'[34] as reported by Containerisation International. As the Economist newspaper commented, 'the industry may be the handmaiden of globalisation, but it is congealing into regional oligopolies'[35], with the top seven lines controlling around 75 per cent of containerships, by the time new buildings are delivered in 2021 according to Drewry Maritime Financial Research. The six largest Container lines (early 2018) based on current TEU capacity/percentage of overall total are given.

The Largest Container Shipping Companies[36]

Maersk Line (Denmark) –	4,265,408 TEU (19.6%)
Mediterranean Shipping Company (MSC), (Switzerland) –	3,190,498 (14.7%)
CMA-CGM Group, (France) –	2,525,777 (11.6%)
COSCO, (China) –	1,856,172 (8.5%)
Hapag Lloyd, (Germany) –	1,543,598 (7.1%)
Evergreen, (Taiwan) –	1,070,825 (4.9%)

Such developments have implications for container terminals, as on most trades, lines operate in partnerships with other lines, sharing ships on which all partners may co-load containers, thus removing the need (and immense cost) for each line to operate its own service and (they argue) allowing a better service and wider geographical range. These are known as alliances and are accepted by, for example, European Union (EU) regulatory authorities on the basis that such cooperation is limited to each line making space provision for others on a vessel and does not involve any commercial liaison. Lines continue to market their own services with their own pricing policies, but fewer, competing alliances of lines inevitably leads to a reduction in choice for customers and also a reduction in the alliances' use of the container terminals they utilize. By mid-2017, rationalization had reduced the industry to only three major alliances, '2M', 'THE' Alliance and 'Ocean' alliance, which, despite many smaller independents remaining, represented over 70 per cent of global container capacity.[37] In this contacting, competitive environment, those hub terminals (like Dubai-Jebel Ali) that have firmly established themselves with shipping lines as regional leaders for performance, cost and suitability are the terminals which will survive best, as calls at other terminals are shelved or downgraded.

In the Gulf – The impact of Shaikh Rashid al Maktoum

With the Sharjah creek closed to all vessels, the regular trade reviews from the Political Agency report that in the last quarter of 1960, no ships called Sharjah and cargo for the city was relayed via Dubai.[38] Dubai was thus able to consolidate its commercial supremacy. Additional work took place to expand the quays inside Dubai creek, but as the 1960s progressed, the growth of business (helped by the lack of any competition from Sharjah) resulted in increasing congestion and lack of space on the wharves. Shaikh Rashid was anxious to ensure that Dubai remained capable of expanding its trade, but he also was aware that the process of lightering (barging), cargo from ships at anchor to the creek wharves was slow and inefficient. 'Shaikh Rashid was convinced that a large modern port would be a natural progression for his city's expansion.'[39] Accordingly, In 1965, the ruler asked William Halcrow and Partners to design a four-berth deep-water port (that is, a port that could allow four large ships to berth alongside the quay at one time), outside the creek mouth, thus avoiding draft and size restrictions which restricted movements to small craft. Concurrently, the success of more exploratory drilling in May 1967 'officially confirmed this morning that the third rig has struck oil', reported the Dubai Political Agency to London on the 29 May 1967,[40] and ensured that there need no longer be concerns about the funds to pay for development activity. The next month, there was 'an enthusiastic signing ceremony on June 5,[41] despite the outbreak of the 'Six Day War' between Israel and Egypt, Jordan and Syria on the same day, followed by a contract signing in October of the same year with contractors Richard Costain, consultants Halcrow, locally represented by the later (in)famous Mohammed al Fayed of Harrods fame,[42] and Lloyds Bank as financiers. Several months into the contract, Shaikh Rashid 'began to doubt the original concept and ordered the designers to draw up plans for 16 berths instead of four',[43] deciding that the design was too small to cater to potential demand. According to George Chapman's memoir, the ruler himself, to save costs and construction time, identified a site outside Dubai as a source for the stone to build breakwaters, which saved over 4 million sterling.[44]

At the end of October 1967, Shaikh Rashid advised Chapman, who had worked with him on shipping matters for over fifteen years, that he wanted Gray McKenzie (GM) to operate the port.[45] Initially Gray McKenzie were not entirely convinced that they should accept, for local political and financial reasons (they would be to blame if their management was not a success and this would jeopardize their other business activities – and they were not convinced it would make money). It also seems likely that the Head Office in London considered George Chapman as so close to the ruler of Dubai that he might leave, to be employed by Dubai to run the new port.[46] However, in the end they saw the benefits of being involved in such an operation and the new port (Mina – (Port) – Rashid) operated by GM as 'Dubai Port Services' (DPS) was inaugurated, though not fully complete, in November 1970, when the BISNCo 'Sirdhana', operating on the Bombay/Karachi Gulf service made the first and its maiden call. The port was fully opened, with fifteen berths, in October 1972.

At this point, it is necessary to review the environment in which Dubai was evolving and also, its position in the then Trucial States, before the formation of the United Arab Emirates (UAE) in 1971. The Emirate had been ruled by the Al Maktoum family since the early nineteenth century and, as we have seen at the beginning of the twentieth century, they took an active part in encouraging entrepreneurial trade. In the 1950s, Shaikh Rashid al Maktoum was acting as regent for his elderly father, becoming ruler in his own right in 1958. The British attitude, not to get directly involved in local matters over which the local rulers held sway, is perhaps summed up in a report submitted by D.M.H. Riches of the

Foreign Office Eastern Department in January 1956. Commenting on the need for improvements to Dubai creek because 'it is the centre for the trade of the coast and for the *entrepot* trade with the Iranian side of the Gulf.... Our action in the case of Dubai is ... what I feel ought to be our true function in all these development projects, namely providing the initiative and organising skill and drive'.[47] In other words, for worthwhile projects, in Dubai promoted by Shaikh Rashid, the British would assist by arranging financing, consultant and construction expertise, if at all possible (as many references in the archives reveal), with British companies. Note that providing money is not mentioned. Fred Halliday sums this general policy up as 'arresting certain changes and encouraging others'.[48]

It is greatly to the credit of Shaikh Rashid that he clearly understood very quickly how to play his part well in this system – focussed as he was, entirely on the future of Dubai. By promoting projects for the benefit of Dubai, discussed not only with local merchants and the *majlis*, but with his long-term and trusted British advisors, he realized that the British at a political level would certainly be in favour. This was becoming particularly apparent, in an increasingly competitive Gulf, opening up at last, to other exporting nations, if there were prospects of British company contracts. It is worth quoting a memo from the Dubai Political Agency to Bahrain in 1967, discussing the impending deep-water port infrastructure project, which illustrates how important the relationship with Shaikh Rashid was, as British power and influence was beginning to decline, and how increasingly he was driving it.

> Shaikh Rashid has never done anything on the development side ... or any commercial enterprise in which he has not been successful. He is prepared to take risks (but takes advice and listens carefully), and his record in meeting his commitments has been extremely good. Politically, British involvement should cement links between Dubai and the UK. *The fact is that Dubai does what it's Ruler says* (my italics) and Shaikh Rashid likes and binds himself to those who have established themselves in his confidence. Conversely, our failure to help ... might turn him away from us. He is nothing if not a realist. Finally, our participation ... would give the lie to the charge that we have utterly neglected the development of the Trucial States.[49]

The history of the British Bank of the Middle East (BBME) in Dubai very much reinforces the picture of an astute Shaikh Rashid making the most of what options and facilities were available to him. As the only (monopoly) bank in Dubai for seventeen years (1946 to 1963) the BBME felt that it had 'obligations' to the state and 'these considerations led (the bank) to play a role ... above and beyond that expected of a normal commercial bank'.[50] The bank had excellent relations with the ruler not only because one of their local senior members of staff (Easa Saleh al Gurg) was a (Dubai National) friend of his but also because of his progressive, liberal economic policies for development and they felt he could be trusted to keep his word and would not – a key point for bankers everywhere – renege on his financial commitments. This, contrasts, as recorded in BBME correspondence, with the economic (and political) concerns about Sharjah – the ruler's debts and a reluctance to settle them; deteriorating finances; attempts to circumvent dealings with the Political Agency by appealing to external sources, coupled with increasingly overt support for Arab nationalist symbols as personified by President Nasser.[51] Christopher Davidson too highlights the commercial decline and political risk-taking of Shaikh Saqr.[52] Clearly, as was felt by the Political Office, Shaikh Rashid, however, was regarded as a progressive, 'safe pair of hands' who could and should be supported in his endeavours, as indicated earlier where the BBME guaranteed the loan from Kuwait for the creek dredging. As part of this agreement, the bank took over the administration of customs dues, thus ensuring that henceforth the ruler would have a clear record of his revenues and also that clear and impartial records were kept of the (mainly import) duties that were paid to Dubai.

Such changes from haphazard to professional records and administration were of great assistance in Dubai's evolution, reinforcing its position as the major entrepot in the lower Gulf, and as with the Political Office, BBME senior staff found themselves involved in Dubai administration. The local BBME manager was co-opted onto the new Port Committee and helped to set up the Dubai Electricity Company (DEC) in 1958, funded by a (considerably oversubscribed) local share offering.[53] This did not pass unnoticed by BBME seniors but the fact that local managers were 'advisors on commercial, industrial and even municipal matters'[54] was regarded as an acceptable price to pay for the banking monopoly and goodwill of the ruler to be maintained. Certainly, they recognized that, as highlighted by a Director Sir Alec Kirkbride in a December 1962 report, 'the ruler (Shaikh Rashid) continues to use the bank as a sort of unofficial department of the administration'.[55] Even in 1970, the departing political agent J L Bullard could report, admiringly, in his valedictory despatch that the ruler (Shaikh Rashid),

> 'revels in his own personal system . . . if new jobs need doing he shares them out amongst his existing advisors. Outsiders are roped in too and such firms as Gray Mackenzie and Halcrow may not realize to what extent their local staff are also unpaid servants of the Shaikh. It is a cheap and simple system and when he is at the top of his form it works brilliantly.'[56]

As with the BBME, so too with the consultant engineers, Sir William Halcrow and Partners, whose representative from 1959, Nevil Allen, advised Shaikh Rashid for nearly twenty years on the infrastructural projects that were to define Dubai's future, such as the Creek improvements, the new Port Rashid, Dubai airport and Jebel Ali port. It was he who received a 5 am phone call in 1972, instructing him to meet the ruler at Jebel Ali (then a barren stretch of land leading to a small hill ('Jebel') near the border with Abu Dhabi) and told to give an estimate for a large port that was to be built there. In an interview given to the Dubai British Business Group (BBG) magazine 'BBG Calling' in 1995, he emphasized that 'the Ruler placed great reliance on his advisors and they responded loyally to this trust'.[57]

All the evidence confirms that once 'into his stride' as formal ruler of Dubai from 1958, it was Shaikh Rashid who, with advice and opinion from a wide range of sources, both Dubai Nationals and expatriates, decided on policy and then very deftly played his cards to ensure that those who could assist in the implementation of such schemes, were supportive, particularly for funding. A visit to London had been arranged in 1959 and Shaikh Rashid used the opportunity to push for more financial assistance for Dubai, returning in August, according to the Dubai Political Agency, advising the Bahrain Residency, 'in excellent spirits and full of plans for the future, one of his first acts after his return was to give instructions for the building of an airport'.[58] He recognized that the bastions of British involvement in Dubai, the Political Office, the BBME, Gray Mackenzie, Halcrow all talked to each other and so by involving them, individually or severally as appropriate, as a form of mutual support group, not only for advice but as implementers of policy, he ensured he was likely to get the political and financial impetus to pursue his development plans. However, he also recognized, and with his own character and demeanour ensured, that these advisors were not only experts in their various fields – shipping, banking, finance, administration, civil engineering – on whom he could depend but were also people who could be trusted to do their best for a fledgling Dubai, people who identified with the emerging state. Such a man as Bill Duff, who, from 1959, worked as head of customs and financial controller and built up the financial infrastructure that provided for the development plans. Quoted in his obituary in the *Financial Times* in 2014 as telling his family 'it's not about the money, how many people can say they helped to build a country?'[59] George Chapman confirms that Shaikh Rashid assembled 'a formidable team of specialists and advisors . . . (but) he didn't have to pay our salaries as we were already being paid by some other organisations'.[60]

Relations with the 'Protecting Power'

Inevitably, we must consider the question of how Shaikh Rashid made his decisions in the context of the prevailing political, Arab Nationalist and 'end of Empire' climate of the time in the Near and Middle East. The conditions in Dubai (and the Trucial States) were unique. The territory was not a colony but a 'protected state' and numbers of (British) expatriates were tiny until the 1960s, 'in 1958/59 my small dining table could accommodate . . . all the British in Dubai',[61] wrote Donald Hawley. There was no huge edifice of British armed forces, other than the military staff at the airport – which was in Sharjah – or bureaucratic presence; the population of Dubai was small, some tens of thousands in the 1950s and 1960s; the political officers came and went, some more effective and influential than others but there was never a long-term British *eminence grise* to raise the hackles (such as Charles Belgrave in Bahrain, advisor for over 40 years to the Al Khalifa ruling family, departing in 1958, at least in part due to local resentments about his over-mighty role). British protection also extended to keeping outside influence and interference at bay in the late 1950s. These factors were, primarily, after the Suez debacle in 1956, Arab nationalist opinions as manifested particularly by the Cairo-based Arab League 'a rival for the hearts and minds of Trucial States Rulers',[62] despite the fact that ironically, it had been created in 1945 with British support, to foster co-operation between Arab states.

This quarantining of the Trucial States ensured that despite the impact of radio propaganda, the physical presence of Nationalist delegations was effectively thwarted, although the ruler of Sharjah, with historical grievance memories, little revenue and the conscious of being displaced commercially and politically by Dubai, flirted with Arab League assistance for some years. But though the Sharjah ruler felt that Arab League promises might turn the tide for his Emirate, neither Dubai nor Abu Dhabi appeared anxious to throw off an external British protection structure which for over a hundred years had protected their rule, particularly as the Arab nationalist republicans, having overthrown ruling monarchies to gain power were unlikely to be better bedfellows, despite appeals to 'Arab Unity'. Mindful of 'the wind of change', British policy from the beginning of the 1950s increasingly recognized that development should be encouraged to prepare the Trucial States for eventual independence. This was spelt out in the instructions to the Gulf Resident Bernard Burrows in 1953, when his instructions from London included stipulations that 'where appropriate, HMG will endeavour to advance the internal independence of the Shaikhdoms, (and) In the Trucial States a common administration would appear to be highly desirable'.[63] As Davidson confirms, 'Fortunately, there was already a functioning Trucial Council, Trucial Army and a Trucial fund . . . as building blocks for the Federation',[64] as the Trucial States Council (TSC) had been set up in 1952. This was initially chaired by the political agent, bringing the rulers together twice a year, to discuss collective matters such as medical services, education and agricultural development, even though they still preferred to deal individually with the agency on behalf of their Emirates. The armed forces were limited to the mainly British-officered Trucial Oman Scouts (TOS), originally founded in 1951 as the Trucial Oman Levies, re-named in 1956, responsible for supporting the individual rulers' police forces, protecting the Sharjah Airforce base and to provide security from banditry. The TOS also provided employment for local men, controlled illegal immigration, helped with road building, established a Radio Station ('The Voice of the Coast') in 1960, and helped with the professional formation of local police forces. 'The force played a vital role maintaining peace and security . . . from the mid-1950s through to the 1960s, eventually founding the formation of the UAE armed forces in 1971.'[65] Significantly, the Trucial States Development Fund, to be administered by the TSC, was initiated under British pressure, very much both to stave off increasing offers of finance to Trucial States members from the Arab League and to demonstrate that (overdue) development projects were being pursued. With financial assistance from Saudi Arabia, equally anxious to avoid Arab League influence in the region, the fund was established in 1965, to be directed by Easa al Gurg from 1971.

Also, in this era of increasing Arab nationalism, the British, in addition to supporting the Trucial States as a whole, through the measures highlighted earlier, were anxious to display a constructively, supportive role in assisting the ruler in developing Dubai, despite the Emirate's negligible resources and population, numbering probably no more than 50,000 until the mid-1960s.[66] Though Shaikh Rashid remained very much focussed on Dubai's affairs rather than on the wider political environment, he was aware of the external pressures and knew how to negotiate the best agreements for Dubai too, by clearly encouraging the belief that he would look for better prices and terms with outside (non-British) companies to encourage better terms from British contractors, knowing that the Political Agency would work to ensure that British companies would avoid losing out to 'foreign' competition.

We must certainly recognize that the constant 'elephant in the room' was the British political agent in the Emirate and his ability to influence or dictate events, but it also seems clear that 'Dubai's driving force was Shaikh Rashid ... with a clear understanding of the need for big infrastructure projects to make Dubai the region's leading centre',[67] with this (British) political support structure behind him and actually manipulated by him, certainly in the days before the creation of a government bureaucracy. As Michael Crawford writes about the relationship with protected states, 'Rather than (British officials) exerting unchallenged control over subordinate political actors, it was more an interactive dance. The Resident could bring considerable influence to bear ... but his role more often consisted of persuasion and negotiation.'[68] This very much echoes the point made by ex-political officer Glen-Balfour Paul, who emphasized the difficulty of balancing getting involved or not getting involved. 'Persuading independent Rulers to accept advice, particularly since progress meant change and the old ways were cherished was never plain sailing.'[69] Shaikh Rashid was effectively working in tandem with British political officers who were increasingly aware of post-imperial decline and the need to work to secure commercial contracts for the UK, in an increasingly competitive world, anxious to support Dubai development because of the economic benefits that would accrue not only to Dubai but to British businesses too. The balance of power was already beginning to shift.

Shaikh Rashid, as a merchant and trader himself and as someone who had travelled in Europe and Asia (for example, London in 1959), took a wider view of the future than many of his compatriots. DPW head, Sultan Bin Sulayem highlighted that 'Shaikh Rashid sent a delegation to Singapore in the 1970s, one of them was Bill Duff (head of Finance and Customs) to gather information',[70] and Daniel Brook argues that Shaikh Rashid was also profoundly influenced by his visit to London and his experience of the vast imperial metropolis, galvanizing his determination to develop Dubai.[71] He was also canny enough to listen to his network of official and unofficial advisors, which enabled him to be aware that Halcrow were being contracted to build Port and Industrial zone projects on both coasts of Saudi Arabia in the late 1970s – Jebel Ali's confirmation in 1976 seems likely to have been, in part, a response to this likely upper Gulf competition – and the necessity of ensuring that Halcrow kept their commitment focussed on Dubai.

A ruling policy – The velvet glove after the iron fist

However, Shaikh Rashid also had to work with and convince his own 'constituency', in Dubai, the inhabitants of the 'city of merchants'. As long-established senior Dubai businessman Saadi al Rais highlighted in an interview in Dubai,[72] the ruling family of Dubai (as *primus inter pares* merchants themselves) had long been closely involved with the local inhabitants, particularly the merchants, in a sort-of early 'Public-Private Partnership (PPP)' a point also explored by Fatma Al-Sayegh[73] and James Onley[74] in their works on the crucial role of merchants in the 'transnational' Gulf. With the removal of the 5 per cent customs duty in 1904 (as part of the raft of measures to encourage Lingah merchants) and the creation of Dubai as a 'Free' port, the ruler farmed out revenue collection to merchants who agreed to remit an agreed sum each year and often lent money to the ruler. As part of this 'ruling bargain' merchants were appointed to the Majlis (advisory council) and as such, representing the various social groupings, were able to act as influencers of policy. Inevitably, some merchants were more successful in business than others. However, as highlighted elsewhere, the collapse of pearling and the rise in the rulers' revenues from other sources (such as fees for oil exploration rights), contributed to the merchants losing influence in the 1920s and 1930s as their economic decline heightened, resulting in a brief 'merchants revolt' in 1938 in which some of the majlis merchants (and dissident Al Maktoums) attempted to preserve its (and their) influence by challenging the Al Maktoum ruler's control and increasing financial independence.

The British Resident in 1956, at a time when there were concerns that after the Suez fiasco and the success of Nasser in Egypt, Arab Nationalism was threatening to affect the Trucial States, wrote to London enclosing a detailed report of the problems in 1938, as some of the 'problem' families were the same as twenty years earlier, emphasizing that the issues were in fact a power struggle between two factions. One faction was that of the ruler (Shaikh Saeed Al Maktoum) and his son (Shaikh Rashid), supported by the hinterland Bedouin, most of the old tribal Bani Yas families, some merchants and the (Shia) merchant families originating in Southern Persia, all of whom were living on the 'Dubai' side of the creek, and; the other ruler's cousin Shaikh Mana and his grouping of some other old (Sunni) families living on the other side of the creek in Deira. It is worth highlighting here that Raymond O'Shea, an RAF Officer based at the base in Sharjah from 1944, wrote of the town divided by the creek, 'Dubai proper where the merchants and wealthier classes live, and Dera (Deira), the fishermen's quarter . . . the houses in Dubai town are larger and more imposing than those in Deira . . . remarkably clean.'[75]

The Residency report focusses on the loss of influence, economic benefits and contracts by the Shaikh Mana faction, but also highlights that a major element of contention for the latter, was the growth in influence of the merchants from Persia, arriving since the early years of the century and particularly again in the 1920s and 1930s, who, together with Banian (Indian) merchants, who were taking business that 'local' merchants felt were theirs by right. As so often where immigrants are concerned, religious (in this case Sunni/Shia) resentments may well have played a part, although most immigrants from Southern Persia were Sunnis re-settling for economic reasons and also because of resentment against the modernizing/ westernizing of Reza Shah in Iran, as Al Gurg[76] and Jahani[77] relate. The British report considered 'this (Shaikh Mana) faction called itself the reforming party, but the reforms they advocated were not especially progressive but rather designed to divest the Ruler of some of the wealth and power that accrued to him for their own wealth and enjoyment'.[78]

This 'Dubai Reform Movement' as Davidson rather generously describes it, and the council they set up to share customs dues, was crushed with some violence by the ruler, Shaikh Said al Maktoum (and his son Shaikh Rashid), who had no intention of transferring or weakening the ruling family's control and some merchant family members (such as the Al Ghurair) went into exile. It is possible to consider the 'reform movement' as a genuine movement to produce a more 'democratic' and equitable form of Government in Dubai by replacing the ruling family with some form of 'popular assembly' (popular in the sense that disadvantaged merchants would have more participation). However, on balance, despite the 'Reform' proposals for more financial control away from the ruler, an education department and a municipal council, which might be categorized simply as attempts to gain the moral high ground while jockeying for power, a more dispassionate assessment of the dispute points more likely to an attempt by disaffected family members and some less successful merchants motivated by the loss of business and resentment of foreign interlopers to improve their financial position and status by forcing regime change. As Albadr Abu Baker emphasizes, 'The figures indicate that the revenue from pearls reached its rock-bottom around the time of these Reform movements. In other words, the movement of the merchants was not an indicator of their historical role, nor their penchant to political reform nor their political prowess; and if it were all of these it should have occurred between 1903 and 1913 when they were at their zenith.'[79] The attempt at regime change was therefore primarily motivated by economically impoverished factions within Dubai, particularly those merchants focussed primarily on pearling. Business families of Persian origin were less affected as their activities were more widely spread (in foodstuffs for example), as Angela Rugh has highlighted.[80]

Whether the British would have permitted the removal of the ruler is open to doubt as Al Gurg comments that, however, the most important consequence was that the lessons of this period were not lost on Shaikh Rashid (who was closely involved in the aggressive counter-reaction to the attempted coup), when he came to power in 1958 after his father's death. Almost immediately, he sought to institutionalize a more co-operative relationship with the merchants through the Majlis, as Al Sayegh[81] emphasizes in her essay, to enhance commercial prosperity by involving them in the wealth distribution and governing process, and he established institutions (such as the Municipal Council and Dubai Port Committee) with the participation of community representatives, that had been demanded in 1938. Even before, as Regent in 1957, he had set up a *baladiya* committee (municipal council) with twenty-two nominated (merchant and other) members to organize the cleaning of streets and to build new market buildings and other public facilities in addition to advising the government.[82] Karen Young has described this refined process as 'the Majlis's mechanisms (consensus decision-making and drawing from pools of leadership talent among a close-knit community, whether tribal, commercial or most importantly, loyal) built a syncretic development project in Dubai that blurred lines between state and private assets'.[83] This 'connected capitalism' and the removal of dissent by including the majlis merchants in the economic growth of Dubai by giving them access to the opportunities (such as agencies and services or construction) offered by foreign companies entering the expanding Dubai market was very much part of Shaikh Rashid's ruling evolution, as part of the 'Ruling Bargain'. One element of this inclusive approach referred to earlier in this chapter, was the dhow-based trade in gold to India, where it could be sold at twice the world-market rate, as a result of the apparently insatiable demand there for gold, used in dowries and for convertible and transportable savings. Gold was flown into Dubai from London or Zurich, and from 1963, deposited in the vaults of the National Bank of Dubai (NBD), established by British retired banker David Mack on behalf of Shaikh Rashid. Gold was then moved on Dubai dhows/launches, and, under cover of night transferred to Indian launches in Indian waters, 'the average return was said to be around eighty percent and . . . everyone in Dubai was in on the business'.[84] The import of gold into India was illegal, but unorthodox methods of shipment and lack of effective enforcement for entry into India, meant that for this trade, 'at its height in 1970, Dubai handled 259 tons, about 20% of the non-communist world's production. All but a handful of Dubai's merchants were involved'[85] – and huge profits were made.[86]

That this approach was by no means assured of success and that there were considerable risks involved in empowering powerful merchant families, some of whom still resentful of the degree of Ruling family control, is shown in the correspondence of the Dubai Political Agency in 1965. In reports to the Gulf Residency in Bahrain, that Shaikh Rashid had established a (much needed) Dubai Chamber of Commerce (DCOC) in July 1965, they expressed surprise that this had taken place at all, although 'recent events in Sharjah (the removal of the ruler by his family with British connivance), have strengthened Shaikh Rashid's hand (and) it is probable that he now feels he can make some concessions to the merchants, quite a few of whom were hitherto critical of his policy'.[87] However, though the DCOC elected 'the potential troublemakers' (ibid) to the posts of Chair, Deputy Chair and Secretary in September, a further report from the DPO in November advises, clearly with some surprise, that 'the chamber is now meeting frequently and conducting its work in a remarkably business-like fashion. The leading merchants appear keen to get to grips with some of the persistent trade problems of Dubai'.[88] As some of the 'plotters' identified in the 1956 report were members of the Al Ghurair (Hamid was exiled in 1956 for gun-running and supporting Saudi claims) and Al Futtaim families, who decades later, are now some of the wealthiest and most successful business empires in Dubai, it seems reasonable to conclude that, as Karen Young observed previously, Shaikh Rashid correctly and perceptively assessed in the majlis (more accurately than the Political Office) that the timing was right for the merchant families not only to be pacified by obtaining more responsibility for and involvement in, the commercial development and activity of Dubai but also for them to see the future commercial and financial opportunities for themselves, if they played a constructive part in the process. However, he continued to choose his course carefully, as increased local merchant activity, as Dubai developed, inevitably led to accusations that non-locals (such as Gray Mackenzie's George Chapman) were 'pulling the strings'. The fact that he faced down such opinions, and that many expatriates (Indians and Europeans and Sudanese) were still occupying official positions of trust a decade after independence, reflects well on both Shaikh Rashid as a believer in choosing the right talent regardless of race – and the expatriates who clearly demonstrated that they were working on behalf of Dubai.

The politicking and responses to it by Shaikh Rashid in the late 1950s and later are also important for another reason, reflecting one of the core reasons for Dubai's success – the tolerance of 'the other' and the acceptance that non-nationals can have a part to play in the future development of the state, regardless (for example) that such people might be Shia, or even Christians. This willingness to work with others in trade and logistics, as well as accepting other Arab nationals and Sudanese, such as the ruler's advisor Mahdi al Tajir in the 1970s (Bahraini) or Dubai Municipality 'Town Clerk' Kemal Hamza from the 1960s for twenty-four years (Sudanese), let alone the expatriate British 'Dubai civil servants' who remained in government positions after 1971 independence, was unusual, apart from other traditional trading cities, in the (certainly inland) tribal xenophobia of the region. Al Rasheed, referencing Al Sayegh reminds us that 'Dubai emerged as an international trading centre under the patronage of an indigenous political leadership and a commercial elite consisting of local Arab, Indian (Banian) and Persian merchant families'.[89] This tolerance and acceptance of 'early globalisation' were very much a feature of the long-standing Gulf mercantile 'transnationalism' described by Onley that linked the Gulf with the wider world and its constructive impact is a lesson that Dubai embraced and has continued to foster, despite the fact that 'the nature of that transnationalism has changed (due to) the politicization of Gulf Arab identity'.[90]

We can therefore confidently assert that Dubai and its rulers were adopting the pragmatic and liberal processes that reflect what we now consider as aspects of globalization, long before the term was coined, focussed on local and transnational merchants and trade. As the ruler's advisor, Mahdi Al Tajir (himself a Bahraini), re-emphasized in a newspaper interview, 'Oil is, and will remain, secondary to trade',[91] with the article already referring to Dubai as, 'a kind of super cash-and-carry centre of the Middle East . . . as a result of its flourishing entrepot trade'. In doing so, the Al Maktoum rulers, particularly Shaikh Rashid, showed both traditional political ruthlessness to beat off internecine competition and increasingly sophisticated political sagacity to pacify and mollify the disquieted merchant elites by weaving them into the fabric of the state as beneficiaries of commercial largesse that they would help to create. With the business elite increasingly bound up in the economic success of Dubai (despite a nervousness about the success of major projects) Shaikh Rashid was able to pursue development strategies, confident that British support would be behind commercial and infrastructure policies that would potentially also benefit British businesses too, and, reflect British Gulf policies in a rosier light at a time of increasing Arab nationalism. He also assembled a team of advisors on financial, municipal, utilities, engineering and maritime and commercial matters, some of whom were employed by companies established in Dubai and whom he had known for several years. Several of these were British, but they were so embedded in the success of Dubai that they saw their roles as dually, promoting their companies' interests as part of the development of Dubai. Such efforts were entirely compatible to the extent that (as was the case with George Chapman) overseas head offices had suspicions about where final loyalties lay. It must also be acknowledged, that without Shaikh Rashid's personal energy and initiatives, however, such developmental activity would have been much more limited, 'he constantly kept an eye on everything that was going on',[92] an energy and attention that was unusual in the Gulf among ruling families.

The need for a bridge crossing the creek became more acute, and merchants in particular, regularly raised the subject at the Majlis, once Dubai's airport opened in 1960 – the bridge opened in 1963. The efforts to build an airport in Dubai, rather than having to travel to the neighbouring state of Sharjah in order to fly any distance, were motivated by irritation that Dubai, as the coast's primary commercial centre in the late 1950s, required business travellers to fly into Bahrain, then on small aircraft (e.g. Avro Ansons operated by Gulf Aviation), to Sharjah, followed by a road journey (on still poor roads) to Dubai. The Bahrain flights to Sharjah were invariably full.[93] There was initially some – in retrospect rather obtuse – opposition from British officials then in Bahrain, who did not wish to pay for another airport when there was a perfectly good one nearby in Sharjah and conscious of what the reaction of Shaikh Saqr in Sharjah would be. However, Shaikh Rashid not only lobbied the Gulf Aviation pioneer Freddie Bosworth to support the case, but also advised the resident in Bahrain directly, that he was prepared to fund the building of an airport himself, as confirmed by Al Gurg,[94] Davidson[95] and Chapman[96]. After tests to ensure that aircraft (up to the size of a Douglas DC3) could land on the compacted sand, 6000 feet long runway in Al Ghusais on the Deira side of the creek, the airport, built by Costain, opened in September 1960, and expanded with a 9000-foot tarmacadam runway and more terminal building, repair and hanger facilities soon after, construction starting in 1963 and completed in 1965.[97] The Arab world's tallest building, the prestigious, commercial and office complex, Dubai Trade Centre, was opened by Queen Elizabeth and also, during her three-day visit in February 1979, she inaugurated Dubai Dry Docks (commencing operations in 1983), built to add further reasons for shipping to call Dubai, despite, or more likely because of, a competing facility, Arab Ship Building and Repair Yard (ASRY), in upper-Gulf Bahrain established in 1977.

Significantly, as emphasized by the examples of Bill Duff (see earlier) and George Chapman, the activities of the British Political Office were increasingly becoming almost an irrelevance, that rarely had any impact on the day to day work of those involved in business or developing Dubai, apart from exceptional major infrastructural projects which needed their assistance for financial and project planning, as Shaikh Rashid grew in confidence and Dubai developed its own momentum. Certainly, once it was apparent, from the late 1960s that the revenue from oil exports was on the horizon, and the days of seeking loans and borrowings were numbered, Shaikh Rashid had already built up his own parallel structure, involving the National and expatriate elites to support his plans. For the last ten years before independence, British official policy was primarily reactive, supporting or acquiescing in the policies pursued by the Dubai ruler.

Elsewhere in the Gulf

In current years, Sharjah and the other Northern Emirates (Ajman, Umm al Quwain, Ras al Khaimah and Fujairah) now play only a modest role in the economic life of the UAE with Abu Dhabi and its oil wealth (60 per cent) and Dubai as the commercial centre (25 per cent) dominating the country's Gross Domestic Product (GDP) of circa USD 371 billion in 2016[98]. Sharjah, with a reported GDP in 2016 of around USD 26 billion,[99] therefore accounts for about 7 per cent of the UAE GDP, with oil and gas revenues accounting for only 1 per cent, the major elements of its economy being property and business services (22 per cent), manufacturing (17 per cent) and wholesale and retail (12 per cent) according to Oxford Business Group[100]. Sharjah, quieter, more conservative (no alcohol is served in the Emirate) and cheaper than Dubai now also acts as a dormitory town for many people working in Dubai, the roads between the two adjoining Emirates jammed with traffic in the morning and evening peak periods. There are three main ports: Khor Fakkan, a major container terminal on the Sharjah and UAE's east coast; Mina Khalid serving the city of Sharjah, just outside the Sharjah Creek with a small container terminal (400,000 TEU in 2016 according to operator Gulftainer's website), general cargo and oil support facilities and Hamriyah, further along the coast acting as a small free-zone port and providing oil and gas support.

As we have seen, from the 1950s and 1960s onwards out-manoeuvered and outperformed by Dubai, Sharjah was penurious and Shaikh Saqr's attempts from the late 1950s increasingly tried to obtain funds from external sources such as Egypt. There was also clear support for Arab Nationalist movements (agreeing to open an Arab League office in Sharjah – though this did not happen), and an increasing frustration with the fact that Sharjah was, developmentally, being left behind. His frequent absences from Sharjah, for example in Lebanon, coupled with increasing familial discontent, as recounted by Hawley and Christopher Davidson, led to his deposition in June 1965 by the British. Officially, this was on behalf of and apparently at the request of Al Qasimi family members, among whom, according to the then commander of the Trucial Oman Scouts, 'he was extremely unpopular . . . one and all wanted him to be deposed'[101] – though this is a version disputed by the current ruler of Sharjah Shaikh Sultan al Qasimi.[102] For the British to intervene and depose a Ruler in the mid-1960s, despite the inevitable, wider, political storm this would create in the Arab world, there was clearly confidence that this was an action that needed to be taken and that could be justified, albeit under the usual excuse of 'complying with the family's wishes'. There had been long-standing tensions between other Al Qasimi family members, who would be only too happy to see him removed, resenting Shaikh Saqr's political policies (which were regarded as foolhardy), his long absences from Sharjah (in Lebanon), the maladministration that had resulted in the creek silting up and the decline of Sharjah's economic and political status. However, the deposition of Shaikh Saqr, also removed any chance that new Arab League overtures, resurrected in 1964, proposing an independent Arab federation (with its capital in Sharjah), backed by copious Arab League development funding, would make any headway.[103] Although this fanciful scheme, aimed astutely at Shaikh Saqr's dream of re-establishing Al Qasimi fortunes, had little chance of popularity away from Al Qasimi territories and was certain to be opposed by Dubai and Abu Dhabi, it seems clear that the British, capitalizing on the ruler's unpopularity, decided to take no chances.

In Abu Dhabi too, by 1965, attitudes towards the ruler were also hardening. 'Matters have gone backwards (in Abu Dhabi, due to) the ruler Shaikh Shakhbut, a paranoiac, who by his avarice, his muddle-headedness, his suspicion and refusal to delegate authority is single-handedly holding his state back' fulminated Abu Dhabi political officer J. Boustead to Bahrain in the annual report for 1964.[104]

Though oil exports commenced from Abu Dhabi in December 1963, the first successful well at Murban Bab having begun operation in May 1960,[105] Shaikh Shakhbut continued to refuse to spend any money on development in the state. Easa Al Gurg, who knew him well, testifies that with age, 'he became, if anything more difficult and less reasonable . . . he bitterly resented the changes which he knew would come to his state . . . he also resisted change for its own sake'.[106] The then political agent in Dubai, Donald Hawley, confirms that initially he assumed 'development in Dubai would lead Shaikh Shakhbut to emulate it, but he seemed unable to rid himself of suspicions of new ways'.[107] Despite the very substantial revenues now being earned from oil revenues and exploration rights, which ex-Eastern Bank representative Neville Green confirms the ruler required in cash, initially in a suitcase, before long, in a truck ,[108] Abu Dhabi remained without roads, hospitals and schools, the Shaikh even destroying a building to be used for a fledgling Municipal Council. In August 1966, the Al Nahyan ruling family with the full support of the British, exiled Shaikh Shakhbut and he was succeeded by his younger brother, the progressive and energetic Shaikh Zayed Al Nahyan, the governor of Buraimi (Al Ain). Shaikh Zayed had a very different character to his brother and he used the vast oil revenues rentier-fashion to develop Abu Dhabi, establishing schools, hospitals and infrastructure, and to assist the less wealthy Emirates. However, Abu Dhabi did not pursue the trading and logistics approach of its neighbour in Dubai, and for as long as Shaikh Zayed lived, until 2004 when he died after being president of the UAE for thirty-three years, Abu Dhabi remained almost entirely focussed on the Oil and Gas industries and being the political and bureaucratic capital of the UAE.

In just over a year, the British had therefore been complicit in removing two Trucial States rulers. The fact that they felt able to do so, despite the strength at the time, of Arab Nationalist feeling in the wider region (Nasser in Egypt, the revolution in Iraq in 1958 and accelerating process of de-colonization throughout the British Empire) seems to reflect three main factors. Firstly, they were confident that the action could be justified, 'for the greater good' of the states concerned, as a result of mal-governance. Secondly, justifiably in the case of Abu Dhabi, it could be argued that development was being stalled, not by British indifference, but by incompetent rulers out of touch with their people – very much in line with the attitude of republican regimes. Thirdly, despite an era when British power and influence were in decline, the legacy of over a hundred years of imperial overlordship was not so easily cast-off by the Trucial and other Gulf states. It is of course significant too, that the British were prepared to be involved in regime change to deal with the inadequacies of the rulers of Sharjah and Abu Dhabi. There was never any suggestion that Dubai, as the paradigm of regional development, might suffer the same fate.

Oman had, for centuries, seen struggles for power and influence between the littoral based trading Sultanates of Ibadi faith and the more insular Imams of the interior, resulting in an effective division of the country, where the control of the Sultan in the mountainous interior of the north was no more than nominal. Similarly, in Dhofar in the south, over 1000 kilometres from Muscat, cultural and political differences remained and only in the first half of the twentieth century did the Sultanate begin seriously to enrol the region as a fully constituent part of Oman, at least in part by Shaikh Said bin Taimur, by the expedient of making his home there. Despite these efforts during the 1940s, disaffection in Dhofar fuelled by instability in Yemen over the border became a serious challenge in the 1950s and 1960s. Also, in the north, even though Sultan Said in 1955 forcibly established control over the interior Imamate – unifying the country definitively for the first time – exiled Imamate supporters, backed by Wahhabi Saudi Arabia,[109] continued their resistance. Shaikh Said resisted the modernization of the state despite the discovery of oil in 1964 and in 1970, when he was deposed by his son Qaboos, the 'large, under-developed country (had) ... three schools, 12 hospital beds, 10km of paved roads, 557 telephone lines'[110] and according to a witness (in 1956), 'promptly at eight in the evening ... the heavy wooden gates of (the capital) Muscat were closed'.[111]

In these circumstances, the efforts of the new Sultan Qaboos were inevitably focussed on maintaining the unity of the state, and building, from scratch, the infrastructure of a state together with an education and healthcare system. He no longer had to concern himself with Zanzibar (independent in 1964) or Gwadar (sold to Pakistan in 1958) but the emergencies in the interior and Dhofar were only resolved at the end of the 1950s and mid-1970s respectively (with British assistance in both and some Iranian in the latter). In these circumstances, despite the dramatic development changes pushed through by Sultan Qaboos, Oman was in no position to compete economically with the other regional states.

Bahrain, throughout the 1960s, continued to act confidently as the major commercial, air-transport and re-export centre of the Gulf, paying little heed to the developments (such as the construction of Port Rashid in Dubai). The realization that a new nimble adversary had arrived in Dubai, competing for shipping and trading business seemed not to trouble the Al Khalifa ruling family, perhaps preoccupied with strikes and demands for greater workers' rights. The country declared independence from Britain in August 1971.

In Qatar, internal dissention among the ruling Al Thani family and disputes about the way oil revenues should be distributed dominated political life in the 1960s, to the detriment of the development of political institutions. The ruling family split over the question of whether to join a federation (with the ex-Trucial States) after the British departure. The question was resolved, in favour of complete independence, when the ruler Shaikh Ahmad was out of the country in September 1971. The following year he was deposed, to be replaced by Shaikh Khalifa. The economic focus rested solely on fossil-fuel exploitation.

Kuwait became independent in June 1961, but its early access to oil revenues, decades ahead of lower Gulf states and the domestic constitutional and rentier bargains after 1962, created a state which not only provided generous help to the (then) poorer lower Gulf states – as the existence still, of 'Kuwait Hospitals' throughout the UAE, and the Creek dredging loans to Dubai can testify – but also invested in local industry and downstream petrochemical infrastructure. The new Government took as its model, European constitutional monarchies and the Al Sabah were confirmed as hereditary rulers, possessing executive authority, and sharing legislative authority with an elected national assembly. Legislation ensured that only the Royal family and Kuwaiti citizens would enjoy the exclusive privileges of the rentier bargain, ensuring a solidarity between rulers and ruler against the increasing numbers of expatriates employed in the developing state.

In 1960, the port of Shuwaikh was inaugurated, adjacent to the centre of Kuwait city, and this multipurpose port continues to act as the major focus for general cargo and containers (despite restricted facilities). The container Terminal at Shuaiba Port (45 kilometres south of Kuwait city), was opened in 1982 with the aim of focussing container traffic at a purpose-built facility, but consignees, long-established in the Shuwaikh Industrial Areas adjacent to the port and close to the city, were reluctant to switch and Shuwaikh continues to handle the majority of container throughputs in the early twenty-first century.

In Saudi Arabia, with the oil price rises in the 1970s, studies of policy direction ordered by King Faisal aimed at 'the creation of two substantial industrial poles, the first at Jubail near the massive Eastern Province oil and gas fields and the second at Yanbu on the Red Sea'.[112] However, at the same time the King aimed at 'keeping as many as possible of the western expatriate community out of (the capital) Riyadh ... and it was only in the late 1970s that foreign banks were allowed to establish themselves in Riyadh. The embassies remained in Jeddah'.[113]

Such was (and is) the Saudi obsession with ensuring that containers did not provide a conduit for illicit goods such as alcohol, drugs, firearms and pornography that customs regulations required all containers arriving in the Kingdom to be opened unpacked and inspected. During the Saudi Seaports chairmanship of Dr Fayez Badr from the mid-seventies until 1995, there was even a concerted effort to insist that shipping lines calling Saudi ports used a specific 'Saudi Box' that not only had the usual container end doors but also opening doors on each side to facilitate inspections. Eventually, this logistically impracticable proposal was quietly dropped as being too costly and difficult to implement. Such policies and the lack of deep-water draft and sufficient and sizeable container cranes, also ensured that international businesses and shipping lines, attracted by container volumes produced by the sheer scale of Saudi industrialization and consumerism continued to set up regional centres in more commercially flexible and business-orientated Dubai.

However, in one respect, Dammam and Saudi Arabia, logistically, were and are still in advance of the whole region as, since October 1951, there has been a railway line between Dammam and Riyadh which from 1981 has carried cargo in containers by rail to the 'inland port' in the capital 'under customs bond' (i.e. to be customs cleared in Riyadh, and not as usual at the (Dammam) port of entry). The line was originally built (by Bechtel during 1947-51) and operated by Aramco, subsequently by the Saudi Railways Organization (SRO) from 1966, and the inauguration of the 'Dry Port' in Riyadh in May 1981 was intended to reduce the numbers of trucks on the roads between Dammam and Riyadh, which had grown considerably in number from the mid-1970s, as well as assisting Riyadh importers by allowing them to clear (take delivery of) their cargo in Riyadh itself, according to the Saudi Railways Website. In practice, however, this far-sighted intermodal approach, based on examples in the United States and Europe as well as the success in the 1970s of the similar bonded system, established by the American company Sealand, operating in Iran from Bandar Shahpour to Tehran, was slow to develop. Customs clearance agents based in Dammam were able to offer cheaper rates and quicker delivery by clearing cargo, un-stuffing containers and delivering cargo to Riyadh consignees by truck, compared with the 'through' intermodal rates in containers by rail to Riyadh (which required a costing for the invariably empty container to be returned to Dammam). Statistics on the Dammam/Riyadh rail volumes have always been difficult to obtain but based on website of the current (private) operators, BAAS International Group (BIG), import volumes in 2015 are likely to be in the region of 350,000 TEU according to their Website. At the time of writing (October 2017) this line remains the only rail-linked intermodal service for containers in the Arabian Peninsula, albeit only for Saudi inland traffic.

By the beginning of the 1970s, Iran seemed to have weathered the political challenges posed by populist politicians and the conservative clerics. The Shah had developed a formidably equipped military, had expanded education for all (including girls), introduced economic and social reforms with the 'White Revolution' from 1963, and expanded the country's industrial sector. Such was the Shah's confidence that he staged a vastly expensive 2500th-year anniversary party in October 1971, for the founding of the Acaemenid empire, equating the Pahlavi dynasty as a worthy heir. Also, in November of the same year the Iranians seized the Abu Musa and Tumbs islands from the newly formed United Arab Emirates, despite agreements that administration of the islands was to be shared. It seemed clear that Iran was determined to be the new Gulf political and economic arbiter after the departure of the British. However, this apparent stability and all-pervasive power would soon prove to be an illusion.

After the revolution in 1958, Iraq underwent a period of instability with a total of four coups d'etat in the next ten years. However, the success of the Baath Party in the coup of July 1968, was to herald a period of stability, in which oil revenues and a well-educated population would make a sizeable contribution. The main port of Basrah, like other such riverine ports worldwide, was increasingly exposed as inadequate as ship sizes increased and in 1967 a 'deep-water' port was opened in Umm Qasr at the mouth of the Shatt-Al-Arab (though still affected by silt accumulation, requiring regular dredging). Umm Qasr was also rail-linked via Basra to Baghdad. However, from 1980 and the start of the Iran/Iraq war, until the early years of the twenty-first century, Iraqi ports, of which only Basra, was of any size, had little impact on the region, cut-off from all but the smallest craft as a result of war damage and no investment with several wrecked ships in the river channels and lack of facilities.

Chapter review

At first glance, Sharjah seemed to be in a position of strength in the Trucial States in the first half of the twentieth century. However, despite Sharjah's apparent status as the HQ of the Trucial States, with the British Political Office located there, an airport and a British air force base; a (creek) port that was superficially similar to that of Dubai and a history of maritime and political suzerainty, weak leadership and much greater impetus and economic initiative from its near neighbour, increasingly saw Sharjah steadily overhauled and overtaken by Dubai. The Political Office moved from Sharjah in 1954; merchants moved to the more active Dubai market; the port, already falling behind Dubai, was allowed to silt up by 1960 and the construction of a new airport in Dubai siphoned off most of the passenger traffic. We should not forget also, the fundamental, economic impact of British merchant houses and commercial concerns, such as Gray Mackenzie, the British India Steam Navigation Company (BI) and the British Bank of the Middle East (BBME), all based in Dubai, 'in shaping and developing international trading patterns'.[114] However, they were only based in Dubai because it was the best place for their businesses. The large infrastructure projects begun in the 1960s and 1970s saw Dubai pull even further ahead, as, even in the decade before independence, it is clear, that companies, merchants and the British Government had placed all their support behind a modernizing and active Dubai, already becoming the regional entrepot. It is hard to argue with their conclusions, reflecting the attitudes and the commercial and infrastructural, developmental approach of a Dubai very different than its quiescent neighbours. Abu Dhabi, under a conservative ruler, made little attempt to change the status quo and even with the accession of the constructive and pragmatic Shaikh Zayed in 1966, focussed on the development of the state –

virtually starting from scratch – and the (admittedly vast) oil reserves, which had been exported since 1963. Dubai's role as the commercial and trading centre of the Emirates and beyond was to remain apparently accepted and unchallenged, even as Abu Dhabi's oil-wealth and influence increased, until the death of Shaikh Zayed in 2004. The two, potential, neighbouring challengers to Dubai were therefore in the formative years of the second half of the twentieth century, politically and commercially inept on the one hand and disinterested then focussed elsewhere on the other.

Wider political developments, particularly the withdrawal of the British from 1971 and the impact of Arab nationalism did not deflect the focus of the Dubai ruler from the desire to push-ahead with the infrastructural improvements to enable Dubai to compete more effectively. In this he was fortunate that this was an era where communications were limited to poor radio connections; Dubai was still a very small player in a region where the larger states were making all the headlines and, until 1971, the British had the responsibility without power for external relations – and thus could be blamed accordingly. Shaikh Rashid was able to proceed with his plans 'under the radar' with few external distractions.

The role of Shaikh Rashid al Maktoum in creating the conditions and pushing through the policies that established modern Dubai cannot be overstated. Sir Bernard Burrows, who, as the Resident in Bahrain from 1953–8, was certainly in a position to know, summed up his impact three decades later.

> 'One of the most successful Rulers was Shaikh Rashid of Dubai. He was a typical merchant-prince, more like those known in history in medieval Europe, who had brought his state to a high level of material prosperity, even before it received any oil revenue. He achieved this by the encouragement of trade and business activity of all kinds, by use of the creek . . . which provided a more or less secure base for a host of local craft.'[115] He updated, rebuilt and built again the port infrastructure to support commercial activity; he secured and then developed on a large scale, a modern airport; the administrative infrastructure was developed and expanded with a modern police force (1957), modernized customs procedures and a court system and the modern municipality. Alhammadi confirms, 'As a result of his efforts Dubai developed superior administrative infrastructure to the other (Trucial States).'[116]

Inevitably, there are questions about the extent to which he acted independently from the influence of the British Political Office in Dubai and the Gulf Residency in Bahrain, although, officially, as set out by Glen Balfour-Paul, British protection over the states 'did not confer . . . any right of interference in (their) internal affairs'.[117] Even if we accept, as we must, that the British Political Office, in the final analysis, was the ultimate source of power (potentially backed up by force), this was rarely used, particularly because, in the case of Shaikh Rashid, there was no reason to interfere. The evidence from contemporaries, both Nationals and expatriates, as well as the (confidential) records at the time from British Government and company sources, which often had very critical views of other contemporaries, show a remarkable convergence of opinion. This consensus reveals a man focussed entirely on the development of Dubai, who was respected for his independence of thought, imagination and energy, who took much counsel from many sources but then made up his own mind on how to proceed, often completely at variance with the (in hindsight) conservative hesitancy of his advisors. Even though he had the benefit of working at a time when there was little competition from a maladroit and declining Sharjah and an Abu Dhabi focussed on oil, disinterested in making the effort to pursue commercial business, this should not diminish the skill with which he fought for Dubai's interests. There is no hint that he was playing to anyone's agenda but that of Dubai. Simply because he was (usually) on good terms with local political agents, reflects more his diplomatic skills to achieve what he wanted, rather than acquiescing in someone else's policy. Skilfully playing on the concerns of the British at the tail-end of empire, with courtesy and charm, he managed to both get the Political Agencies to work on his (Dubai's) behalf, as it would reflect well on British policy (helping stave-off the appeal of pan-Arab nationalism), and because the proposals were fiscally sound and economically sensible, and also used the local British company seniors as sounding-boards and as unpaid advisors to help him start cautiously positioning the building blocks of a modern state. This balancing act was even more impressive when it is clear he had to negotiate his relationship with the Dubai merchant elites, some of whom, fearing economic exclusion from the collapse of pearling and the competition from economic migrants, had been restive throughout the 1940s and 1950s. Shaikh Rashid's achievement in political persuasion and creating the environment for the Dubai merchants to accept and participate in the economic expansion of the Emirate, embedding them in the state-building process, without diminishing the agreed authority of the ruling family, is perhaps the most notable success of all.

Chapter 3

EXOGENOUS IMPACTS AND THE LOGISTICS REVOLUTION (1971–90)

> Ports and port cities have evolved at the intersection of local and global forces.[1]

In January 1968, the British government had announced that Britain would withdraw from the Gulf by the end of 1971. This decision, as a result of 'internal British and Labour Party politics, not the initiation of a particular foreign policy',[2] was greeted with incredulity by the Gulf rulers, who had been assured only months earlier, that Britain had no such intention. Despite efforts for nearly twenty years to produce a more 'federal' approach among the separate Trucial States, long-standing British protection, rivalries and the varying wealth and developmental attitudes of the seven rulers had ensured there was little incentive for them to take such action. The implications of the British action were to focus minds very rapidly. Lengthy negotiations soon commenced to convince the rulers that joining together in a Federal structure with the Emirates of Bahrain and Qatar would provide the best chance for small states to have a more viable future.

Old rivalries soon surfaced, however, with the divisions of powers, locations of ministries and responsibilities proving difficult to distribute among the nine rulers coupled with the complexity of their often-competing external relations. It was difficult to convince the ruling families that were outside the Trucial States to reduce their independent power, as they were used to rule themselves separately under British overlordship for many decades, and increasingly confident of their financial viability. Despite their many common links of ethnicity, language, social customs and religion, there were suspicions, border disputes and economic competition between the states in the Arab Gulf, grown confident of their place in the sun during the longue duree of *Pax Britannica*. By late 1969, both Qatar and Bahrain had quit the joint discussions, and in August 1971 Bahrain declared itself an independent state, secured by the Iranian government waiving any claims to the island in May 1970 following a United Nations (UN) organized referendum. Qatar followed suit a month later, leaving the seven Trucial States to work out a future structure on their own.

With five of the seven virtually penniless, Dubai and Abu Dhabi were to be the prime movers in the declaration of the new federation in December 1971, although the last-minute withdrawal of Ras al Khaimah rather dampened the enthusiasm. Ras al Khaimah finally joined the nascent UAE two months later in February 1972.

Though there were concerns that the new federation would not last, as described by Hawley,[3] to the great credit of both Shaikh Rashid of Dubai and the new president Shaikh Zayed Al Nayan of Abu Dhabi, the structure held together. Shaikh Zayed, who had replaced his arch-conservative brother in a palace coup five years earlier, was very much committed to the new United Arab Emirates and used Abu Dhabi's oil wealth for development not only to develop his own Emirate, but throughout the federation. Frauke Heard-Bey recounts, for example, how already by 1974, 'when the price of oil had quadrupled over seven months, Abu Dhabi contributed the lion's share of the Federal budget'.[4] Reflecting concerns about potential external threats, the fledgling new state moved to cover its flanks by joining the Arab League and the United Nations soon after independence and negotiating an agreement with Saudi Arabia to resolve a long-standing border dispute in 1974. However, as a foretaste of the problems arising to face a new state after the century and a half of British external protection, days before the British departure, Iran seized the disputed Tunbs islands from Ras al Khaimah by force and forced through a partition of Sharjah's Abu Musa island in November 1971. It is significant that this Iranian action took place while the islands were still under the control of these small independent states, rather than later which would have provoked a much more serious breach with the Abu Dhabi and Dubai dominated UAE.

With Abu Dhabi settling into its new UAE capital role and the new internal, federal and international governmental responsibilities that its new position entailed, for post-independent Dubai, it was 'business as usual' with the focus remaining on commerce and infrastructure expansion. The relationship between Dubai and Abu Dhabi remained fragile – many years of separate development and ancient rivalries did not of course disappear overnight despite the efforts and compromises necessary to create the new independent federal state. The nature of the new UAE, deliberately rather loose, vague and decentralized in order to reach an agreement at all, allowed each Emirate to retain control over their own natural resources and thus their own development paths. In practice, this meant that progress towards further federal integration of the seven Emirates was negligible, with Abu Dhabi (admittedly having vast oil revenues) effectively funding the federal budget, with Dubai deliberately making little or no contribution and the other five Emirates nothing at all.[5] The new union was therefore very much 'work in progress' for the first decades of its life with its members making their own way much as they had always done. In these circumstances, there was even more incentive for Dubai to accelerate its commercial and trading infrastructure programme while it still had the independence to do so, in order to ensure that the city would remain the unchallenged business centre of the new enlarged state.

The impact of external instability

By the late 1970s, despite the departure of the British from the Trucial States in 1971 and the creation of the independent UAE, Dubai was continuing to develop, as it had been doing for the previous twenty years, establishing state institutions and the panoply of a modern state, focussing on its trading infrastructure. Port Rashid was expanded, Jebel Ali was under construction (with the first phase opening in 1979) and the airport opened in 1960 was handling rapidly increasing numbers (by 1980, 2.7 million passengers a year.)[6] These facilities were to prove attractive alternative options when the Lebanese Civil War broke out in 1975.

> In the ten years prior to 1975 the Lebanese economy was one of the most dynamic in the Middle East. Regulations impinging on the market for goods and services, labour, capital and trade were limited and tax burdens were light . . . furthermore, Lebanon had an important role as the key economic intermediary between the developed economies of Europe and those of the Middle East. Because of this combination of a stable macroeconomic environment, liberal economics and its role as a regional intermediary, Lebanon enjoyed a strong comparative advantage in the services sector of its economy particularly in Banking, finance, tourism, insurance and trade-related services.[7]

The internecine conflict in Lebanon, lasting fifteen years, destroyed this attractive environment, fragmenting the country, devastating infrastructure, fracturing state institutions and causing a massive flight of financial capital and of people out of the country (with their professional and entrepreneurial skills) to safer, more congenial locations. By the early 1990s, as Lebanon gradually emerged from a generation of self-immolation, it was clear that the regional mantle for providing the various services, in which it had specialized, banking, finance and tourism, had passed from Beirut to Dubai and that the Emirate was also benefitting from many thousands of skilled and well-educated workers who were established and settled with little desire to return to a still uncertain and dystopian Lebanon. There had been other alternatives to choose for businesses (and people), but the reason that Dubai had succeeded in attracting both was that it was creating a similar, reliable and stable business environment in the now burgeoning Gulf. Lebanon's moment in the sun had passed as, almost imperceptibly, the regional business centre of gravity shifted south-east. 'Getting the structure right' infrastructure, an efficient and honest civil service, an effective legal system and a liberal, low-tax, entrepreneurial economic environment was working in Dubai's favour.

Concurrently, on the opposite shore of the Gulf, rising domestic dissention in Iran in the late 1970s resulted in the overthrow of the Shah in 1979 and the establishment of the Islamic Republic. The Arab Gulf monarchies were still coming to terms with this new revolutionary regime as it struggled to establish itself amidst internal discord, when Iran was attacked, opportunistically, by

Saddam Hussein's Iraq in September 1980 in a conflict that was to last for another eight years. Though the Arab states urgently created a regional grouping in 1981, the Gulf Co-operation Council (GCC), as a demonstration of regional solidarity against the perceived threat from Iran and 'to help Shaikhly regimes maintain their grip on power through security and economic means',[8] Dubai's long and carefully maintained relationship with Iran ensured that despite serious regional political differences, concerns about Iranian revolutionary rhetoric and disputes about the islands seized by Iran in 1971, trading activity continued. Some idea of the scale of Dubai's trade with Iran in the period before the war can be gauged by the claim that 'in the early 1970s more than half of about 50,000 trading dhows in Dubai were engaged primarily in the re-export trade with Persia (Iran)'.[9] With major Iranian ports such as Bandar Shahpour (renamed Bandar Iman Khomeini after the revolution) literally in the front-line of hostilities and closed, and others such as Bandar Abbas or Bushire unable to provide the facilities or capacity for the imports needed to sustain a population of over 40 million people, Dubai, maintaining a studied neutrality despite pressure to pursue a more 'Arab solidarity' line, became even more, the major gateway for Iran. The impact of maintaining a trading relationship with Iran is revealed in the UAE (i.e. mainly Dubai) import/export statistics recorded by the IMF during this time, particularly compared with the volumes with the rest of the GCC.

UAE and GCC exports to Iran in USD million

	GCC	UAE
1985	40	68
1986	60	488
1987	47	355
1988	53	251
1989	201	863
1990	264	883
1991	180	1273
1992	505	1444
1993	450	1018

(Source IMF Direction of Trade Statistics)[10]

Even with the political will to maintain trading links with Iran, volumes on such a scale would not have been possible without the ports and logistics infrastructure in which Dubai had invested so presciently.

As a result of the completion of the deep-water, fifteen-berth Port Rashid in 1972, Dubai was increasingly more equipped than other Gulf ports to cope with congestion caused by the post-oil-price cargo boom later in the decade. However, two years later, seeing the impact of development and its future requirements, Shaikh Rashid confirmed a further huge expansion, adding a further 20–22 berths, completed in 1979 – and significantly, converting one of them (Berth 10) into a specialized container berth with two container-handling cranes, opened in 1980. It is worth re-emphasizing here that the new ruler was, as repeatedly confirmed by George Chapman's memoir detailing their friendship over nearly forty years, extraordinarily tenacious in pursuing such projects.

> He wanted to know everything that the job entailed ... and soon was discussing with the engineers the relative merits of training walls, steel piling and explosives .... He was involved every step of the way. He looked, he listened, he had people explain. He was always surrounded by people and set himself a daily agenda that was exhausting, out early in the morning touring the various sites, planning projects, watching progress, asking questions.[11]

With hindsight, the decision to expand the new port seems entirely logical, but at the time there were fears that such grandiose schemes were costly and pointless follies, with no precedents for large port infrastructure projects at that time on such a scale. However, the oil price shocks of 1973-4, when oil prices quadrupled (by 1976-7), as a result of the Arab producers' oil export embargo following the Yom Kippur war with Israel, resulted in a huge increase in imports into the Gulf paid for with oil revenues. Dubai's first oil was discovered in 1966 (the offshore 'Fateh' field), and the first exports took place in 1969. Though volumes were relatively modest, with departing British resident officer Julian Bullard stating at the beginning of 1971 that production was to increase from 100,000 barrels per day to 300,000 within two years,[12] the economy expanded sevenfold between 1968 and 1973.[13] It is worth highlighting that the price of oil in 1970-1 was (only) $ 3.60 per barrel, on which basis Dubai oil revenues were around $ 360,000 per day (or circa USD 2 million per day inflation adjusted with today's values). By 1976, the oil price had risen to circa $ 13.10 and by 1980 $ 37.42.[14] Abu Dhabi's far larger deposits had been on-stream since 1963. Initially, construction material, particularly cement and steel, dominated the import volumes, with steadily increasing amounts of cars and consumer goods. The sheer scale and rapidity in the increase of imports can be shown by the following figures, over just one decade, recorded by the British Bank of the Middle East (BBME) in their annual reports:

Dubai Imports by Value, Pounds Sterling (Million), 1968-77[15]

1968 –   42
1969 –   83
1970 –   84
1971 –   91
1972 –   147
1973 –   234
1974 –   450
1975 –   1013
1976 –   1282
1977 –   1621

Levels of congestion (i.e. ships waiting to berth at the ports) reached absurd levels as huge orders for imports resulted in cargo volumes reaching unprecedented proportions at all Gulf ports. Conventional cargo ships anchored offshore, waited indefinitely to receive permission to berth to discharge general cargo, building material, steel and cement (slowly), at small, inadequate conventional ports. Congestion was so serious that ships would sometimes wait for months before berthing and, for a short time, a system of registration was introduced whereby a ship would 'register' a place in the queue for an indicated date of berthing and then go elsewhere either to discharge cargo at other ports if possible, or register a place at such ports too, before returning to its (established and higher) place in the queue. Dubai was in a better position to cope than others thanks to Shaikh Rashid's 'supply-side driven strategy',[16] and by 1977 the BBME was reporting that there 'was little or no waiting times at Port Rashid'.[17] The problems with congestion and the resultant delays and increases in costs (for importers) focussed attention on new port handling methods, as it was becoming apparent that more cargo was now moving in containers. Crucially, containers were much easier and quicker to handle and remove from the quayside, thus improving productivity and subsequently, reducing congestion. Congestion accelerated the demand for better and bigger ports equipped to handle containers, and the first berths (quays) for containers in Dubai were operational in November 1980, with a full-fledged separate 'Container Terminal' in Port Rashid expanded and completed in 1982. Dubai Port Services (DPS), established in 1970 by George Chapman's Gray Mackenzie Company to manage the port, pioneered the use of computers in the 1980s to cope with the increasing complexity of monitoring container movements.[18] It wasn't the first. Sharjah's small, Mina Khalid, is generally considered to have this accolade in 1976,[19] catering to some of the new container start-ups such as Hellenic Lines who aimed to explore niche opportunities at a time of rapid change.

Building for the future

Significantly, Dubai continued to expand its port (and Container) facilities to cater to the increased volume of trade, particularly with the decision (in 1976) to build Jebel Ali port near the border with Abu Dhabi. The location though logistically sensible, out of the city in a stretch of undeveloped land with space for expansion, also ensured, as highlighted by Ramos,[20] that this area and recently disputed (with Abu Dhabi) territory was definitively part of Dubai. As with the decision in 1973 to build a large skyscraper tower (The World Trade Centre) to house offices and displays for business (when complete in 1979 it was the tallest building in the Arab world), Shaikh Rashid's advisors and the traders in the Majlis[21] urged the ruler to reconsider. 'We all told the Ruler that the Trade Centre was too big and that no-one would use it – and we told him the same thing about Jebel Ali. Of course, we were wrong and he was right on both counts.'[22]

The Jebel Ali project entailed building the largest man-made port complex in the world with 15 kilometres of quay and 67 berths, the first phase of container berths coming on-stream in 1979, the current ruler of Dubai, Shaikh Mohammed Al Maktoum, explaining recently, 'my father told me he was building something for the future, something we might not be able to afford later'.[23] By 1983, the construction of Jebel Ali port was complete, but further expansions, building on the initial decision to place emphasis on the new containerization developments – and equally importantly – the industrial zone and free-zones backing it up, continued and have continued and evolved ever since, fully justifying Shaikh Rashid's decision. Shaikh Rashid was a believer in competition and this attitude extended to the initial choice of Port Operator for Jebel Ali, choosing Sealand, the company founded by Malcolm McLean, with Gray Mackenzie remaining as operator of Mina Rashid. However, the Dubai government, now increasingly in the hands of Shaikh Rashid's sons, was increasingly determined to take over full responsibility itself. In 1984, Gray Mackenzie's contract in Mina Rashid was altered to make them Port Managers with the government taking financial and investment authority. Sealand's contract at Jebel Ali was also on the same basis. (This system continued until May 1991 when the Dubai government decided that competition between its own ports was no longer appropriate when a more coherent long-term strategy was necessary for them and for Dubai and took over full financial and managerial control of both Mina Rashid and Jebel Ali, forming Dubai Port Authority, staffed and managed by industry professionals.)[24]

At first, Jebel Ali's progress was slow, seemingly confirming the fears of many in Dubai and the region that the development was a step too far. There were three main problems. Firstly, shipping lines had concerns about moving to a port operated by a competitor (Sealand) despite repeated assertions by the management that commercial impartiality was maintained. Secondly, Dubai merchants did not at first want to pay the extra costs involved in collecting cargo from Jebel Ali which was much further away (100 km there and back) than city centre Port Rashid, which at the time was already handling containers efficiently. These issues were eventually resolved because most major shipping (container) lines eventually moved from Port Rashid to Jebel Ali as the facilities were better, (and ship sizes were increasing) although concerns about losing customers to lines remaining in Port Rashid remained. Despite misgivings about the competitive impact, major lines such as Maersk and P&O Containers switched, in 1991, conscious that they were making a long-term leap of faith, and lines mitigated the impact for customers and induced consignees to maintain support by (initially) agreeing to competitive haulage rates for containers moving into Dubai city. Also, lines no longer had to worry about the terminal being operated by competitors as in 1991 the Dubai authorities unified the administration of both Jebel Ali and Mina Rashid under one, government-controlled 'Dubai Ports Authority' (DPA).

The third problem, more seriously, was that the region's politics and trade had been convulsed by the Iranian revolution of 1979 and the collapse of the Gulf's largest and seemingly most buoyant economy, replaced by a regime in Tehran whose rhetoric seemed to pose a threat to the Arab states of the Gulf. This uncertain environment had a severe dampening effect on trade and investment in the region, particularly so for Dubai with its longstanding trading links with

Iran. This uncertainty was compounded in September 1980 by Saddam Hussein's decision to take advantage of what was perceived to be a much-weakened Iran following the revolution and invade the ethnically Arab western oil-producing provinces of his neighbour. This gamble did not succeed and, as described in Dilip Hiro's 'The Longest War',[25] the two states fought themselves to a standstill over the next eight years at a cost of over a million military and civilian lives. The economic environment in the Gulf in these circumstances was slow to recover, but as the war dragged on, Dubai, with its excellent infrastructural facilities in the lower Gulf, began to benefit as a safe transport and relay hub, both because of its facilities and competence and also because it was felt to be at a safe distance from hostilities – unlike the upper Gulf ports.

Jebel Ali had been an investment in the future, not least as a post-independence statement that even within the federal UAE, Dubai would continue to maintain and expand its trading traditions. As highlighted, its very location was an affirmation that this was Dubai territory, based on the agreement with Abu Dhabi in 1968 that this disputed area 'would be ceded to Dubai',[26] and also a statement that the new port could serve both Dubai and Abu Dhabi in future as well as maintaining a competitive advantage over such newly announced schemes such as the Saudi Royal Commission development in Jubail on the Saudi Gulf coast.

However, although the impact of Dubai's Jebel Ali was slow to show itself, the development was to be a 'game-changer' for the region, for three main reasons. Firstly, Jebel Ali was a port project purposely designed for the container age on a massive scale, initially with one container terminal, providing by 2017 'a capacity of 19.3 million TEU . . . 28 berths equipped with 102 ship-to-shore cranes'.[27] The facility dwarfed other terminals in the region (as it still does) and in so doing provided the key requisites of shipping lines and their import or export customers – efficiency, speed and convenience – with a customer-focussed professionalism new to the region. Secondly, Jebel Ali was not designed simply to be a port but as part of an interconnected logistics complex, backed up by the Jebel Ali Free Zone (JAFZA) inaugurated in 1985, providing customers both in Dubai, the other Emirates and the wider region, a base to establish their import, export or distribution-to-a-wider-area businesses, linked seamlessly to the port, achieving 500 businesses/customers by 1995 and 1000 by 2000.[28] Thirdly, the sheer scale of the terminal and therefore the ability of shipping lines to operate the largest container ships and to relay containers from one ship to another quickly (and cost-effectively as a result of competitive pricing by the port) transformed the ways of shipping lines serving the Gulf. There was now no need for lines to send increasingly large (and expensive) ships up the gulf, but to provide a better, more reliable and financially more attractive service to customers by trans-shipping/relaying containers in Jebel Ali from large ships onto smaller 'feeder' vessels. Jebel Ali had become a 'hub' port, where larger container ships discharged their containers for relay on to 'spoke' services to other regional ports on smaller container ships.

As a 'hub' port, it became an automatic port of call for all container ships serving the Gulf and (via feeder ships) the wider region including Pakistan, West

Coast India and East Africa with the integrated free-zone providing the facilities for companies to use Jebel Ali for their products as a distribution hub too. Dubai volumes as a proportion of Gulf container throughputs (including outer Gulf hubs) highlight this clearly:

Gulf Container Volumes (million TEU)

Year	Dubai	Other Gulf	Dubai %
1985	0.5	1.1	32%
1995	2.1	2.3	47%
2005	7.6	8.5	47%
2015	15.5	15.6	50%

(Source: Drewry Maritime Research London)

That it was able to do so with such effect was due both to the 'cluster' effect of the intermodal opportunities provided by a closely linked transport and distribution hub and the fact that it was out-competing other ports and cities over a wide area because other centres had failed to provide facilities or performance that were better. The statistics given illustrate both the growth in total volumes and the extent to which Dubai has maintained and extended its proportion of these throughputs, with '(Fordist) precision, efficiency, economy, reliability and speed'[29] and, the appreciation and acceptance of the opportunities provided by containerization, consequent globalization and the increasing multipolar global economy particularly since the latter years of the twentieth century.

Jebel Ali was therefore the cornerstone of Dubai's success in attracting business, having adapted to 'aspects of economic globalization and focused on practical measures of global engagement'.[30] Not only could Dubai offer businesses and their employees a 'package' comprising a safe and comfortable place to base themselves; the best and biggest port in the region with unrivalled shipping-line availability; excellent connectivity through the region's biggest airport and a tax-free, 100 per cent foreign ownership Jebel Ali Free-Zone Area (JAFZA) site without import or re-export duties. Also, as a result of neighbouring states' inactivity or inability, Dubai was able to make the best case for ships to call, relatively unhampered by potentially viable competitors.

This was the case not only in the Gulf but for South Asia and East Africa too. The failure of governments in the very large nations of India and Pakistan to develop infrastructure ensured that as container shipping services evolved, the major (state-owned) ports of Mumbai (India) and Karachi (Pakistan), both handling the majority of their countries' trade, 55 per cent[31] and 60 per cent respectively,[32] remained inefficient and insufficiently transformed for the container age, with archaic bureaucracy and inadequate facilities. Only with the advent of private companies from 1999 onwards in India was real progress made to provide facilities (cranes, new berths, yard areas), which would allow containerized trade to be handled efficiently, despite Jawaharlal Nehru Port Trust (JNPT) in Mumbai, half-heartedly starting the process in 1989. In Pakistan, the (relatively small) Karachi

International Container Terminal (operated by Hutchison Ports only opened in 1998). These late starts allowed and encouraged shipping lines to use Jebel Ali as a hub from the early 1990s, with 'spokes' extending not only to the Gulf but also to India and Pakistan – a large deep-sea vessel from say Europe or Asia relaying containers for Mumbai or Karachi at Jebel Ali onto dedicated feeder services serving those ports. This trans-shipment routing, via Dubai, with an approximate two-day transit to Karachi and four days to Mumbai,[33] was able to deliver containers more regularly, more reliably and more cost-effectively than using more, smaller, higher cost-per-slot ships on a long-distance routing and spending expensive ship-days in inefficient ports. Such logic (to fill the larger ships with 'hub and spoke' cargo rather than simply call-port containers) became ever-more inevitable as ship sizes increased. For companies based in Jebel Ali using the Free Zones as a distribution centre for the whole region (including West Coast India, Pakistan and East Africa), such hub operations simplified their logistical supply-chain procedures. The fact that neighbouring states in the Indian Ocean, not only India and Pakistan but the nations of Africa, either failed to understand the benefits of infrastructure development for their economies or made no progress because of corruption and bureaucracy, simply ensured that Dubai benefitted the more.

Towards a connected-up logistics approach – Jebel Ali and free-zones

Dubai, from the 1960s onwards, as we have seen, invested early in major maritime infrastructural projects, especially Jebel Ali port, 'when Dubai's global aspirations were first realized through port engineering and construction',[34] giving 'an early starter advantage'.[35] However, the advent of containerization (gradually) ushered in a raft of associated changes in the way in which cargo was handled, transported and delivered. The traditional 'break-bulk' (loose cargo) delivery process, whereby cargo was loaded and unloaded at a port (in boxes, crates, bundles etc) having to be delivered to the ship transported and then discharged and collected by whatever means of transport was suitable, gradually receded into history. Containers allowed goods to move, unitized, from 'door to door' and through multi-modal transportation was now possible, rather than the age-old 'port to port' procedure. Dubai's foresight in building the huge Jebel Ali complex allowed the growth of 'hub and spoke' operations by shipping lines (discharging containers from a mega-container-ship in the Dubai hub and relaying those containers for other regional ports on smaller ship (spoke) services). However, the lesson from primarily transhipment centres (whether past such as Lingah, or present, such as (the admittedly very efficient) Khor Fakkan in an enclave of Sharjah on the UAE's East coast) is that without a domestic cargo base to consolidate the need for lines to call, a transhipment port will always be at the mercy of changing trade patterns, new competition or shipping line re-alignment and consolidation.

The first of the free-zones in Dubai, Jebel Ali Free Zone, established in 1985, set out to accelerate the provision of improved facilities for businesses that would build the cargo base in Dubai and, using the established regional shipping hub, to supplement simple relay of cargo with domestic product either produced in Dubai or using the free-zone as a distribution centre for imports destined for the wider region. Such a policy also aimed to develop the logistics industry, appreciating that container shipping hubs and logistics hubs are not always the same, 'the former is the outcome of the carriers' concerns with optimizing their route networks, the latter with managing goods distribution'.[36] However, in Dubai, the two have evolved together.

But what is a 'free-zone', what are its advantages and why is it different from, in this case, the rest of Dubai? Arang Keshavarzian, argues that

> states have established these zones with highly liberal financial and legal frameworks to encourage industrialisation and job creation by promoting foreign investment, export-orientated production and the transfer of- skills. (While) these zones have not always resulted in these ends and have definitely not in the Iran (Kish Island) case . . . the facilities and lowered barriers to trade and finance have made the Southern Gulf a critical node in various transnational networks.[37]

He also argues, as highlighted previously, that in the case of JAFZA, the location was a deliberate attempt to confirm that this was Dubai territory as part of post-federation accommodations with Abu Dhabi. There may well have been some such element in Shaikh Rashid's thinking, but more realistically, it was part of an (expensive and at the time, derided) statement of infrastructural expansion, in a strategically and commercially appropriate position, between the two main Emirates, cementing, literally, Dubai's commercial status. We should also recognize that this was part of the accommodation and negotiations that allowed the UAE to arise from the Trucial States – that Dubai would remain the commercial and trading centre of the new federation. The success of Jebel Ali port and JAFZA equally confirm that though there may have been a variety of rationales, the economic development logic behind them was correct.

As the JAFZA website is keen to emphasize, the free-zone thrives because of Dubai and vice-versa, 'one of the most competitive locations to establish your business and see it grow . . . within the dynamic Dubai market that supports enterprise development while offering one of the most desirable places to live'.[38] So much for the 'boiler-plate' advertisement – the next paragraph highlights the specific advantages of a free-zone – essentially a duty-free enclave within a state – which in the case of JAFZA offers: 100 pc foreign ownership; zero pc corporate tax for 50 years; zero import, re-export duty; zero personal income tax and no restrictions on capital repatriation, currency or foreign employees. Such zones, also called Special Economic Zones (SEZs), or Free Economic Zones (FEZs) as well as other variations, are designed, particularly in emerging economies throughout the world, as specific areas, usually adjacent to seaports, airports or on national boundaries, in which companies do not incur tax at all or at a low level, in order to encourage investment and economic activity. One major difference, and advantage, for a foreign company seeking to establish itself in Dubai, is that in a free-zone (in addition to the benefits listed previously) there is no requirement to have a local partner who by law will own at least 51 per cent of the company, which is a requirement in the rest of Dubai and the UAE (to protect the interests of UAE citizens). Therefore, for international companies trading in the region, being based in JAFZA or other free-zones, allows the advantages of the free-zone economic concessions – a presence in the area's biggest entrepot; the proximity of the region's largest port and airport and the amenable living conditions for (invariably) foreign staff keen to work in Dubai. However, free-zone companies cannot sell directly to the local market, they must have a partnership with a local company (with local majority shareholding) in order to do so. JAFZA website emphasizes the success of this policy of attracting businesses, using the symbiotic relationship between the port and the free-zone(s), by stating that JAFZA started out in 1985 with 19 companies and now has over 7000.[39]

Mehran Kamrava, recently emphasized that 'a busy deep-water port and lucrative architectural practices do not a global city make',[40] thus rather disparagingly dismissing Dubai's efforts and pretensions in this direction. While he has a point, that cities such as Dubai still have some way to go, before they create trends rather than following them, his patronizing remarks are perhaps misguided. The free-zones are very much part of the way in which Dubai has aimed to address the issue of being seen to produce and create rather than simply consume, particularly as, over the years, the range of specialized units has widened to include examples such as Dubai Flower City (horticulture), Dubai Academic City (education), Healthcare City (healthcare provision) and Dubai Multi Commodities Centre. This policy has been extremely successful in further widening and diversifying the economy, continuing until the present day. (The Gulf News newspaper reported in August 2017 that the free-zone sector accounts for '32pc of (Dubai's) total direct trade, driving about USD 135 billion of commerce in 2015. As of 2015, Dubai was home to 20,000 free-zone firms . . . 144,000 people are employed in JAFZA alone'.)[41]

There are other benefits too. These innovative developments, in addition to adding to Dubai's business portfolio, broadening the scope of Dubai's worldwide 'soft-power' presence and increasing the scale of the Emirate's commercial, technical and industrial base, are also a vital source of revenue because of the number of companies, and foreign workers who constitute virtually all of the free-zones' workforce. The government benefits from the various set-up fees for companies, visas, trade licences and various other charges which, once companies are established, provides a steady income stream. Such has been the success of these steadily evolving measures, that three-quarters of the total Dubai Government USD 8.3 billion revenues in 2015, according to a Chatham House Report, consisted of 'fines, services and fees' with 'Dubai . . . a unique example of a Gulf state that has embraced expatriates and turned them into a source of revenue . . . and where expatriates constitute 92% of the population it can be assumed that the bulk of fines and fees are paid by expatriates'.[42] As the Chatham House report also highlights, this innovative policy of taxing (indirectly) and charging expatriates, while successfully creating a major part of the Emirate's income, is also potentially a serious weakness. The prosperity of Dubai is built on the availability and ability of people and companies to continue to pay, effectively for being part of the Dubai success story. If, therefore, the supply of cheap labour dries up or conditions force them to depart, and like Lingah a century earlier (or Bahrain 30 years ago), poor decisions and a weakening competitive position persuades companies to move, lacking natural resources and with a limited, tangible, commercial, technical and industrial base, Dubai might be left exposed as its carefully assembled income streams dry up, as Christopher Davidson discussed in his 2008 work. It would all the more be the reason why, despite weathering the many regional economic and political trials and tribulations over several decades, Dubai's policy has been to continue to widen the base and increase the scale of activity, focussed on the free-zone cities, in more sophisticated industries, to make Dubai indispensable both to business and international institutions.

Jebel Ali Free Zone's success caused free-zones to become regarded as a 'magic bullet' that can instantly transform an economy and unsurprisingly other regions of the UAE followed suit. Ready-made success is, however, far from being the case, although there are now around forty-five free-zones in the UAE, and many others, serving a variety of purposes throughout the region. These range from providing useful opportunities to give employment for local citizens in FZ administrations, economic zones for industries in Saudi Arabia (King Abdullah Economic City),[43] to the attempted rival of Dubai in Iran (Kish Island), now morphed into a destination for domestic tourism[44] in a more 'relaxed' atmosphere than is normal in Iran, after a 'dismal economic failure in terms of attracting foreign investment, developing the manufacturing sector and creating jobs'.[45] In the case of Iran, war, sanctions and an uncertain investment climate have obviously contributed to the problem. Where Dubai has led the way, with economic liberalization and acceptance of 'globalisation', is to innovate by diversifying the range of traditional free-zone activity (such as exporting goods) to include specific centres that retain the traditional free-zone attractions (tax-free/foreign ownership etc) while pursuing very different focussed paths in, for example, new technology, media and information technology that recognize the requirements of a changing world. However, the factors linking them all together – the 'joined-up thinking' – remain the twin logistics centres of Jebel Ali port and the Dubai Airport(s), without which the multi-free-zone concept, developed so successfully, would not have been possible on such a scale. As with all such feed-off, cluster strategies, the ports and airport feed and feed off the free-zones and the free-zones feed and feed off the port and airports. This natural development of Dubai's long-term policies has imitators elsewhere but as yet, no effective regional competitors.

There are critics of the free-zones, who argue that these 'gated fiefdoms'[46] are primarily both a means for the Al Maktoum ruling family to maintain power by generating income and as opportunistic bases for global capitalism to establish itself, less tethered to the controls of a nation state. There is some substance to these claims for, as we have established, the rulers have adopted a variety of measures to ensure that their relationship with their National 'constituents' is maintained by ensuring that their economic benefits continue. It is therefore entirely consistent that they should establish innovative policies, setting up separate free-zone enclaves, used to increase and enhance the economic base, because such policies are the best way of achieving this objective, in a competitive world where there are always other alternatives for international businesses. The Al Maktoum do not stick to old orthodoxy and are not afraid of following the optimum economic logic.

I am arguing, therefore, that in the context of a Dubai, which, as a small city without natural endowments on which to depend, has had to innovate and diversify from its logistics and trading base, the free-zones have been a great success. They have enabled the Emirate to juggle the twin strategy of operating these separate enclaves, with distinctive commercial and legal regulations to attract foreign investment and skills, engaging fully with a globalized world – indeed designed to interface with other centres – while separately maintaining the standard 'onshore' businesses which, requiring a local majority partner, remain, in part, business- and revenue-generating opportunities for local citizens. This two-pronged approach allows both the ability to create environments conducive to the needs of international organizations and businesses, hesitant of relinquishing control to a local partner, while retaining business opportunities throughout the rest of the Emirate, operating under standard UAE conditions and legislation. These enclaves are particularly suitable for attracting the cutting-edge, high-tech organizations that Dubai is keen to attract and for acting as bases for international organizations and regional centres for international businesses. However, as we have seen, free-zones are not always successful. That they are in Dubai reflects the fact not only that their facilities and conditions are attractive and competitive but also that the logistical framework on which they are established was necessary and effective. The success of these policies evolving out of the infrastructure expansion begun in the 1960s can be gauged by the fact that the Global Logistics giant DHL, according to *The Economist* newspaper, ranked 'Dubai/UAE at Number 12 in its 2014 'Global Connectedness Index (GCI), just behind Hong Kong but ahead of France and Italy'.[47] The free-zones and their globalistic approach to the technologies of the twenty-first century exemplify how Dubai has demonstrated that the Gulf can be much more than just a cliched collection of fossil-fuel producers.

Logistics – airports and airlines

Apart from the development of the ports and the subsequent free-zones, without doubt, the most significant milestones and fundamental building blocks emphasizing the determination of Dubai to establish itself as a regional centre, were the creations, first of an airport and second, an airline. By 1980, Dubai airport was handling 2.8 million passengers a year with 61,000 flights and by 1985, having been expanded and with a second runway, the throughputs had increased to 3.8 million passengers on 63,000 flights.[48] This remarkable growth reflected not only the increasing attraction of Dubai as the business centre of the region but also the importance of an airport for an Emirate which had relied on facilities elsewhere until 1960.

It has been highlighted in an earlier chapter that there was already a functioning airport (with a British Royal Airforce base) in the neighbouring Emirate of Sharjah, but this was not the only obstacle facing Shaikh Rashid on his accession in 1958. There appeared not to be sufficient traffic to justify another airport so close to the existing one; there was no agreed site and the British authorities were unwilling to pay for another airport. However, the ruler was clearly determined not to depend on another (separate) Emirate's facility, particularly as the increasing amount of passenger and freight traffic was destined for or moving from Dubai and not Sharjah, with space constraints inevitably affecting Dubai most. Having determined that the British authorities would not object to a Dubai airport if Dubai paid for it,[49] to obtain the money for an airport, 'the first plank of the Ruler's strategy was to tackle the ticketing issue. The Dubai government gave notice that it intended to nationalize the business ... and in January 1959 the Dubai National Air Travel Agency (DNATA) started trading'.[50]

This initiative was more efficient, allowing tickets to be bought directly rather than through third parties and brought money into the government, but space and quotas were still a major frustration for a Dubai that was unable to control capacity and events at an out-of-territory airport. In the late 1950s, the feeder service operated by Gulf Aviation (the forerunner of Gulf Air) from Bahrain used fifteen-seater De Havilland (DH) Heron aircraft and eight-seater DH Doves. With only two or three seats allocated to Dubai on each flight, passengers could wait days to find a seat even to get to Dubai or certainly to leave.[51] Eventually, despite a site near Jebel Ali being considered and then rejected because of the cost, distance (50km) from Dubai centre and the additional cost of building the road infrastructure, a suitable site at Al Ghusais close to the Deira part of Dubai town was chosen. On 3 September 1960, the new airport opened with DNATA acting as sole booking agent, and gaining agencies from Saudia, Middle East Airlines (MEA) and Gulf Aviation. The new facility expanded rapidly as a result of increasing demand, and by early 1961, Gulf Aviation had added two extra Dubai flights a week and agreed to provide an extra Heron flight ad hoc if DNATA would guarantee to fill it. 'By the end of 1961 ... there had been a total of 1072 aircraft movements'.[52] After such a start, there was confidence that Dubai was capable of attracting more business, but this would require the ability to handle larger, heavier aircraft with a runway more resilient than hard-packed sand. Halcrow were set the task of upgrading the airport and in May 1965 an asphalt runway was opened, leading to the arrival of more airlines and much larger-capacity aircraft, including Gulf Aviation's 86-seat DC-4s and from 1967, a regular weekly BOAC VC-10 from London on the back of a commitment from Dubai that a 60 per cent load factor (4,500 seats per year) would be guaranteed. 'Cabin load factors were so consistently high that less than six months later a second weekly service was introduced.'[53]

It would have been easier to compromise and share Sharjah facilities, and easier to wait for more aircraft capacity and easier to take a cautious view on airport expansion. However, as with the policy on the ports, Shaikh Rashid had no desire to have the growth of the Emirate dependent on factors over which Dubai had no control or to be constrained through lack of infrastructure. The confidence in economic growth and, using the same logic that built Jebel Ali port, above all, the creation of the facilities that would serve Dubai in the future by enabling growth through the provision of passenger and freight transport infrastructure produced an airport that could cater to latent demand. The saga of the airport shows all the hallmarks that have accompanied Dubai policy-making and that made it so distinctive from many of their neighbours; determination, innovation and a clear long-term vision of what was required and could be controlled by Dubai, all ruthlessly and professionally pursued. This thorough determination was to become even more manifest in the mid-1980s.

Though increasingly recognized as the burgeoning commercial centre of the Gulf, Dubai, despite maintaining an 'open skies' policy (i.e. no limit on flights by any airline), was increasingly in dispute with the region's major carrier, Bahrain-based Gulf Air. Gulf Air was founded in 1973 by Abu Dhabi, Bahrain, Oman and Qatar to be a regional flag-carrier for all four states. Despite not holding any shares directly but because of the economic and business growth, 'by the 1980s, Dubai was Gulf Air's most profitable operations centre . . . the airline operated more flights into Dubai than any other destination'.[54] Dubai was pressing for more services and more capacity, but without shareholding or management influence on what was after all a 'foreign' airline like the other forty more that served the Emirate – albeit the most important – negotiations made little progress. Gulf Air too wanted more protectionist measures for itself in Dubai and restrictions on other airlines and, in this fractious environment, apparently to put pressure on Dubai and make the point that their views had to be accommodated, Gulf Air published their spring/summer timetable for 1985 which saw 'Gulf Air flights serving Dubai's airport drop from 84 a week to just 39'.[55] Even if we take account of the fact that Gulf Air had several shareholders to satisfy, all with their own agendas, and perhaps the aggressive approach and attitude of an increasingly frustrated Dubai, it is impossible to avoid the conclusion that this extreme negotiating tactic with one of their most important customers was a serious mistake. It proved to be one that was the first misstep into a steady decline, that brought the airline from a position of respected pre-eminence to the relatively minor player of recent decades. We certainly should also not lose sight of the fact, as a likely influencing factor, that Bahrain, where Gulf Air (rising from the foundations of pioneering Gulf Aviation) had its management and HQ, was increasingly anxious about the rise of Dubai as a commercial rival.

Given Dubai's approach to development and commerce, anxious to map out plans without dependence on others, it is at least possible that a confrontation with Gulf Air, so dominant in the region, was bound to happen sooner or later. However, this is by no means certain. The Dubai 'open skies' policy had worked well, attracting over forty carriers by the mid-1980s and, despite economic difficulties (and the Iran/Iraq war), passenger volumes and flight numbers were increasing rapidly as we have noted, with DNATA now well-established and acting as sales and handling agent for most airlines at the efficient and growing airport in the region's increasingly acknowledged rising trading and commercial centre. What point in taking the extreme financial and reputational risk of an airline start-up? There is a clear parallel with container port development here. There are established container shipping lines that have then decided to manage ports (e.g. AP Moller/Maersk Line), as business opportunities, as part of a logistics portfolio and in certain examples to keep logistics control in their own hands. However, the usual process, as we have discussed previously (as Dubai had done), is for a state to set up the best port facilities and operation in the right place for cargo movements, with the focus then being to attract lines by delivering good service – not then by also setting-up a shipping line to serve the port, which would be a very high-risk, high-investment and high-cost strategy, economically and competitively. In the case of Dubai, Gulf Air's clumsy attempt to bludgeon the upstart into submission, only served to produce this very – and most unexpected outcome – the start-up of Dubai's own airline.

Despite the pressure from Gulf Air and the impact of reduced services, negotiations continued, but, in secret, a team under the direction of Shaikh Mohammed Al Maktoum (Shaikh Rashid's son) was assessing the viability of starting an airline, with effect from the start of the Winter Schedules on 25 October 1985. There were no concessions from Gulf Air and the reduced schedules were implemented from March 1985, with erstwhile Dubai flights being routed to and from Sharjah and Abu Dhabi instead, reflecting the political and competitive complexity of Gulf Air shareholder relationships and, clearly, a determination to coerce Dubai with a show of force. Shaikh Mohammed provided a hastily assembled group of aviation professionals with a start-up fund of USD 10 million and, remarkably, as the result of a negotiated arrangement with Pakistan International Airlines (PIA), two wet-leased aircraft (i.e. aircraft supplied with crew members and maintained and insured by PIA) inaugurated the fledgling airline, now christened 'Emirates' (to mitigate any negative reaction from Abu Dhabi), with flights to Bombay and Karachi on 25th October. Significantly, proposed flights within the Gulf from Dubai initially met some 'bureaucratic' obstacles, not least from states with shareholdings in Gulf Air, less committed to open competition than Dubai.

Having determined this policy, expansion moved rapidly, especially as the ruler rejected requests for a reduced 'open-skies' approach to protect the infant and 'demanded that the airline post profits from the very beginning, so as to prove it did not receive subsidies'[56]. For the first ten years Emirates capacity 'grew at 30 percent each year' and by 2010, after twenty-five years, had 50,000 employees worldwide and operates 151 aircraft.[57] In 2018 the airline operates over 250 aircraft, either wide-body Boeing 777 or the super-jumbo Airbus 380 of which it is the world's biggest operator. Passenger numbers grew dramatically:

Emirates Airline Passenger Numbers

1999/2000 over 4 million
2009/2010 over 27 million
2017/2018 over 56 million[58]

The irony is that, without the 'Gulf-air-shock' in 1985, the further economic diversification of Dubai might not have developed in the way that it has. Gary Chapman, president of Group Services and DNATA,[59] is clear that the Gulf Air action was the catalyst that confirmed to the Dubai government the need to ensure that their development strategy could not be derailed by outside parties controlling key logistics elements. Chapman admits that 'at the time, no-one probably realised how big Emirates would become and how influential',[60] but in the decades after 1985, he is quite clear that Emirates 'turned the aviation industry upside down' as the airline's expansion, focussed on creating a market share and heightened customer service (such as the provision of individual video screens for each passenger), helped to expand the market, but also put severe competitive pressure on the 'legacy' carriers, forcing them to improve services too. Employing around 80,000 people in Dubai (in 2018), according to Gary Chapman, the Emirates Group is also now a major part of the integrated Dubai economy, investing in Dubai and acting, through branding and association, as the tangible presence of the Emirate throughout the world. The existence of Emirates and the need for the airline to be successful by sustained expansion, by carrying more passengers and freight, created a need for facilities in Dubai itself, in addition to the recognition that the airline could be a part of the strategy for Dubai. A strategy that would not only showcase Dubai, but also provide the means on Dubai-branded transportation to bring visitors to the Emirate, and, using the expanded airport as a hub, to other parts of the world.

The established and expanded facilities in Dubai, the airport and the fledgling Emirates Airline were to face another major test, as the region, its confidence returning after the end of the Iran/Iraq war in 1988, was again convulsed by the actions of Saddam Hussein, this time attacking his small Arab neighbour Kuwait in August 1990. Though Kuwait had actively supported Iraq in its war after 1982, with Kuwaiti ports functioning as Iraq's major logistics gateway after the closure of Basrah, and Kuwaiti oil tankers being targeted by Iran at sea after 1984, by 1990, relations had soured. Saddam's gamble to invade Iran at a time of perceived weakness had failed and the ceasefire after eight years of war left the borders much as they had been before, despite huge casualties on both sides and economic and civil devastation. Iraq owed Kuwait over USD 14 billion, which it was unable to repay, as a result of the war. There is little doubt, with the benefit of hindsight, that Saddam Hussein calculated a rapid takeover of Kuwait, justified by accusations that it 'was stealing Iraq's oil' by drilling near their common border and also claiming this was a 'natural part of Iraq' carved away by British imperialism (the '19th Province') would both restore his reputation – certainly in the Arab world – by gaining control of Kuwait's sophisticated and efficient oil industry – and remove the issue of debt repayment permanently. He did not anticipate that international opinion, confirmed by UN Resolution 660 and supported by the other Gulf monarchies, increasingly nervous about his future intentions, would refuse to accept the fait accompli invasion of a sovereign state, independent since 1961. The American-led coalition expelled the Iraqis by the end of February 1991, leaving

Kuwait looted and devastated, enveloped in a pall of thick smoke from oil wells set on fire by the retreating Iraqis.

The invasion and its aftermath impacted Dubai in two important ways. Firstly, Jebel Ali was, because of its size and efficiency and its presence in a safe location in the Southern Gulf, close to a major airport (a second runway had been completed in 1984), the primary logistics base. It was used by the coalition forces not only for naval units but also as the logistics supply centre for military materiel, foodstuffs and all kinds of other equipment in the build-up to the coalition onslaught and the re-supply of Kuwait after the liberation in 1991. If there had been any uncertainty before 1990 about the status of Dubai's logistical position in the region, after 'Desert Storm' there was no longer any doubt. The Emirate responded robustly to the challenging conditions of the time with, as highlighted by Mohammed Sharaf,[61] in conversation with the author, when he reminded me that during the conflict, the Dubai government undertook to cover the cost of extra war risk insurance premiums imposed by underwriters (in London) on the hull and machinery values of ships entering the Gulf (once they had passed Hormuz strait). Such additional charges, for seven days cover only applied at a level of 0.5 per cent, for example, would, in the case of a ship with hull and machinery worth $100 million, cost the shipowner an extra $500,000, making the call both risky and completely loss-making. Dubai acted with initiative and pre-emptively to ensure that lines would continue to maintain calls at Dubai's ports – invariably (because of the cost and danger of sailing further up the Gulf) *only* at Dubai's ports. The enforced logistical response to the war helped to cement Dubai's role as the regional distribution hub.

The second major impact of the liberation of Kuwait was to have greater long-term effects. Following the end of the war, the Kuwaiti and Saudi governments, because of the spectacularly ill-judged response of the Yemen and Palestinian governments in supporting or condoning Saddam's invasion actions, reacted by expelling almost all the Yemeni and Palestinian workers who had historically made up a large proportion of their respective blue and white-collar workers. The role of migrants, particularly South Asians, constituting the bulk of unskilled or semi-skilled labour in the GCC states, what Al Shehabi refers to as 'demographic disorder', was already well established by the late 1980s with expanding local businesses anxious to draw more comprehensively on traditional labour markets for familiarity and economic (low-cost) reasons.[62] Indians, for example, were a familiar presence in the structure of lower Gulf states such as Dubai in particular, for long-established trading reasons and in more recent years because of their literacy (particularly South Indians from Kerala) and familiarity with English – essential as local businesses expanded rapidly. Being established particularly in clerical and junior managerial roles and increasingly embedded in the business structures gave such workers, particularly Indians, the ability to continue to recruit continually from their own communities, villages and extended families, rather than from other nationalities. The fact that such workers were anxious to be employed in the Gulf, to make money and escape the stultifying red tape, lack of social mobilization and lack of opportunity in India at the time, coupled with their always temporary status in the Gulf, as 'impossible citizens',[63] undoubtedly contributed to their attraction to employers. Al Shehabi, referencing Baldwin-Edwards, estimates that in late 1990 in the GCC states there were already over 5 million non-Arab migrant workers compared with 2.5 million who were citizens.[64] From 1991 onwards, this imbalance was distorted even further as 'some 350,000 Palestinians were deported from Kuwait and . . . Saudi Arabia also deported hundreds of thousands of Yemenis and the Iraqi communities throughout the GCC experienced the same fate'.[65] In total, as a direct consequence of the invasion, around 2 million Arabs were expelled or displaced. These actions reinforced the role of 'neutral/guestworker' labour, initially from South Asia on short-term visas, rather than from other Arab states in the economies of the GCC.

Dubai's competition

As highlighted in previous chapters, some Gulf ports have been integral parts of the Indian Ocean trading network for centuries, others have risen to prominence only in recent decades, while others still have declined into insignificance. Inevitably, the reasons for these changes reflect political and economic events, changes in trading patterns and commodities – as well as the failure to adapt to changing circumstances. It is very much my contention that Dubai in particular, initially under the rule of Shaikh Rashid al Maktoum, took a proactive stance to logistics and infrastructure development, as 'he needed to do it to survive – for him the most important thing was trade'[66] – not as purely reactive 'one-off' projects, but as part of long-term planning. This approach, considered foolhardy at the time, would lay the foundations for Dubai's future dominance in marine and aviation logistics. However, it would be entirely wrong to suggest that other regional states took no action at all in the post-oil price boom periods from the mid-1970s onwards. Most had their development strategies, based on oil and gas, but were also forced to respond to their lack of modern logistics facilities by building new port and infrastructure projects that were urgently needed to cope with the dramatic inflows of construction material and consumer goods. The difference is that these efforts were simply responses to cope with the additional cargo flows, and not, as with Dubai, the cornerstones of an economic strategy. It is necessary to show how different areas reacted, how they were impacted by internal and external events and how they fared in comparison with Dubai.

In Abu Dhabi, as highlighted earlier, after the accession of Shaikh Zayed in 1966, and independence in 1971, when the city became capital of the new federal state, the focus of activity was on the expansion of the oil industry and spending oil wealth to develop the Emirate (and poorer parts of the UAE). The main commercial activity and the major agencies remained in Dubai and most imported products for Abu Dhabi were routinely routed via Dubai ports and then by sea (vessel or barge). This was entirely logical logistically, to distribute from the main port of call, and secondly, because Abu Dhabi's Mina Zayed (port) was small and ill-equipped (the road between Dubai and Abu Dhabi was of a poor standard until the 1990s). The major, well-established merchants and their agencies were also based in Dubai, with branch offices in Abu Dhabi. The container statistics for Abu Dhabi's Mina Zayed (Port Zayed) illustrate this very clearly compared with volumes in Dubai (TEU), illustrating that for over twenty years or so after the creation of the UAE in 1971, Abu Dhabi was a small market and that Dubai remained unchallenged by Abu Dhabi in its commercial-hub role:

Abu Dhabi and Dubai Comparative Container Volumes

	Abu Dhabi	Dubai
1980	12,289	272,933
1985	25,633	516,325
1990	45,733	913,363

(Source: Drewry Maritime Research London)

In Sharjah, following the deposition of Shaikh Saqr al Qassimi in 1965, the state of familial relations ensured that instability continued, with Shaikh Saqr's successor Khalid in power only for seven years before an attempted, but unsuccessful, coup by the deposed Saqr resulted in Khalid's death during the storming of the Sharjah palace in January 1972. Khalid's successor Sultan, one of his younger brothers, was confirmed by the other rulers and by the Al Qasimi family later in the year. Despite yet another coup attempt in 1987, when Shaikh Sultan's elder brother Abdul-Aziz briefly seized power, a Dubai-brokered agreement returned Shaikh Sultan to the throne, and exiled Abdul-Aziz. The palace coup of 1987 reflected both the residual resentments lingering among the extended Al Qasimi family members and also that Shaikh Sultan was considered to be spending money that Sharjah could not afford, on supposed 'vanity' projects such as museums and the expansion of the airport.[67] A subsequent banking collapse in 1989 and the consequent loans from Saudi Arabia also led to the still-common assumption that the Saudi loans came with conditions attached. This price (supposedly) was that Sharjah should adopt a more religiously austere approach including (more modest) forms of dress, gender segregation and a ban on alcohol consumption (although actually, this latter decision was enacted a decade earlier in 1979).

In fact, there is no evidence to reveal any Saudi 'deal', though the 'fellow-Wahabi' spectre inevitably appears in any such discussions and though the current Sharjah ruler clearly has deeply held beliefs on such subjects, he continues both to allow alcohol to be purchased for private consumption with a licence (and at the large Airport Duty-Free) and keenly endorsing (in a non-Wahabi fashion) women's education and participation in the governance of the Emirate and the UAE. Even Christopher Davidson seemed to accept such rumours about Sharjah, and then to link Sharjah next with Iran, 'likely that Crescent Oil of Iran will supply Sharjah's energy needs in the near future',[68] when Crescent is actually a long-established (1971) Sharjah Company, with what then (2008) seemed a secure negotiated commercial gas contract with the National Iranian Oil Company (NIOC), which to date has, however, not taken place. (Crescent is pursuing a claim for damages having won a case held under International arbitration.) The fact remains that this more conservative approach may have been popular with (some of) Shaikh Sultan's local 'constituency' and more traditionalist expatriates, but clearly has not helped Sharjah to compete with a more laissez-faire Dubai in the 1980s and beyond. Even today it is not difficult to find older UAE residents who remember Sharjah as more 'free-wheeling' than Dubai in the late 1970s and link the failure to provide a viable alternative to Dubai in recent decades with the more 'traditional, patrimonial' style of government, less planned infrastructure and alternative trappings ('25 museums') rather than the economy. (It is of course equally easy to find residents who prefer Sharjah's less frenzied approach to development and who appreciate the ruler's focus on education and cultural activity.)

However, to his credit, Shaikh Sultan did promote, though not with government money, the expansion of Khor Fakkan (in Sharjah's UAE east coast enclave). Managed by local company Gulftainer from 1976, this private company, without government funding, developed the natural deep-water container terminal, which has grown to be one of the largest and most efficient container terminals in the region focussing almost entirely on onward relay/trans-shipment of containers for other destinations. However, despite its relative success, without a local cargo base it failed to inhibit the growth of Dubai's port, and its volumes remained modest in comparison.

Khor Fakkan Volumes (TEU)

1980	23,999
1990	162,620
(2000	1,014,122)

(Source: Drewry Maritime Research London)

In a container shipping world where the very large ships of perhaps 18,000 TEU need to fit in as many end-to-end voyages as possible and physically cannot call all ports, Khor Fakkan allows a useful 'hub and spoke' alternative for serving the wider area. For example, this might include an Eastbound mega-ship from Europe calling Khor Fakkan to discharge containers for other Gulf Ports, East Africa and South Asia, which are then loaded and on-carried by connecting-services smaller ships, allowing the Mega Ship to continue Eastwards after a call of only a few hours. Such hub-ports need to be very efficient in order to compete with local end-user terminals and Khor Fakkan, upgraded with increasingly bigger container cranes (currently 20 in 2017) and other equipment, in addition to the latest container control software is capable of very high productivity, at best, well over 200 moves (of a container) per hour, as evidenced by a highlighted example at the end of 2015 when the terminal handled 8288 containers/13005 TEU in 36 hours during the call of the 18,000 TEU 'CMA-CGM Georg Forster'[69].

Khor Fakkan is unusual in that it has developed as a private company, without direct government impetus, under private management working with the state, using efficiency and its geographical position (outside the Gulf but adjacent to shipping line East/West routes, as with Salalah and Sohar) to provide a partial alternative to Dubai, but it can never hope to challenge the latter's dominance. The fundamental problem for trans-shipment hubs is that without a local city/market to supply and depending almost entirely on relay, 'with little or no traffic base of their own, their status remains highly unstable and carriers can transfer their services to other ports with some ease'.[70] They are at the mercy of factors beyond their control, such as changing trade patterns, shipping line services and ownership, the consolidation of operational consortia into fewer groupings and the fact that maintaining competitive costs and efficiency are essential if the terminal is even to compete and certainly to survive. Khor Fakkan therefore provided, as a large efficient terminal, some benchmarking competition for Jebel Ali, (and was used extensively – until recently – by major carriers) but without a cargo base it could never hope to emulate its Dubai rival. Sharjah city retained its small container terminal (also managed by Gulftainer), but shallow and with limited facilities it handled smaller and feeder vessels only, serving the local market.

Oman's sole international port was Mina Qaboos in the capital Muscat, a long-established natural harbour, but small and constrained by its geographical position, dealing only with limited local imports. Container volume throughputs in 1980 give some idea of the disparity in external trade between Oman and Dubai:

Dubai Container throughputs –   272,933 TEU
Mina Qaboos throughputs –   18,537 TEU

(Source: Drewry Maritime Research London)

In the next decade, however, Mina Qaboos volumes had increased substantially as the Omani economy was expanding as a result of Sultan Qaboos's development policies, despite a gulf-wide depression in the 1980s caused by a collapse in the price of oil, (USD 7 per barrel in January 1986) and the ongoing (September 1980–August 1988) Iran/Iraq war.[71] This downturn affected inner-gulf, particularly upper-gulf, states nearer the hostilities-zones more than Oman, but Dubai volumes, reflecting its now firmly established hub role and as a logistically well-equipped safe-haven, were unaffected and continued to rise. The following throughput figures are shown to illustrate three things; firstly, that Omani volumes continued to rise steadily during the period, albeit modestly, reflecting domestic development; secondly, that upper Gulf states were seriously affected by economic downturn and the protracted adjacent war; thirdly, that Dubai throughputs and share of total regional trade continued to rise by virtue of its position in the lower Gulf, its role as a transhipment centre and its excellent logistics facilities.

Dubai and Mina Qaboos Container Throughputs Comparison

TEU throughputs	1982	1984	1986	1988
Mina Qaboos	44,112	90,175	110,635	147,882
Dubai	323,676	446,616	529,262	627,292

(Source: Drewry Maritime Research London)

These lessons of regional instability, of the role of Dubai in particular, as a distribution hub and the potential choke point of the narrow straits of Hormuz entering the Gulf were not lost either on the Omani government or on shipping lines.

In Bahrain, by the early 1970s, oil production had already peaked, weakening the state's ability to distribute 'rent' and by the early 1980s oil's share of GDP had reduced to around 20 per cent. The state increased the number of licences for Offshore Banking Units (OBU) modelled on those of Singapore; negotiated a higher rental fee from the American forces for the lease of Julfair naval base and also initiated the construction of a causeway linking the island to Saudi Arabia, for trade, tourism – and security. Security was always a major concern because the Sunni ruling Al Khalifa family, in power since the end of the eighteenth century, exercised power, uniquely in the region, over a majority Shia population. Constitutional reform in the early 1970s was unilaterally abrogated by the ruling family in 1975. Also, although Iran had officially renounced any claims to the island in 1970, the new revolutionary regime in Tehran after 1979, openly made approaches to the Shia in Bahrain, who felt themselves to be disadvantaged, resulting in a foiled coup by Shirazi Shi in 1981.[72] Therefore although it is clear that Bahrain was attempting transitioning from oil dependence to a more diversified economy, 'any changes to the domestic political economy of resource distribution pose a direct threat to the security and stability of states in transition (and they are) especially vulnerable to erosion of the ruling bargain . . . if mechanisms for co-opting support and depoliticising society begin to break down'.[73] In Bahrain, not only were the 'internal mechanisms' seriously flawed but external events were conspiring to make it more difficult for the state to maintain a role as a regional centre. The war between Iran and Iraq, not too distant from upper-gulf Bahrain, the downturn in oil prices, depressed Gulf trade and an unstable internal political environment contributed to a degree of nervousness in the island's international businesses. Increasingly, businesses, particularly the large numbers of offshore banks, eyed alternative locations, particularly, stable, dynamic and enticing Dubai.

With a head-start as the Gulf's established business centre in the 1970s, despite internal political concerns, it was not at all apparent that Bahrain would within two decades lose its hard-won and superficially solid reputation as a state taking all the 'right' steps to wean itself away from nearly half a century of oil dependence. However, the 'perfect storm' of exogenous factors over which it had little control; its position in the upper Gulf with major hostilities close by; the rise of a major rival (Dubai) that made bigger and better infrastructure decisions with economic and administrative good-governance policies; and the increasing impact of long-term unresolved, internecine internal dissent, combined to diminish the economic and political status of Bahrain by the end of the 1980s. A seriously misjudged attempt to force Dubai to accept Bahrain and Gulf Air as arbiters of regional air services, backfired spectacularly in 1985 as has been described earlier, when Dubai reacted by setting up its own airline, Emirates, with a professional determination that saw Emirates eviscerate Gulf Air as a competitor. The serious sectarian instability, and the reaction to it, emphasized the extent to which Bahrain had become dependent on Saudi Arabia, relying on Saudi financial, political and military support, diminishing any real hope of winning regional businesses from Dubai.

Not content with syphoning off the airline-hub traffic in the Gulf from Bahrain, Dubai as a port hub in the 1980s completely outpaced the container volumes in Bahrain by virtue of building better and improved facilities and by having a bigger and more dynamic economy. As the following statistics illustrate, Bahrain remained an end-user destination with consistent volumes serving only the island. By the late 1980s, Dubai was well on the way to becoming the Gulf's transhipment hub. Bahrain was no longer a real competitor.

Bahrain and Dubai Container Throughput Comparison

	1980 TEU Volumes	1986 TEU Volumes	1990 TEU Volumes
Bahrain	60,196	80,393	75,066
Dubai	272,933	529,262	913,363

(Source: Drewry Maritime Research London)

The Iraqi invasion of Kuwait in 1990 exacerbated the difficulties with which Bahrain had been contending throughout the 1980s (particularly the Iran/Iraq war), and accelerated the flight to Dubai of many major companies' Gulf Head Offices, such as various Banks and Insurance companies and Inchcape/Gray Mackenzie, with the hostilities close-by providing the 'ideal' opportunity for them to explain the shift. Though the sixteen-mile-long Saudi causeway had as expected provided a valuable filip to the island's economy with 'up to 18 million crossing each year (by the early twenty-first century) . . . (and) on weekends, thousands of Saudis cross the causeway to get away from the strict moral codes enforced in Saudi Arabia'.[74]

At this stage, it is useful to assess what went wrong for Bahrain and why it lost the impetus to Dubai. This occurred despite having a head-start as the established, pragmatic, business centre of the (Arab) Gulf with a well-functioning port and airport and also, as its oil revenues declined in the 1970s, policies initiated to diversify the economy, in advance of other regional states. There are four main factors: firstly, that the diversification measures were not enough to attract the scale of diverse investment that Bahrain needed to offset the decline of oil revenues. Offshore banking for example was prestigious and brought in useful government revenues (from the approximately seventy-five operations in the mid-1980s, some of which had switched from Lebanon) but its trickle-down impact for most Bahrainis was very limited and such an activity, in isolation, was difficult to link to other economy expanding activities. ALBA and ASRY were (and are) successful, but there was little attempt to develop them as part of an integrated strategy, and despite Bahrain's long history, the island never developed fully as a modern, major trading centre. Secondly, the measures adopted to diversify the economy were too late to stave off the competition from a much more dynamic and professional adversary, Dubai, which by building port and airport infrastructure linked with free-zones and 'ease of business' measures, attracted the majority of investment. Thirdly, Bahrain can justifiably claim some degree of ill-luck, by being geographically, near the hostilities of the Iran/Iraq war in the 1980s and the invasion of Kuwait by Iraq in 1990, both of which inevitably inhibited investor confidence in upper Gulf locations. Finally, and most significantly, Bahrain has endured internal political instability with riots and attempted coups for many decades (1981, 1994-9 in particular) as the ruling Sunni Al Khalifa have failed to integrate the two thirds majority population Shia into political discourse, as participants in power sharing.[75] However, the end result is that such continuing civil unrest by the bulk of the population was not and has not been conducive to business confidence, particularly as Bahrain is in competition with Dubai for international investment.[76]

Qatar has never been a major trading nation (with Kamrava highlighting that only the Al Mana and Al Darwish merchant families had sizeable wealth before the oil era)[77] and played little part in the economic and political life of the region until the 1980s, reflected in the port of the capital city Doha, which until the 1990s, lacking equipment and draught for ships to berth, was dependent on containers moving by road from Dubai or on barges operated by the state-owned company Qatar Navigation. Consequently, statistics for throughputs during this time are not available or are unreliable. The Emirate continued to focus on the development of its oil and gas industries.

Kuwait is a small state in the Northern Gulf, independent since 1961, on the border with Iraq, where (easily extractable) oil was first discovered in 1938, with exports commencing in 1946 according to Kuwait Petroleum Corporation Website. The state has a long seafaring and mercantile tradition as recounted by Villiers,[78] and Field,[79] but these elements declined rapidly as the revenues from one of the world's largest oil reserves (nationalized in 1975) increasingly dominated the economy, with the small (measured in two or three hundred thousand even in the 1960s and 1970s), population receiving generous lifelong subsidies.

The fact is that though Kuwait had once been an important trading location, acting as a conduit for Gulf/Levant trade and with trading vessels sailing throughout the Indian Ocean, the arrival of vast oil revenues from the 1940s onwards with rentier payments to all citizens gradually diminished the appetite for and role of all other activities apart from a small number of major merchants and the oil industry – the latter dominated by foreign labour from the 1960s and 1970s. Though Kuwait has acted as a conduit for traffic into southern Iraq, because of poor facilities at Iraqi ports such as Basrah, and because of the damage to Iraqi ports in the almost decade-long Iran–Iraq war (and also for military traffic after the invasion of Iraq in 2003), the ports were never hubs and imports into Kuwait were primarily consumer goods, foodstuffs and oilfield supplies for the domestic economy. The Container throughput statistics (compared with Dubai) for Shuwaikh and Shuaiba from 1980 onwards clearly reveal the slow growth (in TEU):

Kuwait and Dubai Container Volumes Comparison

	Shuwaikh	**Shuaiba**	**Dubai**
1980	50,000	170,796	272,933
1989	124,033	105,065	827,395
(1999	119,348	174,553	2,844,634)

(Source: Drewry Maritime Research London)

There are one or two exceptions to this oil-focussed rentier approach. In 1976, a multi-Gulf-state-owned transport giant, United Arab Shipping Company (UASC), was created from the basis of Kuwait Shipping Company. Owned by the governments of Kuwait, Iraq, Bahrain, Qatar, UAE and Saudi Arabia, it was set up to ensure that the Gulf states participated in the shipping movements to and from the region, then dominated by overseas companies. The company was headquartered in Kuwait and grew its conventional, and subsequent container-ship fleet, to become one of the largest operators worldwide, with (at the end of 2016) a container-ship operating rank of tenth worldwide with fifty-five ships, handling 2.5 per cent of world container ship capacity.[80] UASC was operated on a commercial basis on behalf of the shareholders, from a main office based in Dubai after 1990 (as a result of the Iraqi invasion of Kuwait), with the corporate HQ remaining in Kuwait, until 2017, when the industry surge of amalgamations resulted in a merger with and absorption by German carrier Hapag Lloyd.

Another, originally Kuwait-based logistics success has been Agility, originally established in 1979 as the state-owned Public Warehousing Company (PWC), until privatization in 1997 and still having its corporate headquarters in Kuwait – though main operational offices are overseas. Specializing in commercial logistics, Agility won substantial US military contracts after 2003, enabling the company to expand dramatically, though this success soured as a result of lawsuits from the military alleging overcharging. The legal issues were only finally resolved in May 2017, when, after being suspended from participating in military tendering for seven years, Agility agreed to pay USD95 million to resolve civil fraud claims as part of a global resolution which involved the company pleading guilty to 'theft of Government funds', according to the US Department of Justice Website, 26 May 2017. Presumably this agreement was felt to be worthwhile if it 'closed the chapter' and allowed Agility, now a global logistics force with 22,000 employees in 2017, to participate again in military contracts.

Kuwait endured the long Iran/Iraq war on its doorstep in the 1980s, which severely depressed its economy and put its core oil exports at risk, particularly during the 'Tanker War' of 1987 when Iran tried to stop or restrict oil exports from Iraq and its allies. However, much worse was to follow in 1990, when two years after the end of the war, Saddam Hussein gambled on another invasion, this time of Kuwait. Though American and coalition forces expelled the Iraqis in early 1991, Kuwait city had been looted and vandalized with most of the inhabitants fled or in hiding, Shuwaikh Port's gantry cranes toppled into the harbour and the oil wells destroyed or severely damaged, covering the city in a thick pall of oily smoke (author's eye witness account). The state and the economy slowly recovered as the oil production and extraction industry was repaired, with the twin pillars of state revenue remaining as rent from the oil industry and earnings from the overseas investments of the Kuwait Sovereign Wealth Fund (KSWF), established in 1953 – (and by 2017 having assets of USD 524 billion – the fourth largest such fund worldwide).[81]

In the eastern province of Saudi Arabia, the port of Dammam, from its first inception was created to serve the oil industry and to provide an entry point for other goods into the Eastern Provinces of Saudi Arabia. There was no intention or prospect of acting as a regional distribution centre, with the suspicious and restrictive nature of Saudi cargo-handling regulations giving no opportunity for expansion. (Only in the twenty-first century have facilities expanded with professional independent port managers such as Hutchinson and the Port of Singapore bringing their expertise into joint-ventures with Saudi partners.) Focussed entirely on the Saudi market, Dammam is certainly well behind the Dubai *entrepot*, as shown in the throughput volumes (TEU):

Dubai and Dammam Container Throughput Comparison

	Dammam	Dubai
1980	250,956	272,933
1990	232,456	913,363

(Source: Drewry Maritime Research London)

The nearby Saudi Arabian port of Jubail was established by the Royal Commission in 1975 together with the development of Yanbu (on the Red Sea), as part of the second 'Five Year Plan', but deliberately separate from other activity, according to Pampanini,[82] to avoid entanglement in internal politics. The industrial downstream developments such as the creation of Saudi Arabian Basic Industries Corporation (SABIC), focussing on petrochemicals, resins and fertilizers, have proved to be much more successful than the commercial port. There was simply no commercial requirement for Jubail Container Terminal at the time, though the separate industrial port, serving the oil-industry based Jubail industrial areas, is on a vast scale. However, in the 1980s and 1990s Jubail volumes remained insignificant.

Jubail Container Throughputs (TEU)

1980	4276
1990	7500

(Source: Drewry Maritime Research London)

Iran's ports, such as Bushire and Bandar Abbas (historic 'Gombroon'), as previously described in my first chapter, have a long and distinguished history. The onset of steamers into the Gulf in the mid-nineteenth century ensured that 'BI's fortnightly service (in 1866) between Bombay and the Gulf called at the ports of Bombay, Muscat, Bandar Abbas, Bushire and Basra'.[83] However, any account of Iran's recent history, and certainly that of its involvement in transport and logistics, has to be dominated by the impact of the Islamic revolution in 1978–9, the near-decade-long war with Iraq from 1980 to 1988 (and the UN sanctions imposed on the regime for many years). Michael Axworthy, in his history of Revolutionary Iran, estimates that 'the (Iraq) war had cost Iran about \$200bn . . . . And that GDP had fallen by 1988 to 54% of its peak level in 1976'.[84] In these circumstances, it is easy to forget that in the mid-1970s, modernizing Iran was actively embracing containerization, particularly at the upper Gulf port of Bandar Shahpour, now Bandar Imam Khomeini (BIK), linked by rail with the capital Tehran since the 1930s, with container services from Japan in the 1970s pursued, particularly by Sealand. Containers were discharged at Bandar Shahpour, where a container terminal was inaugurated in 1975, and some moved by rail under customs bond – the passevant system – to Tehran Inland Container Terminal, established in 1972 (according to the Perse Transport Bar Website).[85] Jeuro also inaugurated a 'Trans-Siberian' overland link for containers from Japan and East Asia by rail to the Iranian–USSR border post at Julfa.

Until the revolution and then the war with Iraq, Iran was the region's largest, most populous, with 38 million people, and most rapidly developing country. However, after the revolution, Iran's new status as a pariah state, considered dangerous, hostile and certainly unattractive for outside investment, coupled with the economic impact of the Iraq war, severely restricted opportunities for Iranian ports to attract business at all – let alone increase their regional role. In the intervening four decades since the Revolution, despite the recovery and expansion of some Iranian ports, particularly Bandar Abbas near the mouth of the Gulf (though BIK has never regained its previous pre-eminence), the role of Dubai as a logistics centre has been firmly established and its status as a relay centre for Iranian cargo has not only been indispensable for Iranian consumers – but also it has been a cornerstone of Dubai's emergence as a regional entrepot.

The bilateral relationship between Dubai and Iran is long-standing and strong with many Dubai families having their origins in Iran (see Chapter 1) and these close economic and trading links were reinforced after the revolution when Dubai effectively became Iran's major port for imported goods as economic constraints, sanctions and the impact of consequent Iranian customs and financial restrictions limited direct access for a wide range of imports. Dubai established itself as the re-export centre for Iranian imports because of its port and infrastructure facilities. In practice, this meant that containerized imports for the Iranian market were discharged in Dubai, some re-packed into containers, thus becoming a Dubai/Iran shipment, and also a large proportion of cargo was unpacked into the many small craft and 'dhows' which then on-carried goods to smaller Iranian ports where procedures were 'less rigorous'. Additionally, Dubai's role as the regional supermarket continued (and continues) to attract Iranians who can not only buy a wider range of goods at more attractive prices, but also enjoy a more relaxed atmosphere than in their homeland. The Iranian authorities attempted to stem these ways of circumventing fiscal and customs controls by setting up a duty-free 'offshore' – literally and metaphorically – alternative on the island of Kish, where duty-free goods and a less restrictive lifestyle attracted those Iranians who could not afford or were unable to travel abroad.

In Iraq, historically, the port of Basra was one of the most important centres, stretching back into antiquity as the port for Mesopotamia. In the nineteenth century with the advent of steamship services from India such as that of the British India Line (BI), Basra was the Gulf terminus[86] and the site of the operation of riverine steamers by Lynch Brothers to and from Baghdad.[87] 'Basra was one of the most important Gulf ports . . . with (eg) in 1901-04 goods worth £1.5 million imported from Europe and North America . . . and seaborne exports (which) included wool, cereals, dates, liquorice root and horses . . . '.[88] However, Basra's position, about 100km from the sea, on the shallow and oft-changing channels of the Shatt-Al-Arab, hindered trade as ship sizes increased, and in 1967 a small 'deep-water' port was opened in Umm Qasr at the mouth of the Shatt (though still affected by silt accumulation, requiring regular dredging). Umm Qasr was also rail-linked via Basra to Baghdad.

However, from 1980, the start of the Iran/Iraq war, until the early years of the twenty-first century, Iraqi ports, of which only Basra, was of any size, had little impact on the region, cut-off from all but the smallest craft as a result of several wrecked ships in the river channels and lack of facilities.

Chapter review

Dubai developed focussing on trade and diversified commercial activity supported by long-term and continuous infrastructure development from the 1960s onwards. Oil revenues existed from the late 1960s, but these were used to fund further trading and infrastructure development. Such an approach, as this chapter has shown, was not completely unique (Bahrain started a similar approach earlier), but its constancy and consistency certainly were. The end of Dubai's completely independent status in 1971 with the formation of the United Arab Emirates did not deflect or derail its development approach for several reasons. Firstly, the 'soft-touch' structure of the new unified state maintained Federal control only over foreign policy, immigration and issues of national importance. Individual Emirates were left free to pursue their own economic policies (which effectively meant those of Dubai and Abu Dhabi). Secondly, the fragility of the new structure was such that President Shaikh Zayed sought to avoid confrontations with Dubai, which might have led to the break-up of the new state. Thirdly, the focus of Abu Dhabi was to build up its role as the new capital of the UAE, which involved building a bureaucracy and a foreign policy, the development of Abu Dhabi itself with infrastructure, schools and hospitals, and funds for the poorer Northern Emirates. Abu Dhabi had been receiving increasingly huge inflows of wealth from oil sales and drilling rights – but these were only used for development after the accession of Shaikh Zayed in 1966 – only five years before the UAE's formation. There were therefore several compelling reasons for Dubai to continue its developmental policies with renewed vigour to make its position unassailable – conscious of the new power and wealth of Abu Dhabi.

The reasons why Dubai's actual or potential rivals did not achieve the role of regional entrepot are due to, above all, what Dubai did, and others didn't, in terms of provision of facilities, innovation and continuous development, particularly from a trading perspective, in the wholehearted adoption of containerization and its logistics follow-up. Within the Trucial States, Abu Dhabi focussed on its oil revenues and Sharjah beset with internecine strife and out-performed by Dubai.

As evidenced, the Gulf was far from homogeneous in its approach to development and logistics and transport facilities, but all the states took some action, on the Arab side, in the main, based on the arrival of oil revenues, which in the case of Bahrain (1930s) and Kuwait and Saudi Arabia (1940s) were decades before those in the Trucial States/UAE.

However, once oil revenues were flowing in, neither Saudi Arabia nor Kuwait made any serious efforts to diversify their economies away from oil. Bahrain initially made some progress in its diversification but lack of infrastructural development and more effective competition from Dubai during the 1980s onwards, internal political and ethnic tensions and proximity to regional wars weakened its position. The arrival of larger container-ships, which preferred to turn in Dubai (to avoid expensive/time-consuming additional port calls), would ensure that Bahrain remained a modest market and Bahrain's role as the Gulf Aviation hub diminished from the end of the 1980s as a result of an ill-fated attempt to force emerging Dubai to work within Gulf Air imposed constraints, resulting in the creation of Emirates Airline. In Iraq and Iran, there were two ancient civilizations and substantial modern states, with long-existing trading ports pre-dating the arrival of oil wealth. Iran, by the late 1970s was already experimenting with 'through-container' movements to inland Tehran and ports such as Bandar Shahpour in the north and Bandar Abbas in the south were expanding their container facilities to service this large nation. Iraq's maritime options were more limited and its position at the head of the Gulf and limited coastline mitigated against a role as a hub, but its great oil wealth promised substantial port and logistics development. Such is the speculation, but the actual results were a long stagnation (which continues to resonate), with neither state able to contribute much to the economic and maritime evolution of the Gulf, (and pose as competitors to Dubai) as a result of the Iran Revolution in 1978/79, the subsequent invasion of Iran by Iraq in 1980 and the invasion of Kuwait by Iraq in 1990. These events not only removed Iran and Iraq as major external commercial and logistics players but also weakened Kuwait and Bahrain's development and investment opportunities because of their proximity to hostilities. Their absence allowed Dubai to benefit from both lack of potential competition and also from additional business, (particularly to Iran), which moved over Dubai's ports instead of directly to Iran. Oman, with a long maritime history, but arriving late on to the development path (after Sultan Qaboos' accession in 1970) and with modest fossil-fuel deposits, and Qatar, another late arrival, small but with massive gas reserves are in different categories. In both cases, there was no appreciable development of port or other facilities (until the second decade of the twenty-first century when both have started to emulate the 'Dubai Model').

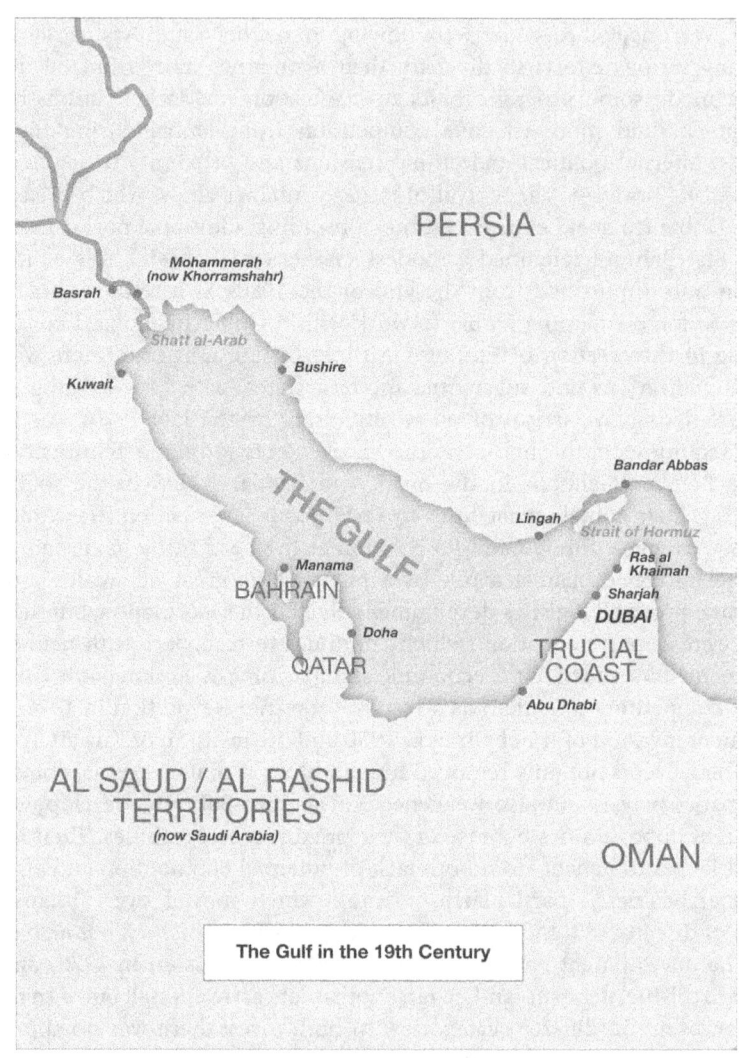

Figure 1 Map of the Gulf in the nineteenth century. (Copyright: William Nuttall)

Figure 2 First ship call at Port (Mina) Rashid, Dubai – MV Sirdhana November 1970. (Copyright: P&O Heritage)

Figure 3 HH Shaikh Rashid al Maktoum, Ruler of Dubai, opening the Port Rashid Container Terminal in November 1980. (Copyright: Len Chapman)

Figure 4 Aerial photograph of Port Rashid circa 1981. (Copyright: Len Chapman)

Figure 5 Containership 'Tor Bay' – Built 1982, overall length 200 metres, capacity circa 2000 TEU (twenty-foot equivalent unit containers). (Copyright: P&O Heritage)

Figure 6 Containership 'CMA-CGM Jacques Saade' – Built 2019/20, overall length 400 metres, capacity circa 23,000 TEU. (Copyright: Rod Riseborough)

Chapter 4

SUCCESS

GOOD LUCK OR GOOD MANAGEMENT? (1990–2004)

A language of commerce, economic liberalism, bargaining and trust that has been the hallmark of Dubai for two centuries.[1]

The driving force behind the creation of modern Dubai, the ruler Shaikh Rashid al Maktoum, died in October 1990. However, the transfer of power within the ruling family was handled smoothly, with Shaikh Rashid's eldest son Maktoum, succeeding his father and maintaining the economic and social initiatives (albeit with his younger brother Mohammed increasingly involved in policy-making). It is possible to label the decade and a half from the early 1990s as the era in which Dubai cemented, consolidated and expanded its position as the most dynamic and successful centre, not only in the region but achieving a worldwide reputation. This was the buoyant 'end of history'[2] era of the apparently solidly established American world order, in which the legend of Dubai was firmly established. Although, inevitably, there are times when factors work in any state's favour, it is only the fact that long-term policies and solid preparation built an effective, diversified economic and bureaucratic structure and infrastructure that allowed Dubai consistently to benefit when deleterious conditions impacted elsewhere.

In this epoch, at the end of the twentieth century, the analysis focuses on three major elements of Dubai's evolution and expansion: the distinctive form of economic model that Dubai adopted; the economic and social implications of the expansion of 'guest-worker' population growth and the way in which Dubai adapted to it; and the surge in the size and sophistication of container shipping and its transformation into a part of the worldwide logistics and intermodal industry.

The major external events contributing to Dubai's success in the 1970s and 1980s were, as we have already assessed, the Lebanese Civil War from 1975 to 1990, the Iranian Revolution of late 1978, the Iran–Iraq war from 1980 to 1988 and the Iraqi invasion of Kuwait in 1990 and the coalition response that expelled it. In the years after 1991, Dubai continued to benefit from the fact that other Gulf economies maintained their focus on oil and gas as the region recovered and re-built after the traumas of the 1980s and the invasion of Kuwait. Within the UAE, Abu Dhabi was using its huge oil wealth to develop its infrastructure and to fund the development of the poorer Emirates, while consolidating its role as the capital and centre of UAE government bureaucracy. Iraq and Iran remained international pariahs, unable even to consider acting as any sort of competition to Dubai as regional centres, but as in the past, Dubai remained the hub from which they were often supplied by sea and air.

Iraqi forces were expelled from Kuwait by the US-led coalition at the end of February 1991, but there was no attempt to follow-up the rout and extend the campaign into Iraq itself, even though this seemed entirely feasible. There were several reasons why this did not occur, the lack of a UN mandate and the hope that internal insurrections in Iraq would overthrow Saddam Hussein being two of them. However, a major factor was also the need to maintain the increasingly fragile relationship with other Arab states whose attitude, in some cases, was one of deep resentment at foreign military intervention. In the complex world of 'Middle East' politics, the invasion had not been universally condemned – the Yemeni government and the Palestinians had actually shown support for the action – 'independent western-baiting, strong Arab leader removes pro-western nouveau-riche plutocrats'. Even in those states which felt potentially threatened, such as Saudi Arabia, the presence of foreign troops on Saudi soil (despite the fact they had been requested to be there, temporarily, to support Saudi forces) exposed deep fault lines between the rulers and increasingly militant, conservative religious radicals.

Radical Islam was not a new phenomenon. In late 1979, there were hundreds of casualties when the Grand Mosque in Mecca was occupied by insurgents aiming to overthrow the Al Saud monarchy because of what they felt was its deviation from the purity of Islam, its corruption and its pro-Western policies. Saudi forces took two weeks to regain control of the sprawling complex. The Soviet Union's invasion of Afghanistan in 1979 and the bitter guerrilla war that continued until the Russian pull-out ten years later also created a large pool of Saudi-funded anti-Soviet Afghan and expatriate Arab fighters. These veterans not only challenged and undermined well-established versions of state/religious authority in several Arab states (including Saudi Arabia) but provided the core and the impetus for groups such as Al Qaeda, which increasingly turned their attention to opposing, by terror attacks, what they saw as the influence of US hegemonic power in the region and elsewhere. Ten years after the expulsion of Iraqi forces from Kuwait, they struck the Twin Towers in New York in September 2001, leading, in part, to an invasion of Iraq in March 2003 as an American-led coalition sought to remove one pillar of the 'Axis of Evil' group that was perceived to support terrorism and have weapons of mass-destruction. By the end of April 2003, hostilities had effectively ended, and the occupation of Iraq began.

What kind of development?

Despite the use of Jebel Ali as a supply base by coalition forces in 1990–1, Dubai was not affected by the increasing radicalization of religion elsewhere. As a tolerant trading centre, welcoming foreign visitors for many decades, and focussed on money-making opportunities, it continued to be regarded as the place in the Gulf to live, work and do business. Largely free from the official political constraints of UAE foreign policy, handled by Abu Dhabi, Dubai maintained its focus on and pursued an increasingly more innovative and wide-ranging economic policy, boosted by the end-of-century economic buoyancy.

Initiatives such as the Dubai Shopping Festival (1996) were aimed at attracting visitors who would spend money in the 'shoppers paradise' and boost hotel numbers, flights on Emirates Airline and increase trade volumes through Jebel Ali. The architecturally dramatic Burj Al Arab hotel was opened (1999) highlighting Dubai's intention to be at the cutting edge of design technology and to be a centre for quality high-end tourism. Innovative and economy broadening measures such as the opening of the Dubai Financial Centre and the inauguration of 'Media City' and 'Internet City' took place in 2000, with the construction of the vast 'Palm' reclamation and development commencing in 2002 and, not forgetting sport, the first Dubai Tennis Championships in 2003.

The containerization revolution that, as highlighted earlier, transformed the shipping industry, the ports industry and the world economy continued to evolve and Dubai, as we have seen, evolved with it by creating the port complex of Jebel Ali. As the container trades evolved rapidly, there were major implications for ports as ships grew in size, trading patterns changed, and technological developments drastically affected the way in which commerce took place. The most significant point here is that Dubai continued during these troubled times, to continue to invest, not only in the infrastructure for containerization, but also in the expansion of the airport and free-zones. This consolidation also, crucially, not only involved the creation and evolution of an effective state with institutions that worked – 'getting the sequence right' in the words of David Runciman[3] but also the increased use of foreign labour, primarily from South Asia, both skilled and non-skilled, resulting in an even more polyglot, multinational, multicultural city. It can be argued therefore that Dubai was, by its actions, to be in the vanguard of the globalization that was to transform the region and the world, but only because it had taken the steps to be so. But what sort of development was it? Al Faris and Soto make a useful summation:

> 'Dubai is an interesting case-study for any resource-dependent economy wishing to achieve sustainable prosperity by engaging in better-balanced growth paths than those typically induced by the mere exploitation of natural resources. (Dubai's) strength has been in identifying such opportunities, devising adequate policies and persevering in their implementation and, most important, providing the institutional environment needed for those policies to flourish.'[4]

Equally Bill Emmott emphasizes, 'globalization has been an outcome, not an objective. It has been an outcome of policies that treated openness as a virtue, including openness to trade, to ideas, to capital, to cultural interplay and, for many, now the most sensitive issue, to migration.'[5] This description fits Dubai's approach very well.

All developing and emerging states evolve uniquely depending on their actions, endowments and circumstances and in the Gulf, most of the economies are regarded as classic 'rentiers' – that is, states that gain most of their revenues from external sources paying 'rent' for resources (in these cases oil and gas). Such states are generally regarded to tend to perpetuate authoritarian government as they do not rely on taxation revenue from their populations and 'do not respond to society'[6] but provide, as Davidson puts it, the 'ruling bargain'[7] – no taxes, cradle to grave benefits, but no political representation. Ayubi has highlighted the supposed debilitating effects of this form of government, stifling development and initiative – a sort of 'cargo-cult' mentality with the population just waiting for the next handouts to arrive.[8] However, assumptions of the demise of the Gulf oil monarchies turned out to be exaggerated (and upheavals such as the 'Arab Spring' of 2011 have shown that many of these regimes are actually rather more flexible, nimble-footed and politically resilient than the republican alternatives), as highlighted, for example, by Greg Gause[9] and Lisa Anderson.[10] Laura Al Katiri uses the term 'Guardian States' to describe (Gulf) rentiers which have 'exceptionally high access to non-tax fiscal revenues . . . oil-based resource rents . . . with a small typically homogeneous national population through which rents are divided',[11] with the state acting as custodian of economic development while ensuring that traditional policies of buying allegiance from domestic groups are maintained through handouts and benefits to the national population. Al Katiri highlights, 'how natural resources wealth can be used to promote welfare and development-enhancing objectives'[12] (compared with other worldwide, resource-rich states), but also the waste of resources and careless, profligate spending. Dubai is not a classic Guardian State using some of these definitions, but its focus on other diversified revenue streams to achieve its objectives, the role of government in shaping the agenda and the promotion of social provision and diversified development makes it at least an outlier.

Dubai's form of development has been different from that of the classic Gulf rentiers, while conforming with elements of modernization theory and Rostow's classic stages of economic growth, 'traditional society, preconditions for take-off, the take-off, the drive to maturity and the age of mass-consumption',[13] because it has not relied primarily on oil and gas rents to fund and expand the economy. Some specialists maintain that Dubai 'cannot be classified as a rentier state',[14] whereas others feel that 'only the type of rent and how it flows have changed, the rentier bargain remains in place'.[15] Their perspectives, I would argue are actually, not too dissimilar. Gray argues that a patrimonial structure remains in place, maintaining a structure that dispenses patronage and services to maintain the well-being of 'Nationals', using the revenues from a diversified economy rather than the now virtually negligible revenues from oil. The 'Kafala' (sponsorship) system still exists, which allows expatriate labour to be employed under the sponsorship of an Emirati company or individual and entails that any business must have a Dubai / Emirati partner who has 51 per cent of the ownership and this can be defined as a form of rentierism. However, it is clear also (as Hvidt asserts) that Dubai policy for the last half-century has manifestly been aimed at growing a broadly based, diverse and job-creating economy based on trading, shipping and services providing opportunities for national citizens, rather than simply 'sitting back' and relying on rent from fossil-fuels.

As Adam Hanieh has highlighted, rentier theory assumes that 'rentier states were predisposed to economic policies that discouraged diversification because they could rely on external rents'.[16] Dubai, on the other hand, adopted a very wide diversification policy initially assisted by the oil revenues from the time of Dubai's first exports (in 1969) – but – and this is the major difference between Dubai and the rest of the Gulf – the revenues were used to prepare for a post-oil future as a regional hub and trading entrepot and ploughed back into infrastructure development. An economy based on external rents was never an end in itself. Though government revenues continued to subsidize the lives of Dubai citizens, increasingly policies were aimed at weaning the population off the assumption that such bounty could continue indefinitely, without some contribution from nationals to the development of the Emirate.

Understanding what sort of development Dubai has pursued helps us to identify how the 'Dubai Model' emerged in the 1990s and why the Emirate was able to be the 'destination of choice' when other regional centres imploded. As we have seen, the pro-business policies of the ruling family, such as encouraging merchants to move to Dubai from South Persia from the early twentieth century onwards (despite concerns about cultural and religious assimilation) established the city-state's reputation. Political scientists such as Alice Amsden, Peter Evans and Mary Ann Tetreault have all worked on emerging economies with Amsden's 'The Rise of the Rest' focussing on the 'late-industrializing' economies in Asia – 'statist' regimes where the government and not the private sector encouraged foreign investment to grow their economies through industrialization.[17] Dubai has used the same principles, but using the models of Singapore and Hong Kong, its policy direction was to build up the port, airport logistic and business infrastructure (promoting private-sector initiatives) throughout the 1960s, 1970s and 1980s to act as a commercial centre for the region, indeed Ahmed Kanna feels that Dubai and Singapore have much in common, emanating from their creation 'in the crucible of the British Indian Ocean Empire',[18] and as indicated earlier, there is no doubt that Dubai took note of the polices that the south-east Asian city-state had employed, to prosper in a competitive environment.

However, the economy of Dubai has evolved and the contribution of the state and that of the private sector to this process has shifted over time. Before the development of the 1960s, the 'non-state sector' consisting of merchants, fishermen, agriculturalists and those involved in pearling constituted what might be called the economy of Dubai (and the region). The ruling family collected taxes from, for example, the pearling businesses, thus elevating them to a vital role in the structure of the state and contributed themselves, by ensuring that commerce and administration ran smoothly and safely. The ruling family was itself involved in trading activity and had close ties with their fellow merchants. These relationships came under strain as merchants became weaker after the collapse of pearling and the ruler became less dependent on their support. There was even an attempt by some economically distressed factions to recover their position and re-distribute what income there was by regime change, as described in a previous chapter, but the policies of Shaikh Rashid al Maktoum from the 1950s onwards, re-established the role and importance of the merchant elite and re-integrated them into the support structure of the state, as emphasized by Fatma Al Sayegh.[19] These well-established, private-sector elites, concerned with their own economic interests, worked within the patrimonial system, occupying senior government positions. Consulted and enriched by the ruling family, as described by Khalid Almeizany, they support the government's political and economic policies, there being 'a strong correlation between the economic wealth of the merchant class and their desire for political change'.[20] There is no doubt that it is the government, not the private sector, that has created and implemented the development policies over the last half century. Hvidt[21] highlights nine key factors which distinguish Dubai's approach:

1. Government-led development (i.e. by the ruler)
2. Fast decision-making
3. Flexible (i.e. not necessarily permanent) labour-force
4. The bypassing of industrialization (i.e. a commercializing and service economy)
5. Internationalization of Service Provision (i.e. focus on quality and professionalism)
6. Creation of investment opportunities
7. Supply-generated demand
8. Market-positioning (i.e. branding)
9. Development in co-operation with international partners (i.e. acceptance of the globalized world)

Dubai is therefore, I would suggest, a 'late-commercialising economy', a 'business-state', a unique example of a developmental state pursuing a distinctive path set out by a proactive series of rulers working in close liaison with the societal and business elites of the Emirate. As Mishrif and Kapetanovic put it, 'Given its unique governance approach, Dubai's model is a deviant case of economic development . . . (reflecting) the nature of the relationship between the ruling family and the merchants.'[22] This approach involves partnerships, innovation, entrepreneurship and the involvement of state-owned enterprises. The government (ruling family in liaison with senior families) sets out parameters and aims to create the conditions to attract private business, an approach which creates a Gulf version of the 'Japan inc'. What this means in practice (as with Japan) is that the whole state and decision-making apparatus, government departments and key institutions and organizations, the public and private sectors interplaying together, 'act with one voice', rather akin to a professional major company. Indeed, the current ruler Shaikh Mohammed has in the past referred to himself as the CEO of Dubai encouraging 'the empowering of employees . . . of listening . . . and the need for consultation and collaboration'.[23] While appreciating that 'he would say that wouldn't he', his definition of his role, certainly confirms that the Dubai state plays the major role in the economy.

> This command economy . . . whose subsistence (is) strategically linked to the success of new industrial and commercial activities . . . as in Singapore, Dubai benefits from Foreign Direct Investment (FDI) and the involvement of international corporations . . . and in both cases the port's economy has been a crucial factor for economic expansion (as) both are hubs for global container transport and this has boosted their commercial growth.[24]

Peter Evans has described the examples of East Asian developing economies where government as well as bureaucracy develops and progresses its aims without having to depend on other elites, but is, nonetheless, 'embedded' with them due to close and deep ties, thus achieving policy coordination. These links ensure that it is listening to a broad range of opinion and also that there is broad consensus on having policies implemented, with the state acting as 'midwife' to promote growth (in the private sector). There are clear parallels with a Dubai that organized government, focussed on high-achieving officials and the implementation of decision-making, as it evolved, providing the framework, as, 'transformation depends on turning structural strengths into the effective execution of a well-selected blend of roles'.[25] The fact is that Dubai defies conventional categorization and as a 'Business State' has worked as the best businesses do, to focus on its core strengths – by innovating and re-shaping its direction with a clear plan, by ensuring that its customers received professional service and by ensuring that there are a wide group of 'shareholders' committed to the same path. 'Developmental states show that state capacity . . . involves entrepreneurship as well . . . and a dense network of ties that bind them to societal allies with transformational goals.'[26] This structure, without doubt, is managed and controlled by the Ruling family, in concert with input from the business elite of the Emirate and the other 'shareholders' in the enterprise, the Dubai citizens, albeit, in the latter case, with consultation that does not emerge from a ballot box. As Michael Herb has highlighted, the ruling family continues to be accorded legitimacy by national citizens and the increasing heterogeneity of the Emirate has actually, aligned this privileged minority even more closely together to preserve culture, traditions and the 'nation'.[27] However, Dubai's development exemplifies the view that policies and institutions trump natural endowments and geography, issues discussed by Acemoglu and Robinson,[28] as in its modernization drive, the Emirate not only invested in education, healthcare and housing but also in the competitive and innovative business strategy to allow it to compete without reliance on fossil-fuels. Mary Ann Tetreault has also emphasized that Dubai has always been a 'competitive state', initiating and implementing policies that would improve competitiveness and always aware of the need and the necessity, to create facilities and conditions that would out-perform others.[29] That Dubai has continued to maintain this attitude is illustrated by the World Bank's (to mid-2017) 'Ease of Doing Business Survey', which puts the UAE in 21st place out of 190 countries (just behind Germany at number 20), with regional rivals trailing well behind: Bahrain (66), Oman (71), Qatar (83), Saudi Arabia (92) and Kuwait (96).[30]

Such an approach works in part on the 'build it and they will come' principle (that is, if you provide the best and competitive facilities they will – sooner or later – be used) and from the 1990s onwards government initiatives increased the options available on this basis – particularly in the real-estate sector as the city expanded in size and population. However, though this 'expansion ahead of demand' approach had been successful in the past (expansion of port Rashid, new airport, Jebel Ali) there is always the chance that over-optimism and miscalculation will create over-capacity when trade and business expansion does not increase as expected.[31] At the beginning of the twenty-first century, there were already concerns that with over-confidence and more than a little hubris, Dubai's economy was over-heating as and in the burgeoning laissez-faire environment, too few controls, particularly on the real-estate sector – seen as a cash-cow because of an influx of investors desperate to be part of the Dubai miracle. In this environment and in the very much 'top-down' ruling and policy styles of the Al Maktoums, the 'can-do' approach is very much part of the ethos of Dubai, to overcome problems despite the lack of resources and despite the difficulties. Laudable though this may be, we have to recognize that this culture is by its nature, reluctant to recognize alternative views, particularly those which run contrary to the more assertive expansionary approach. Inevitably, those who have divergent opinions may be inclined to keep them to themselves for fear of being regarded as 'negative'.

The role of expatriate labour

This is an important subject which not only emphasizes that Dubai's flexible and laissez-faire approach to expand economic activity extends to include large numbers of expatriates without whom the grandiose plans could not work. The attitude reflects not only the non-doctrinaire regional attitude to the large-scale employment of foreigners but also the extent to which Dubai has become a magnet to attract workers from other states (particularly South Asia) where opportunities for work and advancement are poor. The success of Dubai has been built on its ability to attract workers and talent from elsewhere to buttress indigenous entrepreneurs.

Even before 1991, Dubai and the UAE always had a relatively small proportion of expatriate Arab workers, 'protected' as they were until 1971 by British oversight that discouraged movement from other Arab states to avoid political contagion in particular, though small numbers of professionals such as school teachers and administrators were recruited from Egypt, Jordan and Sudan. Contacts with the outside world through trade involved Indian Ocean inhabitants rather than large numbers of Arab nationals. Until the last quarter of the twentieth century, the, always small, population had no need of additional numbers (certainly once the pearling days were over), and later development (when large numbers of manual and clerical workers were needed) relied on traditional manpower suppliers

(Pakistan and India). Al Shehabi, quoting figures produced by Kapiszewski in 2006 illustrates this by showing that in 1985 and 1996 the percentage of Arab workers in the GCC was: [32]

GCC Arab Workers (percentages)

	1985	1996
Saudi Arabia	80	30
Kuwait	70	35
UAE	25	15

However, the invasion of Kuwait in 1990, the (ill-advised) celebratory reaction of states such as Yemen and Palestine and the resultant concern over potential 'fifth-columns' of workers potentially hostile to the regime re-confirmed the preference in Dubai and the Emirates for neutral third country nationals (TCN), particularly from India, Pakistan, Bangladesh and in more recent years from the Philippines and increasingly, anglophone Africa.

Once again, Dubai showed itself to be a Petri Dish for experimenting with policies in the absence of oil and where the bulk of the population are 'guest-workers' with no prospect of citizenship, yet who pay for the privilege of being in Dubai, helping to support the living standards on the minority of Dubai national citizens. During the 1990s, policies were refined and according to a recent Chatham House Report, three quarters of the Dubai Government USD 8.3 billion revenues in 2015, consisted of 'fines, services and fees' with 'Dubai . . . a unique example of a Gulf state that has embraced expatriates and turned them into a source of revenue . . . and where expatriates constitute 92% of the population it can be assumed that the bulk of fines and fees are paid by expatriates'.[33] Dubai has successfully achieved this position by focussing on the merits and benefits of living in Dubai and the possibilities of advancement and better opportunity for foreign employees and their children (able to obtain better, English-speaking education).

It is evident after several decades that this policy is attractive to many men and women in emerging nations (and 'advanced' ones too) who are attracted by the prospect of living in an iconic well-managed city rather than their own often dysfunctional homelands. That there is no prospect of citizenship is something that does not appear to disturb most of such economic migrants, who, fully conscious of the residence 'contract' with Dubai, are often more anxious to escape from political uncertainties and instability and lack of opportunity to focus on a better and more humdrum life for themselves and their children. Many salaried employees at both senior and junior levels have been in the Emirate(s) for decades. For most workers, the prospect of being able to send money back (remittances) to their parents/relatives/families in their homelands is the most important benefit that Dubai can bestow and the impact of this outflow of funds is considerable on the lives of millions in the developing world who depend on it. Though there are relatively few studies as yet, the *Gulf News* newspaper in December 2017 reported that remittances to India in 2017 (my extrapolated figures) would be around USD

5.6 billion and to the Philippines around USD 3 billion.[34] An earlier study by Genc and Naufal estimated that Philippinos and Philippinas in the UAE each remitted (in 2011) around USD 2000 each,[35] which at the time by my estimate, probably constituted about 1.5 per cent of the entire Philippines GDP.

The point being made here is that the mechanisms by which Dubai ensures that the foreign worker population pays for the privilege of being in Dubai are part of the social bargain which on the one hand allows workers from foreign countries to live in Dubai as (always) temporary inhabitants but on the other hand provides such workers (in the main) with the opportunity to provide better financial provision for family in their homelands, better conditions of life and better educational opportunities for their children. Dubai benefits from having skilled enthusiastic workers who are queueing up to have the opportunity to work in the famous city – we should not forget the majority of foreigners in Dubai are there by choice. An article in the Economist in August 2018, referencing United Nations Statistics, shows that from 2000 to 2017 the UAE showed the highest increase in proportion of international migrants, worldwide at over 10 per cent (compared for example with Australia at 6 per cent, Britain at over 5 per cent and the United States at 3 per cent). 'There is a trade-off. Because migrants have fewer rights, Gulf citizens are willing to admit more of them, relative to population, than western countries. Most of the migrants benefit and want to stay.'[36] If Dubai is to continue to maintain competitiveness, it must continue to innovate and change – requiring a regular inflow of talented people. Not all such people will stay for decades but will return home or go on to other locations, having acquired savings and learned new first-world skills in the professional and competitive Dubai melting-pot. The fact that Dubai was such an important trading, shipping and port hub ensured that multinational companies positioned quality staff into the Emirate both to gain more experience and also because as a major centre, there is a powerful competition requiring quality staff performance. As is to be expected, the UAE, particularly Dubai, goes out of its way to emphasize the multicultural attractions of living and working in Dubai and the Emirates. As, for example, highlighted at the UAE pavilion at the 2017 Venice Biennale where 'Rock, Paper, Scissors: Positions in Play' was an exhibit by 'A group of artists, representing the diverse and complex demographics of the UAE' where, 'the potential of play to transform a place into home presents a counterpoint to the mercantile forms of cosmopolitanism that rely on the UAE's (effectively, Dubai's) role as an entrepot'.[37]

Of course, the picture is not always so rosy, particularly for those without skills and qualifications, conditions emphasized in works, by Mike Davis[38] and Syed Ali,[39] for example, which focus on the capitalist, neo-liberal approach that Dubai adopts on the unskilled labour that is imported, like a commodity, for specific projects on a short-term basis. It cannot be denied that the poor and unskilled are often exploited both by agents who recruit them, and the UAE citizens who are complicit in employing them in poor conditions, circumventing the legislation designed to protect such workers.

However, the reality is also that, particularly in this region, areas of South Asia such as India, Pakistan, Bangladesh and Nepal continue to have vast reserves of unskilled manual labour who, often lacking any opportunities at home for work – or work only of the most arduous and unremunerative type – are only too anxious to seek out opportunities elsewhere. A report by Chatham House's Gareth Price focussing on Nepalese workers in the Gulf, particularly in Qatar, emphasizes that 'each day some 1,600 or so Nepalese set off in search of higher wages in foreign lands ... and the average remittance per worker sent home (from Qatar) stands at more than $1,500 a year – twice Nepal's per capita income'.[40] The results from Dubai would show the same. The Chatham House report also stresses that 'if the Gulf adopted western building practices, it would have less need for unskilled labourers. Those workers would be back in South Asia earning less'.[41] This reality is probably true in every part of the world and the accounts highlighted here emphasize that as Hvidt describes, Dubai is able to have a flexible approach to the hiring (and laying-off) of workers, particularly in the changing demands of a global market.

However, once we look more closely at the way in which Dubai has been operating, this bleak 'hire and fire' mentality seems less clear-cut. Firstly, the population of Dubai has actually, been growing each year, and as (based on the available statistics), expatriate labour accounts for about 91 per cent, the 'flexible' labour force is steadily growing, and as a greater proportion of the total and has been for many years (even during the financial crisis of 2007–8).

Total Dubai Population

1995	689,000
2000	862,000
2005	1,321,000
2010	1,905,000

(Source: Gulf Labour Markets & Migration Website)[42]

Expatriates as a Proportion of the Population

2014	212,000 Dubai nationals	/ 2,115,350 expatriates
2015	222,875	/ 2,223,800
2016	233,430	/ 2,465,170

(Source: Dubai Statistics Centre)[43]

There is clearly no evidence here of major downturns in the labour market, reflecting both the fact that the aim is to employ labour for the longer term, with the focus on skilled or semi-skilled people, as part of the focus on the expansion of the various free-zones and trade and logistics activity, but also that unskilled labour, subject to shorter-term visa regulations (two or three years) may be replaced. Technology advances are also leading to automation and less reliance on (more transient) unskilled labour. Al Faris and Soto point out that in Dubai, 'In 1997 only 11pc of GCC, 54 pc of MENA Arabs and 66pc of Westerners were university graduates; in 2009 these had increased to 65pc, 62 pc, and 88 pc respectively'.[44]

Secondly, as evidenced in the figures just seen, the diversified economic policy, maintained for several decades, requires increasing numbers of employees who have a wide range of skills (rather than unskilled workers) and whose employers expect them to remain (in many cases) in Dubai for years. Thirdly, Dubai (UAE) employment laws and regulations are now comprehensive, covering the private sector applying 'to all employees working in the UAE whether UAE Nationals or Expatriates' (UAE Government Website) and including the statutory provisions for emoluments, healthcare, repatriation etc. Of course, implementation and enforcement of such labour contracts may always be effective, but the laws exist and there is considerable external pressure from (Western) governments and NGOs. Fourthly, conditions and salaries for most skilled or semi-skilled workers in 'First-World' Dubai (and other Gulf states) are invariably better than those in other emerging economies, particularly in South Asia, as we have already noted, again ensuring that the better/skilled people can be and need to be, employed for the longer term. There are few, if any, suggestions on how and what the Emirate of a few hundred thousand people should do, alternatively, to provide the labour for its development, in an environment, where for demographic reasons, it is impossible to provide expatriate workers with full citizenship. The reality of the labour market in Dubai that it reflects a diverse and increasingly skilled 'add-value' employment, based in the free-zones, reflecting the diversified nature of the economy, supplemented in particular by the hospitality industry in the Emirate, with conditions that attract talented people from every part of the world. These, working and living conditions for most people in diversified economy Dubai, not only stand up well, in the main, with those in 'third world' states, but also with those in the rest of the Gulf. Naturally, Dubai benefits from this employment policy but millions of non-national workers do too. Until the (worse) conditions improve in other emerging states, Dubai will continue to attract workers of all skill levels who cannot find work at home.

The final point in this review of workers in the economy is 'the elephant in the room', the difficulty of persuading cossetted national young people that they should participate in the competitive and performance-based, private sector. Though Dubai's employment policies for development and the process by which these have been implemented have been successful, to the extent that some other regional states are 'cherry-picking' elements as they seek to diversify from oil and gas, there are some fundamental underlying weaknesses. First, substantial numbers of foreign workers have not automatically resulted in good productivity, though a Dubai Economic Council (DEC) survey in 2010 showed that FTZ companies significantly outperformed their (Dubai non-FTZ) counterparts in terms of productivity, capital investment and qualifications.[45] It is no coincidence that the FTZs have focussed on skilled employment activity and are not constrained by the Kafala system which regulates the participation of expatriates and the employment protection of Dubai (UAE) Nationals, by an Emiratization policy which shelters them from open competition with expatriates – but thus reduces their employability – 'private-sector employers prefer to employ non-nationals because they cost less, have fewer rights and have more market-relevant skills'.[46] Emiratis are therefore overwhelming employed in the public sector – 'around 80 pc are civil servants'.[47] Dubai has, effectively, therefore, a parallel employment system operating within one of the two parallel economic models.

In Dubai, the government has for years been trying to decide how to entice more national young people into the private sector without upsetting the economic success built on professionalism and skills provided by the numbers of expatriate workers. Simply, 'Emiratisating' all private-sector jobs would not be feasible for both skills and sheer numbers reasons, so the policy in the private sector has been a threefold one of:

1. Making certain, useful and appropriate jobs (e.g. public-relations officers of all private companies) reserved for Emiratis.
2. Increasing the required ratio of Emiratis in certain 'suitable' sectors (e.g. particularly Banking and Insurance), which are able to afford (well-educated) Emiratis as reported on HH Shaikh Mohammed Al Maktoum Twitter Feed 25/10/15 – 'we also approved an Emiratisation strategy for the banking and insurance sector, which is the second biggest employer of UAE Nationals'.
3. Continuing to grow the economy to provide opportunities for Emiratis to be employed.

These 'carrot' methods, designed to encourage and persuade Emirati youth to engage with private-sector companies, were supplemented in 2014 by the 'UAE National Service Law' (UAENSL) 'stick', requiring all Emirati males between eighteen and thirty to register for national service, with those having a completed High School Diploma serving (now) for one year, and serving for two years without such a diploma.[48] Though accurate figures are hard to establish, Soto and Rashid, referencing the UAE Labour Force Survey of 2009, highlight that

> as of 2010, about 45% of Emirati – males and females – are active in the labour market...a considerable reserve of manpower that could enter the labour market ... but around 20 pc of males classify themselves as not willing to work. It reflects Emirati society as having a high 'reservation wage' (the minimum salary a person would demand to become active in the labour market.)[49]

The UAENSL clearly represents government efforts to force 'non-participants' to contribute.

In practice, the Dubai government push/pull strategy on employment is probably as realistic as possible, as it seeks to square the dichotomy circle of needing an increasing labour force (both skilled and unskilled) in the FZs and in 'Dubai proper', to grow and vary the economy, particularly in the run-up to the (currently deferred) 2020 World Trade Fair in Dubai, yet weaning young male nationals away from a non-participatory, risk-averse employment culture and transforming them into entrepreneurs – while preserving the 'Ruling Bargain'. Dubai has looked closely at the Singapore blueprint as we have seen, and the following extract could have almost been written about Dubai too. 'The unique *except for Dubai* (my italics) success of Singapore is due to a number of factors: the quality of public provided infrastructures and equipment; financial incentives and the establishment of free-trade zones. The most important factor, however, was the high levels of education and skills of a workforce that could adapt to new technologies and work practices.'[50] Dubai, despite some progress, clearly has some way to go to reach this stage.

In the years after 1990/91, Dubai was able to benefit, as normalcy returned to the Gulf. The capacity of Jebel Ali, the linked-in free-zones, the expanding airport and airline and the living environment attracted more business – and other regional states did not offer any real competition. Dubai policy, since the mid-1980s, had placed more emphasis on growing the trading and ports-related economy by focussing on the free-zones, internal enclaves, where (internationally accepted) English law applied (rather than Sharia), taxes low or non-existent and where ownership (even if non-citizens) did not have to involve a (Kafala) UAE national majority share. Both Sultan Bin Sulayem (personally involved in the initial efforts to develop the Jebel Ali Free Zone (JAFZA) established in 1985) and Mohammed Sharaf (erstwhile chief executive of Dubai Ports World) have emphasized the success and scale, which by the second decade of the twenty-first century, as described on the JAFZA website, has companies 'from over 100 countries, sustaining 144,000 jobs and attracting more than 32% of the UAE's Foreign Direct Investment (FDI) and exceeding 50% of Dubai's total exports . . . of USD 87.6 billion'. However, JAFZA only began to gather real momentum in the years after 1991 for two main reasons. Firstly, the end of the Iran–Iraq war and the removal of Iraq from Kuwait, allowed business confidence in the region to return. Secondly, the Emirate's ports (Port Rashid and Jebel Ali), managed by different operators (Gray Mackenzie and Sealand respectively), who acted as competitors for the same (Dubai) business were rationalized in 1991 into Dubai Ports Authority (DPA), government-owned but commercially independent. This action allowed more focus to be placed on attracting business to under-utilized Jebel Ali and the marketing of adjacent JAFZA to complement it.

Container shipping developments – Size, scale and critical mass

In the rest of the UAE in the 1990s, Abu Dhabi continued to develop its role as the *primus inter pares* – assisting the less wealthy Northern Emirates, expanding its activities as the diplomatic and bureaucratic centre and reaping the financial benefits of its huge oil reserves with production averaging about 2 million barrels a day.[51] Volumes at the Emirate's port of Mina Zayed increased, but at a low level, and Dubai continued to be and expanded its position as the UAE's major trading centre. For example, throughputs (in TEU) are given.

Abu Dhabi (Mina Zayed) and Dubai Container Throughputs

1993 –	Mina Zayed – 102,000	Dubai – 1,700,000
1996 –	Mina Zayed – 237,000	Dubai – 2,200,000
1999 –	Mina Zayed – 360,000	Dubai – 2,800,000

(Source Drewry Maritime Research, London)

Sharjah's east coast container terminal of Khor Fakkan and the container terminal at Fujairah also benefitted from the expansion in trade to the region and their specific roles as relay/trans-shipment centres. Both Khor Fakkan and Fujairah attracted lines who, while continuing to have a major presence in Dubai, wanted an outer Gulf port that could be used as a relay centre for their other services and to consolidate containers to and from those services at a point where they could be consolidated for movements on specific sailings in and out of the Gulf (rather than having all of their services do so). Fujairah's major customer was American President Lines (APL), and Khor Fakkan had United Arab Shipping Company (UASC) and CMA.

Throughout the 1990s, both terminals increased their volumes, but towards the end of the decade, Khor Fakkan gradually overtook Fujairah, which lost regular shipping line calls. By the early part of the new century, Fujairah had abandoned its focus on containers, to focus instead on oil storage and offshore supply services. The throughputs at the two terminals were substantial (in TEU).

Khor Fakkan and Fujairah Container Volumes Compared

1993 –	Khor Fakkan –	446,000	Fujairah – 649,000
1999 –	Khor Fakkan –	989,000	Fujairah – 566,000
2003 –	Khor Fakkan –	1,400,000	Fujairah – 202,000

(Source, Drewry Maritime Research, London)

The competition from these professional terminals (always virtually all trans-shipment cargo) was never going to directly threaten Dubai's position but they gave Jebel Ali some useful competition and also allowed shipping lines to 'benchmark' performance – providing opportunities to pressurize Jebel Ali into improving performance and pricing.

The rapidly expanding size, impact and evolution of the container trades and containerization made an enormous contribution to the continuing expansion of Dubai. In 1990 Container throughputs were 913,000 TEU and in 1993, two years after the formation of DPA, Dubai volumes had nearly doubled to 1.7 million TEU. By 2003, the container throughputs at the Emirate's ports, primarily Jebel Ali, dwarfed those in other Gulf states. Gulf Volumes for the year 2003 were (rounded in TEU):

Gulf Container Volumes in 2003

Dubai –	5,200,000 –	(2,600,000 Transhipment and 2,600,000 Local cargo)
Other UAE –	2,023,000 –	(370,000 Transhipment and 1,653,000 Local Cargo)
Oman –	2,300,000 –	(1,980,000 Transhipment (Salalah) and 300,000 Local cargo)
Iran –	1,035,000 –	(All Local Cargo)
Iraq –	33,000 –	(All Local Cargo)
Kuwait –	503,000	(All Local Cargo)
Bahrain –	176,000 –	(All Local Cargo)
Saudi Arabia (East Coast) –	657,000 –	(All Local Cargo)

(Source: Drewry Maritime Research, London)[52]

The statistics clearly show, even with some distortion provided by the Southern Omani relay terminal at Salalah, that Dubai dominated the region both in 'local' gateway cargo for Dubai itself, and for relaying/trans-shipping containers to other locations. Volumes, in part, reflected the growth in the carrying capacity of container cargo ships, which were getting progressively larger.

The increasing size of container ships, particularly from the late 1990s, was a reaction to the fundamental principle of maritime transport economics, that of economy of scale. The bigger the container ship, the lower the slot/unit cost of each container transported. With the improvement in shore-side container crane availability, new containerships on major routes were built without any container-handling equipment of their own, depending entirely on the facilities at ports. This transition had two important consequences. Firstly, it enabled container ship design to focus on carrying even more containers stacked in 'cell-guides' for easy loading and discharge above and below deck, effectively floating warehouses and secondly, it placed the onus for effective performance in port squarely in the hands of the ports themselves. Without the requisite number of container cranes or quay length or draught (depth of water under the keel of the ship) ships could not load and discharge containers quickly and cost-effectively, requiring ports to regularly update and modernize their facilities or run the risk of losing services to other ports that had. A review of some Maersk Line (often a market leader for innovation), new container ship tonnage from the 1980s onwards, highlights the rapidity with which the container shipping industry was evolving (TEU figures are approximate).

Increasing Container Ship Sizes – Maersk Line Examples[53]

1982 – L Class / 241 metres long / 32 metres width / 44,000 dwt / 2500 TEU (Panamax size = can pass through the Panama Canal)
1988 – M Class / 294 metres long / 61,000 dwt / 4500 TEU
1996 – K Class / 318 metres long / 43 metres width / 90,000 dwt / 7400 TEU (Post-Panamax = too big to transit the Panama Canal)
1997 – S Class / 347 metres long / 105,000 dwt / 8160 TEU
2005 – G Class / 367 metres long / 115, 000 dwt / 9074 TEU
2006 – E Class / 398 metres long / 56 metres width / 158,000 dwt / 15,500 TEU (Super post Panamax)

(As indicated previously, there are now (updated for 2020) several operators such as Hyundai, Maersk, CMA-CGM and MSC for example who operate ships of around 400 metres long, 59 metres width and can carry 21,000 to 24,000 TEU)

The significant point being made here is that if Dubai (or any other major port or hub) wished to ensure that it was able to remain a major port or hub, then such increases in vessel size (and container volume) required the port to continue to: replace its container cranes (as Panamax size ships stacked only around 13 containers across the ship, over which a container crane had to reach, but post-Panamax ships stacked 18 and super post Panamax ships around 22); ensure that quay lengths were increased, to accommodate the biggest ships which over twenty years had grown 150 metres longer; dredge the water depth alongside the berth and in the channel, where the biggest ships would potentially now require 16 metres of water under the keel; and develop container-yard space, IT systems and yard transport to cope with the substantially greater demands posed by thousands rather than hundreds of containers loaded and discharged on each vessel call.

In 2001, having already expanded Terminal 1 at Jebel Ali, the construction of a second terminal opening in 2009, with 8 berths and 29 Quay cranes and Terminal 3 in 2014 equipped with 19 automated Quay cranes capable of handling the biggest Super Post Panamax ships) commenced, according to the port website. Other neighbouring states either did not pursue any development or expansion on this scale.

Demonstrating the extent to which the policy of 'expansion ahead of demand' from the 1990s onwards has evolved and worked successfully to ensure that the regional hub status was not only maintained but expanded is the example of a major carrier, CMA-CGM with the line's schedule advertising export sailings from Jebel Ali as follows (some services calling en-route from origin ports/some services in conjunction with other lines):

CMA-CGM Services from Jebel Ali – February 2018[54]

Weekly EPIC 2 service to UK/Europe via Pakistan, India and the Med (via Jeddah)
Weekly MEDEX service to Pakistan, India thence Spain, Italy and France (via Jeddah)
Weekly MEGEM service to the East Med
Weekly INDIAMED service to Pakistan, India, Jeddah, Djibouti and Egypt
Weekly CIMEX 1 / MEA 1 service to South East Asia and China
Weekly CIMEX 3 / MEA 3 service to Qatar, Dammam and Jubail thence Singapore and China
Weekly CIMEX 5 / MEA 3 service to upper Gulf, South East Asia and China
Weekly MED 2 / MEX 1 service to South East Asia and China
Weekly CIMEX 6 / MEA 4 service to South East Asia and China via Iran
Weekly CIMEX 7 / MEA 5 service to Singapore and China via Bahrain and Dammam
Weekly CIMEX 8 service to China and Korea via Iran
Weekly INDIAGULF service to Iraq, Iran and India
Weekly CIMEX 9 service to Taiwan, China and back via Iran
MIDAS 1 weekly service to India, Sri Lanka, South Africa and West Africa
SWAHILI EXPRESS weekly service to East Africa, Djibouti thence India
NOURA EXPRESS weekly service to East Africa and Somalia
MIDAS 2 weekly service to India, Indian Ocean Islands and South Africa
NOURA EXPRESS 2 weekly service to East Africa

I have listed these eighteen weekly services as a snapshot to illustrate how extensive the coverage is of world markets and particularly, regional markets in the Gulf, Africa, and Asia, by carriers such as CMA-CGM who interlock their services at Jebel Ali so that, for example, containers from Europe to East Africa are loaded on an Eastbound sailing to Asia and relayed on to the on-carrying ship (to Africa) at Jebel Ali. Other major worldwide carriers such as Maersk and Mediterranean Shipping Line (MSC) have similar operations at Jebel Ali, as do lines operating on a smaller scale. The fact that this happens, using a mixture of ships of various sizes, reflects both the ability of Jebel Ali to accommodate these sailings and the seamless trans-shipment of containers in the terminal as well as the nature of globalization in the late twentieth century, 'enmeshed in worldwide systems and networks of interaction'.[55] Dubai's role as a regional supermarket, easily accessible by good-air links and with the regular container shipping services, attracted traders from Africa, for example, who loaded containers with varieties of goods bought in Dubai and Sharjah, then shipped them back home to sell. A hub port and a large 'market' complement and sustain and grow each other, so that import or export containers can be moving:

1. To or from the local market (e.g. for local consumption)
2. Via the port to be relayed onto a connecting vessel bound for another port
3. To or from a facility in a free-zone where it is consolidated with other cargo and re-exported
4. Imported into Dubai, the cargo unpacked (e.g. on the creek) and the 'loose' cargo moved by local (dhow) vessel to smaller local ports

As Dubai became the unchallenged Gulf centre in the 1990s, commercially expansionary initiatives such as 'Dubai Shopping Festival' were launched (in February 1996) to attract more visitors and developments such as Dubai's 'Dragonmart' were planned. Described as being '1.2 km long with 3500 shops ... the largest trading hub for Chinese goods outside mainland China and offers a unique platform for traders of Chinese goods in the ME and North African markets'.[56] This example echoes the 'World's largest wholesale market for cheap, non-technical, mass market goods'[57] to be found in Yiwu, Zhejiang province in Eastern China, closely linked to Ningbo Port (the world's fourth-largest container port). The one (port) does not necessarily create the other (market) – and vice-versa – but there is invariably a symbiotic relationship, growing together and certainly, neither of these trading emporia could exist and flourish where they are without major container facilities / major shipping companies close at hand. The transit time for regular direct sailings from Ningbo to Dubai is just over two weeks, for example as shown on the CMA-CGM website. Equally, as long as the cargo flows remain available and the hub port remains efficient and cost-effective, it will retain its links, but there is a powerful incentive for both the port and the cargo-producing/receiving area (e.g. Dubai and its free-zones) to continue to expand and innovate, to ensure it remains indispensable in a competitive world. As we have seen, there are always alternatives if ports fail to deliver the right performance to end-user customers. The same point applies to markets or centres. If they fail to maintain their performance or attractiveness, they will lose customers to others.

For the core trading and port environment, the impact of containerization created, effectively, a whole new industry of 'intermodalism' (through transportation from origin point to destination involving various modes of transport such as sea, land, rail or air) and 'supply chain management' (the oversight of co-ordinating and integrating the flow of goods from point of origin to destination as efficiently and cost-effectively as possible). Containerization allowed the easier movement of cargo in containers from origin to destination, more quickly, more efficiently and more cheaply. Jephson and Morgen in their history of (Danish) Maersk line illustrate how dramatic these changes were, using the presentation made by a Maersk Line senior (Ib Kruse) in 1996:[58]

1973   4 million TEU involved in moving cargo worldwide
1983   12 million TEU
1993   26 million TEU

(By 2016, volumes had risen to 130 million TEU, with cargo worth more than USD 4 trillion)[59]

Investments by the shipping industry at the time, totalled USD 65 billion and as a result, customers were receiving a much better service at a substantially lower cost, for example (in 1996), as highlighted by Ib Kruse:

1. The Freight costs for moving a TV had reduced from Danish Kroner (DKR) 3,995 to 56.55 (say USD 8)
2. Freight costs for moving a pair of sports shoes from Hong Kong to Denmark = 1.87 DKR (say 3 US cents)
3. Freight costs for a camera worth DKR 3,395 from Japan to Denmark were DKR 0.51 (about 1 US cent)

At the time of writing, these costs have actually reduced further, based on end 2019 rates for containers from China to Europe (which fluctuate) of approximately USD 1700 per 40 foot container[60] giving the freight costs for a flatscreen TV at about USD 2.1 (assuming circa 800 in a 40' container) and about US cents 1.7 per pair of shoes – based on 10,000 boxed pairs in a 40' container. (However, things can change. The Covid Pandemic from the end of 2019 has severely disrupted supply chains and freight prices have (from mid-2020) dramatically increased).

Such efficiencies and thus the ability to reduce freight costs so dramatically were brought about by three factors: firstly, the standardization of container sizes in the industry; secondly, the ability with such standardization to invest in better transportation units, increasingly large ships in particular (economy of scale) and the trucks, trains and handling equipment for 'door to door' movement of cargo; thirdly, the impact of technology, primarily information technology (IT) and communications technology which transformed supply chains by providing enhanced speed, clarity and transparency. As its port(s) increased in size and importance, Dubai, becoming a major world trading centre, was able to be at the forefront of these technological changes and be able to capitalize on them.

In the decades after the Second World War, what has been described as the 'rules based international system' evolved. This, 'framework of liberal political and economic rules, embodied in a network of international organizations and regulations',[61] allowed international trade to thrive by establishing rules and agreements that governed trade throughout the world. Such agreements were only, painstakingly, achieved after years of negotiations between individual countries, trading blocs or combinations of the two and various international organizations such as the World Trade Organization (WTO), World Customs Organization (WCO) and the United Nations Conference on Trade and Development (UNCTAD) to name but three, supplemented by shipping-related organizations such as the International Maritime Organisation (IMO) and the International Chamber of Shipping (ICS). Such bodies and international states throughout the world negotiated the physical, legal and commercial common ground that allowed a container to travel, for example, from a factory in Beijing by road to a port, by sea to Dubai and then by road to the customer inland in the UAE, reliably and (under normal circumstances) unopened, having been sealed at the shipper's premises. These shipments require substantial documentation provided by the exporter, such as a Bill of Lading (B/L), which is the contract for the carriage of goods between the shipper and the (say) shipping line, both acting as a receipt issued by the carrier taking possession of the cargo and acting as a document of title to allow the holder to claim the cargo (usually at the time of arrival). Other documents include a commercial invoice, a packing list (of the cargo being sent) and a certificate of origin (showing that the goods were in fact from the country stated on invoice). The shipping line has to provide authorities at the port of arrival with a cargo manifest and a hazardous goods manifest (lists of cargo, relating to each B/L) loaded at specific ports for discharge at specific ports. Such information paperwork, for customs and, increasingly, security purposes, had (and has) to be provided by the ship several days before arrival, with the potential for delay if the information failed to arrive. It is a complex, often labyrinthine business. For example, Maersk, the world's biggest container shipping line, found that a shipment of avocados from Mombasa to Rotterdam entailed more than 200 communications involving thirty parties. According to the World Economic Forum, referenced in *The Economist*, 'the costs of processing trade documents are as much as a fifth of those of (actually) shifting goods. Removing administrative blockages in supply chains could do more to boost international trade than eliminating tariffs'.[62]

Until the 1990s, virtually all documentation had to be transmitted in 'hard copy' and for shipping company cargo manifests, required in advance by destination ports, this was a difficult procedure – to accumulate all information in hard copies, package it up and despatch (usually by courier, by air). In the era of the fax machine, some information was transmitted using this method, but it was unreliable. The transformation was with the introduction of Electronic Data Interchange (EDI), which is a secure, automatic exchange of electronic documents between organizations, businesses and trading partners, using a standardized format that allows different computer systems to talk to each other. The UN has established the Electronic Data Interchange for Administration, Commerce and Transport (EDIFACT) setting out internationally agreed standards and guidelines.[63]

The important significance for Dubai was that as a major trading hub from the 1990s onwards, its ports, government institutions and companies, benefitted and derived competitive advantage from the fact that technological change was experienced there more rapidly than other places in the region, as various innovations were trialled there first. EDI, for example, transformed the way in which organizations traded and transferred data with each other. Of course, as always, such developments need internal impetus too and Dubai has pursued this path to such an extent that it has established 'Dubai Trade' 'the premier trade facilitation facility that offers integrated electronic services from various trade and logistics providers in Dubai under a single window'.[64] What this means in practice is that DPW itself, Dubai Customs, Economic Zones World (free-zones) are linked through one online portal with shipping lines, shipping agents, freight forwarders and haulage companies for arranging their various services and for payments and invoicing.

All shipping lines, companies and ports and government departments are now entirely dependent on IT systems to run their businesses. Such sophistication, to provide 'seamless' services for customers, is another way in which Dubai seeks to maintain its major entrepot role, as its customers (shipping lines or exporters/importers) become embedded with / used to dealing with Dubai's state-of-the-art procedures and IT systems, to the benefits of the system – and being joined-up smoothly is a major disincentive to change – particularly if competitors do not offer the same technological provisions. The full digitization of trade paperwork, now being trialled by Maersk in conjunction with IBM as highlighted in the 'The Economist' article of 24 March 2018 (referenced earlier) will eventually be 'rolled out' at the shipping line's major hubs (such as Dubai) and will help Dubai to ensure that it remains at the cutting edge of new technology, to promote efficiencies and to be 'ahead of the game' against potential competitors. In an era of rapid technological change where companies such as Amazon and Ali Baba have transformed parts of the traditional distribution chain with a focus on handling data and acting on the information it provides (such as the movement of vast numbers of shipments, where they are and where they are going), to be at the heart of the process is a major advantage.

Throughout the 1990s and beyond therefore, Dubai built on the foundations that it had established and with other potential competitors disinterested in or unable to pursue commercial and trading development, was able to establish the critical mass that more definitively excluded alternatives. As containerization evolved, ships became progressively much larger, requiring expanded facilities if they were to continue to call, Dubai continued to invest in such infrastructure expansion in the ports, free-zones and airports, when others in the region did not or could not. Size matters, and the bigger and better that Dubai became ensured that investors, businesses and individuals would choose the city rather than smaller, less well-equipped, less-proficient alternatives. The impact and development of containerization in Dubai was therefore an enabler that allowed the Emirate in Hoosteval's words, 'the freedom to break out of national borders and become part of globalised networks that connect individuals, firms and nations'. He sums up, 'the proliferation of containers and their infrastructures has become a critical part of wealth creation for cities, regions and nations by making trade a global and not just a domestic phenomenon. States that discount the significance of containers and their infrastructure do so at their peril'.[65]

In the 1990s, Jebel Ali dominated the Gulf shipping horizon with its facilities and capacity well in excess of any competitor. Its size and importance to shipping lines ensured it was at the forefront of technological and logistical developments. However, there were some developments elsewhere as other states learnt the lessons from Jebel Ali's progress and the impact of regional disputes and choke-points.

Activity elsewhere

In Oman, although Mina Qaboos in the capital, Muscat, remained the country's main port, it was small and could not be expanded. In 1996, reflecting the concerns about the 'choke-point' of the Strait of Hormuz, potentially restricting cargo flows in and out of the Gulf, and also the rapidly expanding and evolving nature of the container shipping industry, the Danish Line Maersk (part of the A P Moller Group) agreed to a joint venture with the Government of Oman, Sealand and some private investors to develop Mina Raysut in Salalah in the far south of Oman. The port had seen limited investment from the Omani government in the 1980s but Maersk's decision, 'changing a local port into today's major trans-shipment terminal',[66] was not only the first major port project in Oman but the location of Salalah (outside the Gulf and closer to the core Suez Canal East/West shipping routes) away from the Gulf, was deliberately aimed at linking in with other Maersk/Sealand networked services and acting as a regional hub. The opening of the terminal (managed by A P Moller Terminals) in 1998 allowed Maersk to combine more services more efficiently rather than the many 'point to point' patterns which were still the norm. In setting up such a (new) terminal, it posed a potential challenge to Dubai, though Maersk aimed to use it for linking other services, and the port struggled to attract non-Maersk/Sealand services because of perceived doubts about confidentiality in a terminal managed by a (competitor) line. Having invested in the terminal Maersk had to use it and from 1999 (when Maersk took over and amalgamated with Sealand), volumes rose steadily, albeit, almost entirely transhipment containers (i.e. containers relayed via Salalah en route elsewhere), on interconnecting Maersk services. There was minimal local cargo. Transhipment throughputs increased dramatically, reflecting both the overall growth of Maersk (to become, at the time of writing in 2017, the world's largest container shipping line with 12 million containers carried and over 700 ships operated according to the Maersk Website), and also increased use of owned terminals such as Salalah wherever possible, to keep revenue within the group, rather than using alternative terminals – such as Dubai.

Salalah and Dubai Throughput Comparison

	1999 TEU	2005
Salalah	645,758	2,466,824
Dubai	2,844,644	7,619,219

(Source: Drewry Maritime Research London)

In the final analysis, however, Salalah is purely a seven berth, transhipment terminal with no major hinterland industrial or commercial base backing it up, for the benefit of one line's service network efficiency and relying on (primarily) one line for its volumes. It provides no particular benefit to Oman (other than an admittedly important source of some jobs in the region) and cannot in the foreseeable future, challenge the volumes and role of Dubai.

However, also in Oman in 1999, another very different port development began in the historical port city of Sohar, on the Batinah coast outside the Straits of Hormuz, 'a joint venture between the Port of Rotterdam and Oman, with three major clusters, logistics, petrochemicals and metals (which) will soon be joined by a terminal dedicated to agricultural bulk'.[67] This long-term project was established, using the Dubai blueprint, to create Oman's main container and industrial Zone focus (very much in the image of Jebel Ali) at a more convenient site away from the restricted capital city. The port of Mina Qaboos would eventually be closed (apart from tourist/cruise ships) and cargo operations transferred to Sohar. (This finally took place on the 1st of September 2014.) Sohar's location was also very much designed to compete for container cargo entering the Gulf and to other regional centres (again based on a Jebel Ali template) though one of its major selling points, an Oman rail network, has been shelved, certainly to the UAE, as reported in the International Rail Journal in May 2016.[68] However, the growth of 'local' business backing up the port; transhipment and easy access to the UAE by road are all powerful arguments for lines to consider Sohar as an option instead of Dubai (though intra-GCC disputes and lack of seamless customs procedures mitigate against land movements) and declared throughputs reflect its progress over the last decade.

Sohar Container Throughputs (TEU)

2007	8,225
2010	101,338
2013	203,316
(2015	535,674 – Mina Qaboos no longer operating)
(2016	619,000)

(Source: Drewry Maritime Research London)

As a development that clearly took Dubai and the port and free-zone of Jebel Ali as its model – and a model to be challenged as a direct competitor – Sohar must be considered a major, if not the major competitor to Dubai for container throughputs in the future.

By the early 1990s, Bahrain was no longer posing a serious challenge to the new economic and trading power of Dubai, the (nearby) regional hostilities over the previous decade of course having had a major impact. Port throughputs once again highlight the disparity in performance, reflecting the progress of Dubai as the regional entrepot and hub even a decade after the liberation of Kuwait:

Bahrain and Dubai Container Throughput Comparison

	1991 TEU Volumes	2001 TEU Volumes
Bahrain	84,254	137,500
Dubai	1,400,000	3,501,820

(Source: Drewry Maritime Research London)

Inevitably also, the role of Bahrain as the region's airline hub had been impacted severely by the wars and also by the rise of Emirates Airline as a rival to Gulf Air.

Though airport throughputs figures seem less reliable in earlier years, by the year 2000 according to the airports' own statistics, there is a very wide gap between Bahrain and Dubai in both passengers and air freight and just over a decade later the divide has widened still more.

Dubai and Bahrain Airports – Throughputs Comparison

2000 Passengers / Freight 2011 Passengers / Freight
Bahrain 4 million / 150,000 tonnes 7.8 million / 279,000 t
Dubai 12 million / 563,000 tonnes 51 million / 2,194,264 t

(Sources: Dubai Airports Website and Bahrain International Airport Website)

Politically, Kuwait stands alone in the Arab Gulf in having an elected Parliament 'with actual legislative authority'.[69] Economically it is a rentier state par excellence, depending, as Ghabra highlights, 'on oil for 95% of its revenue and has failed to devise a strategy for economic diversification . . . no Government policies since 2004 to diversify have been implemented (and with falling oil prices) Kuwait has a budget shortfall of $15.3billion in the fiscal year to March 2015'.[70] This apparent paradox reflects the difficult reality of Kuwait's institutions, embodied in the radical constitution of 1962 (just after independence from Britain in 1961), which created a balance of power between the Al Sabah ruling family on one side (maintaining hereditary rule and executive power) and members of the urban community and merchants on the other (sharing legislative power through an elected assembly). Subsequently, this arrangement has often developed into a power struggle between the Al Sabah (government) determined to resist encroachments on its authority and the parliament equally determined to increase its oversight over legislation. Such an antagonistic structure – coupled with a cossetted population so weaned on rentier handouts that the government was even expected to recompense citizens who made bad stock market investment decisions (as in the 1983 Souk al Manakh investment bubble and the 2008 world financial crises) have made long-term planning and contentious policy choices difficult to implement. Such processes also explain why, compared with other Gulf monarchies described earlier, Kuwait's Royal Family has embarked on few soft (or hard) power initiatives, with government revenues earmarked primarily for distribution to Kuwaiti nationals in the various social and tribal constituencies.[71]

After the invasion of Kuwait in 1990 and the expulsion of the Iraqis in 1991, there was inevitably a period of rehabilitation, the most urgent task being to repair the oil fields, set on fire as the invaders retreated, making it possible to resume oil exports, earning revenue for reconstruction. Political life resurfaced, with a new National Assembly elected in 1992, but as Michael Herb has illustrated, the Al Sabah ruling family were edging towards a more absolutist rule earlier in 1990, before the invasion, when the National Assembly was replaced by a more restricted National Council. 'There is no doubt that the Iraqi invasion . . . directly caused the restoration of the 1962 constitution'.[72] The two ports were brought back into operation, and the regular flow of imports resumed, at the usual modest levels of between 200 to 300, 000 TEU per annum. The focus on hydrocarbons continued more than ever.

In Qatar in June 1995, Shaikh Hamad al Thani seized power from his father, promising to implement reforms in the way in which the country's revenues from oil and gas were used for development. Limited provisions for elections were enacted, but only for bodies such as the Chamber of Commerce and for municipal councils. Despite a lengthy consultation for a new constitution begun in 1999 and the approval of its (limited) proposals, such as a part-elected advisory council, in 2003, implementation is still awaited. The Al Thani had no intention of sharing power. As Jill Crystal clarifies, 'power remains uninstitutionalized. There is no meaningful distinction either political or legal between the person of the Emir and the institutions of state. Sovereignty is unlimited'.[73] In the social sphere, Shaikh Hamad was more liberal, allowing women the franchise and, in 1996, establishing the *Al Jazeera* broadcasting station, which was allowed great editorial freedom (apart from criticisms of Qatar). Economically, the rentier system distributed vast oil and gas wealth among the royal family and a Qatari citizen population of less than a quarter of a million. There was no attempt to match what Dubai had created – for most Qataris, at the end of the twentieth century, Dubai was primarily a destination to spend money.

The years after 1990 posed many challenges for the rulers of Saudi Arabia, with internal religious dissention stoked by the presence of foreign troops during the war to remove Iraq from Kuwait, the rise of Al Qaeda and the attack on the World Trade Centre in New York in 2001. The Kingdom was now at the epicentre of world events. However, from the perspective of Dubai, Saudi Arabi remained, as it had been in previous decades, a market and an investor, not a rival.

With the Arab Gulf's biggest population of over 30 million people, and as the world's biggest oil producer, with resultant upstream and downstream industries, Saudi Arabi has pursued, using Alice Amsden's analysis,[74] a mainly statist, late industrializing approach. This was based on oil tied to rentier revenue distribution, very different from the 'late-commercializing' trading entrepot approach of Dubai. Saudi ports in the Gulf were never traditional trading centres on the coastal littorals but emerged only in the late twentieth century to serve the internal economy, growing in line with population expansion, consumer demands and the evolution of petrochemical exports. To illustrate how modest the volumes were, compared with Dubai, Dammam port volumes grew from

232,000 TEU in 1990 – (Dubai – 913,000) to 454,000 in 2000 – (Dubai – 3,000,000).

(Source, Drewry Maritime Research, London)

In Iran, after a decade of hostilities or hostilities on its borders, coupled with a fractious relationship with the Gulf Arab states and the rest of the world, the economy and its ports were in bad shape in the 1990s. The situation became worse with US sanctions imposed in 1995. Bandar Iman Khomeini (BIK), the renamed Bandar Shahpour, near the border with Iraq, was (obviously) in no position to attract or handle container volumes. Even by the year 2000, throughputs were only a few thousand containers. The once major historical port of Bushire also languished with no container volumes to speak of. However, for logistical and security reasons the port of Bandar Abbas in the lower Gulf received investment to allow it to develop as the major entry port for Iran. It was essential to improve the connections between the port and the interior, resulting in a major construction project to build a railway line from Bandar Abbas to Bafgh (on the main line), completed in 1995.[75] As the decade progressed, volumes at Bandar Abbas increased substantially, with some direct calls from shipping lines, but the majority of business routed on feeder ships from Jebel Ali. Volumes were (in TEU):

1990 – 65,000; 1995 – 167,000; 2000 – 418,000;

(Source, Drewry Maritime Research, London).

For Iraq, there was virtually no containerized traffic into the country's ports during this time, as a result of war damage and sanctions. Imports moved over land via Syria, Kuwait or Turkey. However, the Invasion of Iraq between March to May 2003, ensured that Dubai, with its airport and Jebel Ali port, established as the region's paramount entrepot, port and distribution centre could further consolidate its position following the Anglo-American invasion. More significantly, not only was Jebel Ali used as a support base for allied forces, but in the following months and years, Dubai was to become the distribution centre for the rebuilding of Iraq as companies based in Jebel Ali free-zone would co-ordinate shipments there from various parts of the world before on-carrying them to either Kuwait (for transit over the border) or to Umm Qasr port in Iraq, once it began operating again. The Emirate was also the source of a major flow of goods (cars, cigarettes, consumer goods) that moved across to Bandar Abbas in Iran, then by road through Iran to the borders with (semi-independent) Iraqi Kurdistan.

The long-established commitment of Dubai to a liberal, open-door economic philosophy, diversifying the economy away from hydrocarbons and focussing on pro-trade and pro-business policies, exemplified by the investment in infrastructure and the establishment of large modern port and logistic facilities, was very much at variance with the actions of other regional states. However, despite their success, such measures, in isolation, would be insufficient to stave off the challenges facing small open economies from larger 'endowment rich' competitors and in many ways, the more remarkable transformation has been that in the innovative policies which created an airline, free-zones, 'economic cities' and an entire tourism (hotels/shopping/restaurants/sporting events/cultural events) industry from nothing – to supplement and feed/feed off the other economy sectors. These policies were established, refined and expanded in the successful decade of the 1990s.

Chapter review

As Anoushiravan Ehteshami has pointed out, what Dubai does today others follow tomorrow, reflecting the approach of the Ruling family in seeking the opportunities from globalization, 'in sharp contrast to the more cautious and largely sceptical views prevailing across the region.'[76] Indeed, the current ruler, Shaikh Mohammed al Maktoum has often adopted an almost Weberian approach in emphasizing the merits of hard-work and innovation, when comparing Dubai (and the UAE) to others.[77] 'Firstly we should look positively at our abilities and potential... secondly we should look positively at our future... thirdly we should stop waiting... we serve God with action, by striving for betterment, rather than waiting for a miracle... every one of us must toil and labour.'[78] Dubai's transformation was very much due to this use of 'disruptive technologies'[79] attitude of mind, to be competitive, to take action, to adapt and to innovate in new directions. In the years after 1990, Dubai's neighbours, complacently awash with fossil-fuel rents and focussed on recovery from years of disruption and war, did not feel the need to follow this approach.

As part of the focus on Dubai's unique development path, we need to highlight how this 'cluster' policy of adding value and complementary diversified, knowledge and skills-based activities was part of 'a long-term economic strategy for Dubai (that) must build on policies aimed at an improved innovation environment'.[80] Dubai developed, focussing on trade and diversified commercial activity supported by long-term and continuous infrastructure development from the 1960s onwards, recognizing that 'trading networks are a strategic asset'.[81] Some oil revenues existed from the late 1960s, but these were used to fund further trading and infrastructure development. Such an approach, as this chapter has shown, was not completely unique (Bahrain started a similar approach earlier), but its constancy and consistency certainly were. The reasons why Dubai's actual or potential rivals did not achieve the role of regional entrepot are due to above all, what Dubai did, and others didn't, in terms of provision of facilities, innovation and continuous development, particularly from a trading perspective, in the whole-hearted adoption of containerization and its logistics follow-up.

Within the UAE, throughout the 1990s and the beginning of the twenty-first century, Abu Dhabi focussed on its oil revenues and Sharjah made only modest economic progress. In Dubai however, there was concerted investment to improve infrastructural facilities and to innovate.

- Dubai Airport Terminal 2 opened in 1998, expanding airport capacity by 2 million passengers per annum
- The new Shaikh Rashid Terminal opened in 2000, increasing the Airports capacity to 23 million passengers
- Plans inaugurated to expand Jebel Ali port with a second container terminal
- Dubai 'Internet City' was inaugurated in 2000
- Work began on artificial reclaimed developments in 2001, 'Palm Jumeirah' and 'Palm Jebel Ali'
- In 2002, 'Dubai Knowledge Village' and the Dubai International Financial Centre' were inaugurated

With copious oil revenues flowing in, neither Saudi Arabia nor Kuwait had made any serious efforts to diversify their economies away from oil. Bahrain initially made some progress in its diversification but lack of infrastructural development and more effective competition from Dubai during the 1980s onwards in addition to internal political and ethnic tensions and proximity to regional wars weakened its position. Evolution in the container shipping industry and the consequent arrival of mega-container-ships which increasingly preferred to turn in Dubai (to avoid expensive/time-consuming additional port calls) ensured that Bahrain remained a modest market. Equally, Bahrain's role as the Gulf Aviation hub would begin to diminish, as a result of an ill-fated attempt in the mid-1980s to force emerging Dubai to work within Gulf Air imposed constraints, resulting in the creation of Emirates Airline. In Iraq and Iran, there were the two ancient civilizations and substantial modern states, with long-existing trading ports pre-dating the arrival of oil wealth. Iran, by the late 1970s was already experimenting with 'through-container' movements to inland Tehran and ports such as Bandar Shahpour in the north and Bandar Abbas in the south were expanding their container facilities to service this large populous nation. Iraq's maritime options were more limited, and its position mitigated against a role as a hub, but its great oil wealth promised substantial port and logistics development. Such is the speculation, but the actual results were a long stagnation from the 1980s and 1990s (which continues to resonate) with neither state able to contribute much to the economic and maritime evolution of the Gulf (and pose as competitors to Dubai) as a result of the Iran Revolution in 1978/79, the subsequent invasion of Iran by Iraq in 1980 and the invasion of Kuwait by Iraq in 1990. These events not only removed Iran and Iraq as major external commercial and logistics players but also weakened Kuwait and Bahrain's development and investment opportunities. Their absence allowed Dubai from the 1990s to benefit from lack of potential competition and also from additional business (particularly to Iran), which moved over Dubai's ports instead of directly to Iran. Oman, with a long maritime history, but arriving late on to the development path (after Sultan Qaboos' accession in 1970) and with modest fossil-fuel deposits, and Qatar, another late arrival, small but with massive gas reserves are in different categories. In both cases, there was no appreciable development of port or other facilities until the end of the twentieth century when both have started to emulate the 'Dubai Model', in Oman's case with port development (Sohar, Duqm) to offer as relay alternatives to Dubai; and in Qatar's case, a large airport/airline and sports sponsorship Dubai-emulator writ small.

These late-arriving imitators are only now in the early twenty-first century, seeking to 'cherry-pick' portions of Dubai's blueprint, reflecting both the impact that its long-term and innovative policies have had – and the time it has taken for others to catch up. The 1990s were the decade in which Dubai consolidated its position, when most of its potential rivals were inwardly focussed on hydrocarbon wealth, recovering from a decade of conflicts or isolated from the rest of the world. This consolidation and expansion of facilities and institutions was the time when the Emirate created the full linked-up package and critical mass which will make its position the more difficult to dislodge. However, the years at the turn of the century also increasingly saw the growth of a hubris in which Dubai seemed to believe its own rhetoric – that it was infallible and all-prescient – and to lose control of the scale and type of developments that were being agreed, as investors flocked to be part of the Dubai bonanza.

Chapter 5

THE NEW CHALLENGES OF THE TWENTY-FIRST CENTURY (2004–PRESENT DAY)

No region of the globe is so simultaneously localised and globalised, so rooted in unique traditions and yet so interactive with the world.[1]

In the early years of the twenty-first century, Dubai, together with much of the world, continued to forge ahead in what seemed to be an era of trading buoyancy and optimism. Even the occupation of Iraq from late 2003, by American and allied forces, benefitted the Emirate's logistics facilities as the materials for the re-construction of the devastated country's oil fields and infrastructure were routed via Jebel Ali. The city was feted as a paradigm of model capitalist development and vast expansion plans were put into place, involving the creation of new developments on areas reclaimed from the sea. Despite all the evidence of Dubai's achievements, some assessments of the city ascribed its success purely to fortunate circumstances and being in the right place. The ruler of Dubai, Shaikh Mohammed Al Maktoum (perhaps understandably), has commented that 'when they want to diminish your achievements, they attribute them to luck'.[2] In 2004, Shaikh Zayed Al Nahyan, the President of the UAE since 1971 and ruler of Abu Dhabi since 1966 died, succeeded as ruler and president by his son Shaikh Khalifa. This event was to mark the beginning of a shift in the attitude of Abu Dhabi to its position and that of Dubai in the UAE.

In Dubai, the calm and efficient transfer of power from one Al Maktoum ruler to the next, maintaining stability, has certainly contributed to Dubai's reputation and economic evolution. Shaikh Rashid's son Maktoum had assumed power after his father's death in 1990, but to reflect the increasing popularity, status and capabilities of Shaikh Rashid's second son Mohammed, he was officially declared crown prince in 1995. 'Officially Maktoum remained ruler, but Mohammed was effectively the Premier . . . and as a result when Maktoum died . . . in 2006, there was little real transition of power in Dubai.'[3] Shaikh Mohammed Bin Rashid has continued to be ruler of Dubai and prime minister of the UAE since 2006. (The process of careful selection continues with the confirmation of Shaikh Mohammed's eldest (surviving) son Hamdan (born in 1982) as crown prince. A telegenic, Sandhurst-educated poet who goes by the nickname of 'Fazza' and who, online, has millions of 'followers', on Instagram (Fazza @faz3), he is gradually assuming some of his father's responsibilities, as preparation for future leadership).

These calm internal regime transitions were soon to face major external challenges. Firstly, the worldwide economic crisis, to which Dubai, it transpired, was particularly exposed; and secondly, the popular insurrections in the MENA region in 2011, known as the 'Arab Spring'.

The arrangement in place even before the creation of a Federal State in 1971, whereby Abu Dhabi, the biggest and richest Emirate remained quiescent and allowed Dubai, by now a worldwide 'brand', to continue to dominate and define the external perceptions of the Emirates, as it had done for half a century was, early in the new century, to change completely. The new generation of the ruling Al Nahyan family, signalling a distinct shift from the approach of Shaikh Zayed, began to raise the profile of Abu Dhabi, in part by ensuring that public pronouncements from the Emirates came from Abu Dhabi in order that the outside world should recognize that the capital of the UAE was in that city rather than Dubai. Second, Abu Dhabi began to plunder the Dubai playbook by not only seeking prestigious and headline-garnering event sponsorships (such as Formula 1 Grand Prix) but also, with the creation of Etihad ('Union') Airlines at the end of 2003, a determined effort to compete with Dubai's well-established Emirates Airline – as a representative of the UAE. This determination to raise the profile of Abu Dhabi into more tangible areas, with soft-power status projects (such as a Louvre Museum in the city) as highlighted by Stefan Hertog,[4] inevitably creating, though never admitted, head-on competition with Dubai, was to be even more dramatically emphasized with the announcement of the replacement of Mina Zayed by a vast container and port complex, begun in 2008. Mina (Port) Khalifa (named after the Abu Dhabi ruler and UAE president) saw the first stage opened in 2012, backed up by a huge 40 sq. km (Industrial City of Abu Dhabi) industrial zone – only about 60 km from Jebel Ali.

However, the events that secured and formally established Abu Dhabi's undisputed position as the power-centre of the Emirates, confirming the prescient warnings of Christopher Davidson,[5] arose as a result of the Global Financial Crisis in 2007–8. Dubai's expansion, particularly into more speculative spectacular property and reclamation developments, such as the high-end 'Palm' and 'World' projects, left the Emirate fiscally over-exposed 'when Dubai's external debt stood at USD 115 billion, representing about 152% of GDP',[6] without sufficient resources to meet debt obligations on outstanding loans, primarily owed by major Dubai companies sponsored by the Ruling family. Such companies included Nakheel (property), Emaar (property) and Dubai World (ports, property and logistics) with DPW liabilities alone considered to have reached the region of USD 59 billion of which USD 26 billion needed to be restructured. Though the precise details of the 'rescue package' may never be known, Abu Dhabi certainly made major short-term loans, USD 10 billion is the figure usually mentioned,[7] to allow DPW's Nakheel to repay an Islamic Bond (sukuk), but the new relationship between the two Emirates was illustrated in dramatic fashion on 4 January 2010 when the opening ceremony of the world's tallest building in Dubai, unexpectedly christened the 830-metre skyscraper 'Burj Khalifa' rather than the expected 'Burj Dubai'.

The fact that this iconic building, representing and encapsulating the pride, ambition and appetite of Dubai for world attention, should at the eleventh hour, be named after the (Abu Dhabi) President of the UAE demonstrated in no uncertain terms to the outside world the overt and clearly delineated pecking-order that was now in place, but in reality, the fundamental structure of the governance, economy and intra-emirate relationships had settled more firmly into position, rather than radically changed. Abu Dhabi with 87 per cent of the UAE landmass and 96 per cent of the UAE's oil reserves,[8] had been for several decades the wealthiest Emirate, in addition to being the capital of the federation, inevitably therefore, de facto, the most powerful. Pumping over 2.5 million barrels a day for many years, with revenues from oil and downstream petrochemical industries (such as polymers) ploughed into the sovereign wealth fund handled by the Abu Dhabi Investment Authority (ADIA), the world's fourth largest,[9] Abu Dhabi's wealth had long far outstripped that of Dubai. Since independence in 1971, the most important position in the UAE, the presidency, was effectively reserved for Abu Dhabi, acknowledging its pre-eminence, with the prime ministership reserved for Dubai. However, this internal distribution of power was, for decades after the creation of the UAE, obfuscated and concealed by the apparent indifference of Abu Dhabi towards external recognition and their apparent willingness for the Al Maktoum ruling family in Dubai to garner the commercial and soft-power headlines internationally. More clearly from 2004 onwards, it was clear that this policy had changed, and Abu Dhabi was determined to obtain the status and international recognition that it felt was its due.

However, once Abu Dhabi had clearly established its authority and status, the delicate mechanism of interaction between the UAE's major players resumed its course. Dubai and its various companies restructured and repaid their loans and by 2011–2 confidence and momentum in the economy and property market had been restored. The Emirate, as the recognized commercial hub of the UAE, continued its multifaceted economic diversification in preparation for the next major event – World Expo 2020 and Abu Dhabi, as the undisputed Political Capital of the UAE, continued to place focus on its oil and gas industry while establishing the industrial and Mina Khalifa port zone to 'complement' Jebel Ali. Mina Khalifa's size and ability (like Jebel Ali) to take the largest container ships; its new 'super-post-panamax' gantry cranes and the backdrop of the developing heavy industrial zone have persuaded more lines to make direct calls and volumes have increased since its opening in 2012 and the closure of Mina Zayed.

Mina Khalifa Abu Dhabi (TEU) Volumes

Year	Volume
2013	901,772
2014	1,137,679
2015	1,504,293
2016	1,530,446

(Source: Drewry Maritime Research London)

Abu Dhabi's belated assertiveness, in the course of just over a decade, is inevitably in part, a reaction and response to the high-profile international reputation and success of Dubai, a determination to ensure that the capital (and the Al Nahyan family) are no longer overshadowed by their old brotherly adversaries. By combining the oil and gas financial wealth with many elements of the 'Dubai Model' (such as seaports/airport expansion and airline) as well as the professionalism and soft-power policies conducted so successfully by Dubai, Abu Dhabi has emerged from its slumbers to become a major participant in regional and international affairs.

Sharjah remains in the shadow of Dubai. Though it has some (lower end) industry, it is used by many Dubai workers as a cheaper alternative for housing with the consequence that roads between the Emirate and Dubai are heavily congested during the morning and evening peak periods. There has been little effective infrastructure expansion. The ruler has placed his focus on its more traditional and less frenetic reputation with an emphasis on artistic and educational credentials with a variety of museums, the Sharjah Biennial and an annual book fair. Khor Fakkan, despite remaining a large, modern, efficient Container Terminal, has lost much of its business as a result of the consolidation of the shipping industry and its lack of a cargo base.

The other Emirates, Ajman and Umm Al Quwain (UAQ) are very small in size and economic clout, with ports to match. Fujairah, traditionally aligned more with Dubai than its immediate neighbours, was an early proponent (like Khor Fakkan) of a container hub outside the Gulf, handling volumes of over 600,000 TEU per annum at its peak in the mid-1990s. This activity gradually declined, and attention switched instead to offshore supply work and as an oil terminal in the last decade. Dubai Ports World (DPW) managed the container terminal from 2005, although the agreement was terminated early, in 2017.[10] This was probably a sensible decision as, like Khor Fakkan, it lacks a local cargo base of any real size. Ras al Khaimah (RAK), also attempted a brief (and ultimately pointless) flirtation with a container terminal at the start of this century but its small size and inability to compete with the scale and efficient big-ship facilities of Jebel Ali or Khor Fakkan saw its meagre throughputs disappear almost entirely by 2010. Despite this being the case, for reasons that are as yet unclear, the Chinese major Port Operator (Hong Kong based) Hutchinson, has recently announced Terminal operation contracts at UAQ and RAK to add to its existing operation in Ajman.[11] None of these operations, in view of the minimal volumes handled, will have any real impact on Dubai's Jebel Ali in the foreseeable future, but they certainly indicate the increasing impact and influence of China on the region, a focal point of China's 'Belt and Road' initiative.

Downturn and resurgence

As Dubai and the UAE began to adjust to a new UAE President, a new relationship and a new Dubai ruler from 2006, external events convulsed Dubai, revealing 'some weak structural features in the economy of Dubai that need to be identified and addressed'.[12] The global financial crash from 2007–8 onwards was a crisis that exposed the Emirate's (over) dependence on highly leveraged, external debt to fund expansion and its sensitivity to worldwide economic cycles, like all smaller, open economies integrated into world markets. For three or four years, like economies elsewhere, there was a serious downturn in economic activity and major developments failed to take place or were mothballed. However, by 2011–12, Dubai had made a strong recovery with a return to high growth levels as a result of initial government intervention to support banks and improve liquidity, as well as the fundamental strength of the diversified trading, financial services, technological innovation, media and tourism clusters in the region's main commercial centre – not forgetting the financial assistance from brotherly Abu Dhabi.

Once the Global economy started to move again, Dubai moved too because, notwithstanding the mistakes and over-commitment at the beginning of the twenty-first century, the strategic development plans, that had created the infrastructure and institutional framework for a successful growth path, were still in place, and the Emirate was continuing to act as a funnel for international trade, one of the worldwide 'entrepot ports which live by distribution'.[13] There were certainly lessons to be learnt and Al Faris and Soto highlight three weaknesses that need to be addressed in Dubai's development trajectory; firstly, that productivity needs to improve rather than simply adding more cheap labour (and the focus on higher-skills free-zones clearly reflects that this is being addressed); secondly, that the economy 'exhibits significant vulnerability to external shocks'[14] and although this is to a certain extent inevitable, better fiscal and budgeting procedures need to be adopted; thirdly, that there was too much emphasis on (relatively unsupervised) government-related entities (GREs) particularly in the real-estate and construction sectors in promoting economic growth – the property development GRE, Nakheel, for example, which had needed substantial bail-out assistance in the crisis as a result of too much speculative development based on borrowed money.

In some ways, the financial crisis was a useful wake-up call to a Dubai, which, if not exactly complacent, had begun, in its much-feted success, to exhibit signs of over-inflated self-regard. The financial shock serving as a reminder that there were both structural issues that needed attention and that the need to remain innovative and competitive was more important than ever as other regional states began also to diversify using many of the same principles that had built Dubai. In the aftermath of the global downturn, there was also an urgent need to restore the Emirate's reputation for financial competence. Some of the recommendations have already been highlighted, to improve economic performance in the longer term, but others include: better financial transparency and regulation; a better primary and secondary education system; more skills-based/value-added job creation; more focus on exports and re-exports, particularly to widen the scope of commodities (gold is over-represented) and partners (Iran and India predominate); reform the *kafala* system to improve efficiency and quality and flexibility of labour; improving bureaucratic procedures for tourist visitors and among government departments. The next decade will show whether Dubai has the determination and thoroughness to push through these reforms, to avoid the mistakes of the recent past.

By the end of 2010, just as the economy and business confidence had begun to recover, major regional upheavals threatened more destabilization. Described, somewhat optimistically, as the 'Arab Spring', the various anti-government protests that began in late 2010 in Tunisia and spread throughout much of the MENA region in 2011 were motivated by great popular dis-satisfaction with oppressive and incompetent regimes that had failed to improve opportunities for participation in government, end corruption and expand economic opportunities and standards of living. However, each protest was coloured by the local circumstances. In the Gulf area, Shia-majority Bahrain experienced serious disturbances; there was agitation in Saudi Arabia's traditionally overlooked eastern region with its Shia population; demonstrations in various cities in Oman reflected criticism about corruption and lack of jobs, and insurrections began in Syria against the repressive Al Assad regime. In the UAE, there was neither the oppression, poverty or lack of opportunity among the national population nor any real disconnect between them and their rulers, to generate serious dissent. (However, a group of five academics were arrested, to be 'pardoned' soon afterwards, after calling for greater political liberalization.) The Federal government also (perhaps not coincidentally) decided to increase support for the poorer Northern Emirates in March 2011, pledging to invest USD 1.6 billion on infrastructure over three years.[15] Despite the fact that Dubai was essentially unaffected directly by the events of the Arab Spring, the longer-term repercussions, particularly the resultant civil war in Syria and its consequences such as the Qatar crisis, are still being played out.

In the new architecture of the Gulf, created by the Syrian civil war and the schism with Qatar, the newly assertive Abu Dhabi, however, has moved from quiescence to 'the Arab World's most interventionist regime . . . a little Sparta' (according to US Defence Secretary, James Mattis),[16]sending troops to Yemen, setting up military bases in Somaliland and, in concert with Saudi Arabia and Bahrain, blockading Qatar. This approach is not necessarily best for a Dubai that has traditionally eschewed confrontation, and could seriously undermine the UAE's (particularly Dubai's) reputation as a neutral space. A much more active UAE foreign policy, bandwagoning with Saudi Arabia in the proxy cold war against Iran, has taken place during the tenure of the president's younger brother Shaikh Mohammed Bin Zayed Al Nayan (MBZ), as the UAE president Shaikh Khalifa Al Nayan is apparently ill, and has not been seen in public since 2014. It is not clear, as yet, what results this determination to pursue an activist and assertive UAE foreign policy will have – although 2020 saw a pulling back of activity – but such policies are without doubt the antithesis of those pursued by Dubai during the last half century. A contrast perhaps because 'virtually everything in Abu Dhabi has come about because of oil'.[17]

The rapid recovery from the impact of the 2008 financial crisis, reflected the strength of the structure that Dubai had created, institutions, infrastructure and innovation. As has been described, the long-established commitment of Dubai to a liberal, open-door economic philosophy, diversifying the economy away from hydrocarbons and focussing on pro-trade and pro-business policies, exemplified by the investment in infrastructure and the establishment of large modern port and logistic facilities, was very much at variance with the actions of other regional states. This transformational strategy is increasingly being copied, adapted and adopted by Dubai's neighbours as they too seek to diversify their economies and mark-out distinctive identities. By the beginning of the twenty-first century, Dubai had also started to innovate in even more remarkable ways, as the natural extensions to the structures already in place.

Tourism and the establishment of a brand

Perhaps the most startling development of all, confirming Dubai's reputation as the most radical innovator, was the growth from a standing start of a tourism industry, which, according to the statistics website Statista.com, provided Dubai with 14.87 million overnight tourists in 2016, an increase of over 75 per cent from 2010, making the Emirate the fourth most visited city worldwide (using data from Mastercard).[18] The Middle East in general, with some exceptions, and the Gulf in particular until the 1990s, had little or no track record as a major destination for leisure tourists. Excepting more specialized locations such as Egypt or Jordan, there was a perceived lack of distinctive sights, lack of facilities, fears of regional violence and concerns about the cultural and social acceptability of tourists in conservative societies. However, what the Gulf had in abundance was a year-round hot and sunny climate with virtually no rain or cloud cover, very attractive to cold weather residents of northern Europe for example, who had since the 1960s and the onset of mass tourism, increasingly started to visit warm-weather regions such as the Mediterranean for holidays. What was needed was both the tourist infrastructure to accommodate visitors and activities to occupy them, coupled with a marketing effort to persuade potential customers that Dubai was a safe and welcoming destination – no easy task in a region identified with instability and war.

Although, with Dubai's emergence as a commercial centre, basic hotels for business travellers were in existence, 'the true beginning of the hotel industry in Dubai came in 1959, when the Airlines Hotel was established. By the late 1960s, Dubai had more hotels than any other Emirate, due to the fact that its population was growing more rapidly and business was booming, expanding and diversifying.'[19] The 85 room, Ambassador Hotel was opened in 1968 (close to the ruler's office), considered the first notable hotel structure, and 'the ruler of Dubai used the venue for official lunches and dinner banquets until the 1980s'.[20] In the 1980s, there were only a handful of 'Five-Star' hotels in Dubai, such as the Sheraton, The Intercontinental near the Creek and the Hilton adjacent to the World Trade Centre. However, the growth of Dubai's Emirates Airline from the 1990s onwards and the expanded airport ensured that they together (in addition to other airlines) could provide the capacity to carry the increasing numbers of business and, gradually, leisure tourists to fill this limited capacity. For travellers from Western Europe for example, the flight was six or seven hours, and after the fall of the Soviet Union, the flight time from Moscow, for the surge in sun-deprived

Russians to a safe neutral location, was only four hours. From this time onwards, there was a huge hotel building surge to cater to demand. Some indication of the scale of expansion can be shown by highlighting the increase in twenty-five years from 1993. In 1993 there were 167 hotels with 9,383 rooms, but by 2018 this number had risen to 689 hotels (including 197 hotel apartments) with 108,807 rooms (including 24,908 hotel apartment rooms).[21]

As described in the last chapter, in 1996 the 'Dubai Shopping Festival' was launched, essentially an attempt to attract overseas family tourists with lower prices throughout the souqs (markets) and shops and shopping malls of the Emirate for a specified period. The shopping festival was aimed not simply at Europeans but also for travellers from South Asia (who often had family or friends living in Dubai) and for Arab tourists from the Gulf keen to have a 'retail experience' in the famous trading city, an Arab city and a Muslim country, but more relaxed than their homelands. Similarly, Iranian tourists were able to visit to buy a wider range of goods more cheaply and more obtainable than in economically sanctioned Iran, also taking the opportunity to holiday in a less restricted environment close by – with which they had a long and close connection. Such was the success of this innovative idea – persuading people from a wide spectrum of locations to visit Dubai to spend money – that Shaikh Mohammed Al Maktoum could state (in 2014) that the direct economic returns of the festival were estimated at USD 4 billion a year.[22]

By 2008, to cater to increasing demand, not only were two new creek-crossing bridges required (the Business Bay Bridge and the new Maktoum bridge), but a low-cost airline, 'Fly Dubai' was inaugurated, Terminal 3 at Dubai airport was completed, and the 1,500 room Atlantis hotel was launched on the reclaimed Palm development. In 2009, the first stage of the Dubai Metro began operating and the 'Dubai Mall' the world's largest shopping mall opened. Over the succeeding years, there have been more 'bolt-on' efforts to widen the spread of Dubai's attractions, ranging from desert safaris to water-parks and hundreds of hotels and restaurants with celebrity chefs, but the original ethos to attract tourists remains much the same, to market the Emirate as a relaxed and safe place to spend time on the beach in sunny weather in good quality accommodation. The focus has shifted over the years, particularly as Emirates Airline has widened its scale of activity, to include more Asian tourists in addition to those from Europe and Russia, in what is now, even more, a very cosmopolitan city. However, it is important to emphasize that the tourism policy has followed, very much the same, professional logic, as that applied to the free-zones – to determine the environment best-suited to potential customers (in this case tourists), that can involve as many elements of Dubai's infrastructure and activities as possible (airline, hotels) and then implement it. More tourists mean more people flying on Emirates; more Emirates destinations means more visitors using the Hotels and shops of Dubai; more visitors means more spending on goods and services in the shopping malls and hotels built by Dubai and Emirati family companies or foreign companies with a majority local partner; more businesses and economic activity mean more job opportunities for local people (even if the vast majority of tourism/hospitality related jobs are filled by non-locals).

The merit of this approach is that there is now a vast industry, created from nothing, which not only supplies leisure tourism but also provides facilities both for local businesses and their visitors, and international business visitors, in addition to the international conference industry. Dubai's location, midway between Europe and Asia makes it an attractive, easily accessible location for international conferences. A major event booking site shows literally dozens of English language conferences scheduled during the year on a myriad of subjects, ranging from '10th Dental Facial Cosmetic Conference and Exhibition', 'International Child and Adult Behavioural Health Conference', 'Global Innovation Summit', 'Blockchain Investment Technology Conference Middle East', 'The 5th Annual GCC Pharmacy Congress' and 'The 2nd International Oil and Gas Conference'.[23] Dubai's 'connectability' with the logistics facilities on the ground (including the region's first Metro rail system opened in 2009) and the focus of Emirates Airline and most other airlines – because Dubai attracts many leisure and business travellers – has also resulted in winning the right to hold and subsequent preparations for, 'Dubai 2020', the latest in a series of World Trade Fairs, held every five years (the first being held at London's Crystal Palace in 1851). As a result of the Covid pandemic, the Expo (due to open in October 2020) will now open in October 2021, will last for six months, is expected to attract 25 million visitors and the site (near Jebel Al) will cover 438 hectares.[24]

However, despite the successes, it is not hard to see how expansion on this scale, relying on increasing numbers of visitors, has potential drawbacks, even though Dubai is unique in the region in offering such a broad range of activities for business and leisure. Such a reliance on sheer numbers of tourists (and business people) to feed into the treadmill of hotel development is dependent both on potential visitors regarding Dubai as a safe, dependable location and that the stream of arrivals does not diminish because of external factors (such as an economic or political downturn in those markets that supply the visitors). Tunisia and Egypt, whose economies were devastated when their tourist industries lost most of their customers (in 2015 and 2017 respectively), due to security fears, are only the two most recent examples of how perceptions can change very quickly. The continuous provision of new facilities inevitably gives rise to concerns about, 'over-heating' of the real-estate market, something with which Dubai has had experience when the financial bubble collapsed in 2007–8, and clearly, this must be a concern when the dust has settled in mid-2022, after the closure of the (rescheduled) Dubai World Expo fair. However, the experience of Dubai, as we have seen, is that they have become proficient at facing down external economic and political crises over several decades, learning when to retrench and to adapt to circumstances, but always being able to bounce back because of the excellence of their infrastructure, governance and professionalism. In part, this is very much, as detailed in previous pages, because without the cushioning natural resources on which to fall back, Dubai policy makers have had to take long-term, often difficult decisions, trusting in their judgement. This approach, reflected in its liberal economy and society opened to the world, is very different from the intrinsically conservative policies of its fossil-fuelled neighbours, comfortably living off rentier incomes– but comes with the inherent risks.

Business writers have described this approach as strategic trajectory, by creating an asset or assets, improving and expanding those assets, asset acceleration (such as more free-zones/ Emirates Airline expansion) followed by leveraging the assets (different types of free-zones / tourism) to cater for increasing and pent-up demand. Assets can then be re-invested (enhanced and improved) and re-invented (new forms and new directions). This model requires leadership that is innovative and takes calculated risks, a lean organizational structure to accelerate decision-making, open-mindedness to outside ideas and competition, good communication and a professional business culture.[25] This description very much encompasses both the 'business state' mentality of Dubai, recognizing 'that bringing the world into the Emirate will allow it to compete more effectively on an international scale',[26] and the difference between the Emirate and its neighbours, who have tended to a more insular approach focussed on and cocooned by, apparently limitless fossil-fuel revenues.

The strategy to attract more visitors to Dubai needed more than just hotels. It soon became clear that both holiday-makers and other visitors required activities of interest to occupy them – or attract them in the first place. High-profile sporting events not only served as attractions in their own right for visitors but also helped to raise Dubai's profile away from simply 'a desert with a beach', especially as it became clear that the UAE climate in the winter months was attractively sunny and dry but not unduly hot – perfect for outdoor sport. The first events began in a low-key way. The Rugby Sevens competition was sponsored in 1987, by newly founded Emirates Airline, recognizing a popular locally organized competition involving mainly British expatriates and by 1996 had evolved to the extent that Dubai was hosting Rugby Sevens World Cup qualifying rounds. In 1989 the Dubai Desert Classic Golf competition was inaugurated and became part of the European tour events involving many of the world's top professional golfers. The Dubai Tennis Championships followed in 1993, as part of the ATP World Tour, now sponsored by Dubai Duty Free and in 1996, the Dubai World Cup horse race festival began, once again with generous prize money (increased to USD 10 million in 2007), attracting the world's top horse breeders and jockeys. In 2009, the Dubai Cricket Stadium opened. The strategy has succeeded in establishing Dubai as a centre for worldwide sporting events and all these various competitions now attract thousands of spectators who travel internationally to see them or to participate, and also to raise awareness of Dubai and its brands (such as Emirates) that sponsor them. Local businesses also benefit from the events and from the tie-ins to their own activities. As with Dubai's other innovative policies, regional neighbours have now also recognized the value of such high-profile international sporting events and Bahrain (Grand Prix Formula 1 Motor Racing), Abu Dhabi (Formula 1) and Qatar (Tennis and Football) have all hastened to obtain 'an event'. They are acknowledging that not only do such occasions provide a commercial boost but also provide the eagerly sought reputational affirmation of competence and inclusion into the elite club of nations deemed worthy to host the most prestigious international events – Hertog's 'Quest for Significance'.[27] As with other examples, Dubai was a pioneer in this field and pursued and developed the idea, using the best local and international talent.

In 2007 the Gulf Art Fair began, with the Dubai Culture and Arts Authority formed in March 2008. In recent years the scope has widened to encompass more cerebral activities and events, as Dubai seeks to move on to the next stage, to be recognized as a cultural centre in addition to the commercial and sporting reputation it has already established. Events such as Chess Competitions; Arabic Poetry Contests; the Emirates Airline Dubai Literary Festival (now on a very large scale, established for ten years since 2009 and open for a week with over 180 international authors participating).[28] The latest ventures are the Dubai Arts Art District in Al Quoz including scores of art spaces and galleries, pop-ups and performing spaces and the design district, 'that nurtures emerging local talent and provides a home for the region's creative thinkers'.[29] Dubai has clearly determined that to achieve full international respect and 'legitimacy' requires creative endeavour beyond that of the free-zones, it requires artistic, creative and literary heft too, deftly emphasizing and ensuring that local and regional talent, still at the fledgling stage, is fully nurtured and showcased in addition to overseas participants. As with the use of sporting events as vehicles for marketing and establishing a reputation for substance, significance and legitimacy, other neighbours have followed the Dubai trail, with Abu Dhabi (The Louvre) and Qatar (museums showcasing collected works of art) in particular, opting for high-profile arts projects. However, as Qatar has discovered, with accusations of bribery to obtain the football World Cup in 2022 and serious international condemnation about the conditions in which workers building the stadia are having to work, such high-profile events can, if things go awry, end up as a public-relations disaster rather than adding lustre to the national reputation. Even Abu Dhabi experienced substantial criticism during the construction of the 'Louvre' museum, but these experiences merely highlight the importance of such projects to the Gulf states as manifestations of 'national glory', status – and the success of the Dubai model, which the neighbours are only too eager to emulate.

Dubai has itself skated on very thin ice in this respect too, with a reputation in the early years of the twenty-first century for brash, attention-gathering projects such as the 'Palms' and the 'World', offshore reclaimed land, real-estate developments, which even at the time appeared to owe more to hubris than genuine commercial need. Symptomatic of this overheated environment, in which real-estate projects would be oversubscribed and auctioned off to purchasers before work had even started, was the decision to construct the world's tallest building, the 163-storey, 830-metre-tall Burj Dubai. However, the worldwide financial crisis of 2007–8 onwards burst the real-estate bubble enveloping Dubai and construction stopped or was severely curtailed on the offshore island projects. Bailed out by Abu Dhabi, the Burj Dubai was, at its inauguration in 2010 as we have already described, renamed the Burj Khalifa. That this was an embarrassment is no doubt, but it serves as a reminder that Dubai, in making many risky and innovative decisions will get some of them wrong – or at least not as right as they might have been. What is important is not that 'mistakes' are made, but that lessons are learnt and that the position is recoverable. It took several years before it was apparent that Jebel Ali and the free-zones were not white elephants but prescient investments for the future – and within a few years the Burj Khalifa too, has become a successful iconic symbol of modern Dubai.

At the time of writing it is clear that the impact of the Covid pandemic has had a dramatic impact on all these activities but there is no reason why, when the pent-up demand bounce-back gathers momentum, that Dubai should not continue to benefit.

Economic outreach

In 2005, Dubai Ports World (DPW) was formed, amalgamating the separate operations of Dubai Ports Authority (DPA), and Dubai Ports International (DPI) which was established in 1999, 'to manage and operate container terminals and other facilities outside the UAE'.[30] DPI's first venture had been in Jeddah, beginning terminal operations in September 1999, followed soon after by a contract in June 2000, to manage the entire port of Djibouti, with concessions secured in Visakhapatnam in Eastern India in 2002, Constanza in Rumania in 2003 and Cochin (Kochi) in Southern India in 2004. Making an impact of a more tangible nature and one right at the heart of Dubai's logistical ethos, was the decision to move out of the 'comfort-zone', export the expertise that Dubai ports had developed and seek out overseas container terminals to manage. It is no coincidence that the timing of this approach to establish a presence, and compete head-on with established operators, was at the beginning of the twenty-first century, in the buoyant, 'end of history'[31] economic enthusiasm of rampant globalization. Dubai saw the opportunity not just for good commercial benefits by operating and managing container terminals elsewhere, but also to emphasize and expand the professional abilities of its port management by seeking global outreach – and by association enhancing the reputation of Dubai itself, still a largely unknown quantity in many areas at this time. This logic was very much the same as that used to use Emirates Airline as an extension of Dubai quality and professionalism – reflecting the retaining of focus on the trading and ports and shipping-related activity.

There was a determination to grow quickly, but organic growth, picking up opportunities one at a time, could not achieve this objective and many key port terminals were already in the hands of established competitors. Accordingly, the first major foray into becoming a major force in the industry took place later in 2005, when the new DPW took over the terminal operations of the American CSX Corporation (now the parent company of Malcolm McLean's Sealand), adding interests in nine terminals to the portfolio, including operations in Hong Kong, Tianjin, and Yantai in China, Germany, Australia and South America. The absorption of CSX Terminals moved Dubai Ports into the top six global terminal operators and dramatically enhanced its international footprint, in particular by establishing a presence in the fast-growing Asian and Latin American markets.[32] It was the takeover of P&O ports a year later in March 2006 for USD 6.8 billion that really catapulted DPI into one of the world's major Terminal operators, at the same time underlining the economic transition of power away from long-established historic companies such as the UK's P&O into the hands of new, aggressive focussed businesses from other parts of the world.

P&O's terminal activities included operations in Australasia, the UK, India and South Asia, South East Asia, Canada and Continental Europe and their presence in the hands of Dubai ports, pushed DPI into fourth place worldwide, behind traditional major players, Port of Singapore (PSA) and Hutchison Port Holdings of Hong Kong. P&O's terminal assets, also, however, included operations in several American ports, Baltimore, Miami, Newark, New Orleans, New York and Philadelphia. When news broke of the potential arrival of an Arab, Gulf country 'taking control' over (actually only operating and managing) such facilities (ignoring the inconvenient facts that US security and customs would continue in place), there was a major political and furore in the United States over supposed 'security' issues, despite the fact that Republican US president George W Bush fully endorsed the arrangement. This episode, even at the time, served as a salutary reminder both that traditional global powers resented the arrival of new competitors in their own 'back yards', and also that (as evidenced in subsequent elections in the UK, Europe and particularly the US), there was a growing awareness that the impact of globalism was not just in one direction. To their credit, with a minimum of fuss, to assuage the vehement opposition and avoid political embarrassment for the US administration, Dubai Ports, now Dubai Ports World (DPW) since September 2005, on-sold the US terminals to a US entity, American International Group's investment division.

In 2018, Dubai Port World's Marine terminals account for '77 ports in 40 countries'.[33] Certainly, this substantial portfolio reflects the determination of the Emirate to implement its ports and shipping expertise on a broader canvas, also achieving the need to tie in trading and commercial links on a global scale with these other terminals and the container lines that serve them in an environment that increasingly demands 'integrated transport networks'. Inevitably, some businesses have not developed as anticipated (e.g. Kochi Vallarpadam); others have run into political and financial problems (Djibouti), while others are still establishing themselves or only recently acquired (Berbera). However, overall, this policy, of planting the DPW (and thus Dubai) flag on the map has been very successful, with DPW now at number four worldwide based on numbers of TEU handled (2015 data).[34]

1. Hutchison Port Holdings (China) 83.8 million
2. COS CO Pacific (China) 68.7 million
3. Port of Singapore Authority Intl. 64.1 million
4. DPW 62.1 million
5. AP Moeller Terminals (Denmark) 36 million

However, achieving a business on such a scale is not without its pitfalls. In the early heady years, when it was essential to secure new terminal operating and managing contracts, little attention was paid to the price. Terminals in India and elsewhere were secured regardless of cost. As Notteboom and Rodrigue highlight, in 2005 DPW took over CSX Terminals, paying fourteen times the level of Earnings before Interest, Taxes, Depreciation and Amortization (EBITDA). In 2006, the takeover-price paid to P&O ports was nineteen times the EBITDA level.[35] From a commercial perspective, such prices would ensure that a commercial return on the investment would take decades to achieve, at best – but of course, the perspective of Dubai was not entirely purely commercial, it was to establish the business and Dubai as a world-class player, and they were prepared to pay the price to do so. The container terminal operating industry price bubble burst, along with the rest of global speculative finance in 2007–8 and subsequent acquisitions have been more cautious, with an eye on realistic returns. However, the industry is one for the long-term, requiring substantial investment in capital equipment (cranes and quayside handlers), infrastructure and information technology. In an environment where container shipping lines continue to amalgamate, DPW are in a strong position, by virtue of their worldwide scale of operations and ability to negotiate on a worldwide basis and to ensure that lines and consortia continue to operate at their terminals.

The expansion of logistics expertise overseas was followed by Dubai National Air Travel Agency (DNATA), developing its growth in line with the spread and reputation of Emirates Airline, 'one of the world's largest air-service providers . . . at 130 airports every day . . . (with) 63 catering facilities in 13 countries'.[36] Similarly, and again following the 'joined-up-thinking' approach, the government-owned Dubai Holding group is 'a global investment conglomerate operating in 14 countries and employing over 20,000 people'.[37] The group, in line with the points outlined above, states that it aims 'at an innovation driven, knowledge-based economy'[38] and includes companies such as the Jumeirah Group (Luxury Hotels) and others involved in property, finance and media.

The intended impact of all these strategies was and is to continue to build a diverse base of activities, to remain competitive in a competitive global world and to establish a reputation for Dubai – for flexibility, innovation, quality and reliability – not simply in Dubai itself. Such a reputation and deliberate image-setting we can certainly define as a brand, established by using all the multifaceted elements that the Emirate could showcase to the world, be they the Airline (Emirates), architecture (Burj Dubai), resorts, sporting events and a stable, cosmopolitan lifestyle. There is even a Brand Dubai website, 'the creative arm of the Government of Dubai media office (which) develops initiatives aimed at enhancing the look and feel of Dubai to reflect its unique character as one of the world's most developed, fastest growing and culturally diverse cities'.[39] Dubai has realized that it is possible either to sit back and hope the world comes to you or to take control of the narrative and try to shape perceptions by constructive marketing. Once again, the logic is that in a competitive world, challenging to secure commercial and leisure business, from long-established 'brands' with rich endowments etched into global popular consciousness, a newcomer like Dubai has to be proactive to advertise its attractions. Dubai has therefore, very differently, deliberately created a supply of various products (for commerce, tourism, innovation etc.) and needs to market them to ensure there is demand.

These efforts are often linked in with Dubai government companies that are synonymous with Dubai, such as Emirates Airline, to produce a cluster effect of mutual benefit, very much as highlighted earlier – 'Dubai inc.' in the style of 'Japan inc.' in the 1980s, a world where the government and business sector are closely intertwined.[40] Some of the direct measures to promote Dubai have already been discussed, but the indirect promotional efforts are now so extensive that they are almost subliminal. In the UK and Europe and elsewhere, Dubai (Emirates) sponsors: in football, A C Milan, Arsenal and its stadium, Real Madrid, Paris St. Germain, Benfica, Hamburg S V, Olympiacos, and the English FA Cup; in Racing: the Melbourne Cup, the Singapore Cup with major racing stables (Godolphin) in the UK, France and Australia; in tennis, the US Open, The ATP Tour, the Barcelona Open and the French Open. The list goes on to include cricket, rugby, Formula 1 racing and golf. The value of such sponsorships could be seen for example when Real Madrid won the Champions League football final in May 2018, with thousands of images showing the team members emblazoned with 'Emirates' logos.[41]

To establish a brand requires a great deal of focussed attention and established brands are very valuable. The example of Dubai has been so pronounced in this context that whole studies have been published on the phenomenon, 'in which this newly established hub is projecting itself and being Imagined by an international audience and the way in which the results have been obtained'.[42] It is essential to ensure that the brand image created is nurtured consistently in order to maintain perceptions of the product (in this case, Dubai). 'Building consistent and realistic images . . . is paramount because these images create the expectations that need to be met . . . and if they are not, a "place brand" satisfaction gap might occur.'[43] Ill-judged associations, failures in quality and performance delivery can impact on a reputation very quickly and destroy a carefully crafted image, established painstakingly over many years, as the infamous Gerald Ratner case revealed.[44]

So, such a concerted self-publicizing policy has its risks and Dubai can never completely control its image in the outside world but the examples above have succeeded in establishing name-recognition of Dubai throughout the world. The next stage is to make the city's achievements speak for themselves.

These achievements reflect a very proactive approach to globalization, as a natural progression from the way that Dubai and its merchants had always conducted business. By having a strategic plan, by expanding the diversification of its activities, by establishing a brand and by using a non-threatening trade and services approach to other countries, Dubai has adopted a 'virtual noodle bowl' policy – a variety of free-trade agreements.[45] This very wide-ranging set of partnerships and relationships based on commercial benefit has ensured, 'access to extra-regional markets and attempting some control over the unpredictable economic and political forces exogenous (and endogenous) to the region'.[46] Linked with the promotion and sponsoring of sporting and cultural events and the showcasing of Dubai's commercial, touristic or living attractions, highlighted every day by Emirates Airline's presence throughout the world, this seems to exemplify the use of soft power, as defined by Joseph Nye, 'the ability to achieve goals through attraction rather than coercion'.[47] Such is the city's brand reputation throughout the world, as a model for development and achievement from humble beginnings in a short timescale, that Dubai is often used as a yardstick to measure and compare performance elsewhere.[48]

The impact of the financial downturn after 2008 also, usefully, destroyed the unhelpful myth that Dubai owed its existence and success both to luck and its location by illustrating that Dubai was fallible and not immune from making mistakes – but that its core strengths were such that it bounced back quickly. Success has been due to long-term economic diversification and innovation, allowing the Emirate to become the regional commercial centre because businesses 'voted with their feet' to choose Dubai rather than other centres because of the package of benefits – connectivity through ports and airports, wide-ranging business opportunities, business environment, living conditions – that it provided. When other centres or states collapsed or declined due to political and economic mismanagement, internecine conflict or war (Lebanon, Yemen (Aden), Iraq, Iran, Bahrain), Dubai was able to benefit economically because of increased business activity, not because of luck, but because it was the place which had created the best and most stable environment for people and businesses to live. This process took place over decades when the prevailing world or regional political and economic environment was scarcely conducive to large-scale infrastructural investment (e.g. the Lebanese Civil War, the Iranian revolution, ongoing Israeli–Arab confrontations, Iran–Iraq war, invasion of Kuwait by Iraq and 'Desert Storm'), reflecting the fact that this was a long-term policy, carried out in often less than auspicious conditions. However, we must appreciate that this argument also means that Dubai has 'to keep running' to stay competitive and to stay professional and focussed to stave off competitors.

Has Dubai succeeded simply because it is in the 'right place'. What is the right place? Basrah was the pre-eminent Gulf trading centre for centuries at the head of the Gulf (but no longer due to changing trade, changing transport patterns and conflict); Sharjah (next door to Dubai) had potentially better opportunities to become pre-eminent (but did not take them); Lingah and Bushire on the southern Iranian coast were established earlier than Dubai and traded much in the same way than Dubai does now, but declined as a result of mistaken policies and instability; Beirut was regarded as the 'Paris of the Middle East' combining hedonism and commercial and financial nous, until internecine political and religious disputes destroyed its position; Aden was the pre-eminent port in the region for a century as a coaling and replenishment call. All these centres were felt to be 'in the right place' during their heydays – lessons to be learnt by a Dubai that replaced other centres performing similar functions (Lingah) and out-performing other potential rivals (Sharjah, Bahrain) by being more competitive and better at what it did and by adapting to changing circumstances.

For example, it is true that Dubai's position just inside the Gulf (through the Straits of Hormuz 'choke-point') is now considered ideal for larger containerships to discharge large quantities of containers for relay on smaller ships to other Gulf destinations, this was not always the case and until the 1990s container ships would routinely call most Gulf ports as nineteenth-century steamships had done. It is only the fact that Dubai's continuing investment in ports, associated facilities (free-zones) and airports allowed the Emirate to become the 'hub-port' of the entire region when container ship technology and the shipping efficiencies of economy of scale produced the 'mega' container ships, that only Jebel Ali and its free-zones could handle on such a scale more efficiently and more cost-effectively than others. So too with the airport(s) and Emirates Airline, investments and long-term development policy that transformed a desert waystation into the world's busiest international airport hub and the home of a large international airline.

New challenges – new competitors

The history of this Gulf, or any other region, is that conditions change, technology changes but the challenges remain, and some centres adapt and survive, and others don't. In a Gulf where there are now more challenges than ever from competitors adopting many aspects of the 'Dubai Model' and also from external players, 'if the current momentum of greater trade and a more robust military presence continues, it is only a matter of time before China evolves into a more transformative presence across the broader Gulf region and Arabian Peninsula'.[49] With a military presence in Gwadar and Djibouti, and the presence of Chinese port operators and investors in small UAE ports and Omani ports (Duqm) there is no doubt that the 'One Belt, One Road Initiative' has potential implications for Dubai, some good (more trade), some more problematic (Chinese investment in actual or potential rivals). As always, there are many competitors who feel their place is the 'right' one and seek to persuade customers accordingly and only the coming decades will show whether Dubai's efforts will stave off competitors and whether the results of the Global Financial Crisis helped to reform Dubai's weaknesses and re-boot its innovative approach.

There are other concerns, reflecting both external politics and policies and the ways in which they are implemented. Perhaps most serious is the collapse of the Gulf Co-operation Council (GCC) as a result of the Qatar crisis. The GCC was never particularly effective, as highlighted by Legrenzi,[50] but it did at least serve as a regular forum for Gulf Arab leaders to discuss their policies, review their differences and maintain a show of unity. However, 'While the GCC States are united by strong historical, cultural and social bonds, similar religious customs and traditions and deep-rooted political and economic connections, they also remain distinct entities with unique, individual specificities. (However) these national specificities . . . are increasingly diverging rather than converging.'[51] The estrangement of Qatar and the imposition of sanctions by the UAE, Saudi Arabia and Bahrain from mid-2017 – albeit with a re-set of relations early in 2021 – has inevitably impacted Jebel Ali's role as a distribution hub for the Gulf region, as Qatari container movements are now either moving directly into the new Doha port or via Omani ports such as Sohar. Given the entrenched attitudes on both sides of the dispute, it seems unlikely that Dubai will recover these volumes in the near future, possibly not at all and the position of Jebel Ali as the default location for container relay in the area has now been diminished. The impact of the intra-Gulf dispute does not mean that Dubai's entrepot role is as yet under threat, as Qatar for example, is nowhere near capable of reproducing the scale of what Dubai achieves with its port, free-zones and airports. Qatar had also already attempted to distance itself from its neighbour by copycat policies such as airline expansion (Qatar Airways), airport hubbing and cultural and sporting branding; however, it is clear that in the Gulf there is now a fragmentation of the carefully maintained *khaleeji* ('gulf person') and GCC joint approach to the outside world. For the first time in over 30 years, Dubai is therefore having to face real competition from local regional states.

The change from regional states being quiescent or ineffective competitors to outright hostility is a fundamental change, created by regional politics in which Dubai is not the pre-eminent contributor and this issue is echoed by the challenges that Dubai may have to face, not only as a result of the Qatar crisis (which is a spin-off from the Syrian uprising) but also as a result of the UAE's involvement in the war in Yemen. As we have seen, Dubai's approach has been markedly apolitical, an open-to-all approach focussing on trade, logistics and commercial service industries, and controlling its own destiny, resulting in its status as neutral ground. Clearly there would be consequences for Dubai's prosperity if it was felt that this long-standing ethos was being compromised. However, the political structure of the UAE provides Abu Dhabi with the primary voice in foreign policy and there seems little doubt that Dubai will continue to focus on its commercial, trading and tourism role, re-doubling efforts to attract visitors from less-accessed regions – to compensate for fewer Gulf visitors (from Qatar at least). As long-established alignments shift, the challenges for Dubai are becoming more complex and the competition more severe.

Other neighbouring states are stirring themselves. In Oman, the port of Duqm, approximately midway between Salalah and Sohar, is a new (from 2007) vast development port and investment zone for chemicals, petrochemicals and industry, yet another joint venture, this time with the port of Antwerp. The development plan is to build a town of 100,000 inhabitants by 2020, relying on outside investment and significantly, this is primarily being provided by the Chinese with reports of billions of dollars promised.[52] It may be coincidental that the major Chinese political and economic drive in recent years has been the 'Belt and Road Initiative' (BRI), a network of ports and other infrastructure projects which involves Pakistan, where in April 2015 Chinese investment of USD 46 bn was announced, coupled with the (ex-Omani) port of Gwadar (now operated/'owned' by the Chinese Overseas Port Holding Company since 2013) linked to an actual road and rail link through Central Asia. It seems clear that Duqm is part of the wider Chinese investment and influence onslaught in the region, hinging on the BRI, where 'expressions of interest in projects are welcomed and that Chinese investments are expected'.[53]

Oman's, always modest, oil reserves are likely to be exhausted by around 2025[54] and low oil prices in recent years have strained resources, resulting in the 'Dubai Model' development strategies now in place. In January 2020 following the ruler's death, Haitham bin Tariq al Said succeeded his cousin, the long-ailing Sultan Qaboos, who had been receiving cancer treatment[55] facing major challenges in a state which since 1970 had been ruled 'sultanistically' by Sultan Qaboos and his inner circle – personal patrimonial rule individually and paternalistically exercised, in the classic definition, 'without restraint and at his own discretion'.[56] With a budget deficit in 2016 of 21 per cent and the Sultanate's bonds reduced to junk status, there are serious doubts about how Oman will service its debts, and fund spending, as reported in *The Economist* in July and September 2017.[57] However, increasing dependence on China, such as a USD 3.6 billion loan in August 2017 to fund government spending and less solidarity with neighbouring fellow monarchs in the UAE and Saudi are clear signs that the Sultanate's maverick reputation for independent 'balancing' is to continue. Significantly, there were 'Arab Spring' protests of 2011 in Oman in Sohar and Salalah against lack of jobs and opportunities as well as government corruption, clearly indicating that there are undercurrents of disquiet among Omanis. This is a particularly serious issue as Oman has one of the highest birthrates in the world and the population of this arid, low resource country has risen dramatically from an estimated half-million people in 1970, to over 2 million in 2003 and around 4 million in 2016,[58] a young population wanting employment in an economy with empty coffers.

Like Dubai, but in a bigger landscape, Oman looks back at a great tradition of trading and maritime glory. Lack of long-term oil reserves and the success of the Dubai model have persuaded the government to imitate wholeheartedly the policies adopted by its Gulf neighbour – container ports for local and relay traffic with professional partners from overseas; feed off free-zones backing up the ports and industrial diversification. Unlike Dubai, with serious domestic political uncertainty and a much larger indigenous population that wants employment, it faces the challenge of unseating a powerful, well-established competitor, a professional Dubai brand that has joined up 'adding-value-to each-other' components. Whether it can produce the good-governance and economic liberalism that is also at the core of its mentor's success is more open to doubt, especially if the state is mortgaged up to the hilt to China, although in a geopolitically fragmented, multipolar world, with China increasingly replacing the USA as an arbiter of global rules, strong links to China may be an advantage, perhaps as part of the 'belt and road initiative'. Oman is a late arrival to the 'Dubai Model' emulation party, less able in a larger and politically fragile state, to pull together the strands and to 'allow innovation in Government, the empowering of employees ... of listening ... and the need for consultation and collaboration'.[59] The success of Dubai is much more than a few ports and free-zones; it is innovation, flexibility, professionalism and entrepreneurialism – qualities that Oman will need to produce in the future if it is to mount a serious challenge.

Bahrain continues to work at attracting new business to the island, perhaps, inevitably, including borrowing Dubai's sporting portfolio initiatives (succeeding in attracting Formula 1 Motor Racing for the Bahrain Grand Prix) – even persuading the A P Moller Group (Maersk) to develop and operate a new Container Terminal – Khalifa bin Salman Port (KBSP), which opened in 2009, taking over from Mina Salman, intended to be 'the premier transhipment hub for the Northern Gulf' according to the KBSP Website.[60] It is likely that this development is more useful for Maersk, having their 'own' terminal in the Northern Gulf (and Salalah further south) as logistically, in an era of large containerships, serving as few hub-ports as possible, and with the core hub of Dubai en-route to Bahrain, there is no advantage for most lines to serve Dubai and Bahrain with a large mega-containership. This seems to be reflected in the following throughputs:

TEU Throughputs	2009	2012	2014	2016
KBSP Bahrain	217,000	525,309	433,000	421,725

For most carriers, Bahrain is served by transhipment using smaller ships via a lower Gulf hub.

Qatar is a small country of around 2.5 million inhabitants, of whom only around 10pc are native Qataris. With vast natural gas reserves, Qatar is the world's largest liquefied natural gas (LNG) exporter with hydrocarbon exports accounting for around 80 pc of the state's exports over the last twenty years – 'the most carbon-dependent economy among the GCC countries (with) the share of hydrocarbon revenue in total government revenue 89.2 pc and 86 pc in 1994-2003 and 2004-2013, respectively'.[61] Qatar is therefore a classic rentier state and 'Qataris have come to expect the state's generous allowances, up to USD 7000 per month, interest-free loans, free land and nearly guaranteed employment'.[62]

Container volumes for Qatar (Doha) have traditionally moved via Dubai, consequently, statistics for earlier throughputs are unreliable. However, subsequent World Bank statistics[63] show volumes as follows.

In 2007, TEU throughputs were 350,000 (estimated) with Dubai comparably handling 10,653,000 TEU. In 2014, TEU throughputs for Doha were 424,000 (Dubai 15,249,000).

A long-mooted new port was finally completed in September 2017, including, in addition to the new port and container terminal, a base for the Emirate's naval forces and a large economic zone. It is, certainly, no coincidence that the long-standing project was inaugurated (early), only three months after Qatar was effectively quarantined by its neighbours Bahrain, Saudi Arabia and the UAE as a result of bitter disputes about regional politics and relations with Iran. The new deep-water Hamad Port facility was celebrated with speeches forecasting that it would become a regional hub and in the existing stand-off with other regional states, allow Qatar to avoid being economically choked-off.[64] There is no doubt that this port development has allowed Qatar to ride-out sanctions more easily, but equally there is also no doubt that Dubai volumes will be impacted, as some regional container trans-shipment will switch from Dubai, mainly to Oman, as highlighted in The Economist in October 2017.[65] Though Qatar has clearly emulated several strands of the 'Dubai Model', particularly sports branding, culture and airline logistics, there are few signs of Qatar beginning to rival Dubai as an economic, financial and distribution hub, despite attempts, using parts of the Dubai Model approach, to set up challenges (to Dubai) with an airport, and (to Emirates Airline and Etihad Airlines) with an airline, in the shape of Qatar Airways. This policy has had some success with Hamad Airport Doha attracting over 37 million passengers in 2016 (13th on the worldwide list) but still some way behind Dubai, now the number one international airport worldwide, with over 86 million.[66] I would argue, therefore, that Dubai and Qatar have, until recent years, actually pursued policies which, though similar superficially (despite Qatar's vast gas reserves), are based on a very different ethos. Qatar has pursued not only some soft-power strategies, taken from the Dubai playbook, as 'Gulf monarchies have been using their oil wealth to buy the accoutrements of "good citizenship" and "progressiveness" in the international arena through outward-orientated and costly activities',[67] but hard power policies too by trying to become a major diplomatic force – very different from the Dubai approach, focussed on trade and logistics rather than politics. Of course, it has to be said that Qatar as a small independent state has to make different choices (than Dubai, which is now but a part of a wider entity), but significantly, it has belatedly chosen to emulate the route followed by its southern neighbour.

What is significant here is that the 'soft power' policy (the term coined by Joseph Nye in 1990)[68] was actually initiated in the Gulf by Dubai in the 1980s (Emirates Airline, and the Dubai Desert Classic Golf Competition in 1989 for example), as part of the creation of a Dubai brand. Other headline sporting tournaments in Rugby and Tennis and other cultural activities such as the Dubai Book Festival (from 2009), Arab Poetry Festival (from 2009) and the creation of an Arts area in Al Barsha district and the branding of football teams are further examples of this approach. Without the size, population or ability in trading terms to challenge other neighbouring economies, Qatar has, using its oil and gas wealth, eschewed the neutralist approach of the Dubai model and adopted instead what Mehran Kamrava describes as 'subtle power'[69] making an impact with a dynamic and proactive 'punching above its weight' foreign policy backed up by cultural, branding efforts such as the presence of (mainly American) world-class universities (Georgetown, Northwestern), the creation of the Qatar foundation, museums, sponsorship of high-profile sporting teams such as Barcelona, and the winning of the location for the Football World Cup in 2018. However, though all these policies are taken directly from the well-established Dubai blueprint, the Qatari outreach has actually been far from subtle, with not only the Qatar domestic brand tainted by constant reports of ill-treated workers at World Cup sites, and the reported corruption in obtaining the award; but also the 'hard power' policy, of trying to play an independent role on the world stage has, with Qatari meddling in regional conflicts, contributed to the fragmented mixture of well-funded proxy armed groups in Syria and Iraq and the alienation of fellow Sunni GCC monarchies[70].

Fellow Sunni states, Saudi Arabia, the UAE and Bahrain ran out of patience at this separatist line in mid-2017 and imposed an economic blockade (according to the UAE Minister for Foreign Affairs Dr Anwar Gargash, speaking at Chatham House London in July 2017), after Qatari ransom payments to rescue some of their citizens in Iraq ended up in the hands of terror groups.[71] Of course, Qatar is not solely to blame for some of the issues bedevilling the region, and it has robustly defended its policy of reaching out to those states and factions shunned by the Saudi/UAE bloc, but the assertive, proactive, political policy it has pursued, the antithesis of that followed by Dubai in its formative years, shows the risks of failing to walk the regional tightrope carefully enough. Qatar's 'mavericking' policies, perhaps deliberately pursued as an alternative way for a small but wealthy state to secure influence, when despite copying large portions of Dubai's model, challenging Dubai's economic and logistics hegemony was not feasible, also bring into focus, by contrast, the success of Dubai's neutralist 'balancing' approach, focussing primarily on economic and logistics. As Kamrava admits, due to the personalist nature of the Qatari regime and with 'a serious dearth of technical experts across the state machinery to provide input and advice upward, decisions are made without detailed study of their consequences'.[72] At the time of writing, the standoff with other GCC states has officially (January 2021) ended (helped by Kuwaiti brokering), but trust and the return of cordial relations seem unlikely to return for the foreseeable future – an unnecessary destabilizing factor in the fractious politics of the region.

For Dubai too, there are salutary lessons to be learnt here concerning the limitations and weaknesses of Personal Rule and how its continued economic success has been as a result of successive Al Maktoums adopting trade and infrastructure policies tempered by consultation with a wide circle of local constituency opinion and technocrat professionals – and the retaining of a neutral trade-focussed space. The Qatari dispute and the UAE's involvement in foreign wars (Yemen), albeit pursued under the leadership of Abu Dhabi, are certainly placing this approach under unprecedented strain. 'Brand Dubai' is the keystone of Dubai's success with its reputation for smooth-sailing safety and reliability – the confidence for the millions of visitors (in normal times) that there are no nasty surprises lurking around the corner. The Qatari dispute, seriously impacting the regional role of Jebel Ali and the publicity surrounding the unpalatable family shenanigans of Shaikh Mohammed bin Maktoum are useful reminders yet again, that strong positions created over many years can be quickly swept away by careless or ill-considered policies.

In Kuwait, Michael Herb[73] has highlighted the contradiction at the heart of the state, that despite having the only real elected assembly in the GCC and certainly the most assertive, Kuwait has remained the most single-minded rentier in the region with an entirely oil dominated economy, certainly compared with the UAE which, 'undemocratically' has nonetheless created (in Dubai at least) a very different and diversified economic structure. The fact is of course that the Kuwaiti political decision-making structure is inherently antagonistic with (as Herb highlights) the assembly, unable to form the government, being more intent on (for example) opposing diversification policies (which may be un-Islamic – such as building more hotels for foreign visitors), or involving outside investors which might give scope for corruption (among Ministers); or reducing the size of the bureaucracy – less employment and perquisites for Kuwaiti nationals – of whom, in the workforce, 90 per cent work for the state. Perhaps the biggest impact of the Iraqi invasion of Kuwait in 1990 was not on the oil extraction industry which recovered, but on the ability of the state and the government actually to govern. There is a greater degree of political openness in Kuwait, compared with other regional monarchies, although in practise this results mainly in obstructionism and an economic policy impasse as the assembly seeks to preserve itself and its members' interests and to block anything which might undermine them (such as creating a bigger private sector benefitting foreigners). Kuwait has evolved, where the parliament and ruler need to work together to make policy to divide up revenue, but have found it difficult to do so when neither would compromise on their 'rights' and the demarcation of decision-making, whereas the rulers of Dubai identified themselves with the interests of the merchants, co-opting and embedding them into the policy of economic diversification.

The reality is that Kuwait and Dubai have faced similar challenges, of development and policy, but are tackling them (or avoiding tackling them) in different ways. Despite Herb's distinctions, and though I would dispute that Dubai is an 'extreme rentier', which Kuwait certainly is, both depend on large numbers of foreigners (in the UAE 90% and Kuwait 70%); both (post-1990 when large numbers of Arab Yemenis and Palestinians were expelled from Kuwait) depend on 'third-country-nationals' (usually from India, Pakistan, the Philippines and increasingly Africa); both have difficulties in persuading young nationals to enter the private sector; the private sector and support structures in government and domestically is completely dominated by foreign workers in both Kuwait and Dubai; neither state has a perfect record for inequalities or 'human-rights' violations. Indeed, despite the (only for Kuwait citizens) assembly, Kuwait, in particular, has a poor record for employing overseas workers (particularly domestic workers from the Philippines) and for the treatment of Kuwait inhabitants deemed non-citizens (Bidoon). However, the big differences between Dubai and Kuwait are that Dubai, albeit via the ruling family working with the major families, has given its citizens outward-looking opportunities, in a major economic and logistics hub, to participate and compete in a globalized and connected world and to remove the dependence on a volatile and diminishing fossil-fuel. Kuwaitis seem unable, as yet, to unglue themselves from the apparent safety of distributed oil money (and the SWF receipts), to diversify and to compete in the new world of a globalized economy – though proposals to develop Bubiyan Island close to Iraq continue (for several years now) to re-surface periodically.

In Saudi Arabia, the economy therefore continues to revolve around oil – precarious in an era of low prices – and despite efforts to boost the role of the private sector and wean young Saudis off rentier support, an annual Ministry of Labour report on labour statistics quoted by Faisal Kattan, reveals that the number of Saudis employed in private industry remains stuck at around 10 per cent despite decades of 'Saudisation'.[74] The announcement of 'Vision 2030' by the government in 2016, a blueprint for economic diversification, based on reducing oil-dependence and cutting state costs, failed to prevent the Kingdom's foreign reserves in April 2017 dropping 'below $500 billion . . . . From a peak of $730 billion in 2014 . . . prompting the International Monetary Fund (IMF) to warn that the Kingdom may run out of financial assets needed to support spending, within five years'.[75] Extensive financial support for Saudis as part of the rentier 'bargain' and the military costs of an increasingly assertive regional military role (in Yemen for example) will continue to strain the resources of a state increasingly under pressure to reform – women drivers are the first faltering steps. But despite its size and until recent years, a longstanding and often bitter border dispute with the UAE,[76] Saudi Arabia is not challenging Dubai's role as the regional business centre and has no wish to do so for social, religious and structural reasons.

The arrival of Crown Prince Mohammed Bin Salman Al Saud (MBS) as the effective ruler (recorded by the media in November 2017 as stating that he wanted Saudi Arabia to be like Dubai only bigger) is bringing changes, as the need to diversify and the urgent need to provide jobs for young Saudis has reached a critical level, despite being bolstered by the world's second-largest oil reserves, and an economy focussed on 'hydrocarbon extraction, processing and utilisation'.[77] Though utterly different from Dubai in background, size, population and development and Dubai's success, focussed on trade and political soft power, it is significant that even Saudi Arabia is now regarding the small Emirate as a blueprint for the future. With Sovereign Wealth Fund assets of over $750 billion, according to the Sovereign Wealth Fund Institute, a large population (about 33 million) and a large landmass, the Saudis see themselves as the regional political leaders, emerging as a force in their own right from the protective shadow of the United States, with all the risks inherent in this role. However, the rise of MBS has created more uncertainty and instability, as a result of his aggressive policies. Supported (though less so over the last year) by the Crown Prince (and acting ruler) of Abu Dhabi, Mohammed Bin Zayed (MBZ), the Saudis are now involved in war in Yemen, are imposing sanctions on Qatar, and are enduring international opprobrium, as a result of the October 2018 murder of the Saudi journalist Jamal Khashoggi in Istanbul. MBS and MBZ are considered to have close personal ties, with the older Emirati considered supposedly (by those in Abu Dhabi?) as MBS's mentor. It may be that MBS has a different view. However, both perceive the Muslim Brotherhood as a political threat and believe that the Sunni oil-monarchies must adopt a more assertive approach to counter what they see as increasing (Shia) Iranian influence, that has already enveloped Iraq, Syria and Lebanon, and threatens Yemen. However, the way in which this approach has been pursued has alienated neighbours and split the Gulf Co-operation Council (GCC). The political fall-out and turbulence resulting from these policies do not help a Dubai which relies on visitors and inward investment.

Iran, despite relations with the outside world remaining fractious, still accounted for 12pc of the UAE's (i.e. Dubai's) non-oil exports, worth USD 12 billion in 2013 and 16.6 pc in 2014. The UAE economy was reported to stand to benefit by USD13 billion if sanctions were lifted,[78] reflecting the still vital link between Dubai and this large populous nation. The removal of sanctions turned out to be only temporary. However, as a result of the policy of placing emphasis on facilities nearer the entrance to the Gulf for security reasons, the Iranian port of Bandar Abbas (Shahid Rajaee) has been considerably expanded. The Container Terminal (originally set up in 1983), now has 16 Container Gantry Cranes with the latest phase adding two deep-water berths (of 17m draft), which would allow the latest 'Mega-Containerships' to berth according to the Shahid Rajaee Port Website. As Iran's (only) major container port, volumes have steadily increased, though the impact of sanctions, and weaker oil prices affected growth.

As a result of the war with Iraq and the need to reduce dependency on inner-Gulf ports, the decision was taken to develop the port of Chahbahar, outside the straits of Hormuz on the Indian Ocean, close to the border with Pakistan. Lack of money and lack of connections from the port to the rest of Iran ensured that progress was negligible, but in 2016, India and Iran signed an agreement that would refurbish the port and expand container-handling facilities.[79] There is little doubt that this is a (belated) attempt by India, offering the prospect of better links to landlocked states such as Afghanistan, to try to counter the already well-advanced Chinese 'Silk Road' ('one belt-one road') initiative intended to integrate Central Asia, West Asia and the Middle East into a cohesive economic area, with the Pakistani (increasingly Chinese orientated), port of Gwadar (only 50 miles away across the border) a core link between the maritime and overland connections. Chahbahar container volumes continue to be minimal, reflecting the lack of any industrial or commercial base.

Chahbahar Container Throughputs (TEU)

2010	16,961
2013	15,000
2016	20,441

(Source: Drewry Maritime Research, London).

Despite its size and (now around 80 million people) population, Iran remains an anomaly in the Gulf because of its lack of integration with the other regional states. The Arab Sunni states continue to have concerns about the extent of Shia Iran's political and religious ambitions in the region, in recent years exacerbated by the apparent increasing Iranian influence in Iraq, Syria (the so-called Shia crescent) and even Yemen. The chances of Iran being fully reintegrated into regional systems seem minimal, particularly as external relations with major Western economies remain fraught, and the Qatar crisis and the war in Yemen, is evidence of how seriously, perceived spreading Iranian influence is taken by Saudi Arabia and Abu Dhabi. It seems likely that the future will continue to see a geo-political struggle for influence between Saudi Arabia and Iran, especially as the Saudis, 'despite the (US) tougher line on Iran . . . question how committed the US is to a long-term security presence in the area'.[80] In these circumstances, Dubai ports are likely to continue to remain a major conduit for Iranian official and unofficial containerized trade, maintaining the role they have played officially and unofficially for several decades.

In Iraq, following the American-led invasion of 2003, there were cautious attempts by overseas port-operating companies to work in Umm Qasr and the UAE's Gulftainer (GTL), working on behalf of the Iraqi Port Authority (IPA), eventually initiated a small container terminal, in 2008, using Mobile Harbour Cranes to handle containers on the existing quays, backed by a securely fenced-off container-yard for storage of containers and container un-stuffing. This project was then followed up by GTL in 2012, by the first purpose-built container terminal, part-funded by the World Bank,[81] and in 2015 a logistics centre to support the re-burgeoning Iraqi oil and gas sector. Other, privately operated terminals have also been inaugurated, including those of Philippines Company ICTSI and France's CMA. In 2017, the Gulftainer Terminal handled the largest container ship yet to call at Iraqi ports, the 5500 TEU 'YM Wealth' operated by Yang Ming Lines (YML) of Taiwan.[82]

Such has been the success of the re-establishment of Iraqi container throughputs by sea, as a result of improving, professional container terminals and the scale of imports involved in the re-building of Iraq and of re-equipping the oil and gas companies with material to enable them to set up new operations in the south of Iraq to boost oil and gas extraction, that some services (like YML) are calling Umm Qasr direct, in this case from the Far East. As we have seen, some container volumes continue to enter Iraq via the Kuwait gateway (though other traditional gateway routes into Iraq such as via Syria, Jordan or via Turkey have now either closed or been curtailed), but Iraqi volumes through Umm Qasr have rebounded dramatically in recent years, since the opening of new terminals after 2008:

Umm Qasr Container Throughputs in TEU

2012	439,000
2013	571,122
2014	689,881
2015	895,373
2016	1,056,737

(Source: Iraq Port Authority courtesy of Gulftainer Company Ltd. Sharjah, UAE)

Iraq lacks a true deep-water port on the Gulf. Basrah is no longer a viable port for containers. Umm Qasr continues to be draft restricted in the channel due to the presence of a sand bar and, with the continual depositing of silt by the combined flows of the Tigris and Euphrates rivers, needs constant dredging. Such constraints, domestic politics and the continuing territorial and jurisdictional disputes, with its neighbours Kuwait and Iran curtailing its ability to provide alternative sites, limit its ability to develop the port for mega-container ships and commercial cargo logistics facilities. However, there has been remarkable progress since 2008 in Umm Qasr, very much based on the blueprint of the regional exemplar Dubai, with the arrival of professional facilities backed up by support logistics – absolute necessities when providing service to the time-constrained oil and gas companies with Iraqi government contracts. However, despite the avowed hopes of some Iraqi politicians, suggesting to the author, as container facilities again started operating effectively after 2008, that 'Umm Qasr could, in future, provide the hub for through rail services of containers to Europe from Asia', there is no doubt that Dubai ports and the oil industry regional logistics bases in the Dubai free-zones will continue to dominate logistics for Iraq in the foreseeable future.

If we set out the container volumes for Gulf ports in 2016 and compare them with those in 2004 (and those at the beginning of the economic transformation of the region in 1980), we can see at a glance how throughputs at Dubai have grown more than others. This expansion illustrates the extent to which Dubai at the beginning of the twenty-first century continued to build on the structures it had established, to diversify the economic base (in TEU rounded):

Gulf Container Throughputs

	2004	2016	(1980)
Dubai	6,400,000	14,800,000	(273,000)
Other UAE	2,400,000	5,000,000	(66,000)
Oman	2,500,000	4,000,000	(18,000)
Iran	1,240,000	1,300,000	(20,000)
Iraq	36,000	1,050,000	-
Kuwait	580,000	1,000,000	(220,000)
Bahrain	193,000	420,000	(60,000)
Saudi Arabia (East)	758,000	2,300,000	(60,000)

(Source: Drewry Maritime Research London)[83]

Many of the volumes for other ports indicated in the table are first relayed via Dubai.

Despite the emergence of Abu Dhabi as the dominant power in the UAE, from 2004 onwards, the impact of the Global Economic Crisis in 2007–8 and after, and the consequences of the 'Arab Spring' of 2011, Dubai has continued to invest and innovate. The investment in facilities and the continued expansion to keep up with technological change has required a degree of faith in the policy and vision to maintain the much-expanded trading-hub Dubai in the future. Also, what is clear to us now – that containerized transport completely dominates world trade with ships carrying 20,000 containers and huge port complexes serviced by scores of gantry cranes – was not at all clear in the 1970s and 1980s. However, Dubai invested then and – equally importantly – has continued to invest in technology and infrastructure to ensure its position was maintained. As Hoosteval has emphasized, 'Infrastructure bottlenecks slow the economy. By investing in container infrastructure, a nation can stimulate its economy.'[84] He also stresses the importance of integrating new technology and associated functions, such as customs clearance procedures and the impact this can have on the economy, quoting World Bank studies that found that 'each additional day that a product is delayed prior to being shipped reduces trade by more than one percent'[85].

World Bank 2018 benchmarking statistics for the Logistics Performance Index (LPI), incorporating Customs efficiency, infrastructure, international shipments, logistics competence, container and cargo tracking and tracing and timeliness, place the UAE (i.e. mainly Dubai) at a ranking of 9 worldwide.[86] However, what Dubai also developed and, more importantly, continued to develop was an enabling commercial strategy that by producing the largest and most efficient port and free-zone complex in the region created the optimum entrepot intermediary 'between primary-exporting hinterlands and regional, imperial and world economies'[87] and such infrastructure 'reflecting and driving broader trends towards a more globalized world'.[88] The opening of Al Maktoum International Airport (or 'Dubai World Central' – the name says it all), close to Jebel Ali, at the end of 2010 is just the latest effort to enhance and expand the logistics and commercial opportunities available.

The success of the JAFZA model has led to a policy of creating these free-zone enclaves (or 'cities' as many of them are now designated), often earmarked for specific purposes, as always, with the view of creating the right conditions to attract foreign investment or as a base for regional operations. In mid-2017, there were twenty-seven free-zones in Dubai, including JAZFA, ranging from Dubai Silicon Oasis to Dubai Media City and Dubai Knowledge Park to International Humanitarian City (IHC).[89] The latter example, IHC (established from 2004 onwards), is a good illustration of the way in which Dubai has expanded the role of traditional free-zones to encompass distinctive forms of activity. In this case the IHC acts as a regional base for relief operations, hosting, according to its website, forty-eight non-profit operations, thirteen commercial members and nine UN agencies.[90] Adam Hanieh emphasizes, 'virtually all the humanitarian assistance to the key conflict zones in the Middle East is now co-ordinated through Dubai's IHC. The UNHCR for example holds its largest global stockpile of relief items . . . at IHC.'[91] Such an operation not only contributes to the range of activities that sustains Dubai in terms of cargo movement and employment but, by providing a major centre for International Organizations such as UNICEF, WHO, UNHCR and WFP, also brings additional benefits, by enabling Dubai to be seen as a serious international player of substance, rather than just a port on the edge of the desert. Becoming the recognized, regional centre for the logistical control and distribution of aid and disaster relief throughout the wider region, has only come about because of the quality and capabilities of the free-zones and the Ports and Airport infrastructure. The presence of such organizations also adds lustre to the Emirate's reputation and international standing.[92]

Similarly, Dubai Media City (DMC), launched in 2001, 'encompasses a media community of over 20,000 people working in over 2000 regional and international media companies'[93] and acts as a regional centre for companies such as the BBC, CNN, ITN and Al Arabiya among many others; Dubai Silicon Oasis is a technology park founded in 2005, 'to facilitate and promote modern technology based industries';[94] Dubai Internet City (DIC) announced originally in 1999, 'with the vision of making Dubai a hub for ICT innovation, knowledge development and new ideas for a digital future . . . the MENA region's largest ICT hub'[95] and

Dubai Multi Commodities Centre (DMCC) founded in 2002, 'to establish Dubai as a hub for the global commodities trade . . . Global Free Zone of the Year for three years running according to the Financial Times fDi magazine'[96]. These examples, in particular, reflect the policy aim to make Dubai a centre of innovation, at the cutting edge of new technology and IT and as a major international hub for specific trading activities. Pulling together these elements, 'government driven initiatives have focussed on the relevance of KM (Knowledge Management) . . . and emphasized the importance of working towards knowledge-based work, a knowledge-based economy and a knowledge-driven society . . . so that Dubai serves as a hub interfacing between Europe, the USA and Asia'.[97]

Chapter review

This determined and focussed approach on ports and trading policy and infrastructure was therefore maintained and enhanced at the beginning of the twenty-first century, as was the welcoming approach to the wider world, 'Dubai . . . made a point of welcoming foreigners'.[98] Because other regional centres were either less interested in commerce and diversification because of ample oil wealth, or, were diverted because of internal and external factors, Dubai became even more, the commercial and port distribution centre of the region. By regularly updating and enhancing its facilities, as (for example), the containerization industry evolved, with more and bigger cranes and enhanced information technology, trading businesses, shipping companies and overseas company representative offices established their offices in the Emirate as bases to serve both Dubai and the wider region and once there, became embedded, less likely to transfer to another centre. With increasing expertise attracting other specialists in all areas of a very diversified economy, Dubai became the hub from which not only goods were relayed to other ports and airports, but the 'go-to' place for professionalism and efficiency.

The position of and challenges for Dubai are, of course, now very different than those of the independent Trucial Statelet (until 1971), and the de-facto freedom of action that it enjoyed until the early twenty-first century. However, within the federal structure of the UAE, Dubai continues to enjoy the right to pursue internal commercial policies and its position as the commercial centre of the UAE and the Gulf remains undiminished.

Is the regional trading and distribution position that Dubai has secured so painstakingly over the last forty or fifty years sustainable over the next half-century? There have always been challenges and we have established that the Emirate consolidated its development by taking risks, unwilling to sit back and depend on fossil-fuel resources to sustain it. Chatham House has correctly divined that, 'in the cracks which geopolitical fragmentation is opening up, there is more space, opportunity and compulsion for antagonists to compete'[99] as other regional states belatedly diversify, pursuing many of the innovations that Dubai pioneered. Dubai will need to continue to innovate in order to sustain its regional entrepot supremacy.

Making the right decisions for Dubai and the UAE, both nationally and internationally, are therefore still, important tasks for the ruling Al Maktoum family, in an ever more complex world and where Abu Dhabi clearly now has both the ability and the will to dominate the federation. However, Dubai has shown that 'the ruling families can credibly reform without ending the monarchy',[100] with 'the triumph of the Dubai Model', without anyone 'kicking away its ladder'[101] or coercing its citizens.[102] The ruling family continues to be awarded legitimacy by its national citizenry, with the increasing heterogeneity of the Emirate, actually aligning this privileged minority even more closely together, with the ruling family to ensure the maintenance of continued success as well as, culture, traditions and 'nation'. Nonetheless, the dangers of over-confident hubris as shown by the financial crisis in 2007–8, the risks of ill-judged policies and the need to continue to ensure that heed is taken of contrary opinions outside the charmed, inner-court circles are very real concerns for a Dubai that needs to be even more competitive and focussed if it is to maintain the innovative leadership of the past.

CONCLUSION

This book has sought to show that, when other emerging Gulf regional states were content simply to pump crude and live off the rentier income, particularly in the 1960s and beyond, Dubai invested in ports, airports and infrastructure as foundations for a diversified economy. That it did so was unusual and distinctive. There were no precedents for the expansion of port facilities and projects such as the Dry Dock in 1973, and these initiatives were much derided at the time, when the prospect of Dubai becoming one of the world's biggest container ports and commercial centres within a couple of decades seemed inconceivable. A laissez-faire business environment that created free-zones, bigger airports and an airline followed, together with a raft of other innovations, attracting external investment to a place that had also, crucially, created a safe and reliable governance structure. Dubai recognized the modern globalized world as an opportunity and not a threat, because it had always accepted, being part of the long-established Indian Ocean trading networks, that openness to others was a benefit, and for nearly 200 years its trade-orientated approach has created a neutral, apolitical space. Dubai had the self-confidence to work with and compete with the outside world, its diversification efforts spread, both domestically and throughout the globe, unconfined to specific regions or blocs, usefully foreshadowing the rise of geopolitical fragmentation and multipolarity in recent years.

These efforts were based on the expansion of its infrastructure, primarily the ports and airports, wholeheartedly accepting the challenges of the container revolution in cargo shipping during the 1970s. The resultant expansion of trade in Dubai, its creation of the role of Gulf hub and entrepot and the participation in global supply chains, benefitting also from resultant technology transfer as global trade grew dramatically at the end of the twentieth century, was a deliberate policy. It allowed the Emirate, lacking resources/endowments, the opportunity to avoid the (traditional emerging economy) process of creating a heavy-industry base itself, but building on its traditional strengths and attitudes, acting as a commercial centre, a conduit and servicing centre for the outside world instead. This was not a simple one-track approach. The economic infrastructure stimulated economic development and reduced dependency on other rivals. Without the fossil-fuel resources of neighbours, such a policy had its risks, however, recognizing the need to be multifaceted and to be able to compete in an increasingly hi-tech world, the Emirate worked to ensure that it would excel at and be indispensable in transport, trading, commerce, finance and IT. It had to be the best to ensure it was the preferred location for people, organizations and businesses. The fact that over the last four or five decades, Dubai has become the acknowledged centre of the Middle East for communications, commerce, finance, media, new-technology innovation and the centre for business and international organizations such as UNESCO, WHO or World Food Programme (WFP) is evidence that it has done so. The distinctiveness of Dubai is that it recognized the opportunity to enhance its position in the regional and international economy by pursuing such policies, competing with the established institutions of the outside world, when others hesitated, were incapable or were indifferent. Dubai (and the UAE) also had stable governance and growth-orientated policies over the long term, which allowed successful challenges to existing competitors. Indeed, such is its impact, influence and reputation for impressive scale and achievement that a reference to Dubai is often used as a comparison with other dramatic developments in logistics or construction throughout the world, to show how impressive they are.

It is my contention that the factor that shaped the development of Dubai more than anything else was the containerization revolution and the infrastructural framework which supported it. Containerization changed everything. Without Dubai's wholehearted endorsement of containerization and the infrastructure, processes and attitudes that flowed from it, there would have been no vast Jebel Ali terminal, no free-zones and no embedding of Dubai in the mainstream of a globalized world. Containerization, as a new 'disruptive' technology, allowed Dubai to develop its trading entrepot infrastructure to become more competitive and professional, and to harness the new skills required in a rapidly changing economic environment, to focus on costs, efficiency and customer service. The new global market that containerization ushered in required more complex solutions to the movement and distribution of goods. No longer was it sufficient simply to have cargo solutions which dealt with loose boxes and crates discharged on a quayside, which any port could do one way or the other. Containerization entailed 'intermodal' transport which required professional logistics solutions to handle and relay thousands of containers, requiring state-of-the-art information technology procedures. Containerization created the opportunity for linked-up free-zones – designed to provide an environment where external trade would be enhanced by a more liberal fiscal and bureaucratic regime. The consequent development of the free-zones as centres for innovation and as the focal points for international organizations, and the creation of tourism and airlines, all very much owe their origins to the skills, confidence and techniques brought about by the adoption of containerization. Containerization ensured that Dubai is now part of the profoundly integrated and interdependent world economy which has come to rely on the multi-modal supply chains which are the bedrock of modern economies, and the provision of services in finance, media, information technology and transport and tourism.

But why did Dubai pursue this approach and why was there such a policy of adopting new ideas? With a trading tradition stretching back many decades, the policy of Shaikh Rashid Bin Saeed Al Maktoum in the middle of the twentieth century was to improve the established infrastructure that would enable Dubai to compete more effectively. His predecessor, Shaikh Maktoum Bin Hashar Al Maktoum, half a century earlier in the 1900s, was perhaps the first to give Dubai a reputation for innovative thinking. He successfully marketed the attractions of the Emirate to discontented merchants and traders in Southern Persia, who could have transferred their skills anywhere in the region, initiating the foundations of the city's future, regional and entrepot status. For Shaikh Rashid, throughout his rule, conscious of other regional states' revenues from oil and gas, the focus of his thinking was on what would improve, secure and enhance Dubai's position as a trading centre. Firstly, he expanded the facilities of the Creek, on which the very existence of the city depended, to handle traded goods more effectively; secondly, he instigated the building of a port outside the creek to handle increasing cargo volumes more quickly and efficiently; and, thirdly, to improve air-links, he insisted on having Dubai's own airport, rather than depending on that of rival Emirate, Sharjah. However, the 'big ideas' of Shaikh Rashid and his successor sons were to recognize that if Dubai was to compete with and outperform its rivals in order to prosper, even more innovative and radical ideas were required – to be pursued thoroughly and professionally – leading to the creation of the giant Jebel Ali port, the focus on new-technology containerization, the 'adding-value' free-zones, a much-expanded airport and, subsequently, Dubai's own airline.

It would have been entirely possible for Dubai, certainly after the creation of the new UAE state in 1971, to assume a more limited role within the federation, commensurate with its modest oil revenues (which had been available from the late 1960s). So why did they persevere with expansionist new ideas? We should not lose sight of the fact that until 1971 Dubai and the other pre-UAE Trucial States were separate, competing and often on not entirely cordial terms with each other. The new federal UAE certainly did not remove these competitive instincts and Dubai was already considered the commercial centre. The approach of Shaikh Rashid and subsequent Dubai Rulers to development was to build a state which would be the best and most effective trading and transport hub in the region following its historical legacy, rather than depend on others or simply distribute the revenues from oil. At this point, we should also recognize the pragmatic, nation-building statesmanship of the first UAE president Shaikh Zayed of Abu Dhabi, who did not seek to prevent the efforts of his feisty neighbour – recognizing the value of Dubai to the new federation.

It is worth reiterating that there was no inevitability that Dubai would succeed in these endeavours, initially relying on borrowed finance and pursuing expansion plans, considered foolhardy at the time, in the 1970s and 1980s when the Gulf was still a minor player in international trade. However, the vast purchasing power of the Gulf economies from the late 1970s onwards, as a result of much higher oil prices, and Dubai's approach as a 'late-commercialising' economy, coincided with the radical change in international cargo shipping, brought about by containerization. Having invested in the much-expanded port facilities, Dubai was able to capitalize on the huge increase in imports into the Gulf brought about by the oil wealth, now being carried in containers.

The fact that its sizeable and efficient container terminals were positioned in the Southern Gulf was undoubtedly a factor in Dubai's success, but shipping lines and their export and import cargo-business customers have always required more than just a port in a particular location – and containerization/intermodalism re-emphasized this. They need facilities such as an efficient ship operating/handling service, fast customs clearance and integrated IT links to keep costs down with port infrastructure that expands in line with ship size and design – and that provides a good service to their customers. If shipping lines do not receive the right service in the right place at the right time, they lose their customers – there are always alternative ports – and we should therefore be clear that Dubai's reputation grew, and container volumes grew, because of the good service that it gave, operationally and commercially (better than others), and the facilities, constantly upgraded, that it provided. Innovation in the ports extended beyond the decision to focus on containerized cargo, with Dubai Port Services (DPS), established to operate and manage Port Rashid in 1970, pioneering the use of computers in the early 1980s, to cope with the rapid increase in container volumes and the increasing complexity of the monitoring of their movements.

Further innovation extended from providing efficient and professional ports to the adjacent storage and distribution facilities, on the basis that customers would be attracted by ease of access and streamlined customs and administration procedures. This 'integrated logistics' of container ship links/container terminals/ transport/warehouses and distribution with the resultant free-zones, made attractive to external investors by a raft of 'business friendly' incentives and the lack of majority local-ownership restrictions for re-exported goods, expanded the volume of business through Jebel Ali port as its role as a hub-port developed. Shipping lines determined that a Dubai call was a necessity and as container- ship sizes grew, call-port policies changed, with shipping lines adopting a 'hub and spoke' policy. This saved time and cost by using Dubai as a hub for the large main-line ships, with smaller feeder-ships relaying containers to other Gulf (and regional) ports. Airport and airline expansion provided the linked-up connections to ensure that passengers could travel to and from Dubai easily. Subsequent imaginative developments expanded the free-zone concept to create enclaves focussing on technological innovation and the knowledge economy, while the establishment of Emirates Airline in 1985 helped to kick-start a tourism industry out of apparently inauspicious surroundings, and began the process of creating a 'Dubai brand' by marketing and selected sponsorship, particularly in sports and the arts.

Of course, not all the policies were successful. Sometimes the judgement- calls were flawed – the over-expansion into over-hyped real-estate developments in the early years of the twenty-first century, typified by the 'Palm' and 'World' reclamations, is perhaps the prime example, but Dubai had always had to take risks in order to maintain a lead over possible competitors. In retrospect, the Jebel Ali complex, Dubai Dry Docks and Emirates Airline projects, all derided at the time of their inceptions, have proven to be cornerstones of Dubai's development. Even the Burj Khalifa tower, inaugurated in 2010 having been abruptly re-named from the original 'Burj Dubai', apparently a symbol of Dubai's hubris and failure, is now an iconic and popular landmark. Distinctively in the region, Dubai proactively determined to engage, co-operate and, where necessary, compete with the globalized world on equal terms with no inferiority complex, rather than hanging back to await and react to developments. Dubai grew as a commercial, trading and transportation centre because of innovative ideas. These ideas were to take commerce, trade and transport logistics seriously, invest in them with finance and people and aim to be the best when neighbouring states focussed myopically on oil revenues and were not interested in making diversification efforts. By focussing on 'disrupting technologies', not only the technology itself, such as containerization, that transformed the competitive logistical landscape, but in the attitudinal approach to marketing the different types of the services that Dubai could provide and matching them up with what the market (their customers) required, the Emirate's policy was distinctly different. Creativity and re-invention produced one of the world's biggest container ports within twenty years; the world's biggest international airport in an area barely on international airline itineraries as a destination until late in the twentieth century; and the creation of the established centre for regional business and international organisations.

One of Dubai's greatest innovations was to understand that their customers, in a competitive world, had choices, and by maintaining professionalism, the understanding of what their customers needed – and providing it – they would compete more effectively. Significantly, Sultan Bin Sulayem, the chairman of Dubai Ports World (DPW), when interviewed in Dubai in 2017, responded on the point of innovation and change, very specifically when asked about the biggest challenges ahead. He considered technological change, the prospect of unforeseen changes, radically altering the business model and ways of doing business as the greatest threat. Ironically, as an established international company, DPW, like Dubai itself, now has to consider the prospect of 'disruption'.

Dubai's multifaceted approach to development was also distinctive because of the role of institutions, not only the ruling structure, the 'connected capitalism' involving the accepted authority of the ruling family and their embedding of the local merchants to participate in the diversified commercializing of the economy. Institutions also entailed establishing an administrative structure with legal frameworks, effective government institutions that were free of corruption and where professionalism was regarded as important. Effective institutions are, of course, important for all states, and for emerging economies, they can make the difference between enabling and encouraging foreign investment and international businesses. Diversifying Dubai needed to attract investment and to be a reliable, competent and secure base where businesses and their people would feel confident to establish themselves for the longer term. In a region beset by conflict and with no international reputation (whether justified or not), for a disciplined business approach, this was no easy task. However, Dubai achieved this feat, to become the unchallenged business centre at the epicentre of a wide region, by not only creating the liberal business environment and facilities (ports and airports) that made them work but also establishing the institutions that instilled personal and professional confidence. The Emirate was thus able to benefit from the Lebanese Civil War, the Iranian Revolution, the Invasion of Kuwait by Iraq, and even more distant conflicts such as Chechnya and Afghanistan, as businesspeople and traders re-located to Dubai, not only because of the business environment and the opportunities but also because of reliable and secure institutions.

Providing such comparative advantages, where social, religious, political or economic conditions in many states provided distinct disincentives to remain or to return, attracted both talent and investment. We should recognize that Dubai received this inflow when there were many other alternative destinations, in the wider region, but few providing the tantalizing combination of welcoming economic liberalism in a safe, congenial environment, backed up by largely impartial and effective civil administration and – by many standards – a solid legal and arbitration system. Living in such a place would also provide (both male and female) children with a good (often English language) education. Effective and impartial institutions attract, as the heterogeneity of Dubai testifies. It is easy to overlook the fact that for many inhabitants in emerging economies, the ability to live in such conditions, access such facilities and be able to aspire to better themselves and their children are invariably very difficult to achieve. Dubai provides this opportunity.

The greater transparency afforded by reliable institutions, which have professional connectivity with international organizations, provides the security which businesses, investors and those establishing regional centres require, which has allowed the establishment, not only of businesses but also of the multi-national organizations, using Dubai as a regional centre (such as Oracle, Google, Samsung, IBM, etc), and International bodies such as UNICEF and UNHCR. These institutions have located to Dubai, and inward investment has been that robust, in part, because of the legal and financial rigour of institutions and lack of corruption, compared with other emerging economies, where such issues continue to exist on a major scale.

Some regional specialists have reservations about whether the new cities of the Gulf, primarily Dubai, have the substance to make a real contribution as centres of production, creativity, information, goods and services. I think there is abundant evidence, which I have described, to suggest that Dubai is already well on the way to fulfilling these criteria, as a logistics centre, as a financial centre and as a centre for education, media and technology, in addition to the innovations it has pioneered internationally, in aviation and as a Ports manager throughout the world. The important factor often ignored is the question of attitude – why Dubai acted as it did. In my view, from its earliest days, it has made the efforts and tried to out-perform others by being better and more professional at what it does, to strive, rather than sit back, to compete rather than concede, to be the best rather than perform half-heartedly. Without this 'attitude', Dubai would have allowed Sharjah to continue to be the major location for the Trucial States – not bothered to improve the creek, saved money by not building Jebel Ali, allowed Gulf Air to determine who could travel to Dubai and when, failed to continue to expand its container facilities and free-zones, and never thought of creating a tourist industry from scratch.

This attitude of mind, this competitive instinct, to take on the established centres, to have the confidence to introduce new techniques and new technology and use them to out-perform established international players was already apparent when other states, with a cargo-cult mentality that relied on others to produce and supply everything else, were content to focus solely on oil and gas. Such attitudes were born out of the trading heritage which Dubai continues to regard with pride, a heritage of dealing with the outside world, with a flexible tolerance of religion and origin and, no sense of inferiority or xenophobic disdain. A conviction that trading links were not only mutually beneficial commercial propositions, but also commitments to peaceful intercourse.

The Rulers of Dubai, as 'Merchant Princes' themselves, and remembering the lessons of the past, (Lingah 1902 and Dubai in the late 1930s for example), also appreciated the need to maintain close relations with and provide opportunities for, the merchant community on whom the prosperity of the trading city depended. Unlike Kuwait, for example, where familial elites, determined to have a share of the rentier income from oil, forced the ruling family, to concede their exclusive revenue distribution rights, and to make concessions in the political administration of the Emirate, in Dubai, relations between the Al Maktoums and the merchant elite have remained close for decades. This relationship was a constructive symbiosis, embedding the merchants in the prosperity of Dubai, a 'trickle down', inclusive approach, reflecting an appreciation that the trading community was Dubai and that success for Dubai was based on the merchants, and by extension, the investors and business people who came to the city. The infrastructure expansion, initially Port Rashid and then Jebel Ali, the airport and airline, was aimed at creating the facilities to make Dubai the region's undisputed trading and business centre for the future, reinforcing the attitudinal ethos that had long sustained it, supporting, encouraging and enabling national and multi-national merchants in their businesses.

Dubai and the Al Maktoum ruling family, like everyone else, had no conception that containerization from the 1970s onwards would, by cutting costs dramatically and by standardisation, create a worldwide economic restructuring that would increase trade flows exponentially, and, by enabling globalisation, transform the world – and the Gulf. However, their attitude to this shipping and logistics revolution, as competitive 'newcomers', aligned very closely with that of the new carriers who were to dominate the shipping industry in the future. As Marc Levinson stresses, in his history of the containerization industry, the new companies had very different skill-sets from their predecessors. They were more transnational and, because of the nature of the new industry, focussed on the logistical challenges of moving containers efficiently, seeking out new markets, marketing and information systems, more than traditional maritime knowledge. As the demise of traditional carriers and ports throughout the globe was to show, reacting too slowly or ineffectively to the radical changes that containerization brought about would ensure that customers and the businesses that supplied them would shift support to better alternatives. Tradition no longer counted, cost savings and efficiencies, provided by the new lines and new ports, became even more paramount, as container volumes increased, and ship sizes grew inexorably. Dubai's Jebel Ali, itself a new start-up, alone in the region, provided the quality of product, service and the scale required by lines and customers grappling with the huge, unanticipated growth in trade volumes and the need to provide integrated intermodal transport. As also, with the decisions to expand the airport and to initiate Emirates Airline, Dubai's attitude to investment and pursuing long-term interests was very far from conservative reticence, rather one of seizing opportunities with 'disruptive technology' and radical change, to move far ahead of the competition.

Why would Dubai do this? In a region of rentier states, dependent and solely focussed, in the main, on oil and gas revenues, Dubai, in contrast, particularly from the 1960s onwards, was exceptional in the way that it adopted a very different strategy of economic diversification, developing and strengthening its logistics infrastructure to expand and compete. Innovation was vital, to develop and evolve more effectively, while ensuring that its institutions were fit for purpose in order to keep ahead of the competition. It was essential also, not to lose the distinctive competitive attitude that welcomed outsiders, was determined to work with them, or compete with them as professionally as possible. The unique 'Dubai Model' was therefore never a 'one size fits all' plan, but was a result of policies that, above all, accepted and interacted with a changing and more globalized world; learning from others (like Singapore) and accepting the implications of interconnected local and worldwide activities.

From its early days, Dubai adopted an unusually well-developed cosmopolitanism, accepting the outside world and its varied representatives as valued interlocuters in trade. However, it is unlikely that Dubai would have been able to maintain this attitude or to be able to develop as it did without the external protection of the British for nearly 150 years. Embedded in the trading and maritime connections of Empire the useful legacy of this long connection has today, for example, been retained in the predominance of the English language as a most convenient connector with the outside world and its use in education as a medium of instruction. This shelter, and the peace that it supplied, with protection from, for example, Wahabi religious and Saudi, Iranian or Iraqi territorial expansionary incursions, affected all the small Arab states and allowed their independence. The British umbrella provided the opportunities, but Dubai, as an initially insignificant town with minimal resources, using initiative and innovation, took most advantage of what it offered. However, the British connection eventually worked in two ways, as a significant factor in the survival and success of the Al Maktoum monarchs and Dubai itself, and then, from the 1960s onwards, rather differently, with the British realization that the balance of power was changing and that Britain needed Dubai, as a market and opportunity for British goods, services and for inward investment of financial surpluses, as much as Dubai needed Britain. In the final decade of British protection, the constructive development plans of Shaikh Rashid, to prepare Dubai for the competition in years to come from states with infinitely greater financial resources, were very different from the attitudes of other Trucial States. It is worth stressing, too, that these were indeed the plans of Shaikh Rashid, not those hatched up by the British or others. The evidence of contemporaries and in archive records is that Shaikh Rashid was making the plans, to improve Dubai's ability to compete and often, it was his advisors or the British political officials, who attempted to dissuade him from what were seen as costly and unnecessary ventures.

His successors as rulers, sons Maktoum and in particular, Mohammed, have continued and expanded the developmental measures set in motion by Shaikh Rashid. Dubai remains an example of patrimonial monarchical governance where policies are primarily determined by the ruler and senior family members, albeit in concert with a group of senior non-family advisors. Great attention continues to be paid to ensuring that the relationship with both Dubai business families and Dubai nationals in general is maintained and that their concerns are heard. The choice of the telegenic and personable Shaikh Hamdan bin Mohammed as Crown Prince in 2008 is very much part of the process of ensuring a smooth transition of power, with a lengthy and increasing participation for him in the business of government. However, this system of government is very much dependent on the personable attributes of the ruler who is the final decision-maker. There may be some potential checks and balances from a variety of senior Dubai figures, but the Ruler can decide to listen to their advice – or not. Inevitably there must be questions about how strongly opposition to particular courses of action are argued if these are against the views of the Ruler, and contrary attitudes are regarded as signs of weakness or disloyalty. The Al Maktoum rulers have negotiated their way skilfully – albeit with some missteps – through treacherous waters over the recent decades to maintain the reputation and apolitical ethos of Dubai, and the challenges they face as part of the UAE in an increasingly complex geo-political environment are certainly not getting easier. In recent years, the role and influence of Abu Dhabi has grown, providing financial succour at times of need – and pushing a more active and interventionist foreign policy which have resulted in economic downsides for Dubai. Adverse publicity about family matters have also dogged the Al Maktoums – though whether such stories have any impact on visitors and investment is open to doubt. Dubai needs to continue to take the bold decisions that have carried it and the UAE forward. It is also absolutely necessary that the ruling family continues to listen to advice from a wide variety of sources if they are to make the right decisions – most of the time – in the complex and challenging future.

The development of Dubai was aided by the exogenous economic and political factors in the region, such as the civil war in Lebanon, conflict and revolution in Iraq and Iran and the different developmental policies and attitudes of neighbouring states. However, it is also evident that Dubai was able to capitalize on these events only because they had taken the institutional and attitudinal steps to create a stable, reputable and innovative environment and created the infrastructural facilities to which people and businesses would gravitate as a result of problems elsewhere. This was not just luck. This was a thorough and professional approach which perceived that success is dependent on being competitive and that being competitive requires the provision of the best facilities and service – continually. The ports needed to be upgraded to cope with larger container ships; the airport needed expanding to cater for larger aircraft and more passengers – with another (Al Maktoum) airport established now near Jebel Ali too; the basic logistics of the free-zones of early years needed transforming into high-tech enclaves of computer-controlled intermodalism; and the huge growth in tourism required professional quality facilities, service, sales and marketing.

All these policies relied on the fact that Dubai had never shied away from interaction with the outside business world, to encourage and welcome outsiders for the benefit of the Emirate and its merchants and people. This attitude was very different from the oil and gas mono-culture rentier neighbours, who actively either discouraged external trade or were indifferent to it. In recent years this attitude has changed and, recognizing, at last, the weakness of one-crop economies, all the Gulf states have embarked on policies of diversification, to some extent. They are using exactly the same blueprints as those pioneered by Dubai; ports, airports/airlines, more commercial activity and free-zones/innovation-hubs – with a dash of international sporting activity & culture in a 'search for significance'. But, as yet, none of them have diminished the role of the Gulf entrepot, which continues to bestride the region, with its mix of light-touch, economic liberalism, professionalism, cosmopolitanism and re-invention.

As we have seen, Dubai's approach has not been without its flaws. Hubris and mis-calculations blighted the trajectory during the financial crisis from 2008, but the strength of the underlying structure (and financial lifelines from Abu Dhabi) enabled the Emirate to rebound from 2012 onwards, albeit with the clear understanding that Abu Dhabi was now in the unchallenged political driving-seat.

So, in conclusion, has Dubai, in its unique developmental path, contributed distinctively to the region and beyond? I believe it has.

First, by displaying a trade-focussed, co-operative attitude to dealing with outsiders, it has demonstrated that mutually beneficial interaction, working within internationally agreed rules and regulations, (such as customs regulations and those relating to intercontinental through-container movements), can work effectively for economic development. The success of Dubai is testament to the beneficial impact of the 'rules based international systems' prevailing since the mid-twentieth century. These, adopted by Dubai in the wake of the containerization revolution in particular, allowed the Emirate to participate in and become part of worldwide growth that in three or four decades brought millions out of extreme poverty and increased average life expectancy in the poorest nations by a decade. If Dubai can do it, so can others. We should not underestimate the attractiveness of a state which created building blocks of good governance, an effective civil service and legal system – and comprehensive education for all children – elements so significantly lacking in many other emerging states, many of whose most capable citizens have sought to travel to and remain in Dubai. Why did the Emirate take these steps? – because they worked in creating an economy that outpaced any competitors.

Second, even emerging economies without great endowments, like Dubai, can become viable centres, by focussing on their strengths, adopting a professional approach to customers and by investing in infrastructure, backed up by impartial and robust bureaucratic and legal frameworks. An essential element of this approach is to recognize that it is necessary to compete, for customers and investment and that competing requires professionalism. Things can change; trading patterns, political affiliations, new-rising powers, technological transformation, complacency, can all play a part in transforming the landscape. As has been illustrated, just over fifty years ago, Dubai was a small town of a few score thousand people on a small sandy creek. During the intervening years it has eclipsed older, bigger centres, as a result of the policies it has adopted.

Third, its success reveals how essential is innovation and imagination. The enthusiastic adoption of revolutionary containerization technology which transformed cargo movements; the introduction of new technology in the ports and airports to transform manual systems into automated networks linked to customers; the re-imagining of free-zones into centres for technological development; the creation of a complete tourist industry from inauspicious surroundings; the creation of Dubai airport as a worldwide passenger distribution hub and the imaginative leap to establish Dubai as a brand in itself, its reputation promoted by sporting and cultural events and backed up by its own airline. A reputation for imagination and innovation attracts like-minded, capable people and goes a long way towards ensuring that economic diversification continues to expand. In a brave new world where, according to McKinsey Global Institute, the amount of data crossing borders was 148 times larger in 2017 than in 2005, and the trade in services has grown 60 per cent faster than the trade in goods, being a major hub for commerce and services is a great advantage – but this only happens if the right conditions are met.

The aim of this book has been to show how Dubai's distinctive and innovative policies produced the regional entrepot we see today. These achievements were predicated on a neutralist, apolitical, trade-focussed approach – to be better than other competitors. This trod softly and delicately around regional or international disputes, maintaining cordial relations with all, within the UAE from 1971 and as part of a Gulf Co-operation Council, (GCC) from 1981, which, if not particularly effective, at least tended to move in policy directions which reflected the world views of its Sunni monarchical members. At the time of writing, the Qatar crisis from 2017 (a side-effect of the Syrian uprising) and the increasing assertiveness of Abu Dhabi-dominated UAE foreign policy, aligned to Saudi Arabia, have fragmented this delicate balance in the region, as boycotted Qatar, now, with its own new port, also seeks other allies, such as Turkey and Iran, to circumvent the Dubai entrepot. Even though a Kuwaiti-brokered 'peace' was signed in January 2021, still-evident mistrust and suspicions make it likely that previous well-established trading links and patterns may never return. Economically challenged Oman is (with Chinese investment) developing its ports of Duqm and Sohar as alternatives to Jebel Ali, allowing Qatar containers to transit its ports; and Chinese influence, both political and economic, is adding to the regional contestation, linked to the 'Belt and Road

Initiative' (New Silk Road), with investments and 'partnerships' in Pakistan, the UAE and the Red Sea. This external super-power involvement, financing potential regional rivals (such as Gwadar in Pakistan or Duqm in Oman), is creating new challenges for a Dubai that was sheltered under British or American umbrellas for nearly two centuries and prospered by focussing on trading and as a service centre rather than taking sides. Qatar's wealthy population and economy now side-step the logistical channels established via Dubai for decades and choose other alternatives. Maintaining its consistent approach, and 'keeping its head down', Dubai continues to maintain its focus on its innovative strengths and separateness, and leaves Abu Dhabi to make the external political moves. This has to be a sensible policy as the competitive arena is now therefore less stable and more complex, than ever before. In the coming years, Dubai will certainly need to marshal all its innovative skills, and the critical mass of achievement and reputation, it has established if it is to surmount these latest challenges.

Significantly, also, even the recalcitrant rentiers have, in recent decades, belatedly recognized the need to diversify their economies, with the 'Dubai Model' blueprints as a guide. Fossil-fuel prices and reserves have declined and alternative supplies, (shale gas), or energy sources, such as solar and wind power – in a world where climate change is increasingly accepted as a reality – are increasingly viable alternatives. Perhaps most significantly of all, although its circumstances and development are unique, Dubai's trajectory is undoubtedly a showpiece for emerging states, as an example of what can be achieved, by an Arab state which works as well as 'Western' countries, and where attitude and application in a multinational environment count more than origin, caste or ethnicity. As a poster-child for successful globalization, encouraging by example an improvement in policy by less-capable governments, aware that isolation no longer works, that diversification is essential and that their citizens can make comparisons – this has been Dubai's paradigm achievement.

The most significant recent challenge is of course the impact of the worldwide Covid pandemic, which, throughout 2020 and 2021, has caused virtually every nation, and certainly those in Europe, Asia and America, to suspend or severely limit international travel. Such restrictions have had a dramatic effect on the tourism and services industry on which Dubai is so dependent, including Emirates Airline and the much-feted 'Dubai 2020' Trade Fair (now postponed until October 2021). The Dubai economy contracted by around 7 per cent in 2020 according to official figures, even though DPW container volumes were reported as 'virtually the same as 2019' overall. It seems likely that, as in 2008, an influx of funds from Abu Dhabi will have been necessary to cover borrowing repayments and increased indebtedness. Like other major economies, Dubai and the UAE are aiming to vaccinate their way out of the disaster – emerging yet again as a safe haven – and with commendable efficiency, it has inoculated about half the population by mid-March 2021. 'Toe-in-the-water' exhibitions have again begun (such as 'Art Dubai' 2021) in late March 2021, operating in a Covid-secure, limited capacity environment to highlight, with the 15th annual fair, that if it was not exactly 'business as usual', Dubai was on the way back as a leisure hub.

In fact, for all the reasons expounded in this book, when the 'bounce-back' happens, Dubai should benefit even more from being a 'tried and tested' location for the millions of people who will be desperate once more to travel on holiday and spend 'retail-therapy' money in a safe and reliable location. Based on past experience (such as the post-financial crisis recovery), Emirates Airline, with its enormous fleet size, will certainly recover after a torrid year, as passenger numbers rebound, with perhaps more synergies and consolidation with already ailing Etihad Airline; Jebel Ali port and the free-zones will of course weather the storm, as flexible labour policies will increase worker numbers to handle the container volumes and free-zone activity increase in the post-pandemic surge and Dubai hotels and restaurants will be full again once more. Post-Covid, the Dubai brand will still be intact – its resilience carried through by the infrastructure, innovation and institutions that have sustained it over so many decades.

NOTES

Introduction

1. Jim Krane, *Dubai* (New York: St Martin's Press, 2009), 69.
2. In the container shipping industry, containers are either twenty feet or forty feet long. A twenty-foot container is known as a TEU – twenty-foot equivalent unit (a forty-foot container is therefore 2 x TEU), and this terminology is used statistically.
3. 'Soaring Ambition', *The Economist*, 10 January 2015, 43.
4. Anoush Ehteshami, *Dynamics of Change in the Persian Gulf* (London: Routledge, 2013), 13.
5. A rentier state is one which derives all or most of its revenues from the 'rent' of its resources (e.g. oil and gas) to external parties.
6. https://data.worldbank.org
7. Martin Hvidt, 'The Dubai Model', *International Journal of Middle East Studies* 41, no. 3 (August 2009).
8. Hazem Beblawi, and Giacamo Luciani, *The Rentier State* (New York: Routledge, 1987).
9. Nazi Ayubi, *Over-Stating the Arab State: Politics and Society in the Middle East* (London: I B Tauris, 1995).
10. Matthew Gray, *A Theory of Later Rentierism in the Arab States of the Gulf* (Doha: Georgetown University, 2011).
11. Ashraf Mishrif, 'Challenges of Economic Diversification in the GCC Countries', in Ashraf Mishrif and Yousuf Al Balushi (eds.), *Economic Diversification in the Gulf Region: Comparing Global Challenges* (Singapore: Palgrave Macmillan/Gulf Research Centre Cambridge, 2018), 1.
12. Christopher Davidson, *After the Shaikhs: The Coming Collapse of the Gulf Monarchies* (London: Hurst, 2012).
13. Samuel P. Huntington, *Political Order in Changing Societies* (New Haven: Yale, 1968). Huntington set out the dilemma for monarchical rulers – facing pressure to liberalize in a changing world – how to do so without losing the ability to continue to rule as monarchs.
14. According to *The Times* on 7 November 2017, Prince Mohammed Bin Salman, Crown Prince of Saudi Arabia has declared, as part of his modernization drive, that he wanted Saudi Arabia to be like Dubai, only bigger.
15. Michael Herb, *All in the Family: Absolutism, Revolution and Democracy in the Middle East Monarchies* (New York: Suny Press, 1999).
16. Juan Linz, *Totalitarian and Authoritarian Regimes* (Boulder: Lynne Rienner, 2000).
17. Russell Lucas, 'Monarchical Authoritarianism: Survival and Political Liberalisation in a Middle Eastern Regime Type', *International Journal of Middle Eastern Studies* 36, no. 1 (February 2004).

18 Andrea Rugh, The Political Culture of Leadership in the United Arab Emirates (Basingstoke: Palgrave Macmillan, 2007).
19 Eva Bellin, 'The Robustness of Authoritarianism in the Middle East', *Comparative Politics* 36, no. 2 (January 2004).
20 Abbas Al Lawati, 'Expatriates in the Gulf', in Jane Kinninmont (ed.), *Future Trends in the Gulf* (London: Chatham House, 2015).
21 Joseph Nye, *Soft Power: The Means to Success in World Politics* (New York: Public Affairs Press, 2005).
22 May Seikaly and Khawla Mattar (eds.), *The Silent Revolution: The Arab Spring and the Gulf States* (Berlin: Gerlach Press, 2014).
23 Toby Matthiesen, *Sectarian Gulf* (Stanford: Stanford University Press, 2013).
24 Julian Walker, 'Personal Recollections of Indigenous Sources', *Liwa Journal* 4, no. 8 (December 2012): 20. Julian Walker was a British Diplomat who after years of effort, produced the first internal boundary maps (the 'jigsaw') of the Trucial States in the 1960s.
25 Anita Burdett (ed.), *Records of Dubai Volumes 1-7 1761-1960* (Cambridge: Cambridge University Press Archive Editions, 2000).
26 Wilfred Thesiger, *Arabian Sands* (London: Longmans, Green, 1959).
27 John G Lorimer (ed.), *Gazetteer of the Persian Gulf* (Calcutta: Government Printing Press, 1908).
28 George Chapman, *Memoirs* (Unpublished manuscript 2018).
29 Frank Broeze, 'Dubai: From Creek to Global City', in Lewis Fischer and Adrian Jarvis (eds.), *Harbours and Havens: Essays in Port History in Honour of Gordon Jackson* (St John's Newfoundland: International Maritime Economic History Association, 1999).
30 Mehran Kamrava (ed.), *Gateways to the World: Port Cities in the Persian Gulf* (London: Hurst, 2016).
31 Marc Levinson, *The Box: How the Shipping Container Made the World Smaller and the World Economy Bigger* (Princeton: Princeton University Press, 2008 Paperback).
32 Shaikh Sultan Al Qasimi, *The Myth of Arab Piracy in the Gulf* (London: Routledge, 1988). Shaikh Sultan is currently (2018) the Ruler of Sharjah in the UAE.
33 Frauke Heard-Bey, *From Trucial States to UAE* (Dubai: Motivate Publishing 1982 & 3rd reprint, 2013).
34 Donald Hawley, *The Trucial States* (London: Allen and Unwin, 1970).
35 Jonathan Raban, *Arabia Through the Looking Glass* (Glasgow: Collins, 1979), 164-8.
36 Michael Field, *The Merchants* (London: John Murray, 1984), 60.
37 Abbas Makki, *Rashid: The Man Behind Dubai* (Dubai: Reading for All Publishers, 1990).
38 Graeme Wilson, *Rashid's Legacy* (London: Media Prima, 2006).
39 Easa S Al Gurg, The Wells of Memory (London: John Murray, 1998).
40 Abdul Sherriff, *Dhow Cultures of the Indian Ocean* (London: Hurst, 2010).
41 Stephanie Jones, *Two Centuries of Overseas Trading* (Basingstoke: Palgrave Macmillan, 1986).
42 James Onley, *Britain and the Gulf Shaikhdoms 1820-1971: The Politics of Protection* (Doha: Georgetown University School of Foreign Service in Qatar, 2009).
43 Broeze, *Dubai*, 1999.
44 S. J. Ramos, *Dubai Amplified: The Engineering of a Port Geography* (Farnham: Ashgate, 2010).
45 Kamrava, *Gateways to the World*, 2016.

46 Paul Dresch, 'Societies, Identities and Global Issues', in Paul Dresch and James Piscatori (eds.), *Monarchies and Nations: Globalisation and Identity in the Arab States of the Gulf* (London: I B Tauris, 2005), 1.
47 Christopher Davidson, *Dubai: The Vulnerability of Success* (London: Hurst, 2008), Back Cover.
48 Asraf Mishrif and Harun Kapetanovic, 'Dubai's Model of Economic Diversification', in Ashraf Mishrif and Yousuf Al Balushi, *Economic Diversification in the Gulf Region: Comparing Global Challenges* (Singapore: Palgrave Macmillan/Gulf Research Centre Cambridge, 2018), 89.
49 Jim Krane, *Dubai* (New York: St Martin's Press, 2009).
50 Syed Ali, *Dubai: Gilded Cage* (New Haven and London: Yale University Press, 2010).
51 Martin Hvidt, 'The Dubai Model', 2009.
52 Mike Davis, 'Fear and Money in Dubai', *New Left Review* 41, no. 3 (September/October 2006).
53 Ha-Joon Chang, *Kicking away the Ladder: Development Strategy in Historical Perspective* (London: Anthem Press, 2002).
54 Abdilhadi Khalaf, Omar Al Shehabi, and Adam Hanieh (eds.), *Transit States: Labour, Migration & Citizenship in the Gulf* (London: Pluto Press, 2015).
55 Shaikh Mohammed Bin Rashid Al Maktoum, *Flashes of Thought* (Dubai: Motivate Publishing, 2014).
56 Jones, *Two Centuries*.
57 George Blake, *BI Centenary* (London: Collins, 1956).
58 Michael Q Morton, 'The British India Line in the Arabian Gulf 1862–1982', *Liwa Journal Abu Dhabi* 5, no. 10 (December 2013).
59 Percival Griffiths, *A History of the Inchcape Group* (London: Inchcape, 1977).
60 Nelida Fuccaro, 'Rethinking the History of Port Cities in the Gulf', in Lawrence Potter (ed.), *The Persian Gulf in Modern Times* (New York: Palgrave, 2014). There are other works by Fuccaro on the same theme.
61 Kamrava, *Gateways to the World*, 2016.
62 Brian Cudahy, *Box Boats* (New York: Fordham University Press, 2006).
63 Frank Broeze, *The Globalisation of the Oceans* (St John's Newfoundland: IMEHA, 2002).
64 Lance Hoosteval, *Globalization Contained: The Economic and Strategic Consequences of the Container* (New York: Palgrave Macmillan, 2013).
65 Rose George, *Deep Sea & Foreign Going* (London: Portobello Books, 2014).
66 Horatio Clare, *Down to the Sea in Ships* (London: Chatto & Windus, 2014).
67 Davidson, *Dubai*, 2008.
68 Edward Said, *Orientalism* (New York: Pantheon Books, 1978). Said's seminal work highlighted, in his view, the presumption of Western superiority, Eurocentric prejudice against and patronizing assessments of the Oriental (often Middle Eastern) world.

Chapter 1

1 Phillip Steinberg, *The Social Construction of the Ocean* (Cambridge: Cambridge University Press, 2001), 8.

2. James Onley and Sulayman Khalaf, 'Shaikhly Authority in the Pre-Oil Gulf', *History and Anthropology* 17, no. 3 (September 2006).
3. Davidson, *Dubai*, 13.
4. Anthony Phillips, and Jason Sharman, *International Order in Diversity: Trade and Rule in the Indian Ocean* (Cambridge: Cambridge University Press, 2015), 6.
5. Abdul Sheriff, *Dhow Cultures of the Indian Ocean* (London: Hurst, 2010).
6. Alan Villiers, *Sons of Sinbad* (London: Hodder & Stoughton, 1949).
7. Lawrence G. Potter, *The Rise and Fall of Port Cities in the Persian Gulf in Modern Times* (New York: Palgrave, 2014), 135.
8. Nelida Fuccaro, 'The Making of Gulf Ports Before Oil', *Liwa Journal* Abu Dhabi 2, no. 3 (June 2010).
9. Hawley, *The Trucial States*, 129.
10. Ibid., 318.
11. Glenn Balfour-Paul, *The End of Empire in the Middle East* (Cambridge: Cambridge University Press, 1991), 5.
12. Andrea B. Rugh, *The Political Culture of Leadership in the UAE* (Basingstoke: Palgrave Macmillan, 2007).
13. Hawley, *The Trucial States*, 78.
14. Penelope Tuson, *The Records of the British Residency and Agencies in the Persian Gulf* (London: India Office Library, 1979), xiii.
15. Al Qasimi, *The Myth of Arab Piracy*, xv.
16. Charles Belgrave, *The Pirate Coast* (London: G Bell & Sons, 1966).
17. John B. Kelly, *Britain and the Persian Gulf 1795–1880* (Oxford: Clarendon Press, 1968), 19.
18. Daniel T. Potts, 'Trends and Patterns in the Archaeology and Pre-Modern History of the Gulf Region', in J. E. Peterson (ed.), *The Emergence of the Gulf States* (London: Bloomsbury, 2016).
19. Heard-Bey, *From Trucial States*, 281.
20. Noura S. Al Mazrouei, *The UAE and Saudi Arabia: Border Disputes and International Relations in the Gulf* (London: I B Tauris, 2016), 4.
21. Al Qasimi, *The Myth of Arab Piracy*, 225.
22. Charles E. Davies, *The Blood Red Flag: An Investigation into Qasimi Piracy 1797-1820* (Exeter: University of Exeter Press, 1997), 294.
23. Phillip Macdougall, *Islamic Seapower in the Age of Fighting Sail* (Woodbridge: Boydell Press, 2017), 199.
24. Muna M. Alhammadi, *Britain and the Administration of the Trucial States 1947–65* (Abu Dhabi: Emirates Center for Strategic Studies and Research, 2013).
25. Wilson, *Rashid's Legacy*, 30.
26. Kristian C. Ulrichsen, *The Gulf States in International Political Economy* (Basingstoke: Palgrave Macmillan, 2016), 18.
27. Rosemary S. Zahlan, *The Making of the Modern Gulf States* (Reading, MA: Ithaca, 1998), 27.
28. Davidson, *Dubai*, 14.
29. Husain Al Baharna, *British Extra-Territorial Jurisdiction in the Gulf 1913–1971* (Slough: Archive Editions, 1998), 9.
30. James Onley, *Britain and the Gulf Shaikhdoms 1820-1971: The Politics of Protection* (Doha: Georgetown University School, 2009), 3.
31. Willem Floor, *The Persian Gulf: The Rise and Fall of Bandar-E-Lengeh, The Distribution Center for the Arabian Coast* (Washington: Mage Publishing, 2010), 153.

32 Lewis Pelly, 'A Visit to the Port of Lingah, the Island of Kishm and the Port of Bandar Abbass', *Royal Geographical Society of London,* Proceedings 8, no. 6 (London: 1863/1864): 265/266.
33 Floor, *The Persian Gulf*, 44.
34 David Roberts, 'The Consequences of the Exclusive Treaties', in B. R. Pridham (ed.), *The Arab Gulf and the West* (London: Croom Helm, 1985), 13.
35 Hawley, *The Trucial States*, 195.
36 Lorimer, *Gazetteer,* Vol. ii, 1438.
37 Dionisius A. Agius, *Seafaring in the Arabian Gulf and Oman: The People of the Dhow* (London: Kegan Paul, 2005), 103.
38 Ibid., 105.
39 Norman Lewis, *A Voyage by Dhow* (London: Jonathan Cape, 2001), 47.
40 Jones, *Two Centuries*, 6.
41 Martin Stopford, *Maritime Economics* (Abingdon: Routledge, 2009).
42 Morton, *British India Line*, 41.
43 Stephanie Jones, 'British India Steamers and the Trade of the Persian Gulf 1862–1914', *Great Circle Journal* 7, no. 1 (April 1985).
44 Jones, *Two Centuries*, 81.
45 Freda Harcourt, 'British Oceanic Mail Contracts in the Age of Steam 1838-1914', in D. M. Williams (ed.), *The World of Shipping* (Basingstoke: Palgrave Macmillan, 1997).
46 Percival Griffiths, *A History of the Inchcape Group* (London: Inchcape, 1977), 70.
47 Ibid., 71.
48 George Chapman, *Unpublished Manuscript*, 2018: 20. George Chapman, resident in Dubai since 1951, worked for Gray Mackenzie & Co. (GM), as 'Wakeel' (Agent). GM in Dubai handled all the cargo movements, the mail deliveries, insurance claims and agency work, as well as acting as general agents for many imported goods.
49 Nelida Fuccaro, *Histories of City and State in the Persian Gulf: Manama since 1800* (Cambridge: Cambridge University Press, 2012), 59.
50 J A Saldanha, *Precis of Commerce and Communication in the Persian Gulf 1801–1905* (Calcutta: Government Printing House, 1906).
51 Jones, *Two Centuries*, 86-7.
52 Lorimer, *Gazetteer*, 2467.
53 Anita Burdett, *The GCC States National Development Records – Communications and Transport 1860– 1960 Volume 5* (Cambridge: Cambridge University Press Archive Editions, 1996), 153–62.
54 Ibid., 154.
55 Lorimer, *Gazetteer*, Vol.1, 774.
56 Al Gurg, *The Wells of Memory*, 5.
57 Lorimer, *Gazetteer*, 2596.
58 Floor, *Bandar-E-Lingeh*, 102.
59 Ibid., 101.
60 Lorimer, *Gazetteer*, 2612.
61 Morton, *British India Line*, 55.
62 Heard-Bey, *From Trucial States*, 191 and 243–4.
63 D. N. Muir, 'Early Mail Transport in and From the Gulf 1798-1939', *Liwa Journal Abu Dhabi* 5, no. 10 (December 2013).
64 Floor, *Bandar-E-Lingeh*, 154.

65 Fatma Al Sayegh, 'Merchants Role in a Changing Society: The Case of Dubai 1900–1990', *Middle East Studies* 34, no. 1 (1998).
66 Wilson, *Rashid's Legacy*, 36.
67 James Onley, 'Transnational Merchants in the 19th Century Gulf', in M. Al Rasheed (ed.), *Transnational Connections and the Arab Gulf* (London: Routledge, 2014), 72.
68 Robert Johnson, 'The Great Game and Power Projection', in J. R. Macris, *Imperial Crossroads* (Annapolis: Naval Institute Press, 2012), 34.
69 Lorimer, *Gazetteer*, 369–70.
70 Balfour-Paul, *End of Empire*, 102.
71 Lorimer, *Gazetteer*, 743.
72 Ibid., 2252.
73 Dubai Port World, *Dreams of the Sea: The Dubai Maritime History Project* (Dubai: Explorer Publishing, 2014), 18.
74 Julian Walker, 'Social and Economic Developments in Trucial Oman in the First Half of the Twentieth Century', *Liwa Journal* 2, no. 3 (June 2010): 43.
75 Anita Burdett, *Records of Dubai* (Cambridge: Cambridge University Press Archive Editions, 2000): 558/559.
76 Ibid., 603.
77 J. E. Belt, and H. S. Appleyard, *A History of Frank C Strick and his Many Shipping Enterprises* (Kendal: World Ship Society, 1996).
78 W. A. Laxon and F. W. Perry, *BI: The British India Steam Navigation Company* (Kendal: World Ship Society, 1994).
79 Davidson, *United Arab Emirates*, 182.
80 Walker, *Social and Economic Developments*, 46.
81 UK National Archives, FCO 8/1509 (Dubai Political Agency to FCO London 30 December 1969).
82 George Chapman (Ex *Wakil* in Dubai and Gray Mackenzie MD), self-published, *Those Were the Days* pamphlet 1993. Chapman and the Gray Mackenzie company were responsible (to the Ruler), for the barges that moved cargo from the cargo ships anchored offshore to the Dubai harbour in the creek.
83 George Chapman, *Memoirs*, 2018, 30.
84 UK National Archives (UKNA) Halcrow Report, FO 371/114696, January 1955.
85 UKNA FO 371/114696, Bahrain to London, 31 January 1955.
86 UKNA FO 371/114696, Dubai to Bahrain, 4th November 1955.
87 Al Gurg, *The Wells of Memory*, 75.
88 British Bank of the Middle East (BBME), Dubai Office Letters to London, 68/2, 25 June 1956.
89 BBME Letters, 68/29, 10 February 1957.
90 BBME Letters, 68/31: 95, 25 February 1957.
91 Chapman, *Manuscript*, 36.
92 Ibid.
93 UKNA Halcrow Report, FO 371/114696. January 1955.
94 Christopher M. Davidson, *Dubai: The Vulnerability of Success* (London: Hurst, 2008), 87.
95 UKNA, FO 371/114696, Bahrain to London, 31 January 1955.
96 Donald Hawley, *The Emirates: Witness to a Metamorphosis* (Norwich: Michael Russell, 2007), 211.
97 UKNA, FO 1016/837, Bahrain to London, 15 May 1965.

98   Anita Burdett, Quoting Bahrain Residency to London, 30 April 1948, *Records of Dubai 1761–1960* (Cambridge: Cambridge University Press Archive Editions, 2000), 569.
99   Ibid., 570.
100 Ibid., 587.
101 BBME, 68/2, Dubai Office to London, 25 June 1956.
102 Chapman, *Memoirs*, 37.
103 Davidson, *Dubai*, 156.
104 Hawley, *The Emirates*, 21.
105 UKNA, Bahrain Residency to Foreign Office (FO) London, Annual Report for 1954, 14.
106 UKNA, Bahrain Residency to FO London, Annual Report for 1955, 28.
107 UKNA, Bahrain Residency to FO London, Annual Report for 1956, 12.
108 UKNA Bahrain Residency to FO London, Annual Report for 1959, 10.
109 George Hourani, *Arab Seafaring* (Princeton: Princeton University Press, 1995).
110 Tim Severin, *The Sinbad Voyage* (London: Little Brown & Son, 1982).
111 L. P. Funsch, *Oman Reborn* (New York: Palgrave Macmillan, 2015).
112 J. Jones and N. Ridout, *A History of Modern Oman* (New York: Cambridge University Press, 2015).
113 R. Alston and S. Laing, *Unshook Till the End of Time: A History of Relations between Britain and Oman* (London: Gilgamesh Publishing, 2014).
114 Jones and Ridout, *A History of Modern Oman*, 64.
115 Jones, *Two Centuries*, 23.
116 Ibid., 95.
117 UK National Archives, Bahrain Residency to FO London, 26 February 1960, Ref: FO371/148967.
118 Alan Villiers, *Sons of Sinbad* (London: Hodder & Stoughton, 1949) and Michael Field, *The Merchants* (London: John Murray, 1984). Villiers sailed on the Dhows which sailed from Kuwait to East Africa, bringing back mangrove poles for buildings.
119 Kamrava, *Gateways to the World*, 53.
120 Jones, *Two Centuries*, 83.
121 G. Blake, *BI Centenary* (London: Collins, 1956).
122 J. Bellini, *Pioneering Spirit: The Story Behind Inchcape's Remarkable Journey* (London: Artesian Publishing, 2010) and P. Griffiths, *A History of the Inchcape Group* (London: Inchcape, 1977).
123 Jones, *Two Centuries*, 97.

Chapter 2

1 Marc Levinson, *The Box: How the Shipping Container Made the World Smaller and the World Economy Bigger* (Princeton: Princeton University Press, 2008), xiv.
2 *The Economist Newspaper Online*, 'Why Have Containers Boosted Trade so Much?' May 22, 2013.
3 G. Harlaftis, S. Tenold and J. Valdaliso, *The World's Key Industry: History and Economics of International Shipping* (London: Palgrave Macmillan, 2012), 268.
4 Ibid., 1.
5 Thomas Friedman, *The World is Flat* (London: Penguin Books, 2005).

6. Tim Harford, 'What We Get Wrong about Technology', *Financial Times Weekend FT*, July 8, 2017, 16/17.
7. 'Thinking Outside the Box', *The Economist*, April 28, 2018, 18.
8. R. Parkinson, *Dreadnought: The Ship That Changed the World* (London: I B Tauris, 2015).
9. www.portoffelixstowe.co.uk/50-years/history/
10. Frank Broeze, *The Globalisation of the Oceans* (St John's Newfoundland: International Maritime Economic History Association, 2002), 9.
11. Craig Martin, *Shipping Container* (London: Bloomsbury, 2016), 38.
12. Matthew Heins, *The Globalisation of American Infrastructure* (New York: Routledge, 2016), 30.
13. Broeze, *Globalisation*, 52.
14. A. G. Jamieson, *Ebb Tide in the British Maritime Industries: Change and Adaptation 1918–1990* (Exeter: Exeter University Press, 2003), 85.
15. Richard Woodman, 'Voyage East: A Cargo Ship in the 1960s', in Sam Ignarski (ed.), *The Box: An Anthology* (London: EMAP, 1995), 3.
16. Y. Kaukiainen, 'The Advantages of Water Carriage: Scale Economies and Shipping Technology', in G. Harlaftis, S. Tenold and J. Valdaliso, *The World's Key Industry* (London: Palgrave Macmillan, 2012), 84.
17. GRT, now referred to as GT, is the standard measurement of the space, the enclosed capacity of a ship. The DWT is a measure of how much mass/weight a ship can carry without including the weight of the ship itself.
18. Vernon Rolls, *The Far Eastern Freight Conference 1879* (London: Conference Administration Services, 2005), 9.
19. David and Stephen Howarth, *The Story of P&O* (London: Weidenfield and Nicolson, 1986), 172.
20. Levinson, *The Box*.
21. David Burrell, 'In the Beginning', in Sam Ignarski (ed.), *The Box: An Anthology* (London: EMAP, 1995).
22. A. Donovan and J. Bonney, *The Box that Changed the World* (East Windsor, New Jersey: Commonwealth Business Media, 2006).
23. A. Klose, *The Container Principle: How a Box Changes the Way We Think* (London: MIT Press, 2015).
24. Oliver E. Allen, 'The Man Who Put Boxes on Ships', in S. Ignarski, *The Box: An Anthology* (London: EMAP, 1995).
25. Brian Cudahy, *Box Boats* (New York: Fordham University Press, 2006), 35.
26. A. Klose, *The Container Principle: How a Box Changes the Way We Think* (London: MIT Press, 2015), 161.
27. Matthew Heins, *The Globalisation of American Infrastructure* (New York: Routledge, 2016).
28. Ibid., 14.
29. Levinson, *The Box*, Chapter 9.
30. Ibid., 181.
31. Allen, *Man Who Put Boxes on Ships*, 19.
32. Jamieson, *Ebb Tide*, 35.
33. Rolls, *FEFC*, 59.
34. Janet Porter, 'Four Weddings and a Funeral', *Containerization International*, November 2016, 21.
35. 'The Other Handover', *The Economist*, 15 July 2017, 54/55.

36 Alphaliner website, https://alphaliner.axsmarine.com/PublicTop100/, Accessed 15 February 2018.
37 Flexport Blog website, 'What are Ocean Alliances', by Nerijus Poskus, www.flexport.com/blog/what-are-ocean-alliances/, Accessed 28 November 2017.
38 Wilson, *Rashid's Legacy*, 97.
39 Chapman, *Memoirs,* 111.
40 UK National Archives (UKNA), FO 1016/839/1391/67c, Dubai to London dated 29 May 1967.
41 UKNA, FO 016/ 839, Report from Dubai Agency, 5 June 1967.
42 Chapman, *Memoirs*, 111.
43 Ibid., 112.
44 Ibid.
45 UKNA, FO 016/839 Dubai Agency to FCO London 1 November 1967.
46 Chapman, *Memoirs*, 84.
47 UK National Archives, FO 371/114696 (Internal memo from D. M. H. Riches, 7 January 1956).
48 Fred Halliday, *Arabia Without Sultans* (London: Penguin Books, 1974), 56.
49 UK National Archives, FO 1016/839 (Dubai Political Agency to Bahrain Residency 20 April 1967).
50 Geoffrey Jones, *Banking and Oil: The History of the British Bank of the Middle East, Vol II* (Cambridge: Cambridge University Press, 1987), 135.
51 As recorded earlier, BBME report to London, 68/2 of 25 June 1956, records the Sharjah Ruler's 'lack of co-operation with the Political Agency'. A report of 30 January 1956, 68/17, highlights that the Sharjah Ruler has debt problems.
52 Davidson, *Dubai*, 86/87 and 250.
53 Graeme Wilson, HSBC: *70 Years in the UAE* (London: Media Prima, 2016).
54 Jones, *Banking and Oil*, 155.
55 Ibid.
56 UK National Archives, FCO 8/1510 (J. Bullard, Dubai Political Agency to FO London, 10 December 1970).
57 Nevil Allen, Interview in Dubai British Business Group Magazine, 'Dubai Calling' in 1995, on website www.dubaiasitusedtobe.com, Accessed online 10 June 2017.
58 Alan De Lacy Rush, A., quoted in, *The Ruling Families of Arabia Vol 1* (Cambridge: Cambridge University Press Archive Editions, 1991).
59 Obituary, 'William (Bill) Duff: Financial Supervisor', *The Financial Times*, 17th May 2014. Bill Duff was recruited by Shaikh Rashid al Maktoum in 1960 as his financial advisor. For the next 30 years working closely with the Ruler, he helped to develop the economic infrastructure, particularly the departments of Finance and Customs.
60 George Chapman, *Memoirs*, 119.
61 Donald Hawley, *Desert Wind and Tropic Storm* (Norwich: Michael Russell, 2000), 48. Hawley was the British political agent based in Dubai from 1958 to 1962.
62 Michael Q Morton, *Keepers of the Golden Shore: A History of the UAE* (London: Reaktion Books, 2016), 165.
63 Penelope Tuson (Ed.), *Records of the Emirates, Volume 9* (Cambridge: Cambridge University Press Archive Editions, 1990), 10–11.
64 Davidson, *Dubai,* 56.
65 AlHammadi, *Britain and the Administration of the Trucial States 1947–1965*, 75.
66 Gulf Labour Markets and Migration Website, www.gulfmigration.eu/uae-dubai-estimates-of-total-population-by-sex-1953-1968-census-dates-2006-2013/

67 Frank Broeze, 'Dubai from Creek to Global Port City', in Lewis R. Fischer and Adrian Jarvis, *Harbours and Havens* (St Johns Newfoundland: IMEHA, 1999), 172.
68 M. Crawford, 'Religion in the Gulf 1700-1971', in J. E. Peterson (ed.), *The Emergence of the Gulf States* (London: Bloomsbury, 2016), 146.
69 Balfour-Paul, *The End of Empire in the Middle East*, 111.
70 Sultan Ahmed Bin Sulayem, Chairman of Dubai Port World, Interview in Dubai June 2017. SBS has been at the heart of Dubai decision-making for decades and was instrumental in setting up the Jebel Ali Free-Zone in 1985.
71 Daniel Brook, *A History of Future Cities* (New York: Norton, 2013).
72 Saadi Abdul Rahim Hassan Al Rais, Interview in Dubai November 2017. SAR is the Group MD of his 100-year-old family company and has been a cornerstone of the Shipping and Trading community in Dubai for many years. He is on the Board of Dubai World.
73 Fatma Al Sayegh, 'Merchants Role in a Changing Society', *Middle East Studies* 34, no. 1 (1998).
74 Onley, "Transnational Merchants in the 19th Century Gulf".
75 Raymond O'Shea, *The Sand Kings of Oman* (London: Methuen & Co. 1947), 145–7.
76 Gurg, *Wells*, 1988, 6.
77 K. Jahani, 'Sanctioning Iran: The View from the UAE', in *Al Nakhlah Journal* (Medford: Tufts University, Fletcher School, Spring 2011).
78 A. Burdett, *Records of Dubai* (Cambridge: Cambridge University Press Archive Editions 2000), 7 (Quoting Bahrain Resident to London FO 371/120557, October 1956).
79 A. Abu Baker, 'Political Economy of State Formation: The United Arab Emirates in Comparative Perspective' (PhD Dissertation, University of Michigan, 1995), 99.
80 A. B. Rugh, *The Political Culture of Leadership in the UAE* (Basingstoke: Palgrave Macmillan, 2007).
81 Al Sayegh, *Merchants*, 1998.
82 Morton, *Keepers*, 145.
83 Karen Young, *The Political Economy of Energy, Finance and Security in the UAE* (Basingstoke: Palgrave, 2014), 67.
84 Freddie De Butts, *Now the Dust has Settled* (Padstow: Tabb House, 1995), 187. Freddie De Butts was commander of the Trucial Oman Scouts at the time and presumably had a good idea of what was going on.
85 Frank Broeze, 'Dubai: From Creek to Global Port City', in L. Fischer and A. Jarvis (eds.), *Harbours and Havens: Essays in Port History in Honour of Gordon Jackson* (St. John's Newfoundland, IMEHA, 1999), 173.
86 This period in Dubai's history was turned into a novel about gold-smuggling. Mixing some fact, and the use of real characters (such as Shaikh Rashid), plus others thinly disguised, with a great deal of imagination, but close enough to the truth, was to get the book 'banned' in Dubai. Robin Moore, *Dubai* (London: Barrie and Jenkins, 1976).
87 UK National Archives, Dubai to Bahrain Residency, FO 371/179925, 24 July 1965.
88 UKNA FO 371/179925, 6 November 1965.
89 M. Al Rasheed, *Transnational connections and the Arab Gulf* (London: Routledge, 2014), 6.
90 Onley, *Transnational Merchants*, 78/79.
91 Mahdi Al Tajir (Director of the Ruler's Office), quoted in The *Times* Newspaper supplement to celebrate the formation of the UAE, 21 December 1971.

92 Chapman, *Memoirs*, 42.
93 Ibid., 65/66.
94 Al Gurg, *Wells of Memory*, 104–6.
95 Davidson, *Dubai*, 95.
96 Chapman, *Memoirs*, 67.
97 Dubaifaqs website, www.dubaifaqs.com/dubai-airport.php.
98 Santander Trade Reporthttps://en.portal.santandertrade.com/analyse-markets/united-arab-emirates/economic-political-outline, Accessed 5 December 2017.
99 Invest Group website, www.investingroup.org/snapshot/282/sharjahs-economic-outlook-united-arab-emirates, Accessed 5 December 2017.
100 Oxford Business Group website, www.oxfordbusinessgroup.com/news/sharjah-year-review-2016, Accessed 5 December 2017.
101 Freddie De Butts, *Now the Dust has Settled* (Padstow: Tabb House, 1995), 192.
102 Shaikh Sultan Al Qasimi, *My Early Life* (London: Bloomsbury, 2011), 225/226.
103 Davidson, *Dubai*, 248–50.
104 UK National Archives, J Boustead, Abu Dhabi Annual Report to London for 1964.
105 Abu Dhabi National Oil Company website, www.adnoc.ae, Accessed 28 November 2017.
106 Al Gurg, *Wells of Memory*, 75.
107 Hawley, *Desert Wind*, 61.
108 Interview with Neville Green (Regional Eastern Bank Representative in the 1960s), London, November 2017.
109 D. Commins, *The Gulf States: A Modern History* (London: I B Tauris 2012).
110 M. B. M. Al Yousef, *Oil and the Transformation of Oman 1970-1995* (London: Stacey International 1995), 23.
111 James Morris, *Sultan in Oman* (London: Faber and Faber 1957), 153.
112 A. H. Pampanini, *Cities in the Arabian Desert: The Building of Jubail and Yanbu* (Westport, CT: Praeger, 1997), xiv.
113 Michael Field, *The Merchants* (London: John Murray, 1984), 52.
114 Crawford, *Religion in the Gulf*, 147.
115 Bernard Burrows, *Footnotes in the Sand* (Wilton: Michael Russell, 1990), 55/56.
116 Muna M Alhammadi, Britain and the Administration of the Trucial States 1947–1965 (Abu Dhabi: Emirates Center for Strategic Studies and Research, 2013), 83.
117 Balfour-Paul, *End of Empire*, 5.

Chapter 3

1 Kamrava, *Gateways to the World*, 3.
2 Frauke Heard-Bey, *Trucial States to UAE* (Dubai: Motivate Publishing edition, 2013), 337.
3 D. Hawley, *The Emirates* (Norwich: Michael Russell, 2007), 46–7.
4 Heard-Bey, *From Trucial States*, 381.
5 Davidson, *Dubai*, 220–2.
6 Airport Guides Website, www.dubai-dxb.airports-guides.com.
7 R. Sab, 'Economic Impact of Selected Conflicts in the Middle East: What Can We Learn from the Past?' *International Monetary Fund (IMF)*, Working Paper 14/100, 2014, 17. www.imf.org/external/pubs/ft/wp/2014/wp14100.pdf

8   M. Legrenzi, *The GCC and the International Relations of the Gulf* (London: I B Tauris, 2011), 3.
9   S. Siavoshi, Article on Dubai (1996) in *Encyclopedia Iranica*, www.iranicaonline.org/articles/dubai.
10 International Monetary Fund (IMF) Direction of Trade Statistics, www.imf.org/en/data.
11 Chapman, *Memoirs*, 2018, 32/33 and 98.
12 UK National Archives, FCO 8/1510 (132/71), Dubai to London, Review of 1970, Annex, 10 December 1970.
13 Rosemary Zahlan, *The Origins of the United Arab Emirates: A Political and Social History of the Trucial States* (London: Macmillan, 1978).
14 Inflation Data Website, Historical Crude Oil Prices, https://inflationdata.com/inflation/inflation_Rate/Historical_Oil_Prices_Table.asp
15 British Bank of the Middle East (BBME), Annual Reports from Dubai to London, 1968–1977.
16 S. Ramos, *Dubai Amplified: The Engineering of a Port Geography* (Farnham: Ashgate, 2010), 96.
17 BBME Annual report to London for 1977.
18 'Computers, Containers but No Memory', *Dubai as It used to be*, Website, www.dubaiasitusedtobe.com. Manual paper-based systems were initially used in all container terminals to monitor the status (empty/full/export/import) and location of containers. They rapidly became overwhelmed by the sheer increase in throughputs and the complexity of determining of where containers were and at what stage of the operation they should be allocated. Some ports were unable to cope and collapsed into chaos (Mumbai in the 1990s). Others such as Dubai began to trial computer-based systems, improving accuracy, efficiency and the speed of ship and container handling. This benefitted, shipping lines, ports – and most importantly – customers.
19 Gulftainer Website, www.gulftainer.com/terminals/uae/sharjah-container-terminal, Accessed 15 June 2017.
20 Ramos, *Dubai Amplified*, 107.
21 Wilson, *Rashid's Legacy*.
22 Interview with George Chapman, Dubai, June 2016.
23 Shaikh Mohammed Bin Rashid Al Maktoum, *Flashes of Thought* (Dubai: Motivate Publishing, 2014), 93.
24 *Emirates 24/7*, Business Website, 4 February 2013, www.emirates247.com 'DP World Handled 100 Million Containers in 10 Years', Accessed 12 December 2017.
25 Dilip Hiro, *The Longest War: The Iran-Iraq Military Conflict* (London: Routledge, 1990).
26 Ramos, *Dubai Amplified*, 107.
27 DP World Website, www.dpworld.ae/en/content/15/173/jebel-ali-history, Accessed 14 December 2017.
28 JAFZA Website.
29 D. Schubert, 'Seaport Cities: Phases of Spatial Restructuring and Types and Dimensions of Redevelopment', in C. Hein (ed.), *Port Cities: Landscapes and Global Networks* (London: Routledge, 2011), 56.
30 K. C. Ulrichsen, *The Gulf States in International Political Economy* (Basingstoke: Palgrave Macmillan, 2016), 5.
31 Karachi International Container Terminal Website, www.kictl.com, Accessed 9 February 2018.

32 Jawaharlal Nehru Port Trust Mumbai Website, www.jnport.in.gov, Accessed 9 February 2018.
33 Ports. Com Website, www.ports.com, Accessed 9 February 2018.
34 Stephen Ramos, 'Dubai's Jebel Ali Port: Trade, Territory and Infrastructure,' in C. Hein (ed.), *Port Cities and Dynamic Landscapes* (London: Routledge, 2011), 233.
35 Kamrava, *Gateways to the World*, 45.
36 E. Gouvernal, V. Lavaud-Letilleul, and B. Slack, 'Transport and Logistics Hubs: Separating Fact from Fiction,' in P. Hall, R. J. McCalla, C. Comtois, and B. Slack (eds.), *Integrating Seaports and Trade Corridors* (Farnham: Ashgate, 2011), 65.
37 A. Keshavarzian, 'Geopolitics and the Geneology of Free Trade Zones in the Persian Gulf,' *Geopolitics* 15, no. 2 (2010): 267.
38 Jebel Ali Free Zone (JAFZA) website, www.jafza.ae/about-us/why-dubai-why-jafza/, Accessed 8 May 2018.
39 JAFZA website.
40 Mehran Kamrava, 'Contemporary Port Cities in the Persian Gulf,' in M. Kamrava (ed.), *Gateways to the World: Port Cities in the Persian Gulf* (London: Hurst, 2016), 78.
41 *Gulf News*, 'Free-zones a Cornerstone of UAE Success,' 16 August 2017, https://gulfnews.com/business/property/free-zones-a-cornerstone-of-uae-success-1.2074856, Accessed 9 May 2018.
42 A. Al Lawati, 'Expatriates in the Gulf, in Jane Kinninmont (ed.), *Future Trends in the Gulf* (London: Chatham House, 2015), 24.
43 King Abdullah Economic City Website, www.kaec.com, Accessed 10 May 2018.
44 Kish Island Free Zone Website, www.economic.kish.ir/en, Accessed 10 May 2018.
45 Keshavarzian, *Geopolitics*, 271.
46 Ibid., 268.
47 'Soaring Ambition,' *The Economist*, 10 January 2015, 46.
48 Dubai Airport Website, http://www.dubaiairport.com/DIA/English/TopMenu/About+DIA/Facts+and+Figures/
49 Al Gurg, *The Wells of Memory*, 102–6.
50 Dubai National Air Travel Agency (DNATA), *DNATA: Half a Century* (Dubai: DNATA, 2009), 37–8.
51 Ibid.
52 Ibid., 57.
53 Ibid., 62.
54 G Wilson, *Emirates: The Airline of the Future* (Dubai and London: Media Prima, 2005), 11.
55 DNATA, 125.
56 Davidson, *Dubai*, 110.
57 Khaleej Times Newspaper Dubai 2010, Special Report on Emirates, '25 Great Years.' The growth quote is from founding figure Maurice Flanagan on Page 15. The statistics on Page 10.
58 Statistita Website, www.statistita.com/statistics/300253/number-of-passengers-emirates-airlines/, Accessed 19 June 2018.
59 Interview with Gary Chapman (Emirates Group President, Services and DNATA), London, June 2018.
60 Ibid.
61 Mohammed Sharaf, chief executive of Dubai Ports World (DPW) 2005–2016, Conversation with the author, Dubai 2015.

62 O. Al Shehabi, 'Histories of Migration to the Gulf,' in A. Khalaf, O. Al Shehabi, and A. Hanieh (eds.), *Transit States* (London: Pluto Press, 2015), 23.
63 N. Vora, *Impossible Citizens: Dubai's India Diaspora* (London: Duke University Press, 2013).
64 M. Baldwin-Edwards, 'Labour Immigration and Labour Markets in the GCC Countries: National Patterns and Trends,' London School of Economics (LSE), *Kuwait Programme on Development, Governance and Globalisation in the Gulf States*, Number 15, 2011).
65 Al Shehabi, *Histories of Migration*, 25.
66 Sultan Ahmed Bin Sulayem, Chairman of DP World, Interview in Dubai, June 2017.
67 Davidson, *Dubai*, 252.
68 Ibid., 255.
69 Gulftainer Website Media Centre, 15 December 2015, www.gulftainer.com/press-release/khorfakkan-container-terminal-exceeds-4000-moves-in-a-12-hour-shift/
70 E. Gouvernal, V. Lavaud-Letilleul and B. Slack, 'Transport and Logistics Hubs: Separating Fact from Fiction,' in P. Hall, R. J. McCalla, C. Comtois and B. Slack (eds.), *Integrating Seaports and Trade Corridors* (Farnham: Ashgate, 2011), 72.
71 A. R. Walker, 'Recessional and Gulf War Impacts on Port Development and Shipping in the Gulf States in the 1980s,' *Geographic Journal* 18, no. 3 (April 1989): 273–84.
72 T. Matthiesen, *Sectarian Gulf* (Stamford: Stamford University Press, 2013), 14.
73 K. C. Ulrichsen, *Insecure Gulf* (London: Hurst and Co. 2011), 77.
74 Matthiesen, *Sectarian Gulf*, 30.
75 K. C. Ulrichsen and G. P. Parolin, 'Re-Weaving the myth of Bahrain's Parliamentary Experience,' in M. A. Tetreault, G. Okruhlik and A. Kapiszewski (eds.), *Political Change in the Arab Gulf States* (Boulder: Lynne Rienner, 2011).
76 The second-class role of the Shia in Bahrain and the failure of integration, reform and conciliation resulted, of course, most recently in the 'Arab Spring' insurrections of 2011. Fellow Sunni monarchs in the Gulf sent troops to assist Bahrain forces contain what many Gulf Sunnis felt was an Iranian backed plot aimed at regime change. New York Times Website, 15 March 2011, www.nytimes.com/2011/03/15/world/middleeast/15bahrain.html.
77 Mehran Kamrava, *Qatar: Small State, Big Politics* (Ithaca and London: Cornell University Press, 2013).
78 Alan Villiers, *Sons of Sinbad* (London: Hodder and Stoughton, 1949), an account of the Kuwaiti trading dhows sailing to and from East Africa in the 1930s and 40s.
79 Michael Field, *The Merchants* (London: John Murray, 1984).
80 Alphaliner Website, https://alphaliner.axsmarine.com/PublicTop100/
81 Sovereign Wealth Fund Institute Website, www.swfinstitute.org/sovereign-wealth-fund-rankings/.
82 A. H. Pampinini, *Cities in the Arabian Desert: The Building of Jubail and Yanbu* (Westport, CT: Praeger 1997), 67.
83 Jones, *Two Centuries*, 83.
84 Michael Axworthy, *Revolutionary Iran* (London: Penguin Books, 2014), 296.
85 Perse Transport Bar website, www.perse-iran.com/home/breifhistory
86 G. Blake, *BI Centenary* (London: Collins, 1956).
87 J. Bellini, *Pioneering Spirit: The Story Behind Inchcape's Remarkable Journey* (London: Artesian Publishing, 2010) and P. Griffiths, *A History of the Inchcape Group* (London: Inchcape, 1977).
88 Jones, *Two Centuries*, 97.

Chapter 4

1. Karen E. Young, *The Political Economy of Energy, Finance and Security in the UAE* (Basingstoke: Palgrave, 2014), 6.
2. F. Fukuyama, *The End of History and the Last Man* (London: Free Press/Macmillan 1992). This seminal work put forward the case that Western democracy and capitalism – the US-led world order – had triumphed following the collapse of the Soviet Union at the end of 1991.
3. David Runciman, part of book review of 'Political Order and Political Decay' by Francis Fukuyama, in the *Financial Times, FT Weekend*, 26 September 2014. Runciman's point was that it was essential first, to establish the proper framework of state institutions (an impartial and honest civil service and an effective and impartial legal system for example), if any (emerging) state was to have a long-term future.
4. A. Al Faris and R. Soto, *The Economy of Dubai* (Oxford: Oxford University Press, 2016), 330.
5. Bill Emmott, 'New World Order', *Financial Times Weekend*, 18/19 March 2017.
6. G Luciani, *Political Liberalisation and Democratisation in the Arab World* (Boulder: Lynne Reinner, 1998), 211.
7. Davidson, *Dubai*, 4.
8. N. Ayubi, *Over-Stating the Arab State: Politics and Society in the Middle East* (London: I B Tauris, 1995).
9. F. G. Gause, 'Kings for all Seasons: How the Middle East's Monarchies Survived the Arab Spring', *Brookings Center Doha*, Analysis Paper Number 8, September 2013.
10. Lisa Anderson, 'Absolutism and the Resilience of Monarchy in the Middle East', *Political Science Quarterly* 106, no. 1 (Spring 1991).
11. Laura Al Katiri, 'The Guardian State and its Economic Development Model', in *The Journal of Development Studies* 50, no. 1 (2014): 23.
12. Ibid., 31.
13. W. W. Rostow, *The Stages of Economic Growth* (Cambridge: Cambridge University Press, 1960), 4.
14. Martin Hvidt, 'The Dubai Model', *International Journal of Middle East Studies* 41, no. 3 (2009).
15. M. Gray, 'A Theory of Later Rentierism in the Arab States of the Gulf', *Center for International and Regional Studies*, CIRS Occasional Paper No 7 (Doha, Qatar: Georgetown University, 2011), 27.
16. Adam Hanieh, 'Theorizing the Arabian Peninsula Roundtable: Capital and Labour in the Gulf States: Bringing the Region Back In', Jadaliyya Electronic Rountable, April 2013, www.jadaliyya.com, Accessed September 3, 2017.
17. Alice Amsden, *The Rise of the Rest* (New York: Oxford University Press, 2001).
18. A. Kanna, 'The Trajectories of Two Asian Tigers: The Imperial Roots of Capitalism in Dubai and Singapore', in X. Chen and A. Kanna, *Rethinking Global Urbanism: Comparative Insights from Secondary Cities* (London: Routledge, 2012), 35.
19. Fatma Al Sayegh, 'Merchants Role in a Changing Society: The Case of Dubai 1900–1990', *Middle East Studies* 34 , no. 1 (1998).
20. K. Almezaini, 'Private Sector Actors in the UAE and their role in the Process of Economic and Political Reform', in S. Hertog, G. Luciani and M. Valeri, *Business Politics in the Middle East* (London: Hurst, 2013), 65.
21. Hvidt, *Dubai Model*.

22 A Mishrif and H Kapetanovic, 'Dubai's Model of Economic Diversification', in A. Mishrif and Y. Al Balushi (eds.), *Economic Diversification in the Gulf Region: Comparing Global Challenges* (Singapore: Palgrave Macmillan/Gulf Research Centre Cambridge, 2018), 97.
23 Shaikh Mohammed Bin Rashid Al Maktoum, *Flashes of Thought* (Dubai: Motivate Publishing, 2014).
24 R. Marchal, 'Dubai: Global City and Transnational Hub', in M. Al Rasheed (ed.), *Transnational Connections and the Arab Gulf* (London: Routledge, 2014), 97.
25 P. B. Evans, *Embedded Autonomy: States and Industrial Transformation* (Princeton: Princeton University Press, 1995), 249.
26 Ibid.
27 M. Herb, *All in the Family: Absolutism, Revolution and Democracy in the Middle East Monarchies* (New York: State University of New York Press, 2014).
28 D. Acemoglu and J Robinson, *Why Nations Fail: The Origins of Power, Prosperity and Poverty* (New York: Crown Press, 2012).
29 M. A. Tetrault, *The Economics of National Economy in the UAE* (New York: MEPC, 2000).
30 World Bank, Ease of Doing Business Index, https://data.worldbank.org/indicator/IC.BUS.EASE.XQ
31 A famous case is the bankruptcy sale of Ciudad Real Airport in Spain for Euros 10,000 in 2015. The airport, speculatively intended at the beginning of the twenty-first century, as another gateway to Madrid and central Spain, never opened and cost over Euros 1 billion to build. www.bbc.co.uk/news/world-europe-33578949 18th July 2015.
32 Al Shehabi, *Histories of Migration*, 2015, 21.
33 A. Al Lawati, 'Expatriates in the Gulf: Temporary but Permanent', in J. Kinninmont (ed.), *Future Trends in the Gulf* (London: Chatham House, 2015), 24.
34 Gulf News Money, www.gulfnews.com/business/money/uae-expat--remittances-reach-dh121-1-billion-in-9-months-1.2140876 .
35 I. Genc and G. Naufal, *Expatriates and the Labour Force* (London: Palgrave Macmillan, 2012), 83.
36 'Crossing Continents', *The Economist*, 25 August 2018, 15.
37 National Pavilion of the UAE Booklet, Venice Biennale 2017, 2.
38 M. Davis, 'Fear and Money in Dubai', *New Left Review* 41 (2006).
39 Syed Ali, Dubai: *Gilded Cage* (New Haven and London: Yale University Press, 2010).
40 G. Price, 'A Future built by Sweat of Overseas Workers', *The World Today*, Chatham House 74, no. 3 (June/July 2018), 36.
41 Ibid., 37.
42 Gulf Labour Markets and Migration, www.gulfmigration.eu/uae-dubai-estimates-of-total-population-by-sex-1953-1968-census-dates-2006-2013/.
43 Dubai Statistics Centre Website, www.dsc.gov.ae/en.
44 A. Al Faris and R Soto, *The Economy of Dubai* (Oxford: Oxford University Press, 2016), 248.
45 Ibid.
46 J. Kinninmont (ed), *Future Trends in the Gulf* (London Chatham House, 2015), 18.
47 Al Faris and Soto, *The Economy of Dubai*, 337.
48 A. Khokhar, 'UAE National Service: A Revisit', Al Tamimi and Co (Dubai Legal Company), www.tamimi.com May 2016, Accessed 27 February 2018.

49 R. Soto and Y. Rashid, 'Labour Markets in Transition', in A. Al Faris and R. Soto (eds.), *The Economy of Dubai* (Oxford: Oxford University Press, 2016), 242.
50 E. Gouvernal, V. Lavaud-Letilleul and B. Slack, 'Transport and Logistics Hubs: Separating Fact from Fiction', in P. Hall, R. J. McCalla, C. Comtois and B. Slack, *Integrating Seaports and Trade Corridors* (Farnham: Ashgate, 2011), 77.
51 Trading Economics website, https://tradingeconomics.com, Crude Oil Production statistics.
52 Figures supplied by Drewry Maritime Research London, to the author in 2018.
53 C. Jephson and H. Morgen, *Creating Global Opportunities: Maersk Line in Containerization 1973–2013* (Cambridge: Cambridge University Press, 2014), 95, 177 and 248.
54 CMA-CGM Website, www.cma-cgm.com/products-services/line-services , for Week 7 2018, Accessed 9 February 2018.
55 D. Held, and A. McGrew, *The Global Transformation Reader* (Cambridge: Polity Press, 2000), 3.
56 Dragonmart Dubai Website, www.dragonmart.ae/en/dragon-mart, Accessed 26 February 2018.
57 Ecomcrew Website, www.ecomcrew.com/yiwu-guide-the-largest-wholesale-market-in-the-world, Accessed 26 February 2018.
58 Jephson and Morgen, *Creating Global Opportunities*, 246.
59 www.worldshipping.org 2017 Update, Accessed 10 November 2018.
60 Freightos.com website.
61 'Challenges to the Rules-Based International Order', Chatham House London Conference 2015, 1.
62 'Pulp Friction', *The Economist*, 24 March 2018, 77.
63 United Nations Economic Commission for Europe (UNECE) website, www.unece.org/cefact/edifact/welcome.html.
64 Dubai Trade Website, www.dubaitrade.ae, Accessed 8 March 2018.
65 L. Hoosteval, *Globalization Contained: The Economic Consequences of Containerization* (New York: Palgrave Macmillan, 2013), 71.
66 Jephson and Morgen, *Creating Global Opportunities*, 252.
67 Sohar Port and Free-Zone Website, www.soharportandfreezone.com .
68 *International Rail Journal* Website, 3 May 2016, www.railjournal.com/index.php/middle-east/oman-suspends-railway-project.html.
69 M. A. Tetreault, 'Bottom-Up Democratisation in Kuwait', in M. A. Tetreault, G. Okruhlik and A. Kapiszewski (eds.), *Political Change in the Arab Gulf States: Stuck in Transition* (Boulder: Lynne Reiner, 2011), 92.
70 S. Ghabra, 'Identity and State in the Gulf: The Case of Kuwait', in M. C. Thompson and N. Quillian (eds.), *Policy Making in the GCC: State, Citizens and Institutions* (London: I B Tauris, 2017): 39.
71 Hertog, 'A Quest for Significance', and Michael Herb, *The Wages of Oil: Parliaments and Economic Development in Kuwait and the UAE* (Ithaca: Cornell University Press, 2014).
72 Michael Herb, 'The Origins of Kuwait's National Assembly', *LSE Kuwait Programme*, Paper Series No. 39, March 2016.
73 Jill Crystal, 'Coalitions in Oil Monarchies: Kuwait and Qatar', *Comparative Politics*, July 1989, 427–43, 440.
74 Alice Amsden, *The Rise of the Rest* (New York: Oxford University Press, 2001).
75 'Iran's Railway Revolution', *Global Construction Review* website, www.globalconstructionreview.com/markets 14 December 2015.

76 A. Ehteshami, *Geopolitics and Globalization in the Middle East: Old Games, New Rules* (London: Routledge, 2007), 36.
77 M. Weber, *The Protestant Ethic and the Spirit of Capitalism* (London: Penguin Edition, 2004). Weber argued that sober, hard-working, rational Protestantism was the most conducive to market-driven economic success.
78 Shaikh Mohammed Bin Rashid Al Maktoum, *Reflections on Happiness and Positivity* (Dubai: Sh. Mohammed Bin Rashid Executive Office, 2017), 50–3.
79 Clayton Christensen, *The Innovator's Dilemma: When New Technologies Cause Great Firms to Fail* (Harvard: Harvard Business School, 1997). Christensen, one of the great 'business gurus' distinguished between two different types of change. One was 'sustaining technology' (enhancing existing systems, procedures, technology to become better), and 'disruptive technology' (that changes the entire landscape of an industry by solving problems in new ways with new thinking and (often) different people). Dubai is a classic example of the use of 'disruptive technology' (such as containerization) – when the challenge for companies (or states) is often to recognize that there is a challenge at all.
80 A. T. Al Sadik and I. A. Elbadawi (eds.), *The Global Economic Crisis and Consequences for Dubai* (New York: Palgrave Macmillan, 2012), 21.
81 R. Marchal, 'Dubai: Global City and Trans-National Hub', in, M. Al Rasheed (ed.), *Transnational Connections and the Arab Gulf* (Abingdon: Routledge, 2014), 99.

Chapter 5

1 R. Springborg, 'Introduction', in A. Al Sharekh and R. Springborg (eds.), *Popular Culture and Political Identity in the Arab Gulf States* (London: Saqi Books/SOAS, 2008), 13.
2 Shaikh Mohammed Bin Rashid Al Maktoum, quoted in *What's On Dubai* website, www.whatson.ae/dubai/2017/11/10, Accessed 2 January 2018.
3 Davidson, *Dubai*, 145.
4 Hertog, 'A Quest for Significance.'
5 Davidson, *Dubai*.
6 B. Nandwa and A. T. Al Sadik, 'Public Debt Management and Fiscal Sustainability', in A. Al Faris and R. Soto (eds.), *The Economy of Dubai* (Oxford: Oxford University Press, 2016), 62.
7 BBC News – Business, 25 November 2010, www.bbc.co.uk/news/business-11837714.
8 US Energy Information Administration Website, https://www.eia.gov/, Accessed 7 March 2018.
9 Sovereign Wealth Fund Institute Website, www.swfinstitute.org/sovereign-wealth-fund-rankings/, Accessed 26 September 2017.
10 Zawya (Thomson Reuters) Website, www.zawya.com, 'Dubai's DP World, Port of Fujairah end concession agreement', 16 April 2017.
11 Hutchison Ports Website, https://hutchisonports.com/en/.
12 A. T. Al Sadik and I. A. Elbadawi (eds.), *The Global Economic Crisis and Consequences for Development Strategy in Dubai* (New York: Palgrave Macmillan, 2012), 2.
13 M. Pearson, 'India Ocean Port-Cities: Themes and Problems', in R. Mukherjee (ed.), *Vanguards of Globalization: Port Cities from the Classical to the Modern* (Delhi: Primus Books, 2014), 67.

14 A. Al Faris and R. Soto, *The Economy of Dubai* (Oxford: Oxford University Press, 2016), 331.
15 www.reuters.com/article/emirates-budget/ 11 October 2011.
16 James Mattis, quoted in 'The Gulf's Little Sparta', *The Economist*, 8 April, 2017, 38.
17 H. Askari, *Collaborative Colonialism* (New York: Palgrave Macmillan, 2013), 44.
18 Statista Website, www.statista.com/statistics/284636/visitor-arrivals-in-dubai-from-international-destinations/, Accessed 18 May 2018.
19 Aisha S. Al Qaydi, 'Historical Overview of the Rise and Development of the Hospitality Industry' (in the UAE). *Liwa Journal*, Abu Dhabi 7, no. 15 (June 2016): 22.
20 Ibid., 26.
21 Dubai Statistics Centre (DSC) website, www.dsc.gov.ae, Dubai in Figures/Construction and Housing/Completed Buildings.
22 Shaikh Mohammed Bin Rashid Al Maktoum, *Flashes of Thought* (Dubai: Motivate Publishing 2014), Chapter 32.
23 Eventbrite Website, www.eventbrite.com/d/united-arab-emirates-dubai/conferences/, Accessed 21 May 2018.
24 Bureau International Des Expositions Website, www.bie-paris.org/site/en/2020-dubai, Accessed 21 May 2018.
25 J. Sampler and S. Eigner, *Sand to Silicon: Achieving Rapid Growth Lessons from Dubai* (London: Profile Books, 2003).
26 Ibid., 175.
27 Hertog, 'A Quest for Significance'.
28 Emirates Airline Festival of Literature Website, https://www.emirateslitfest.com/, Accessed 23 May 2018.
29 Dubai Design District Website, www.dubaidesigndistrict.com, Accessed 23 May 2018.
30 DP World Website, www.dpworld.com/2011/our-history.html, Accessed 25 May 2018.
31 F Fukuyama, *The End of History and the Last Man* (London: Free Press/Macmillan, 1992).
32 CSX Press Release announcing the deal in December 2004, www.phx.corporate-ir.net/, Accessed 25 May 2018.
33 DP World Website, www.dpworld.com/our-business/marine-terminals/, Accessed 25 May 2018.
34 Port Technology International, www.porttechnology.org/news/the_top_5_terminal_operators_in_2016, Accessed 29 May 2018.
35 T. Notteboom, J.-P. Rodrigue, Chapter 13, 'Emerging Global Networks in the Container Terminal Operating Industry', in, T. Notteboom (ed.), *Current Issues in Shipping Ports and Logistics* (Antwerp: UPA, 2011).
36 DNATA Website, www.dnata.com/media-centre/dnata-celebrates-25-years-of-international-growth (Release on 11 July 2018)
37 Dubai Holding website, www.dubaiholding.com/en/who-we-are/, Accessed 22 August 2018.
38 Ibid.
39 Brand Dubai Website, www.branddubai.com, Accessed 30 May 2018.
40 Investopedia Website, https://www.investopedia.com/terms/j/japaninc.asp, Accessed 30 May 2018.
41 Emirates Airline Website, https://www.emirates.com/ae/english/about-us/sponsorships/, Accessed 30 May 2018.

42 R. Govers and F. Go, *Place Branding: Glocal, Virtual and Physical Identities, Constructed, Imagined and Experienced* (Basingstoke: Palgrave Macmillan, 2009), 73.
43 Ibid., 242.
44 Gerald Ratner had established a multi-million-pound high-street jewellery chain in the UK, a well-known brand. However, at a, now famous, after-dinner speech in 1991, he referred very disparagingly to the quality of his company's products, leading to the complete collapse of the share-price and the group.
45 J. Bhagwati, 'US Trade Policy: An infatuation with Free-Trade Agreements', Columbia University Discussion Paper Number 726, 1995.
46 S. Katada and M. Solis, *Cross Regional Trade Agreements* (Heidelberg: Springer, 2008), 147.
47 Joseph Nye, *Soft Power: The Means to Success in World Politics* (New York: Public Affairs, 2004), x.
48 For example, Tim Moore, 'An Invasion of Anoraks', *Financial Times* 11/12 March 2017, Page 7. The article references plans to develop Keflavik Airport in Iceland 'into what some in the industry are calling, the Dubai of the North'.
49 G. F. Gresh, 'A Vital Maritime Pinch-Point: China, the Bab al-Mandeb and the Middle East', in, *Asian Journal of Middle East and Islamic Studies* 11, no. 1 (March 2017): 45.
50 M. Legrenzi, *The GCC and the International Relations of the Gulf* (London: I B Tauris, 2011).
51 C. Bianco and G. Stansfield, 'The Intra-GCC Crises: Mapping GCC Fragmentation after 2011', *International Affairs*, Chatham House 94, no. 3 (May 2018).
52 Times of Oman Website, April 22, 2017, www.timesofoman.com/article/107373/oman/chinese-firms-commit-$31billion-investment-in-duqm-free-zone.
53 A. H. M. Nordin and M. Weissman, 'Will Trump Make China Great Again?: The Belt and Road Initiative and International Order', *International Affairs* 94, no. 2 (March 2018).
54 K. C. Ulrichsen, *Insecure Gulf* (London: Hurst and Co. 2011).
55 Foreign Policy Website, www.foreignpolicy.com/2017/04/03/the-oman-succession-envelope-please.
56 H. E. Chehabi and J. J. Linz (eds.), *Sultanistic Regimes* (Baltimore: Johns Hopkins University Press, 1998), 7.
57 *The Economist*, 'Uneasy Sits Qaboos', July 8 (2017): 43 and 'A Port in the Storm', 2 September 2017, 44.
58 J. E. Peterson, 'Oman Faces the Twenty-First Century', in M. A. Tetreault, G. Okruhlik and A. Kapiszewski (eds.), *Political Change in the Arab Gulf States* (Boulder: Lynne Rienner, 2011).
59 Shaikh Mohammed Bin Rashid Al Maktoum, *Flashes of Thought* (Dubai: Motivate Publishing, 2014), 53.
60 Khalifa bin Salman Port Website, www.mtt.gov.bh.
61 International Monetary Fund (IMF) Country Report, Qatar, April 2017, Pages 3 to 4.
62 A. J. Fromherz, *Qatar: A Modern History* (London: I B Tauris, 2012), 112.
63 World Bank Website, https://data.worldbank.org.
64 Reuters Website, 5 September 2017, www.reuters.com/qatar-port/qatar-says-new-port-will-help-circumvent-arab-sanctions-idUSKCN1BG1RP.
65 *The Economist*, 'Economic Gulf', 21 October 2017, 53.
66 Airports Council International (ACI) Website, www.aci.aero.

67 Stefan Hertog, 'A Quest for Significance: Gulf Oil Monarchies' International 'Soft Power' Strategies and their Local Urban Dimensions', *LSE Kuwait Programme*, Series Number 42 (March 2017): 5.
68 Joseph Nye, *Soft Power: The Means to Success in World Politics* (New York: Public Affairs, 2004).
69 M. Kamrava, *Qatar: Small State, Big politics* (Ithaca and London: Cornell University Press, 2013).
70 *Financial Times*, 'How Qatar Seized Control of the Syrian Revolution', 17 May 2013. A long, prescient article about Qatari maverick meddling in Syria, in the aftermath of the Arab Spring.
71 *Financial Times*, 'The $1bn Hostage Deal that Enraged Qatar's Gulf Rivals', 5 June 2017.
72 Kamrava, *Qatar*, 172.
73 Michael Herb, *The Wages of Oil: Parliaments and Economic Development in Kuwait and the UAE* (Ithaca: Cornell University Press, 2014).
74 F. Kattan, *A Review and Critique of the Saudisation Narrative in Policy Making in the GCC* (London: I B Tauris, 2017).
75 *Bloomberg* Website, 'Saudi Reserves Drop Below $500bn', www.bloomberg.com/news/articles/2017-05-28.
76 N. S. Al Mazrouei, *The UAE & Saudi Arabia: Border Disputes & Intl. Relations* (London: I B Tauris, 2016).
77 C. M. Henry and R. Springborg, *Globalization and the Politics of Development in the Middle East* (Cambridge: Cambridge University Press, 2010), 318.
78 *The National* Newspaper Abu Dhabi, www.thenational.ae/business, 6 August 2015.
79 Journal of Commerce Website, www.joc.com, 9 May 2016, 'India, Iran Moving Forward on Re-developing Chahbahar Port'.
80 J. Kinninmont, 'Middle East Gets Messier', *The World Today* (London: Chatham House, October/November 2017), 18.
81 Gulftainer Website, www.gulftainer.com/terminals and World Bank Website, www.ppi.worldbank.org/snapshots/.../umm-qasr-container-terminal-berth-8-10-and-11-5838.
82 World Cargo News, www.worldcargonews.com, 24 July 2017.
83 Statistics supplied by Drewry Maritime Research London to the author, 2018.
84 L. Hoosteval, *Globalisation Contained: The Economic and Strategic Consequences of the Container* (New York: Palgrave Macmillan, 2013), 58.
85 Ibid., 59.
86 World Bank Website, https://lpi.worldbank.org.
87 Martin Hvidt, 'The Dubai Model: An Outline of Key Development-Process Elements in Dubai', *International Journal of Middle East Studies* 41, no. 41 (August 2009): 400.
88 M. Heins, *The Globalisation of American Infrastructure* (New York: Routledge 2016), 236.
89 Gulf News Website, https://gulfnews.com/guides/life/community/ 15 August 2017, Accessed 9 May 2018.
90 International Humanitarian City Website, www.ihc.ae, Accessed 9 May 2018.
91 Adam Hanieh, *Money, Markets and Monarchies: The GCC and the Political Economy of the Contemporary Middle East* (Cambridge: Cambridge University Press, 2018), 264.
92 Hertog, *A Quest for Significance*.
93 Dubai Media City website, www.dmc.ae, Accessed 9 May 2018.

94 Dubai Silicon Oasis Website www.dsoa.ae, Accessed 9 May 2018.
95 Dubai Internet City Website, www.dic.ae , Accessed 10 May 2018.
96 Dubai Multi Commodities Centre Website, www.dmcc.ae, Accessed 10 May 2018.
97 D. Weir, N. A. Sultan, B. D. Metcalfe, and S. A. Abuznaid, 'The GCC Countries as Knowledge-Based Economies: Future Aspirations and Challenges', in N. A. Sultan, D. Weir, and Z. Karake-Shaloub (eds), *The New Post-Arab Gulf: Managing People and Wealth* (London: Saqi Books, 2011), 85.
98 Michael Field, The Merchants: *The Big Business Families of Arabia* (London: John Murray, 1984), 60.
99 Adam Ward, 'Insights from the Director's Office', *Chatham House, London*, December 1, 2017.
100 Michael Herb, *The Wages of Oil: Parliaments and Economic Development in Kuwait and the UAE* (Ithaca: Cornell University Press, 2014), 195.
101 H.-J. Chang, *Kicking Away the Ladder: Development Strategy in Historical Perspective* (London: Anthem Press, 2003).
102 Eva Bellin, 'The Robustness of Authoritarianism in the Middle East', *Comparative Politics Journal* 36, no. 2 (2004).

BIBLIOGRAPHY

Primary sources

1) Interviews

Al Rais, S. H., Chairman of Rais Hassan Saadi Company. Interview in Dubai November 2017.
Bin Sulayem, Sultan, Chairman of Dubai Ports World (DPW). Interview in Dubai June 2017.
Chapman, Gary, Emirates Group President, Services and DNATA. Interview in London June 2018.
Chapman, George, previously 'Wakil' in Dubai and Managing Director, Gray Mackenzie Dubai). Interview in Dubai, June 2016.
Green, Neville, previously Eastern Bank and Standard Chartered Bank in the Trucial States/UAE, Interview in London November 2017.
Sharaf, Mohammed, previously CEO of Dubai Ports World. Conversations with the author London and Dubai 2016.
Stewart, Mel, previously Halcrow Director. Interview in Sharjah June 2017.

2) Unpublished memoirs / records

Chapman, George, *Memoirs,* unpublished manuscript and *Reminiscences* and *Those Were the Days* pamphlets (circa 1993).
Rolls, V., *The Far Eastern Freight Conference 1879–2004*, Internal publication, London: Conference Administration Services, 2005.

3) Archival compilations

Burdett, A., *The GCC States National Development Records – Communications and Transport 1860–1960 – Volume 5*, Cambridge: Archive Editions of Cambridge University Press, 1996.
Burdett, A., *Records of Dubai Volumes 1–7*, Cambridge: Archive Editions of Cambridge University Press, 2000.
Tuson, P., *The Records of the British Residency and Agencies in the Persian Gulf*, London: Indian Office Library, 1979.
Tuson, P., *Records of the Emirates*, Cambridge: Cambridge University Press Archive Editions 1990.

4) Statistics

British Bank of the Middle East (BBME), Dubai Office Letters to London, References: 68/2 (25/6/1956); 68/29 (10/2/1957); 68/31 (25/2/1957) and Annual Reports 1968–1977. HSBC Archives London,. Accessed May 2017.

Drewry Maritime Research, London. Gulf port volume statistics.
Gulftainer Company Sharjah, Iraq Port Statistics.

5) Archival sources

National Archives UK (1955) Ref: FO 371/114696 Halcrow Reports, 12 January 1955.
National Archives UK (1955) Ref: FO 371/114576 Bahrain Residency to FO London 15 April 1955.
National Archives UK (1955) Ref: FO 371/114696 Bahrain Residency to FO London 31 January 1955.
National Archives UK (1955) Ref: FO 371/114696 Dubai to Bahrain Residency 4 November 1955.
National Archives UK (1956) Ref: FO 371/114696 FO Eastern Dept. Memo 7 January 1956.
National Archives UK (1956) Ref: FO 371/120540 Bahrain Residency to FO London 7 May 1956.
National Archives UK (1958) Ref: FO 371/132748 Bahrain Residency to FO London 21 March 1958.
National Archives UK (1959) Ref: 371/140064 Bahrain Residency to FO London 2 February 1959.
National Archives UK (1960) Ref: 371/148896 Bahrain Residency to FO London 11 February 1960.
National Archives UK (1960) Ref: 371/148967 Bahrain Residency to FO London 26 February 1960.
National Archives UK (1965) Ref: FO 1016/837 Bahrain Residency to London 15 May 1965.
National Archives UK (1965) Ref: FO 371/179925 Dubai to Bahrain Residency 24 July, 27 September and 6 November 1965.
National Archives UK (1967) Ref: FO 1016/839 Dubai to Bahrain Residency 26 April 1967.
National Archives UK (1967) Ref: FO 1016/839 (1391/67c) Dubai to London FO, 29 May 1967.
National Archives UK (1967) Ref: FO 1016/839 Dubai to FO London 5 June 1967.
National Archives UK (1967) Ref: FO 1016/839 Dubai to FO London 1 November 1967.
National Archives UK (1956) Ref: FO 371/120633 (1956) and 157047 (1971).
National Archives UK (1969) Ref: FCO 8/1509 Dubai to FCO London 30 December 1969.
National Archives UK (1970) Ref: FCO 8/1510 Dubai to FO London 10 December 1970.

6) Miscellaneous

National Pavilion of the UAE, Brochure, Venice Biennale 2017.
Peat Marwick Mitchell, *The Gulf Pattern*. Business forecast for 1977–1982 produced for Gray Mackenzie and Co. London: PWM, 1978.

Secondary Sources

Abdulla, A., "The Arab Gulf Moment in The Transformation of the Gulf" in D. Held and K. Ulrichsen (eds), *The Transformation of the Gulf: Politics, Economics and the Global Order*, Oxford: Routledge, 2013.

Abu-Baker, A. S. S., 'Political Economy of State Formation: The United Arab Emirates in Comparative Perspective', PhD Dissertation, University of Michigan, 1995.
Abu Dhabi National Oil Company (ADNOC) Website www.adnoc.ae, Accessed 28 November 2017.
Acemoglu, D. and J. Robinson, *Why Nations Fail: The Origins of Power, Prosperity and Poverty*, New York: Crown Press, 2012.
Agius, D. A., *Seafaring in the Arabian Gulf and Oman: The People of the Dhow*, London: Kegan Paul, 2005.
Airport Council International (ACI) Website www.aci.aero, Accessed 4 September 2017.
Airport Guides Website www.dubai-dxb.airports-guides.com, Accessed 9 January 2018.
Al Baharna, H., *British Extra-Territorial Jurisdiction in the Gulf 1913-1971*, Slough: Archive Editions, 1998.
Al Faris, A. and R. Soto, *The Economy of Dubai*, Oxford: Oxford University Press, 2016.
Al Gurg, E. S., *The Wells of Memory*, London: John Murray, 1998.
Alhammadi, M. M., *Britain and the Administration of the Trucial States 1947-1965*, Abu Dhabi: Emirates Center for Strategic Studies and Research, 2013.
Ali, Syed, *Dubai: Gilded Cage*, New Haven and London: Yale University Press, 2010.
Al Katiri, Laura, 'The Guardian State and its Economic Development Model', *The Journal of Development Studies* 50, no. 1 (2014): 22-34.
Al Lawati, A., 'Expatriates in the Gulf: Temporary but Permanent', in J. Kinninmont (ed.), *Future Trends in the Gulf*, 23-6, London: Chatham House, 2015.
Allen, N., 'Interview in "Dubai Calling" the Dubai British Business Group Magazine 1995', Aaccessed online 10 June 2017 via www.dubaiasitusedtobe.com
Allen, O. E.(1994), 'The Man Who Put Boxes on Ships' and Burrell, D. (1994), 'In the Beginning', both in S. Ignarski (ed.), *The Box: An Anthology Celebrating 25 Years of Containerization and the TT Club*, London: EMAP, 1995.
Al Maktoum, M. Bin Rashid, Shaikh, *Flashes of Thought*, Dubai: Motivate Publishing, 2014.
Al Maktoum, M. Bin Rashid, Shaikh, *Reflections on Happiness and Prosperity*, Dubai: Sh. Mohammed Bin Rashid Executive Office, 2017.
Al Mazeini, K., 'Private Sector Actors in the UAE and Their Role in the Process of Economic Reform', in S. Hertog, G. Luciani, and M. Valeri (eds), *Business Politics in the Middle East*, London: Hurst, 2013.
Al Mazrouei, N. S., *The UAE and Saudi Arabia: Border Disputes and International Relations in the Gulf*, London: I B Tauris, 2016.
Alphaliner Website https://alphaliner.axsmarine.com/PublicTop100/, Accessed 15 February 2018.
Al Qasimi, Sultan, Shaikh, *The Myth of Arab Piracy in the Gulf*, London: Routledge, 1988.
Al Qasimi, Sultan, Shaikh, *My Early Life*, London: Bloomsbury, 2011.
Al Qaydi, A. S., 'Historical Overview of the Rise and Development of the Hospitality Industry', (in the UAE), *Liwa Journal*, Abu Dhabi, 7 no. 15 (June 2016): 19-36.
Al Rasheed, M., (ed.), *Transnational Connections and the Arab Gulf*, London: Routledge, 2014.
Al Sadik, A. T. and I. A. Elbadawi (eds), *The Global Economic Crisis* and *Consequences for Development Strategy in Dubai*, New York: Palgrave Macmillan, 2012.
Al Sayegh, Fatma, 'Merchants Role in a Changing Society: The Case of Dubai 1900-1990', *Middle East Studies* 34, no. 1 (1998): 87-102.
AlSharekh, A. and R. Springborg (eds), *Popular Culture and Political Identity in the Arab Gulf States*, London: Saqi Books/SOAS, 2008.

Al Shehabi, O., 'Histories of Migration to the Gulf', in A. Khalaf, O. Alshehabi ,and A. Hanieh (eds), *Transit States*, London: Pluto Press, 2015.

Alston, R. and S. Laing, *Unshook Till the End of Time: A History of Relations Between Britain and Oman*, London: Gilgamesh Publishing, 2014.

Al Tamimi and Co. Website www.tamimi.com, A Khokhar, May 2016, *UAE National Service: A Revisit*, Accessed 27 February 2018.

Al Yousef, M. B. M., *Oil and the Transformation of Oman 1970–1995*, London: Stacey International, 1995.

Amsden, A., *The Rise of the Rest*, New York: Oxford University Press, 2001.

Anderson, L., 'Absolutism and the Resilience of Monarchy in the Middle East', *Political Science Quarterly* 106, no. 1 (Spring 1991): 1–15.

Askari, H., *Collaborative Colonialism*, New York: Palgrave Macmillan, 2013.

Axworthy, M., *Revolutionary Iran*, London: Penguin, 2014.

Ayubi, N., *Over-stating the Arab State: Politics and Society in the Middle East*, London: I B Tauris, 1995.

BAAS Group Website – www.big.sa.com/logistics-port-services, Accessed 10 October 2017.

Bahrain Port Khalifa Website www.transportation.gov.bh/content/khalifa-bin-salman/port, Accessed 24 August 2017.

Bahrain Port Website www.bahrainport.com/doing-business-with-us/120-statistics-data-html, Accessed 23/8/2017.

Baird, A. J., 'The Development of Global Container Transhipment Terminals', in J. Wang, D. Olivier, T. Notteboom, and B. Slack (eds), *Ports, Cities and Global Supply Chains*, Aldershot: Ashgate Publishing, 2007.

Baldwin-Edwards, M., 'Labour Immigration and Labour Markets in the GCC Countries: National Patterns and Trends', London: LSE No. 15. Kuwait Programme on Development, Governance and Globalisation in the Gulf States, 2011.

Balfour-Paul, G., *The End of Empire in the Middle East*, Cambridge: Cambridge University Press, 1991.

BBC News - Business – www.bbc.co.uk/news/business-11837714 - 25 November 2010.

BBC News Online, www.news.bbc.co.uk/1/hi/business/4789368.stm, Accessed 25 May 2018.

Beblawi, H. and G. Luciani, *The Rentier State*, New York: Routledge, 1987.

Belgrave, C., *The Pirate Coast*, London: G Bell and Sons, 1966.

Bellin, E., 'The Robustness of Authoritarianism in the Middle East: Exceptionalism in Comparative Perspective', *Comparative Politics* 36, no. 2 (2004): 139–57.

Bellini, J., *Pioneering Spirit: The Story Behind Inchcape's Remarkable Journey*, London: Artesian Publishing, 2010.

Belt, J. and H. Appleyard, *A History of Frank C Strick and His Many Shipping Enterprises*, Kendal: World Ship Society, 1996.

Bianco, C. and G. Stansfield, 'The Intra-GCC Crises: Mapping GCC Fragmentation after 2011', *International Affairs*, Chatham House 94, no. 3 (May 2018): 613–36.

Blake, George, *BI Centenary*, London: Collins, 1956.

Bloomberg Markets Website 'Saudi Reserves drop below $500 bn', www.bloomberg.com/news/articles/2017-05-28, Accessed 10/10/2017.

Brand Dubai Website, www.branddubai.com, Accessed 30 May 2018.

Broeze, Frank, *The Globalization of the Oceans*, St. Johns Newfoundland: IMEHA, 2002.

Broeze, Frank, *Dubai*: 'From Creek to Global Port City', in L. R. Fischer and A. Jarvis (eds), *Harbours and Havens: Essays in Port History in Honour of Gordon Jackson*, 159–90, St. Johns Newfoundland: IMEHA, 1999.

Brook, D., *A History of Future Cities*, New York: Norton, 2013.
Bureau International Des Expositions Website, www.bie-paris.org/site/en/2020-dubai, Accessed 21 May 2018.
Burrell, D., 'In the Beginning', in S. Ignarski, (ed.), *The Box: An Anthology Celebrating 25 Years of Containerisation and the TT Club*, London: EMAP, 1995.
Burrows, B., *Footnotes in the Sand*, Wilton: Michael Russell, 1990.
Chang, H.-J., *Kicking Away the Ladder: Development Strategy in Historical Perspective*, London: Anthem Press, 2002.
Chehabi, H. E., and J. J. Linz (eds), *Sultanistic Regimes*, Baltimore: Johns Hopkins University Press, 1998.
Christensen, Clayton, *The Innovator's Dilemma: When New Technologies Cause Great Firms to Fail*, Harvard: Harvard Business School Press, 1997.
CIA World Factbook - www.cia.gov/library/publications/the-world-factbook/rankorder/2244rank.html
Clare, Horatio, *Down to the Sea in Ships*, London: Chatto and Windus, 2014.
CMA-CGM website, www.cma-cgm.com/products-services/line-services/flyer/CIMEX3
Coker, C., *Can War be Eliminated?* Cambridge: Polity Press, 2014.
Commins, D., *The Gulf States: A Modern History*, London: I B Tauris, 2012.
Crawford, M., 'Religion in the Gulf 1700–1971', in J. E. Peterson (ed.), *The Emergence of the Gulf States*, London: Bloomsbury, 2016.
Crystal, Jill, 'Coalitions in Oil Monarchies: Kuwait and Qatar', *Comparative Politics* 21, no. 4, (July 1989): 427–42.
CSX Press Release, December 2004, www.phx.corporate-ir.net, Accessed 25 May 2018.
Cudahy, Brian, *Box Boats*, New York: Fordham University Press, 2006.
Davidson, C. M., *The United Arab Emirates: A Sstudy in Survival*, London: Lynne Rienner, 2005.
Davidson, C. M., *Dubai – The Vulnerability of Success*, London: Hurst, 2008.
Davidson, C. M., *After the Shaikhs: The Coming Collapse of the Gulf Monarchies*, London: Hurst, 2012.
Davies, C. E., *The Blood Red Arab Flag: An Investigation into Qasimi Piracy 1797–1820*, Exeter: University of Exeter Press, 1997.
Davis, M., 'Fear and Money in Dubai', *New Left Review* 41, no. 3 (September/October 2006): 47–68.
De Butts, F., *Now the Dust Hhas Settled*, Padstow: Tabb House, 1995.
Donovan, A. and Bonney, J., *The Box that Changed the World*, East Windsor: Commonwealth Business Media, 2006.
D P World, *Dreams of the Sea – The Dubai Maritime History Project*, Dubai: Explorer Publishing, 2014.
D P World Website, www.dpworld.ae/en/content/15/173 Jebel Ali History, Accessed 10 June 2017.
DP World Website, www.dpworld.com/2011/our-history.html, Accessed 25 May 2018.
DP World Website, www.dpworld.com/our-business/marine-terminals/, 25 Accessed May 2018.
Dragonmart Website www.dragonmart.ae/en/dragon-mart, Accessed 26 February 2018.
Dresch, P., 'Societies, Identities and Global Issues', included in P. Dresch and J. Piscatori, *Monarchies and Nations: Globalisation and Identity in the Arab States of the Gulf*, London: I B Tauris, 2005.
Drissi, A., *Dubai, the New Arab Dream*, Paris: IFRI, 2006.

Dubai Airport Website, http://www.dubaiairport.com/DIA/English/TopMenu/About+DIA/Facts+and+Figures/, Accessed 6 June 2018.
Dubai As It Used To Be Website, www.dubaiasitusedtobe.com, 'Computers, Containers, but No Memory', Accessed 10 July 2018.
Dubai Design District Website, www.dubaidesigndistrict.com, Accessed 23 May 2018.
Dubaifaqs Website www.dubaifaqs.com/dubai-airport.php, Accessed 15 March 2018.
Dubai Holding Website, www.dubaiholding.com/en/who-we-are/, Accessed 22 August 2018.
Dubai International Humanitarian City, www.ihc.ae/, Accessed 9 May 2018.
Dubai Internet City Website, www.dic.ae/, Accessed 10 May 2018.
Dubai Media City Website, www.dmc.ae/en, Accessed 9 May 2018.
Dubai Multi Commodities Centre Website, www.dmcc.ae/, Accessed 9 May 2018.
Dubai National Air travel Agency (DNATA), *DNATA: Half a Century*, Dubai: DNATA 2009.
Dubai National Air Travel Agency (DNATA) Website, www.dnata.com/media-centre/dnata-celebrates-25-years-of-international-growth. Press Release on 11 July 2018, Accessed 22 August 2018.
Dubai Ports Website www.dubaiports.ae/corporate/media-centre/fact-sheets/detail/dubai-airports, Accessed 23/8/2017.
Dubai Silicon Oasis Website, www.dsoa.ae/, Accessed 9 May 2018.
Dubai Statistics Centre (DSC), www.dsc.gov.ae/en, Accessed 22 February 2018.
Dubai Statistics Centre (DSC), www.dsc.gov.ae Dubai in Figures 2018/Construction and Housing/Completed Buildings, Accessed 31/8/2018.
Dubai Trade Website www.dubaitrade.ae, Accessed 8 March 2018
Ecomcrew Website www.ecomcrew.com/yiwu-guide-the-largest-wholesale-market-in-the-world.
(The) Economist Newspaper Online, www.economist.com, 'Why Have Containers Boosted Trade So Much? 22 May 2013; 'What is China's Belt and Road Initiative?' 15 July 2017, www.economist.com/blogs.
(The) Economist Newspaper, 'Soaring Ambition', 10 January 2015, 43.
(The) Economist Newspaper, 'The Gulf's Little Sparta', 8 April 2017, 38.
(The) Economist Newspaper, 'Uneasy sits Qaboos', 8 July 2017, Page 43.
(The) Economist Newspaper, 'A Port in the Storm', 2 September 2017, 44.
(The) Economist Newspaper, 'Economic Gulf', 21 October 2017, 53.
(The) Economist Newspaper, 'Pulp Friction', 24 March 2018, 77.
(The) Economist Newspaper, 'Thinking Outside the Box', 28 April 2018, 18.
(The) Economist Newspaper, 'Crossing Continents', 25 August 2018, 15.
Ehteshami, A., *Globalization and Geopolitics in the Middle East: Old Games, New Rules*, London: Routledge, 2007.
Ehteshami, A., *Dynamics of Change in the Persian Gulf*, London: Routledge, 2013.
Emirates Airline Website, www.emirates.com/english/about/history.
Emirates Airline Website, https://www.emirates.com/ae/english/about-us/sponsorships/, Accessed 30 May 2018.
Emirates Airline Festival of Literature Website, https://www.emirateslitfest.com, Accessed 23 May 2018350.
Emirates 24/7 Business Website (4 February 2013), '*DP World Handled 100 Million Containers in 10 Years*', Accessed 12 December 2017
Emmott, Bill, 'New World Order', *Financial Times Weekend*, 18/19 March 2017.
Energy Information Administration Website www.eia.gov/petroleum/, Accessed 29 September 2017

Evans, Peter B., *Embedded Autonomy: States and Industrial Transformation*, Princeton: Princeton University Press, 1995.
Eventbrite Website, www.eventbrite.com/d/united-arab-emirates-dubai/conferences/, Accessed 21 May 2018.
Field, Michael, *The Merchants*, London: John Murray, 1984.
Financial Times Newspaper, 'How Qatar Seized Control of the Syrian Revolution', 17 May 2013, Accessed 20 June 2017; 'William (Bill) Duff: Financial Supervisor', Obituary, 28 February 2014, Accessed 10 May 2017; 'China Eencircles the World with One Belt One Road Sstrategy', 3 April 2017, www.ft.com, Accessed 18 October 2017; 'The $1bn Hostage Deal that Enraged Qatar's Gulf Rivals', 5 June 2017, Accessed 4 April 2018.
Flexport Blog, www.flexport.com/what-are-ocean-alliances/, 'Guide to Ocean Alliances', Accessed 28 November 2017.
Floor, W., *The Persian Gulf: The Rise and Fall of Bandar-E Lengeh, The Distribution Center for the Arabian Coast*, Washington: Mage Publishers, 2010.
Foreign Policy Website, www.foreignpolicy.com/2017/04/03the-omani-succession-envelope-please, Accessed 18 August 2017.
Friedman, T., *The World is Flat*, London: Penguin Books, 2005.
Fromherz, A. J., *Qatar: A Modern History*, London: I B Tauris, 2012.
Fuccaro, N., 'The Making of Gulf Ports Before Oil', Abu Dhabi: Liwa *Journal of the National Centre for Documentation and Research*, no. 3 (June 2010): 19–32.
Fuccaro, N., *Histories of City and State in the Persian Gulf: Manama since 1800*, Cambridge: Cambridge University Press, 2012.
Fuccaro, N., 'Rethinking the History of Port Cities in the Gulf', in L. Potter (ed.), *The Persian Gulf in Modern Times: People Ports and History*, New York: Palgrave, 2014.
Fukuyama, F., *The End of History and the Last Man*, London: Free Press/Macmillan, 1992.
Funsch, L. P., *Oman Reborn*, New York: Palgrave MacMillan, 2015.
Gause, F. G., 'Kings for Al Seasons: How the Middle East's Monarchies Survived the Arab Spring', Doha: Brookings Center Analysis Paper no. 8 (September 2013): 1–30.
Genc, I. and G. Naufal, *Expatriates and the Labour Force*, London: Palgrave, 2012.
George, Rosemary, *Deep Sea and Foreign Going*, London: Portobello Books, 2014.
Ghabra, S., 'Identity and State in the Gulf: The Case of Kuwait', in M. C. Thompson and N. Quilliam (eds.), *Policy Making in the GCC: State, Citizens and Institutions*, London: I B Tauris, 2017.
Gouvernal, E., V. Lavaud-Letilleul and B. Slack, 'Transport and Logistics Hubs: Separating Fact from Fiction', in P. Hall, R. J. McCalla, C. Comtois and B. Slack, *Integrating Seaports and Trade Corridors*, Farnham: Ashgate, 2011.
Govers, R. and F. Go, *Place Branding: Glocal, Virtual and Physical Identities, Constructed, Imagined and Experienced*, Basingstoke: Palgrave Macmillan, 2009.
Gray, M., *A Theory of Later Rentierism in the Arab Sstates of the Gulf*, Georgetown University: Doha, Qatar, 2011.
Gresh, G. F., 'A Vital Maritime Pinch-Point: China, the Bab al-Mandeb and the Middle East', in *Asian Journal of Middle Eastern and Islamic Studies* 11, no. 1 (March 2017): 37–46.
Griffiths, Percival, *A History of the Inchcape Group*, London: Inchcape, 1977.
Gulf Labour Markets and Migration Website www.gulfmigration.eu/uae-dubai-estimates-of-total-population-by-sex-1953-1968-census dates-2006-2013/, Accessed 16 February 2018.
Gulf News Website, https://gulfnews.com/guides/life/country/, 15 August 2017, Accessed 9 May 2018.

Gulf News Money Dubai – UAE Expat remittances reach Dh 121.1 billion in 9 months, 14 December 2017, www.gulfnews.com/business/money/uae-expat-remittances-reach-dh121-1-billion-in-9-months-1.2140876, Accessed 10 February 2018.

Gulftainer Website Media Centre 15 December 15, 2015, www.gulftainer.com/press-relea se/khorfakkan-container-terminal-exceeds-4000-moves-in-a-12-hour-shift/, Accessed 27 December 2017; Iraq website, www.gulftainer.com/terminals/iraq/iraq-container-t erminal/, Accessed 24 October 2017 and www.gulftainer.com/terminals/uae/sharjah-container-terminal, Accessed June 2017.

Halliday, F., *Arabia Without Sultans*, London: Penguin Books, 1974.

Hanieh, A., 'Theorizing the Arabian Peninsula Roundtable: Bringing the Region Back In', *Jadaliyya* Online Roundtable, www.jadaliyya.com, 22 April 2013.

Hanieh, A., *Money, Markets and Monarchies: The GCC and the Political Economy of the Contemporary Middle East*, Cambridge: Cambridge University Press, 2018.

Hapag-Lloyd Website (24 May 2017) www.hapaglloyd.com/en/press/releases/2017/05/hapag-lloyd-and-uasc-complete-merger-html, Accessed 20 September 2017.

Harcourt, F., 'British Oceanic Mail Contracts in the Age of Steam 1838–1914', included in D. M. Williams (ed.), *The World of Shipping*, Aldershot: Ashgate, 1997.

Harford, Tim, 'What We Get Wrong About Technology', London: Financial Times Weekend Magazine July 8/9 July, 2017.

Harlaftis, G., S. Tenold, and J. Valdiso (eds), *The World's Key Industry: History & Economics of International Shipping*, London: Palgrave Macmillan, 2012.

Hawley, Donald, *The Trucial States*, London: Allen and Unwin, 1970.

Hawley, Donald, *Desert Wind and Tropic Storm*, Norwich: Michael Russell, 2000.

Hawley, Donald, *The Emirates: Witness to a Metamorphosis*, Norwich: Michael Russell, 2007.

Heard-Bey, Frauke, *From Trucial States to UAE*, Motivate: Dubai 1982 – third reprint, 2013.

Heins, M., *The Globalisation of American Infrastructure*, New York: Routledge, 2016.

Held, D. and A. McGrew, *The Global Transformation Reader*, Cambridge: Polity Press, 2000.

Henry, C. M. and R. Springborg, R., *Globalization and the Politics of Development in the Middle East*, Cambridge: Cambridge University Press, 2010.

Herb, M., *All in the Family: Absolutism, Revolution and Democracy in the Middle East Monarchies*, New York: State University of New York Press, 1999.

Herb, M., *The Wages of Oil: Parliaments and Economic Development in Kuwait and the UAE*, Ithaca: Cornell University Press, 2014.

Herb, M., 'The Origins of Kuwait's National Assembly', London: LSE Kuwait Programme, Series No. 39, March 2016.

Hertog, S., '"A Quest for Significance: Gulf Oil Monarchies" International "Soft Power" Strategies and their Local Urban Dimensions', London: *LSE Kuwait Programme* Series no. 42, March 2017.

Hiroo, D., *The Longest War: The Iran-Iraq Military Conflict*, London: Routledge, 1990.

Hoovestal, L., *Globalization Contained: The Economic and Strategic Consequences of the Container*, New York: Palgrave Macmillan, 2013.

Hourani, George, *Arab Seafaring*, Princeton: Princeton University Press, 1995 edition.

Howarth, David and Stephen, *The Story of* P&O, London: Weidenfeld and Nicolson, 1986.

Huntington, S. P., *Political Oorder in Changing Societies*, New Haven: Yale University Press, 1968.

Hutchison Ports Website https://hutchisonports.com/en/, Accessed 27 December 2017.
Hvidt, M., 'The Dubai Model: An Outline of Key Development Process Elements in Dubai', *International Journal of Middle East Studies* 41, no. 3 (August 2009): 397–418.
Ignarski, Sam, *The Box: An Anthology Celebrating 25 Years of Containerization and the TT Club*, London: EMAP, 1995.
Inflation Data Website, Historical Crude Oil Prices, https://inflationdata.com/inflation/Inflation_Rate/Historical_Oil_Prices_Table.asp, Accessed 4 September 2018.
International Monetary Fund (IMF) Direction of Trade Statistics www.imf.org/en/data, Accessed 9 January 2018.
International Monetary Fund (IMF) Website www.imf.org *Qatar Country Report No. 17/89*, Accessed 4 September 2017.
International Rail Journal 3 May 2016 www.railjournal.com/index.php/middle-east/oman-suspends-railway-project.html, Accessed 17 August 2017.
Invest in Group website www.investinggroup.org/snapshot/282/sharjahs-economic-outlook-united-arab-emirates, Accessed 5 December 2017
Investopedia Website, https://www.investopedia.com/terms/j/japaninc.asp, Accessed 30 May 2018.
Jahani, K., 'Sanctioning Iran: The View from the UAE', *Al Nakhlah Journal*, Spring 2011, Medford: Tufts University Fletcher School, 2011, 1–20.
Jawaharlal Nehru Port Trust website www.jnport.in.gov, Accessed 9 February 2018.
JAFZA Website, www.jafza.ae/about-us/history-vision-promise/, Accessed 3 December 2017 and www.jafza.ae/about-us/why-dubai-why-jafza/, Accessed 8 May 2018.
Jamieson, A. G., *Ebb Tide in the British Maritime Industries: Change and Adaptation 1918–1990*, Exeter: Exeter University Press, 2003.
Jephson, C and H. Morgen, H, *Creating Global Opportunities: Maersk Line in Containerization 1973–2013*, Cambridge: Cambridge University Press, 2014.
Johnson, R., 'The Great Game and Power Projection', included in J. R. Macris, *Imperial Crossroads*, Annapolis: Naval Institute Press, 2012.
Jones, G., *Banking and Oil: The History of the British Bank of the Middle East Vol II*, Cambridge: Cambridge University Press, 1987.
Jones, J. and N. Ridout, *A History of Modern Oman*, New York: Cambridge University Press, 2015.
Jones, Stephanie, 'British India Steamers and the Trade of the Persian Gulf 1862–1914', *The Great Circle, Journal of the Australian Association for Maritime History* 7, no. 1 (April 1985): 23–44.
Jones, Stephanie, *Two Centuries of Overseas Trading*, Basingstoke: Palgrave Macmillan, 1986.
Journal Of Commerce Online 9 May 2016, www.joc.com 'India, Iran moving forward on redeveloping Chahbahar Port', Accessed 18 October 2017.
Kamrava, M., *The Political Economy of Rentierism in the Persian Gulf*, New York: Cambridge University Press, 2012.
Kamrava, M., *Qatar: Small State, Big Politics*, Ithaca and London: Cornell University Press, 2013.
Kamrava, M. (ed.), *Gateways to the World: Port Cities in the Persian Gulf*, London: Hurst, 2016.
Kanna, A., 'The Trajectories of Two Asian Tigers: The Imperial Roots of Capitalism in Dubai and Singapore', in X. Chen and A. Kanna (eds), *Rethinking Global Urbanism: Comparative Insights from Secondary Cities*, London: Routledge, 2012.
Karachi International Container Terminal (KICT) Website www.kictl.com, Accessed 9 February 2018.

Katada, S. and Solis, M., *Cross Regional Trade Agreements*, Heidelberg: Springer, 2008.
Kattan, F., *A Review and Critique of the Saudisation Narrative in Policy mMaking in the GCC*, London: I B Tauris, 2017.
Kelly, J. B., *Britain and the Persian Gulf 1795–1880*, Oxford: Clarendon Press, 1968.
Keshavarzian, A., 'Geopolitics and the Geneology of Free-Trade Zones in the Persian Gulf', *Geopolitics* 15, no. 2 (2010): 263–89.
Khalaf, A., O. Al Shehabi and A. Hanieh, *Transit States: Labour, Migration and Citizenship in the Gulf*, London: Pluto Press, 2015.
Khaleej Times Special Report, '25 Great Years: 1985–2010' (The Story of Emirates Airline), Dubai 2010.
Khalifa Bin Salman Port Bahrain Website, www.mtt.gov.bh, Accessed 9 April 2018.
King Abdullah Economic City Website, www.kaec.com, Accessed 10 May 2018.
Kinninmont, J., *Future Trends in the Gulf*, London: Chatham House, 2015.
Kinninmont, J., 'Middle East Gets Messier', *The World Today* (October/November 2017): 17–18, London: Chatham House.
Kish Island Freezone Website, www.economic.kish.ir/en, Accessed 10 May 2018.
Klose, A., *The Container Principle: How a Box Changes the Way We Think*, London: MIT Press, 2015.
Krane, J., *Dubai*, New York: St Martin's Press, 2009.
Kuwait Petroleum Corporation Website - www.kpc.com.kw/InformationCenter/Pages/Kuwait-Oil-History.aspx
Laxon, W. and Perry, *BI: British India Steam Navigation Company*, Kendal: World Ship Society, 1994.
Legrenzi, M., *The GCC and the International Relations of the Gulf*, London: I B Tauris, 2011.
Levinson, Marc, *The Box: How the Shipping Container Made the World Smaller and the World Economy Bigger*, Princeton: Princeton University Press, 2008 Paperback.
Lewis, N., *A Voyage by Dhow*, London: Jonathan Cape, 2001.
Linz, Juan, *Totalitarian and Authoritarian regimes*, Boulder: Lynne Rienner, 2000.
Lorimer, J. G., *Gazetteer of the Persian Gulf*, Calcutta: Government Printing Press, 1908.
Lucas, R., 'Monarchical Authoritarianism: Survival and Political Liberalization in a Middle East Regime Type', *International Journal of Middle East Studies* 36 (February 2004): 103–19.
Luciani, G., *Political Liberalisation and Democratisation in the Arab World*, Boulder: Lynne Reinner, 1998.
Macdougall, P., *Islamic Seapower During the Age of Fighting Sail*, Woodbridge: Boydell Press, 2017.
Maersk Line Website www.maerskline.com/en/about/profile, Accessed 24 August 2017.
Makki, A. A., *Rashid, The Man Behind Dubai*, Published in Dubai, 1990.
Marchal, R., 'Dubai: Global City and Transnational Hub', in M. Al Rasheed (ed.), *Transnational Connections and the Arab Gulf*, London: Routledge, 2014.
Martin, Craig, *Shipping Container*, London: Bloomsbury, 2016.
Matthiesen, T., *Sectarian Gulf*, Stanford: Stanford University Press, 2013.
Meyer-Reumann Report of 2 April 2012, www.lexarabiae.meyer-reumann.com, Accessed 17 October 2017
Mishrif A, 'Challenges of Economic Diversification in the GCC Countries', in A. Mishrif and Y. Al Balushi, *Economic Diversification in the Gulf Region: Comparing Global Challenges*, Singapore: Palgrave Macmillan/Gulf Research Centre Cambridge, 2018.
Mishrif, A. and H. Kapetanovic, H., 'Dubai's Model of Economic Diversification', in A. Mishrif and Y. Al Balushi, *Economic Diversification in the Gulf Region: Comparing*

Global Challenges, Singapore: Palgrave Macmillan/Gulf Research Centre Cambridge, 2018.

Moore, Robin, *Dubai*, London: Barrie and Jenkins, 1976.

Morris, James, *Sultan in Oman*, London: Faber and Faber, 1997.

Morton, Michael Q., 'The British India Line in the Arabian Gulf 1862–1982', *Abu Dhabi: Liwa Journal of the National Centre for Documentation and Research* 5, no. 10 (December 2013): 40–63.

Morton, Michael Q., *Keepers of the Golden Shore: A History of the UAE*, London: Reaktion Books, 2016.

Muir, Douglas, N., 'Early Mail Transport in, and from, the Gulf 1798–1939', Abu Dhabi: *Liwa Journal of the National Centre for Documentation and Research* 5, no. 10 (December 2013): 3–24.

Nandwa, B. and A. T. Al Sadik, 'Public Debt Management and Fiscal Sustainability', in A. Al Faris and R. Soto (eds), *The Economy of Dubai*, Oxford: Oxford University Press, 2016.

The National Newspaper Website www.thenational.uae, *UAE Economy to Ggain $13bn from Lifting of Iran Sanctions*, dated 6 August 2015, Accessed 17 October 2017.

New York Times Website www.nytimes.com/2011/03/15/world/middleeast/15bahrain.html, Accessed 23/8/2017.

Nordin, A. H. M. and Weissman, M., 'Will Trump make China Great Again? The Belt and Road Initiative and International Order', *Oxford, Chatham House: International Affairs* 94, no. 2 (March 2018): 231–49.

Notteboom, T., and J.-P. Rodrigue, 'Emerging Global Networks in the Container Terminal Operating Industry', in T. Notteboom (ed.), *Current Issues in Shipping, Ports and Logistics*, Antwerp: Antwerp University Press, 2011.

Nye, J., *Soft Power: The Means to Success in World Politics*, New York: Public Affairs, 2004.

Onley, J. and Khalaf, S. Khalaf, 'Shaikly Authority in the Pre-Oil Gulf', *History and Anthropology* 17, no. 3 (September 2006): 189–208.

Onley, J, 'Britain and the Gulf Shaikhdoms, 1820–1971: The Politics of Protection', Doha: Center for International and Regional Studies, Georgetown University School of Foreign Service in Qatar. Occasional Paper no. 4 (2009): 1–44.

Onley, J, 'Transnational merchants in the 19th Century Gulf', in M. Al Rasheed (ed.), *Transnational Connections and the Arab Gulf*, London: Routledge, 2014.

O'Shea, R., *The Sand Kings of Oman*, London: Methuen, 1947.

Oxford Business Group Website, www.oxfordbusinessgroup.com/news/sharjah-year-review-2016, Accessed 5 December 2017.

Pampanini, A. H., *Cities in the Arabian Desert: The Building of Jubail and Yanbu*, Westport, CT: Praeger, 1997.

Parkinson, R., *Dreadnought: The Ship that Changed the World*, London: I B Tauris, 2015.

Parolin, G. P., 'Reweaving the Myth of Bahrain's Parliamentary Experience', in M. Tetreault, G. Okruhlik and A. Kapiszewski (eds), *Political Change in the Gulf Arab States*, Boulder: Lynne Rienner, 2011.

Pearson, M., 'Indian Ocean Port-Cities: Themes and Problems', in R. Mukherjee (ed.), *Vanguards of Globalization: Port Cities from the Classical to the Modern*, Delhi: Primus Books, 2014.

Pelly, Lewis, *A Visit to the Port of Lingah, the Island of Kishm and the Port of Bandar Abbass* (Proceedings of the Royal Geographical Society of London Volume 8 No 6, 1863–1864): 265–67.

Perse Transport Bar Website www.perse-ir.com/home/briefhistory
Peterson, J. E., 'Oman Faces the Twenty-First Century', in M. Tetreault, G. Okruhlik and A. Kapiszewski (eds), *Political Change in the Arab Gulf States*, Boulder: Lynne Rienner, 2011.
Peterson, J. E., 'The Age of Imperialism and its impact on the Gulf', in J. E. Peterson (ed.), *The Emergence of the Gulf States*, London: Bloomsbury, 2016.
Phillips, A. and J. C. Sharman, *International Order in Diversity: War, Trade and Rule in the Indian Ocean*, Cambridge: Cambridge University Press, 2016.
Port of Felixstowe Website https://www.portoffelixstowe.co.uk/50-years/history/, Accessed 6 February 2018.
Porter, Janet, 'Four Weddings and a Funeral', *Containerisation International* (November 2016): 21–4.
Ports.Com Website www.ports.com, Accessed 9 February 2018.
Port Technology International, www.porttechnology.org/news/the_top_5_terminal_operators_in_2016, Accessed 29 May 2018.
Potter, L. G. (ed.), *The Persian Gulf in History*, London: Palgrave Macmillan, 2009.
Potter, L. G., *The Rise and Fall of Port Cities in The Persian Gulf in Modern Times*, New York: Palgrave, 2014.
Potts, D., 'Trends and Patterns in the Archaeology and Pre-Modern History of the Gulf Region', in J. Peterson (ed.), *The Emergence of the Gulf States*, London: Bloomsbury, 2016.
Price, G., 'A Future Built by Sweat of Workers Overseas', *The World Today*, Chatham House 74, no. 3 (June/July 2018): 34–8.
Raban, J., *Arabia Through the Looking Glass*, Glasgow: Collins, 1979.
Ramos, S. J., *Dubai Amplified: The Engineering of a Port Geography*, Farnham: Ashgate, 2010.
Ramos, S. J., 'Dubai's Jebel Ali Port: Trade, Territory and Infrastructure', in C. Hein, *Port Cities and Dynamic Landscapes*, London: Routledge, 2011.
Reuters Website 5 September 2017 www.reuters.com/...qatar-port/qatar-says-new-port-will-help-circumvent-arab-sanctions-idUSKCN1BG1RP, Accessed 25 October 2017
Roberts, D., 'The Consequences of the Exclusive Treaties', in B. R. Pridham, *The Arab Gulf and the West*, London: Croom Helm, 1985.
Rostow, W. W., *The Stages of Economic Growth*, Cambridge: Cambridge University Press, 1960.
Rugh, A. B., *The Political Culture of Leadership in the United Arab Emirates*, Basingstoke: Palgrave Macmillan, 2007.
Runciman, David, book review of Francis Fukuyama, 'Political Order and Political Decay', Financial Times, London, 26 September 2014.
Sab, R., 'Economic Impact of Selected Conflicts in the Middle East: What can we Learn from the Past?'" International Monetary Fund (IMF) working paper 14/100, 2014. www.imf.org/external/pubs/ft/wp/2014/wp14100/pdf, Accessed 15 September 2017.
Salalah Port website www.salalahport.com, Accessed 17 August 2017.
Saldanha, J. A., *Precis of Commerce and Communication in the Persian Gulf 1801–1905*, Calcutta: Government Printing House, 1906.
Sampler, J. and S. Eigner, S. *Sand to Silicon: Achieving Rapid Growth Lessons from Dubai*, London: Profile Books, 2003.
Santander Trade Report https://en.portal.santandertrade.com/analyse-markets/united-arab-emirates/economic-political-outline, Accessed 5 December 2017.
Sato, S., *Britain and the Formation of the Gulf States*, Manchester: Manchester University Press, 2016.

Saudi Aramco Website www.saudiaramco.com/en/home/about/history.html, Accessed 27 September 2017.
Saudi Railways Website www.saudirailways.org/sites/sro/pages/en-us/aboutus, Accessed 9 October 9, 2017.
Schubert, D., 'Seaport Cities: Phases of Spatial Restructuring and Types and Dimensions of Redevelopment', in C. Hein (ed.), *Port Cities: Dynamic Landscapes and Global Networks*, London: Routledge, 2011.
Seikaly, C. and K. Mattar, K. (eds), *The Silent Revolution: The Arab Spring and the Gulf States*, Berlin: Gerlach Press, 2014.
Severin, T., *The Sinbad Voyage*, London: Little Brown and Co, 1982.
Shahid Rajaee Port (Bandar Abbas) Website www.shahidrajaee.pmo.ir/en/home, Accessed 18 October 2017.
Sheriff, Abdul, *Dhow Cultures of the Indian Ocean*, London: Hurst, 2010.
Siavoshi, Sussan, 1996 Article on Dubai in *Encyclopedia Iranica*, www.iranicaonline.org/articles/dubai, Accessed 9 January 2018.
Sohar Port Website www.soharportandfreezone.com, Accessed 1 August, 2017.
Soto, R. and Y. Rashid, Y., 'Labour Markets in Transition' in A. Al Faris and R. Soto, *The Economy of Dubai*, Oxford: Oxford University Press, 2016.
Sovereign Wealth Fund Institute Website – www.swfinstitute.org/sovereign-wealth-fund-rankings/, Accessed 26 September 2017.
Stanley-Price, N., 'Imperial Airways and the Airfield at Sharjah 1932–1939', *Abu Dhabi: Liwa Journal of the National Centre for Documentation and Research* 5, no. 6 (December 2011): 24–38.
Statistita Website, www.statistita.com/statistics/284636/visitor-arrivals-in-dubai-from-international-destinations, Accessed 21 May 2018.
Steinberg, Phillip, *The Social Construction of the Ocean*, Cambridge: Cambridge University Press, 2001.
Stopford, M., *Maritime Economics*, Abingdon: Routledge, 2009.
Tarayam, A. O., *The Establishment of the United Arab Emirates 1950–1985*, Beckenham: Croom Helm, 1987.
Tetreault, M. A., *The Economics of National Economy in the UAE*, New York: MEPC, 2000.
Tetreault, M. A., 'Bottom-Up Democratisation in Kuwait', in M. A. Tetrault, G. Okruhlik and A. Kapiszewski (eds), *Political Change in the Arab Gulf Sstates: Stuck in Transition*, Boulder and London: Lynne Rienner, 2011.
Thesiger, W., *Arabian Sands*, London: Longmans, Green, 1959.
Times of Oman Website 22 April 2017 www.timesofoman.com/article/107373/oman/chinese-firms-commit-$31billion-investment-in-duqm-free-zone, Accessed 17 August 2017
Tull, M., 'Australian Ports Since 1945', in L. R. Fischer and A. Jarvis (eds.), *Harbours and Havens*, 111–38, St Johns Newfoundland: IMEHA, 1999.
UAE Government Website www.government.ae/en/information-and-services/jobs/employment-laws-and-regulations, Accessed 22 February 2018.
Ulrichsen, K. C., *Insecure Gulf*, London: C Hurst and Co., 2011.
Ulrichsen, K. C., *The Gulf States in International Political Economy*, Basingstoke: Palgrave Macmillan, 2016.
UNECE Website www.unece.org/cefact/edifact/welcome.html, Accessed 8 March 2018.
US Department of Justice Website 26 May 2017 – www.justice.gov/opa/pr/defence-contractor-resolves-criminal-civil-and-administrative-liability-related-food
Villiers, A., *Sons of Sinbad*, London: Hodder and Stoughton, 1949.

Von Bismarck, Helene, *British Policy in the Persian Gulf 1961–1968*, Basingstoke: Palgrave Macmillan, 2013.
Vora, N., *Impossible Citizens: Dubai's Indian Diaspora*, London: Duke University Press, 2013.
Walker, A. R., 'Recessional and Gulf War Impacts on Port Development and Shipping in the Gulf states in the 1980s', *Geographic Journal* 18, no 3 (April 1989): 273–84), www.jstor.org/stable/41144890, Accessed 17 August 2017
Walker, Julian, 'Social and Economic Developments in Trucial Oman in the First Half of the 20th Century', *Abu Dhabi: Liwa Journal of the National Centre for Documentation and Research* 3 (June 2010): 33–47.
Walker, Julian, 'Personal Recollections of Indigenous Sources', *Abu Dhabi: Liwa Journal of the National Centre for Documentation and Research* 4, no. 8 (December 2012): 18–28.
Weber, M., *The Protestant Ethic and the Spirit of Capitalism*, London: Penguin Books, 2004.
Weir, D., N. A. Sultan, B. D. Metcalfe, and S. A. Abuznaid, 'The GCC Countries as Knowledge-Based Economies: Future Aspirations and Challenges', in N. Sultan, D. Weir and Z. Karake-Shaloub (eds), *The New Post-Oil Arab Gulf: Managing People and Wealth*, London: Saqi Books, 2011.
What's On Dubai Website, www.whatson.ae/dubai/2017/11/10, Accessed 2 January 2018.
Wilson, G., *Rashid's Legacy*, London: Media Prima, 2006.
Wilson, G., *Emirates: The Airline of the Future*, London and Dubai: Media Prima, 2009.
Wilson, G, *HSBC: 70 Years in the UAE*, London: Media Prima Amazon Kindle Edition, 2016.
Woodman, R, 'Voyage East: A Cargo Ship on the 1960s', in S. Ignarski (ed.), *The Box: An Anthology*, London: EMAP, 1995.
World Bank, Ease of Doing Business Index, https://data.worldbank.org/indicator/IC.BUS.Ease.XQ, Accessed 12 June 2018.
World Bank Website – Umm Qasr www.ppi.worldbank.org/snapshots/…/umm-qasr-container-terminal-berth-8-10-and-11-5838, Accessed 24 October 2017.
World Bank Website, https://data.worldbank.org, Accessed 5 September 2017.
World Bank Website, https://data.worldbank.org (International LPI), Accessed 4 September 2018.
World Cargo News Website, www.worldcargonews.com/htm/w20170724.343624.htm, Accessed 24 October 2017.
World Population Review, www.worldpopulationreview.com/countries/oman-population, Accessed 18 August 2017.
Young, K. E., *The Political Economy of Energy, Finance and Security in the UAE*, Basingstoke: Palgrave, 2014.
Zahlan, R., *The Origins of the United Arab Emirates: A Political and Social History of the Trucial States*, London: Macmillan 1978.
Zawya (Thomson Reuters) Website, www.zawya.com, *Dubai's DP World, Port of Fujairah end Cconcession Aagreement* (16 April 2017), Accessed 7 March 2018.

INDEX

Abu Dhabi
   growth of   136–8, 140
   relationship with Dubai   72, 136
   significance of   10, 16, 29, 35–6, 62–4,
      67–9, 86, 90, 100, 107, 120,
      133, 135
Acemoglu, D.   113
Aden   1
Agility   97
Agius, Dionisius   22
Airlines Hotel   141
Ajman   21, 29, 62, 138
Al Baharna, Husain   21
Al Faris, A.   109, 117, 139
Al Fayed, Mohammed   51
Alfred Holt   47
Al Ghusais   85
Al Gurg, Easa Saleh   7, 8–9, 55, 58, 61, 63
Ali, Syed   10, 116
Al Katiri, Laura   110
Al Khalifa family   65, 94, 96
Allen, Oliver   46
Al Maktoum, HH Shaikh Mohammed   7,
      10, 77, 87, 112–13, 133, 135,
      142, 173
Al Maktoum, Shaikh Maktoum bin
      Hashar   26, 28, 167
Al Maktoum, Shaikh Mohammed Bin
      Rashid   135
Al Maktoum, Shaikh Rashid Bin
      Saeed   1, 6, 8–10, 32–3, 39, 40,
      56, 68–9, 72, 74, 76, 77, 85–6,
      90, *104*, 112, 166–7, 172–3,
      187 n.59
   death of   107
   impact of   50–4
   relations with protecting power   54–6
   ruling policy and   57–62
Al Maktoum, Shaikh Said   58
Al Maktoum International Airport   162
Al Mazrouei, Noura   18

Almeizany, Khalid   112
Al Nahyan, Shaikh Zayed   63, 67–8, 72,
      90, 100, 135
Al Nahyan Bani Yas (Abu Dhabi)   20
Al Nahyan family   63
Al Nayan, Shaikh Khalifa   140
Al Nayan, Shaikh Mohammed Bin
      Zayed   140, 158
Al Qaeda   108
Al Qasimi, Abdul-Aziz   91
Al Qasimi, HH Shaikh Sultan   8, 17, 18,
      62–3, 91, 92, 180 n.32
Al Qasimi, Shaikh Saqr   35, 40, 53, 62,
      63, 91
Al Rais, Saadi Abdul Rahim Hassan   57,
      188 n.72
Al Rasheed   60
Al Sabah family   130
Al Said, Haitham bin Tariq   153
Al Saud, Mohammed Bin Salman   158,
      179 n.14
Al Sayegh, Fatma   57, 58, 60, 112
Al Shehabi   89, 90, 115
Al Tajir, Mahdi   60
Al Thani, Shaikh Hamad   131
Al Thani family   65
Aluminium Bahrain (ALBA)   37, 95
Ambassador Hotel   141
American International Group   147
American President Lines (APL)   121
American Standards Association   47
Amsden, Alice   111, 131
Anderson, Lisa   110
Antwerp port   152
AP Moller   87, 128
Arabian American Oil Company
      (ARAMCO)   38
Arabian Sands (Thesiger)   5
Arabia through the Looking Glass
      (Raban)   8
Arab League   55

Arab Shipbuilding and Repair Yard (ASRY)   37, 61, 95
Arab Spring   4, 110, 136, 140, 192 n.76
Askold (ship)   29
Associated Container Transport (ACT)   47
Atlantis hotel   142
Australia   48, 146
Axworthy, Michael   98
Ayubi, N.   110

BAAS International Group (BIG)   66
Bahrain
   Dubai and   94–6, 129–30
   as independent state   71
   Iran and   94
   significance of   17, 23, 24, 32, 34, 35, 37, 52, 54, 61, 63, 65, 86, 101, 133–4, 153–4, 192 n.76
Baldwin-Edwards, M.   90
Balfour-Paul, Glen   16, 56, 68
Bandar Abbas (Gombroon) (Iran)   8, 17, 23, 39, 74, 98, 99, 132, 159
Bandar Imam Khomeini (BIK) port (Iran)   39, 74, 99, 101, 131
Bandar Shahpour port. *See* Bandar Imam Khomeini port (Iran)
Basrah (Iraq)   1, 17, 23, 24, 26, 39–40, 67, 96, 150, 160
   port of   99–100
Beirut   1
Belgrave, Charles   18, 54
Belt and Road Initiative (BRI) (New Silk Road)   152, 175–6
Ben Line   47
Bill of Lading (B/L)   126
Bin Sulayem, Sultan Ahmed   56, 120, 169, 188 n.70
Blue Star   47
Bombay   31
Bonney, J.   45
Bosworth, Freddie   61
Boustead, J.   63
Box, The (Levinson)   11
Box Boats (Cudahy)   11
Brand Dubai website   148
break-bulk delivery process   80
Britain and the Gulf Shaikhdoms 1820-1971 (Onley)   9

British and Commonwealth   47
British Bank of the Middle East (BBME)   1, 33, 52–3, 67, 75, 76, 187 n.51
British bureaucratic records   7
British 'Dreadnought' Battleship   42
British India Line (BI)   30, 99
British India Steam Navigation Company (BI)   24, 25, 67, 98
British Political Agency   35
Broeze, Frank   11, 41–3
Brook, Daniel   56
'build it and they will come' principle   114
Bullard, J. L.   53, 75
Burdett, Anita   5, 25, 31
Burj Al Arab hotel (Dubai)   109
Burj Khalifa   145–6, 168–9
Burrell, D.   45
Burrows, Bernard   55, 68
Bushire   17, 18, 23, 26, 39, 74, 98, 131, 150

'Cabinet Survey of Shipping in the Gulf for 1907'   25
cargo operations, as piecemeal   43–4
Chahbahar pot (Iran)   159
Chapman, Gary   88
Chapman, George   6, 24, 33, 35, 51, 54, 61, 75, 183 n.48, 184 n.82
Chatham House Report   82, 115, 117
China   36, 124, 138, 146, 151, 153, 175–6
Christensen, Clayton   196 n.79
Ciudad Real Airport (Spain)   194 n.31
Clare, Horatio   11
CMA   121
CMA-CGM carrier   123
connected capitalism   80–4, 169
Containerisation International   50
containerization   41, 79, 99, 190 n.18
   amalgamation process and   49–50
   Broeze on   42–3
   cargo shipping environment prior to   45
   comparison with conventional cargo system   46, 49, 80
   efficiency of   47–8, 125, 126
   impact of   48, 124, 126
   worldwide   42

integrated logistics of   168
lines and   50, 126
onset of   45–6
shipping developments   120–7
significance of   6, 42, 80, 109, 124–5, 161, 166–8
standardization and   44, 125, 171
unit of   179 n.2
COSCO   49
cosmopolitanism   8, 16, 27, 30, 116, 142, 148, 172
Crawford, Michael   56
Crescent Oil   91–2
Crystal, Jill   131
CSX Corporation   146
Cudahy, Brian   11, 46
Curzon, Viceroy of India   29

Dammam (Saudi Arabia)   39, 66
  port of   97–8, 131
Danish Line Maersk   125, 128
Davidson, Christopher   4, 9, 12, 20, 53, 55, 58, 61, 62, 83, 91, 110
Davies, Charles   19
Davis, Mike   10, 116
Dead Weight Tons (DWT)   186 n.17
De Butts, Freddie   188 n.84
demographic disorder   89
Dhahran   39
Dhofar   64
Dhow Cultures of the Indian Oceans (Sherriff)   9
disruptive technology   196 n.79
D. M. H. Riches   51
Doha (Qatar)   96, 154
Donovan, A.   45
Drewry Maritime Financial Research   50
Dry Port (Saudi Arabia)   66
Dubai (Ali)   10
Dubai (Davidson)   10
Dubai (Krane)   10
Dubai
  Abu Dhabi and   72, 136
  Bahrain and   94–6, 129–30
  beginnings of   15–22
  challenges and competitions for   151–63
  China and   151
  creek in   32–3, 167
  Dammam and   98, 131
  development of   109–14
  distinctiveness of   166
  domination of   3
  downturn and resurgence of   138–41
  formative years of   5–6
  as independent Shaikhdom   29–30
  infrastructure development beginnings in   32–3
  Iran and   74, 77–8, 99, 142, 159–60
  Iraq and   132, 160–1
  Kuwait and   96, 157, 171
  maritime economy of Gulf and   22–8
  and Mina Qaboos container throughputs compared   93
  oil price during the initial years in   75
  open skies' policy of   86, 87
  as port hub   95
  Qatar and   131, 154–5
  Salalah and   128
  Saudi Arabia and   131
  Sharjah and   138
  shipping and logistics literature of   11
  significance of   1–2
'Dubai 2020' World Expo fair   143
Dubai Amplified (Ramos)   9
Dubai Arts Art District   145
Dubai brand   88, 153, 155, 168, 177
Dubai British Business Group (BBG)   53
Dubai Chamber of Commerce (DCOC)   59
Dubai Culture and Arts Authority   145
Dubai Dry Docks   61
Dubai Economic Council (DEC) survey   118
Dubai Electricity Company (DEC)   53
Dubai Financial Centre   109
Dubai Internet City (DIC)   162
Dubai Mall   142
Dubai Media City (DMC)   162
Dubai Model   3, 13, 101, 111, 134, 172, 176
  twenty-first century challenges and   138, 145, 151, 153, 155, 164
Dubai Model, The (Hvidt)   10
Dubai Multi Commodities Centre (DMCC)   163
Dubai National Air Travel Agency (DNATA)   85, 148

Dubai Ports Authority (DPA)   77, 120, 146
Dubai Port Services (DPS)   51, 76, 168
Dubai Ports International
 (DPI)   146, 147
Dubai Ports World (DPW)   138,
 146–8, 169
Dubai Reform Movement   58
Dubai Shopping Festival   109, 124, 142
Dubai Silicon Oasis   162
Dubai Trade   127
Dubai Trade Centre   61
Duff, Bill   54, 56, 61, 187 n.59
Duqm port (Oman)   152, 175, 176

'Ease of Doing Business Survey'   113
East India Company (EIC)   17, 36
economic outreach   146–51
Economist, The (newspaper)   41, 50, 84
economy of scale, logic of   49
Egypt   141, 143
Ehteshami, Anoushiravan   132
Electronic Data Interchange (EDI)   126
Electronic Data Interchange for
 Administration, Commerce and
 Transport (EDIFACT)   126
Ellerman Lines   47
Emirates airline
 Dubai Literary Festival   145
 significance of   12, 87–8, 94, 129, 141,
  142, 144, 146, 149–51, 168, 177
Encounter Bay (ship)   48
English East India Company   8
entrepot role   3, 13, 165, 166, 167, 174, 175
 containerization and   52, 53, 60, 67
 Dubai origin and   21, 27, 32, 37
 efficient management and   111, 116,
  127, 129, 131–3
 logistics revolution and   82, 98–100
 twenty-first century challenges
  and   139, 152, 162, 163
Etihad Airlines   136, 177
Evans, Peter B.   111, 113
'expansion ahead of demand'
 policy   114, 123
expatriate labour, role of   114–20

Faisal, King of Saudi Arabia   65
Far Eastern Freight Conference
 (FEFC)   44, 49

Fear and Money in Dubai (Davis)   10
Felixstowe port (UK)   42, 48
Field, Michael   8, 96, 185 n.118
fixed costs   49
Flashes of Thought (Al Maktoum)   10
Fly Dubai airline   142
France   84
free zones
 advantages of   81–3
 criticism of   83–4
 significance of   81
Frere, Bartle   24
Friedman, Thomas   41
*From Trucial States to United Arab
 Emirates* (Heard-Bey)   8
Fuccaro, Nelida   9, 16
Fujairah   62, 138
 and Khor Fakkan port
  compared   121, 138
Fukuyama, Francis   193 nn.2–3
Furness Withy   47

Gargash, Anwar   156
Gateways to the World (Kamrava)   9
Gause, Greg   110
Gazetteer of the Persian Gulf (Lorimer)   5
George, Rose   11
Germany   146
Ghabra, S.   130
Globalisation of the Oceans, The
 (Broeze)   11
globalization   41, 79, 126, 132, 149
 early   60
Gombroon. *See* Bandar Abbas
government-related entities (GREs)   139
Gray, M.   110
Gray Mackenzie Company   6, 24, 31, 37,
 51, 54, 67, 76, 77, 184 n.82
Gray Paul and Company   24
Green, Neville   35, 63
Griffiths, Percival   24
Gross Tonnage (GT)   186 n.17
'Guardian States'   110
Gulf, economic activity of   22–32
Gulf, in nineteenth century   *102*
Gulf Air   86–8, 94, 129
Gulf Art Fair   145
Gulf Aviation   85
Gulf container throughputs   *161*

Gulf Container Volumes (2003) *121*
Gulf Co-Operation Council (GCC) 3, 74, 90, 175
   Arab workers *115*
   collapse of 151, 158
Gulf News (newspaper) 115
Gulftainer 92, 93, 160
Gwadar port (Pakistan) 176

Halcrow and Partners 32, 33, 51, 53, 54, 56, 85
Halliday, Fred 52
Hamad Airport Doha 155
Hamad Port (Qatar) 154
Hamdan bin Mohammed, Shaikh 135–6, 173
Hamriyah port (Sharjah) 62
Hamza, Kemal 60
Hanieh, Adam 111, 162
Hapag Lloyd (Germany) 44, 49, 97
Harbours and Havens 9
Harrison Line 47
Hawley, Donald 8, 22, 35, 54, 62, 63, 72, 187 n.61
Heard-Bey, Frauke 8, 18, 27, 72
Herb, Michael 4, 113, 130, 156
Hertog, S. 136
Hiro, Dilip 78
Historical Institutionalist approach 4
HMM Algeciras (ship) 1
Hong Kong 84, 111, 146
Hoosteval 11, 127, 161
'hub and spoke' cargo 80, 92, 168
Huntington, Samuel P. 179 n.13
Hussein, Saddam 78, 88, 97, 108
Hutchinson 98, 138
Hutchison Port Holdings (Hong Kong) 147
Hvidt, M. 10, 110, 112, 117
Hyundai Merchant Marine (HMM) 1

Ib Kruse (Maersk Line) 125
Ideal X (ship) 1
India 20, 26, 31, 79, 89, 116, 148, 159
   gold import into 59
   intermodal transport 45, 48, 66, 79, 107, 124
   containerization and 166, 168, 172, 174

International Chamber of Shipping (ICS) 126
International Humanitarian City (IHC) 162
International Maritime Organisation (IMO) 126
International Organisation for Standardization (ISO) 46
Internet City (Dubai) 109
Iran 39, 66–7, 83, 91, 98–9, 131–2, 134
   Bahrain and 94
   as pariah state 99, 108
   relationship with Dubai 74, 77–8, 99, 142, 159–60
Iraq 39–40, 67, 134
   Dubai and 132, 160–1
   invasion of Kuwait 88–9, 95, 97
Iraqi Port Authority (IPA) 160
Isfahan 17, 23
Italy 84

Jahani, K. 58
Japan 44, 112
Jawaharlal Nehru Port Trust (JNPT) (Mumbai) 79
Jebel Ali Free Zone (JAFZA) 78, 79, 120
   significance of 80–2, 162
Jebel Ali port (Dubai)
   CMA-CGM services from 123
   connected-up logistics approach and 80–4
   domination of 127
   as game-changer 78
   as hub port 78–80, 124, 151, 168
   change in position of 151–2
   Iraq invasion of Kuwait and impact on 89
   significance of 1, 12, 47, 53, 73, 76–8, 108, 109, 114, 121, 123–4, 132, 136, 172
Jeddah 39, 146
Jephson, C. 125
Jones, Stephanie 9, 37
Jordan 141
Jubail Container Terminal 98
Jubail port (Saudi Arabia) 98
Jumeirah Group (Luxury Hotels) 148
Just-in-Time (JIT) 48

Kafala (sponsorship) system   110, 118
Kamrava, Mehran   82, 96, 155, 156
Kanna, Ahmed   111
Kapetanovic, H.   112
Karachi   31, 79
Karachi International Container
    Terminal   79–80
Keflavik Airport (Iceland)   198 n.48
Keir, William   18
Kelly, J. B.   18
Keshavarzian, Arang   81
Khalifa, Shaikh   135
Khalifa bin Salman Port (KBSP)
    (Bahrain)   154
Khashoggi, Jamal   158
Khor Fakkan port (Sharjah)
    and Fujairah compared   121, 138
    significance of   33, 62, 80, 92–3, 138
    volumes   92
Kirkbride, Alec   53
Klose, A.   45
Krane, Jim   10
Kuwait   1, 3, 33, 38, 65, 88–9, 96–7, 130, 156–7
    and Dubai compared   96, 157, 171
    impact of liberation of   89
    Iraqi invasion of   88–9, 95, 97
Kuwait Shipping Company   97
Kuwait Sovereign Wealth Fund
    (KSWF)   97

Lansdowne, Lord   29
Lebanon   73
Legrenzi, M.   151
Levinson, Marc   6, 11, 41, 45–7
liner shipping industry, in mid-twentieth
    century   41
    and Al Maktoum
        impact of   50–4
        relations with protecting
            power   54–6
        ruling policy and   57–62
    containerization and   42–50
    Gulf and   62–7
Lingah   21, 23, 31, 32, 83, 150
    decline of   26–8
Linz, Juan   4
Liverpool   48
Lloyds Bank   51

Logistics Performance Index (LPI)   162
logistics revolution   71–2
    airports and airlines and   84–90
    connected-up logistics approach
        and   80–4
    Dubai's competition and   90–100
    external instability impact and   73–6
    Jebel Ali port and   76–80
'Longest War, The' (Hiro)   78
Lorimer, J. G.   5, 22, 25–7, 30
Lucas, R.   4
Lynch Brothers   99

Macdougall, Philip   19
Mack, David   59
Mackinnon Mackenzie and Company   24
McKinsey Global Institute   175
McLean, Malcolm   1, 45–6, 77
Maersk   49, 77, 126–8, 154
Maersk Line   87, 122, 125
Majlis's mechanisms   58–9
Makki, Abbas   8
Martin, Craig   46
Matthiesen, Toby   5
Mattis, James   140
Media City (Dubai)   109
Mediterranean Shipping Company
    (MSC)   1, 49, 123
Merchants, The (Field)   8
Mina Khalid port (Sharjah)   62, 76
Mina Khalifa port (Abu Dhabi)   137
Mina Qaboos port (Oman)   93, 128, 129
Mina Rashid   77, *103*
Mina Salman port   37
Mina Zayed port. *See* Port Zayed
Mishrif, Ashraf   3, 112
Mohammerah (Khorramshahr)   26
Moore, Robin   188 n.86
Moore, Tim   198 n.48
Morgen, H.   125
MSC Oscar (ship)   1, 44, 49
Mumbai   79
Muscat   23, 36–7
Myth of Arab Piracy in the Gulf, The
    (Al Qasimi)   8

Nakheel   139
National Bank of Dubai (NBD)   59
National Iranian Oil Company (NIOC)   91

Nedlloyd (Netherlands)   44
Nejd   38
Nepal   117
New Zealand   48
Ningbo Port (China)   124
Nippon Yusen Kaisha (NYK) (Japan)   44
Notteboom, T.   148
Nye, Joseph   150

Offshore Banking Units (OBU)   94
oil-curse approach   3
Oman   36–7, 64, 86, 128, 129, 134, 152–3, 175
Onley, James   9, 21, 28, 57, 60
open skies policy   86, 87
O'Shea, Raymond   57
Overseas AST   33
Overseas Containers Limited (OCL)   47–9
Oxford Business Group   62

Pahlavi, Shah Muhammed Reza   39, 66
Pakistan   31, 79, 152, 176
Pakistan International Airlines (PIA)   87
Pampanini, A. H.   98
Panamax ships   122
pearling, significance of   22–3
Pelly, Lewis   21
Peninsular and Oriental Steam Navigation Company (P&O) (UK)   44, 47, 77, 147
Perpetual Maritime Truce (1853)   16
Philippines   116
Port Line   47
Port of Singapore (PSA)   98, 147
Port Rashid (Dubai)   44, 53, 73, 74, 77, *104*, 114, 168
Port Zayed (Abu Dhabi)   90–1, 120, 136
Potter, L. G.   15
Potts, D.   18
Price, Gareth   117
private sector, policy of   119
Protestantism   196 n.77
Public Warehousing Company (PWC). *See* Agility
Puerto Rico   46

Qaboos, Sultan of Oman   64, 93, 153
Qatar   33, 37–8, 65, 86, 96, 117, 131, 134, 145, 152, 154–6, 175
   as independent state   71, 155
Qatar Airways   155
Qatar Navigation   96
Qawasim   16–19, 21

Raban, Jonathan   8
radical Islam   108
Ras al Khaimah (RAK)   16–18, 20, 29, 34, 62, 72, 138
Rashid (Makki)   8
Rashid, Y.   119
Rashid's Legacy (Wilson)   8
Ratner, Gerald   198 n.44
Records of Dubai (Burdett)   5
rentier states   154, 172
   meaning of   179 n.5
   rentier theory and   111
   significance of   110, 131
Richard Costain   51, 61
ring-fencing, of Arab Shaikhdoms   29
"Rise of the Rest, The" (Amsden)   111
Riyadh   66
Robinson, J.   113
Rodrigue, J.-P.   148
Rolls, Vernon   49
Rugh, Andrea   17
Runciman, David   109, 193 n.3

Said, Edward   181 n.68
Salalah   122, 128, 153
Saudi Arabia
   Bahrain and   94
   Dubai and   131
   significance of   18, 37, 38–9, 55, 65–6, 90, 91, 97–8, 108, 157–8
Saudi Arabian Basic Industries Corporation (SABIC)   98
Saudi Railways Organization (SRO)   66
Saudi Royal Commission   78, 98
Sealand company   47–8, 66, 77, 99, 128, 146
Sectarian Gulf (Matthiesen)   5
Severin, Tim   36
Shaikhdoms, significance of   21–2
Shaikh Mana faction   57–8
Shaikh Shakhbut   63

Sharaf, Mohammed 89, 120
Sharjah 170
 creek in 34, 35
 Dubai and 138
 significance of 8, 20, 27, 29–31, 33–5,
  50, 54, 55, 61, 62, 67, 69, 85,
  91–3, 100, 133, 150
Shatt-Al-Arab 40, 100
Sherriff, Abdul 9
Shiraz 17, 23
Shirazi Shi 94
Shuaiba Port (Kuwait) 65, 96
Shuwaikh port (Kuwait) 65, 96, 97
Singapore 43, 94, 111
slot cost 49
Sohar (Oman) 153
 port 36, 129, 175
Soto, R. 109, 117, 119, 139
South America 146
Sovereign Wealth Fund (Saudi
 Arabia) 158
spoke services, significance
 of 78, 80
sporting events, high-profile 144
SS (steamship) Sirdhana 44, 51
Statista.com 141
Stopford, Martin 23
stowage plan and cargo 43
Strick Line (Europe) 31
sustaining technology 196 n.79

Taimur, Sultan Said Bin 37, 64
Tanker War (1987) 97
Tehran 23
Tehran Inland Container
 Terminal 99
Tetreault, Mary Ann 111, 113
Thesiger, Wilfred 5
Tianjin (China) 146
Tor Bay (ship) 49, *105*
tourism and brand establishment 141–6
transnationalism 57, 60, 171
trans-shipment hubs, problem for 93
trans-shipment routing 80
Trucial Oman Scouts (TOS) 55, 62,
 188 n.84
Trucial States, The (Hawley) 8

Trucial States
 quarantining of 55
 significance of 5, 18, 32, 33, 34, 100,
  180 n.24
 treaties as beneficial to 21
Trucial States Council (TSC) 55
Trucial States Development Fund 55
Tunisia 140, 143
Two Centuries of Overseas Trading
 (Jones) 9

UAE National Service Law
 (UAENSL) 119
UK National Archives (UKNA) 5, 7
Umm Al Qaiwain 29, 62
Umm Al Quwain (UAQ) 21, 62, 138
Umm Qasr (Iraq) 67, 100, 132, 160–1
UNHCR 162
United Arab Emirates (UAE) 51, 62, 66,
 73, 116, 133
United Arab Shipping Company
 (UASC) 97, 121
United Nations Conference on Trade and
 Development (UNCTAD) 126
US Federal Maritime Board 46–7

Villiers, Alan 96, 185 n.118
virtual noodle bowl policy 149

Wahabis 18, 19, 36, 38, 64
Walker, Julian 5, 30, 31, 180 n.24
Waterman and Lykes lines (USA) 44
Weber, M. 196 n.77
Wells of Memory, The (Al Gurg) 9
Wilson, Graeme 8, 28
World Customs Organization
 (WCO) 126
World Is Flat, The (Friedman) 41
World Trade Organization (WTO) 126

Yang Ming Lines (YML) (Taiwan) 160
Yantai (China) 146
Yemen 89, 159
Yom Kippur war 75
Young, Karen 59

Zanzibar 36, 37

www.ingramcontent.com/pod-product-compliance
Lightning Source LLC
Chambersburg PA
CBHW062219300426
44115CB00012BA/2134